❀

DISCOVERERS, EXPLORERS, SETTLERS

❀

DISCOVERERS, EXPLORERS, SETTLERS

The Diligent Writers of Early America

WAYNE FRANKLIN

Send those on land that will show themselves
diligent writers
SAILING DIRECTIONS of
Henry Hudson

The University of Chicago Press
CHICAGO AND LONDON

The University of Chicago Press Chicago 60637
The University of Chicago Press, Ltd., London

98 97 96 95 94 93 92 91 90 89   6 5 4 3 2

Library of Congress Cataloging in Publication Data

Franklin, Wayne.
    Discoverers, explorers, settlers.

    Includes index.
    1. America—Early accounts to 1600.   2. America—
Discovery and exploration.   3. America in literature.
I. Title.
E141.F7   970'.01   79-4390
    ISBN 0-226-26071-2 (cloth)
    ISBN 0-226-26072-0 (paper)

❦ CONTENTS ❦

LIST OF PLATES
vii

ACKNOWLEDGMENTS
ix

PROLOGUE
xi

INTRODUCTION
Language and Event in New World History
1

1 DISCOVERY NARRATIVE
An Adventure of the Eye Alone
21

2 EXPLORATORY NARRATIVE
Many Goodly Tokens
69

3 SETTLEMENT NARRATIVE
Like an Ancient Mother
123

CONCLUSION
179

EPILOGUE
A Wilderness of Books
204

NOTES
211

INDEX
241

✤ PLATES ✤

Plates follow page 210 of text

1. J. T. de Bry, English sportsmen in the New World, 1618
2. Thomas Jefferson, chart of Old World and New World animals, 1788
3. Thomas Jefferson, map of proposed western territories, 1783–84
4. Thomas Jefferson, chart of the Virginia Indians, 1788
5. Jonathan Carver, map of North America, 1778
6. John Bartram, view of his house and garden, 1758
7. Lewis Evans, map of the middle colonies, 1749
8. William Bartram, watercolor of the *Franklinia Alatamaha,* 1788
9. William Bartram, view of the Alachua savanna in Florida, 1775
10. T. de Bry, shipwreck and survival in Veragua, 1595
11. Samuel Urlsperger, map of Savannah, 1735
12. Peter Gordon, view of Savannah, ca. 1734
13. Thomas Holme, plan of Philadelphia, 1683
14. Robert Mountgomery, plan of the Margravate of Azilia, 1717
15. John White, a terrapin, 1585
16. T. de Bry, Spanish justice in Florida, 1595
17. T. de Bry, John White's "Secota," 1590
18. J. B. M. le Buteaux, view of New Biloxi, 1720
19. William Byrd, plat of North Carolina lands, ca. 1733
20. Samuel Jenner, map of Eden in Virginia, 1737
21. Raphaelle Peale, *A Deception,* 1802
22. John White, Eskimo woman and child, ca. 1577
23. John White, Eskimo man, ca. 1577
24. John White, Frobisher's fight with the Eskimos, ca. 1577
25. Thomas Ellis, view of an iceberg, 1578
26. James Beare, world map, 1578
27. John Vanderlyn, *The Death of Jane McCrea,* 1804
28. J. T. de Bry, Pocahontas and the aggressions of Argall, 1618
29. Matthew Merian, the Jamestown massacre, 1634
30. Robert Vaughan, map of "Ould Virginia," 1624

❦ ACKNOWLEDGMENTS ❦

I AM GRATEFUL TO THE INSTITUTIONS OR PRIVATE OWNERS WHO have allowed the reproduction of items in their possession; specific credits will be found in the illustration section below. I also want to thank Joyce McCarten, of *Smithsonian* magazine, and Lisa Lieberman, of the Historical Society of Pennsylvania, for their aid in locating one of the items I wished to reproduce—McCarten, moreover, for loaning me a photograph of it. Betty Child, of the New York Graphic Society, and Galina Gorokhoff, of the Yale University Art Gallery, likewise lent their help in tracking down another item, while Linda LaPuma, of the Rare Book Room at the University of Illinois Library, checked on one that remains elusive. Among the many other people who provided help in these matters, I must single out Carolyn A. Sheehy, of the Newberry Library, and Douglas W. Marshall, of the William L. Clements Library at the University of Michigan.

For his enduring aid and encouragement, I wish to express my deep gratitude to Thomas L. Philbrick, of the University of Pittsburgh, who first helped me to investigate the early writings of America. That this book exists at all is due to him more than to anyone else except its author. The disclaimer which usually follows such statements—that the author alone is responsible for all remaining errors and shortcomings—is particularly appropriate here, for I did not have the heart to inflict on Professor Philbrick yet another version of my wanderings. He must remain a guiding spirit deprived of the blue pencil he should have had.

It was in the classroom that this book really took the shape it has here, and I must try to express my thanks to the many students at the University of Iowa whose demands on my time really have been gifts of their own. I particularly want to mention Lynn Angstadt, who read an earlier version of the book and contributed much to my further work; and Alan Axelrod, who helped me prepare an earlier set of plate materials.

I reserve my final thanks for Karin Franklin and our son Nathaniel, who have traveled with me across the literal American landscape and through the long journey of this book about other travelers. They know what it is that words always leave out, and how many other things the working with words itself leaves undone.

❧ PROLOGUE ❧

IN A LETTER WRITTEN FROM JAMAICA IN 1503, CHRISTOPHER Columbus described to Ferdinand and Isabella the shipwreck of his squadron, his soul, his earthly life. At one point in the doleful catalog he remarked: "On the day of Epiphany I reached Veragua, completely broken in spirit."[1] This book is a study of such statements, of their origins in European experience in the New World, of their consequences for what finally emerged as an identifiable American culture. I am convinced that statements of this sort are an abstract of nearly five hundred years worth of Western life, a paradigm of New World event and language. And I hope to demonstrate, by examining the records of American travel and their place in the culture at large, that from the start language and event in America have been linked almost preternaturally to each other.

In 1492 America was, from the European standpoint, simply an event. But in 1493 it became a collection of words. The letter which Columbus wrote on his return from the West gave to the act of his voyage the shape of a narrative whole. What made this process of narration particularly important for America was a set of intertwined circumstances. Columbus did not know, in many senses, what he was writing about. He had not recognized his landfall for what it finally turned out to have been. He never knew that he had "discovered America," and hence could not articulate his achievements in precisely that manner. But he could articulate, at least, the smaller events and his sense of their meaning. Language gave him a way of fixing experience, a means of exploring further his literal explorations.

But language had another function, too. For all that Columbus did not know in 1493, those to whom he wrote knew even less. If one can see in his first act of expression, and in those which followed, a growing realization of what he had done and what had been done to him, one sees in the reception of his documents (and the thousands of similar reports which were to follow from other hands) the constitution of America in European minds as a verbal construct, an artifact. Columbus stood between Spain and America like a witness between a jury and those facts which he alone knew.

His writing was itself an act of discovery, a mediation of things eastward through words. Within thirty years Hernán Cortés would write from Mexico a series of long letters to another Spanish ruler, and would place at the end of his first report an inventory of fifty-two items which he was sending along with his prose. His actual abstract of Mexico, the tangible if exotic freight of goods, was mirrored in the very structure of his language. In the case of Columbus, the native word "Veragua" stood out in his Spanish like a sign of all that was strange and almost untellable, of what was beyond the pale of his audience at home.

Like Columbus, Cortés would adopt toward his audience a certain extreme posture, a distant tenacity. Where he stood in a literal sense became as well his rhetorical ground. He, too, had lost his ships—but had burned them himself, believing that a voluntary shipwreck would justify both his future deeds and the pose which he took when he explained them to the king. He was praying for (or rather betting on) an Epiphany, whereas Columbus thought that he had lost one; yet, like the earlier voyager, he was himself beyond the confines of Old World space. He was almost, except for a legal fiction, outside the law. And his long reports to Charles V thus became his means of reentering, or perhaps extending, the bounds of expected and acceptable action. In his beginning was the deed, and then followed the crucial word, the polemical attack on others in the Indies, the conciliation of those at home.[2]

The chapters below follow out some of the implications of these circumstances. I would point out here, however, one final fact. That attenuation of space and language which can be discovered in Columbus, Cortés, and so many later New World travelers was to become in time an independent feature of American (and particularly United States) rhetoric. Writers in America have not always written for Europe, yet the literal structure which one finds in the reports of Columbus emerged in a surprisingly short period of years as a figure for the writer's inward stance in the New World, for the shape of an American prose addressed to a wide range of topics and audiences. The traveler had as his final authority the fact of his separate existence: this was, indeed, the cause for his being an author at all. What was fact became metaphor. Henry Thoreau was to open *Walden,* the account of an exploration begun not on Epiphany but on a local version of that holy day, the Fourth of July, with an assertion of his special standing: "When I wrote the following pages, or rather the bulk of them, I lived alone, in the woods." The implicit response of Columbus to this later declaration was the final line of that last report which he sent, in Thoreau's words, "to his kindred from a distant land": "Written in the Indies on the island of Jamaica, 7 July 1503."[3] This was his letter to a world that never wrote to him. And it was even doubtful, as he noted, whether what he wrote would reach his intended audience—not because, like Emily Dickinson in Amherst, he kept it hidden away, but rather because he was sending it "by way of Indian messengers" and it would be "a great miracle" if it arrived.[4]

❦ INTRODUCTION ❦

Language and Event
in New World History

It is impossible to dream long in a land of such palpable realities.
John Stillman Wright, *Letters from the West* (1819)

ONE BORDER BETWEEN LANGUAGE AND EVENT IS THE POINT AT which a traveler sets down some fact as a cluster of words. Hence the statement of Columbus in 1503: "On the day of Epiphany I reached Veragua, completely broken in spirit."[1] But this is more than a fact, or is a collection of kinds of fact. If it seems to tell a quite simple story, we must note that any tale tends not merely to narrate, but also to explain, whatever it embraces. Even the relation of its parts, or the sequence of its details, has more than a narrative purpose.[2] One may say of that statement from Columbus, for instance, that if he really was at Veragua, it was *not* Epiphany— which in a sense the rest of his sentence suggests.[3] There have been great incongruities in this voyage (as in his whole career), and his letter becomes a conscious inventory of them, a tale which attempts to comprehend what has occurred. Statements throughout the text have the tensely balanced structure seen in the "Veragua" sentence: an assertion of the expected order of things, a location in space and time, an assessment of the real order of events and feelings. "Epiphany" in this case is neither just a date nor just a spiritual occasion, neither pure fact nor pure symbol. It describes instead a meeting point of human (and divine) scheme with the temporal world. By implication, this holy day would be the perfect moment for the realization of the voyager's goals; but by implication, too, it here threatens to become simply another unit of secular time.

"Veragua" seems at first like the means by which that threat is expressed, but in fact it has its own spiritual suggestions. Curiously, it is a possible Spanish compound with intriguing connotations (*ver,* to see; *vera,* border, edge; *veras,* reality, truth—and *agua,* water). Columbus himself states, however, that the term is a native one, and he provides for it earlier in his letter a gloss which is even more   1 attractive than any which might be invented from the Spanish: the inhabitants of Nicaragua, he writes, "gave me the names of many places on the sea-coast where they said there was gold and goldfields too. The last of these was Veragua, about twenty leagues away" (Cohen, 287). Suddenly the tension of his later statement is enriched: the day of the Lord's manifestation, the arrival at a place of promised earthly reward, the sense of a letdown, of bare survival—a time, an event, a place, an emotional state. We thus have a structure of ironic modification that centers on a verb which is not without coloration in a world where simple arrival is hard to achieve, and which balances across itself an established European occasion and a realized New World feeling—which transmits through the place which it touches, through that exotic and promising word "Veragua," a complete reversal of expectation. To arrive in such a fashion is to be still distant from what was sought. Yet there is a strange completion here nonetheless, for Veragua itself had impelled the voyage which ended so bitterly along its shore—its role in reality (and in the sentence) was to act as both a departure and a conclusion, a shifting point of reference for the traveler. One may say that everything Columbus did from the first moment he heard this place-name until he found the place itself was an education in language, in the relation of words to things in America.[4]

In Columbus, as in other travel writers, that relation is a complex and involved affair. Though we tend to think of such figures as preeminent "men of action" for whom writing was a necessary rather than a chosen task, their view of what they wrote in fact was quite sophisticated. And they often turned to writing with an urgency which suggests that it was a means of self-understanding, an essential way of shaping their lives after the fact. They seem, too, to have been painfully aware of the many problems which language posed for people separated as they were from their own world. There was the almost universal issue of native languages, to begin with, and hence the constant need for translation (and guesswork) as well as for some conceptual grasp of the proliferation of tongues in the New World.[5] The contact with native groups was a form of cultural shock which was expressed most poignantly in the initial failure of even a verbal understanding between red and white. Likewise, the profusion of unknown natural objects in America placed an extra burden on the traveler's mind and language, as did the frequently tangled web of European events in this

2 hemisphere of strange peoples and strange sights. Wherever he

turned, the New World traveler seemed to be faced with strains on the one cultural tool by which he might hope to organize his life and explain it to others who had not shared in it.

Such strains first appeared when a European could find neither the proper words nor suitable Old World analogues for American facts. Thus Cortés had to admit in one of his letters to Charles V that the palace of Montezuma was "so marvelous" that it would be "impossible to describe its excellence and grandeur." This disclaimer is, of course, a description of sorts, since we know from it something about the building which Cortés professes himself unable to portray. And it has a certain conventional tone which one might find in comments about any exceptional *Old* World structure. But Cortés will not let his reader rest with a sense of the excellent and grand qualities of the palace. He goes on: "Therefore, I shall not attempt to describe it at all, save to say that in Spain there is nothing to compare it with."[6] There is here a struggle beyond any convention, a sense of the new which the writer will not abridge. Even more touching, for the insight which it offers into the dilemma faced by Cortés, is his attempt to describe the native market in Mexico City. He begins by listing the items sold in it ("lime, hewn and unhewn stone, adobe bricks, tiles, and cut and uncut woods of various kinds," states one catalog; "onions, leeks, garlic, common cress and watercress, borage, sorrel, teasels and artichokes," runs another), but then concludes in a thick-tongued apology—"Finally, besides those things which I have already mentioned, they sell in the market everything else to be found in this land, but they are so many and so varied that because of their great number and because I cannot remember many of them nor do I know what they are called I shall not mention them" (103–4). At the limits of his known world, Cortés appears to have encountered the boundaries of his familiar language, and of the culture implicit in it.

The literary situation of the New World traveler, even in periods much later than that of Cortés, was to be rich in such themes. The struggle to include New World phenomena within the order of European knowledge, and to do so by "naming" them, remained at the heart of the form well into the nineteenth century. But it would be misleading to describe this problem of "inexpressibility" (or others related to it) only as a literary issue. The difficulty with words was, finally, a difficulty with the things to which particular words referred, or for which no appropriate Europeans terms could be found. The challenge which Cortés faced when he tried to write about his experience reflected the ones which arose when he tried to act in the world that he could not easily describe. Indeed, the recognition that his language was inadequate to what he perceived was itself an event, a consequence of his voyage which became a kind of "static" in his medium—and hence a sign of his general position in America. As actor and author alike, he underwent a formidable cognitive test. If we can view his political career in the New World as an attempt to make the void of American space (and the interstices of Spanish authority there) yield power, we likewise can see his literary efforts as an allied attempt to fill the almost aggressive silence of the West with words, to convert "noise" into meaningful sound.[7]

In some ways, the stylistic problems which Cortés and other American travelers discovered when they tried to write about their experience were the indirect result of their historical uncertainties. But style in the broader sense, as world view, itself had an effect on the making of history. Particularly in colonial settings, where the replication of old forms is a controlling impetus to new action, language develops a priority of its own. As the means by which colonial agents make their reports to the home government (and do so with a clear understanding of what they are expected to say), language comes to exert a subtle influence on how life in the colony is conceptualized, even perceived or carried on. The range of admissible statement predetermines both the manner of reportage and the conduct of those affairs which will be subject to review. That Cortés knew in general what Charles V would like to hear (as well as what his own opponents in the New World were likely to tell the monarch) certainly affected how he addressed the issues raised by his bold departure from expected action. Moreover, such canons of allowable speech also shaped the manner in which he perceived and acted in the world of Mexico. The reportable was the feasible and the conceivable as well. The special languages of colonial order, of Old World government, of Christianity, of, finally, perception itself—all these dialects surrounded Cortés like a series of expanding yet constraining rings, each of them forcing on him a decorum of act and word. His attempt to persuade Charles V that his expedition was legal was aimed at including his accomplishments within such limits. The problem of "naming" native culture thus was extended into the very heart of all he did in

4 America.[8]

As a vehicle of political and intellectual control, European language imposed similar strictures on any traveler in America. But it also possessed, even in these functions, a certain reassuring power. Removed from the tangible environment of their culture, travelers came to rely on this most portable and most personal of cultural orders as a means of symbolic linkage with their homes. More than any other emblem of identity, language seemed capable of domesticating the strangeness of America. It could do so both by the spreading of Old World names over New World places, people, and objects, and by the less literal act of domestication which the telling of an American tale involved. Moreover, it could provide voyagers just departing for America with a set of articulated goals and designs by which the course of Western events actually might be organized beforehand. This ability to "plot" New World experience in advance was, in fact, the single most important attribute of European language. Like the expectations about what a New World report ought to contain (or omit), it entailed a faith in the almost magical power of words which was part of a larger European assumption about the immutable correctness of Old World culture. The imperative in either case was for the traveler to resist that corruption of home order for which the distance was a synonym. But the plot of any given undertaking was concrete in a way that the generalized canons which Cortés recognized were not. It suggested that certain acts were to be performed, certain ends pursued, certain desires fulfilled. By its own articulate understanding of the present venture as a type of the whole colonial effort, it provided for a detailed test of Old World perceptions. The voyager was converted into a conscious hero of European order, and the ideal sketch of his future career became a romantic allegory of victory in the West.

Under the best of conditions, such a sketch should have been fleshed out by the voyage which it described. The final report already was implicit in the initial design, and in so much detail that the traveler's career should have moved from the word through a circle of experience which would lead him once more to a point of verbal composition. The burden of this circular route would be, in the simplest sense, the endurance of European intent through all the trials of realization. The completed report would indicate that Old World words indeed could control American events, that art could organize a multitude of unseen (and perhaps even unforeseen) circumstances. The predicted plot would cease to exist only in

5

a conditional mood; it would become fully indicative, an accomplished fact.

Particularly in the New World, however, the art of prediction proved to be a very uncertain thing. Few European "artifacts" were as subject to loss or perversion here as the word, especially the word which was aimed at a prior formulation of some actual fate. American travel books tell us, most of all, about the enormous Old World energies which went into the attempt at controlling the West by means of the symbol system of language. As structures of language in their own right, they offer a double commentary on this general effort. And in their own imperfection as texts—their frequent lack of literary polish, their incompletion and outright loss, their often eloquent concern with the failures of verbal art—they portray that effort as at best a mixed success. The nervous silence of Cortés over the sheer profusion of Mexican things hints at a wild energy in native culture for which his own origins, and the language in which those origins are embodied, have left him radically unprepared. More poignantly, the desperate condition of Columbus on Jamaica borders on a silence of a quite different sort, a collapse of personality triggered by psychic and spiritual displacements far beyond those of Cortés. The rich ambiguity of his "Epiphany" stems from a sense of disorientation which makes that word and the whole cultural order it implicates—the "plot" of redemptive history which he hoped to extend by his voyages—seem merely verbal. It is as if the word has lost its best connotations and has begun to acquire a set of almost satanic meanings, meanings that suggest the power of American facts to alter the most essential of Old World definitions. The juxtaposition of "Epiphany" and "Veragua" becomes a model of the loss of control to which so many American travelers found themselves subjected. We sense here the discovered plot of colonial life—not the grand plot of idealized experience, the easy passage through a strange place, but rather the steady attrition of all such formulas, the slow accumulation of a knowledge won at great expense. What is almost inexpressible for Columbus is not the phenomenal surface of America but the spiritual depths of his own being. The question no longer concerns what the new lands are; it centers instead on who the voyager is, on how his experience has altered his essential nature. His location thus matters only as a sign of his identity. And his language, difficult and even eccentric, mirrors the extremity of his actual fate. It also suggests the degree

to which the tensions between word and thing, art and fact, self and experience, were to become the heart of future New World life, and future American writing.

More than anything else, the West became an epistemological problem for Europe. Though the influx of American gold upset the economy of Spain, its biggest beneficiary, and though the imperial struggle to which America gave birth disrupted the already tense political situation in the whole of Europe, it was simply the fact of "another" world which most thoroughly deranged the received order of European life.[9] The issue was not merely an informational one. It involved so many far-reaching consequences that the very structure of Old World knowledge—assumptions about the nature of learning and the role of traditional wisdom in it—was cast into disarray. While colonial expansion was succeeding in the West, Europe in many ways was retreating from the implications of its American involvement. Faced with a flood of puzzling facts and often startling details, the East was almost literally at a loss for words. Having discovered America, it now needed to make a place for the New World within its intellectual and verbal universe.[10] Like the voyagers who had accomplished this feat, Europe itself was in a state of confusion, a kind of panic which was the natural result of perceptual stress.

But the European discovery also had its more positive surfaces. Such a tangible venture into the unknown typified the modern desire to test received ideas by reference to experience. The finding of new lands (once their newness was accepted) was seen as a signal proof that the ancients had been woefully ignorant of their world, and that contemporary achievements did not reflect uniformly the supposed devolution of culture since classical times.[11] The uncertainty caused by a rapid rearrangement of geographical learning thus might be a promise of future advances. And any new voyages partook in varying degrees of this sanguine exultation. Even if it suggested that a systematic understanding of the world would be hard to construct, the expansion of knowledge about the physical universe emerged as a confident sign that innovation was a worthy and fruitful cultural asset. To depart from the shores of Europe was to depart as well from the confines of ancient error and scholastic deduction.

It was from his sense of this benign meaning which European involvement in America might have that Francis Bacon, primary theorist of a new epistemology and staunch opponent of medieval scholasticism, extrapolated Columbus himself into a symbol of bold modernity. His voyager was decidedly not the man of terminal doubt and despair whom we encounter in the Jamaica letter of 1503. He was instead a figure of hopeful departures, a man whose discovery of a "new world" suggested the possibility that "the remoter and more hidden parts of nature" also might be explored with success. The function of Bacon's *Novum Organum*—his title recalled both *mundus novus* and *novus orbis terrarum*—was to provide for the scientific investigator the kind of encouragement which the arguments of Columbus prior to 1492 had provided for a Europe too closely bound to traditional assumptions. Just as Columbus had sought to convince his contemporaries that, in Bacon's view, "new lands and continents might be discovered besides those which were known before," so Bacon himself was trying to "offer hope" that other new facts might be discovered and understood.[12]

Given his high anticipations, it is understandable that Bacon should have distorted the career of Columbus. But Bacon recognized in his own sphere an uncertainty akin to that which Columbus and other voyagers in fact encountered. He noted that "the universe to the eye of the human understanding is framed like a labyrinth," and he went on to elaborate the metaphor which he derived from classical myth into a figure with distinctly modern overtones. It became, in fact, an image of the traveler's difficult path through nature rather than a reference to the contrived mazes of human art. The labyrinth of the world, he wrote, presented "on every side so many ambiguities of way, such deceitful resemblances of objects and signs, natures so irregular in their lines and so knotted and entangled," that progressing in it was a very difficult task. Moreover, since "the way . . . through the woods of experience and particulars" had to be located "by the uncertain light of the sense," perception itself might prove to be a labyrinth of false understandings about an ambiguous world. To make matters worse, those who pretended to "offer themselves for guides" through the woods were in fact so "puzzled" in their own right that they actually might "increase the number of errors and wanderers." The only solution—modest in nature but radical in implication—was to be "guided by a clue," a detail culled from the vast world of experience. One had to insure that "the whole way from the very first perception of the senses" would be kept clear of waylaying distractions. Hence one had to have "a sure plan" for finding that path (12–13).

Ideally, the *Novum Organum* was to be such a plan. But Bacon's own way had been an uncertain one, as he noted: "I have committed myself to the uncertainties and difficulties and solitudes of the ways and, relying on the divine assistance, have upheld my mind both against the shocks and embattled ranks of opinion, and against my own private and inward hesitations and scruples, and against the fogs and clouds of nature, and the phantoms flitting about on every side, in the hope of providing at last for the present and future generations guidance more faithful and secure." The despair which resulted from such a lonely condition became one of the abiding themes of his book. But it was balanced by Bacon's insistence that the desired renewal (or "instauration") of learning could be achieved only by accepting the doubt which an exposure to experience required. By such means, by "dwelling purely and constantly among the facts of nature," one might hope to lead people "to things themselves, and the concordances of things"— and hence away from the traditional errors produced by habits of inattentive speculation (13–14). One had to enter experience with a full recognition of its deceits, and one's own shortcomings; the despair had to be faced and accepted. But it was Bacon's final point that the world could be trusted to yield in return for one's labors a sense of order beyond doubt, a sense of "concordance."

Columbus and other travelers offered hope precisely on this last point. Their experience provided Bacon with a body of richly concrete images by which he could express his otherwise rather vague method. Yet their use was not merely decorative. Among other things, Bacon was constructing a model of travel itself as a worldly and intellectual act: the great discoverer was his hero as much as his metaphor. Indeed, to turn the argument around, we can say that science was a metaphor for exploration as well as vice versa, that Bacon's use of Columbus provided travel with a philosophy which it had not previously had. It was as an example of the subject-object problem which consumed Bacon's interest that the traveler became a significant figure for him. Separated from that cultural context which, in Bacon's view, so often warped the individual's sense of the natural world, a traveler appeared to enjoy a certain primary contact with the universe. His very separation was a hopeful sign, even if it also represented the possibility for despair that Bacon recognized, the possibility for utter disorientation.

Most germane here is Bacon's view of language, and particularly of the bearing between words and things. In a very real way, words were the villain of his new method, for the library as a symbolic enclosure of authority stood opposite to that "road" which he urged his readers to pursue.[13] By breaking through the enclosures of traditional space, the American traveler also was breaking the bonds of received language. He was penetrating through words to the things which they so often misrepresented, as well as through the texture of fantasy and speculation which had its only real existence in human speech. Though verbal themselves, his reports were composed in a language of events which was hard, concrete, specific—polar to the language used by those "talkers and dreamers who...have loaded mankind with promises" (85). The traveler's disclosure might be broken and uneven, fragmentary and problematic; but these traits would be its signal strength, since (like the "short and scattered sentences" of "the first and most ancient seekers after truth" [84]) they would make his form reflect the actual, honest condition of experience. The science of travel pointed one to an uncertain exegetical path through the given world, not toward an edifice of wit akin to that "fabric of human reason which we employ in the inquisition of nature"—"badly put together and built up, and like some magnificent structure without any foundation" (3). The verbal results of travel, like Bacon's own tentative "aphorisms," would be of value insofar as they suggested the mystery and discontinuity of life itself. The source of literary style was to be the style of experience which Bacon advocated; in the literal New World or the "new continent" of knowledge (104), words were to be the signs of things. And words in this sense finally would move beyond doubt: for, Bacon wrote, "a method rightly ordered leads by an unbroken route through the woods of experience to the open ground of axioms" (80).[14]

The actual traveler's route, of course, rarely was "unbroken." Bacon's stress on the exemplary innovations of Columbus points us, in fact, to that moment in 1503 when, faced with the accumulated "uncertainties and difficulties and solitudes" of his own way, the voyager found himself so far beyond the bounds of his known world that knowledge and words alike were threatened with a severe breakdown. His situation then was a paradigm of the losses which European culture as a whole was to incur in its passage across the ocean. Yet some of those losses were to become for later times the hopeful sign of American distance and difference: the "badly put together and built up" structure of Old World order seemed to

10

have suffered a needed renovation during its transport to America. The grand journey which had produced New World culture thus was seen in part as an act of Baconian growth, a set of related departures which, taken together, composed a plot of stunning comic success.

The motives behind the fabrication of this plot were related to those which moved Bacon himself. The panegyrics with which America was loaded down, particularly after the Revolution (that most conspicuous and conscious New World departure), suggest by the very pitch of their expression that Americans in fact were aware of the doubtful way they had pursued already and still were to follow. To assert not only that the movement west was benign, but also that it was in essence one movement—united in all its reaches, converging in its shape—was to give to the diverse and often fugitive events of early New World history an aesthetic composure which might "offer hope" against the sense of anomie and despair inherent in the experience of transplantation. That the United States came to be itself synonymous with the feeling of "hope" was both a mark of honest western exultation and a sign of the need to be exultant in the face of spatial and cultural uncertainties. Like any individual traveler, the expanding nation felt the continual stress of new facts. When the Federalist Fisher Ames responded to Jefferson's purchase of Louisiana by exclaiming, "We rush like a comet into infinite space," he was voicing a sense of dislocation by no means confined to members of the antifrontier faction. As we shall see later, Jefferson himself had his own fears about the West.[15]

Rushing into space, for all the anxiety it might cause, was an established American custom. Travel had served from the beginning as an actual and a metaphoric link among countless individuals and groups. And it would continue to perform similar functions for at least the next hundred years. "If God were suddenly to call the world to judgment," wrote the Argentine educator and statesman Domingo Sarmiento in 1847, "He would surprise two-thirds of the population of the United States on the road like ants. . . . In the United States you will see evidence everywhere of the religious cult which has grown up around that nation's noble and worthy instruments of its wealth: its feet."[16] As long as one could assume that all this motion was not in the main a dispersion of energies and individuals—that it aimed at some agreed-upon social goal—one might view it as a sign of America's "arrival." But agreement about the destination was far less than universal. What was clear was that people were on the move (and on the make), that transience had emerged as a central fact of American life.

The sense of community does not necessarily require a high degree of literal stability in a population. But a high level of movement certainly is not the best condition under which to develop sustained and sustaining values. A persistent paradox in America has been the focus of communal energies on a set of actions and attitudes which are extracommunal by nature. Of these focal points perhaps none has been more pervasively evoked than the traveler's pose, the Columbian stance of eager discovery. As Bacon's argument suggests, the traveler is almost by definition an iconoclast; his departure, even if he goes in the service of "home" purposes, hints not merely at the general authority of experience, but also (and more subversively) at the prospective power of individual life beyond the horizon. The American ritual of travel thus was centered from the start on an act which was antiritualistic in essence, which pointed the single traveler or the small group away from the very place where the continual reenactment of significant deeds would help to solidify communal ties.

One solution to this particular paradox was the investment of travelers with a weight of social conscience that in reality they often lacked. The figure of the pioneer, for example, became a conveniently sanitized American traveler, a person whose primary interest supposedly lay in the almost holy replication of social form. Opposite to this forerunner was the white renegade, the denier of home order; and in between the two was an array of figures whose loyalties were mixed or unclear: the solitary man like Daniel Boone, who despite his longing for solitude was an agent of expansion; the fugitive from home, to whom a certain indulgence was extended; the degenerate wanderer, whose path led to a complete inversion of settled values. This cast of national characters was rich in its range, though rather narrow in its meaning. And conspicuously absent from it was that waylaid traveler about whose existence the records of early America offer abundant evidence. So strong was the need to control the possibility for loss in New World experience (except as the deserved condition of certain stereotyped opponents) that Columbus himself became a man of delayed but final victory. Writing in the wake of the Revolution, Joel Barlow went so far as to resuscitate him in *The Vision of Columbus,* and to reveal to him by that poem "the numerous blessings which have arisen to mankind from the discovery of America." Acknowledging the

12

mistreatment to which Columbus was subjected in his own era, Barlow sought to dismiss that fact by extending the plot of his life—by making the Revolution itself an installment of his glorious Discovery.[17]

Barlow's rather absurd gesture back to 1492 was the act of a single literary artist. Yet it was typical of a dispersed cultural attempt to emphasize the supposed continuities of American experience. The ability of language to map out a literal traveler's future way was converted in such visions into a power of retrospective plotting. The vocabulary of American memory was selected according to the needs of present life, and in this process the active historical quality of much early New World writing was hidden beneath a new aesthetic or even mythological surface. The whole of colonial life acquired an exalted meaning; it became almost a literary "action," a comedy which was to be repeated with greater finish and sophistication (so the assumption ran) throughout the glorious future.

Such attempts at communal memory and definition resulted, ironically, in a militant forgetfulness, a refusal to read in the national past the record of any terminal disorientation. The sufferings of the "pioneers" became, by a kind of sacrificial arrogation, acts of pious devotion to the brighter American future enjoyed by their memorialists.[18] There were, to be sure, significant hesitations—especially as historians and literary figures began to investigate seriously, in the later nineteenth century, what Washington Irving called (regarding his researches on Columbus) the "complete labyrinth" of early New World prose.[19] But in the popular mind the American story was a simple affair, a tale of progressive achievements and solidified order. Even the narratives of wilderness disaster could be seen as integral parts of a victory, touches of pathos finally clarified by the record of subsequent white possession. Almost nowhere in the popular press was the panegyric decorum broken, and it reached, too, into the efforts of people less easily swayed by such fashionable understandings. Even a "new" historian like F. J. Turner, who sought to convert local history from a stronghold of provincial piety into a means of close and critical knowledge, and who lamented in 1893 the ignorance which partly allowed Americans to draw easy lessons from their past, in fact shared the common sense of New World history as a series of linked and enlarging plots. Industrialization was for him the final stage in an action which began in 1492. And if Turner himself sounded in his Columbian Exposition speech a note of termination which made the era of Columbus seem distant, perhaps unreachable, he averred in an earlier draft of the address that with "a connected and unified account of the progress of civilization across this continent" would come both a "real national self-consciousness" and a sense of "the significance of the discovery made by Columbus."[20] Though he called for detailed research and for a historical vocabulary attentive to the facts of New World experience, he applied to events a certain prior language which was orthodox and hence, in many ways, blinding.

It should not be necessary now to argue for the inadequacy of such partial views. A new grasp of the difficult tensions exhibited by frontier culture has developed, from many perspectives, over the past two decades. But with a few exceptions relatively little has been done with that "labyrinth" of early American travel books in which were recorded—with all the biases and blindspots one might imagine, but also with a certain unexpected freshness—the conflicting sights and sounds and events of colonial experience.[21] The range of such materials is very broad both in time and space, and the widely varying concerns and backgrounds of early American travelers may seem to induce a Baconian "despair" in the modern reader accustomed to more tidy literary categories. My own work with these texts, however, has convinced me that some "paths" may be found through the "woods"—as well as that paths ought not be our sole concern, for we need the sanitive experience, in reading as in other activities of life, of that which goes beyond our own boundaries. It is my hope that what I have to say about our earliest cultural records, and about the difficult conditions which produced them (or which they themselves helped to produce), will strike a balance between theory and detail, between our modern penchant for abstract knowledge and any given writer's engagement with some particular historical world. I will be happy if this book serves well as an invitation to my readers for their own further discovery of our first literature—as a guide not to America itself, but rather to the almost countless imaginings of that place which constitute, even from 1492, the distinctive quality of New World writing.

To trace the history of those imaginings from book to book, and within each separate geographical region, would be an almost impossible task. My reading of these works has been extensive enough 14 to suggest to me the usefulness of some such historical survey. Yet I am not convinced that this kind of study, even if possible, would be the most helpful. For one thing, it would force on our understandings a necessarily chronological arrangement of the material which surely would conceal other connections between single works or between different kinds of writing. Despite their nature as historical documents—their primary concern, that is, with something other than their own form, structure, and meaning—early American travel books *are* artifacts, and they thus have a claim to our attention outside the occasions which gave them birth. Indeed, their historical origins can be understood best when we keep in mind those principles of textual integrity which literary critics, more than historians, tend to recognize. Even the critic, however, is a "particularist": for the best artwork often is judged to be that which occupies some solitary ground, is notable precisely because it stands out from any body of matter to which it can be related. If the historian puts such texts to use by extracting from them whatever verifiable facts they record, the critic uses them most happily when they are "self-verifying"—when, in other words, their artful completion makes unnecessary any appeal to some external actuality. Neither approach is invalid, but neither one on its own will allow us to make sense of the travel book as a form of writing, or as a cultural pattern which, by virtue of its very formal design, yields facts and meanings other than those discovered by the historian or the critic.[22]

What we need for this collection of texts is a combination of the two approaches: a means of isolating aesthetic strategies which by their repetition (and variation) from work to work come to suggest something about the actual world in which they were created. We need, that is, a manner of understanding which will emphasize the shared assumptions of early American travelers about both their active careers and their artistic efforts. My own method here seeks to provide at least a hint as to how such an understanding may be developed. The particular texts that I discuss at length have been chosen for their exemplary rather than their extraordinary nature; they are few in number, when one considers exactly how many other texts might be used, but it is my belief that these works— arranged in the sequence which they here create—offer us a relatively complete guide to the large field of early American prose. Other readers might have chosen other works for discussion, and might have emphasized other aspects of them. But I hope that what I have to say about any given text will help explain ones which I do not discuss or even mention, and that those who follow out my argument will amplify it with their own further examples. The final section of my study provides a brief survey of the rich primary materials of early New World travel, and this survey may prove of help to those people who, whether general readers or specialists, wish to investigate the field more widely. Since it seems to me, moreover, that the present study may be suitable as a handbook for college classes devoted to early American literature and history, or to American Studies, the concluding section will perform double duty for the student whose previous contact with the records of colonial American life has been comparatively slight.

The manner of approach pursued here has the virtue of simplicity. Instead of attempting a full survey of the material, I have tried to discriminate three essential forms of the travel book—the narratives of discovery, exploration, and settlement. A formal method such as this one is valuable, I think, because it allows us to locate with some precision the larger structures of cultural intent which are expressed, with various mixtures, in particular works. The three postulated forms, it should be stressed conspicuously, are "ideal" constructs never encountered purely in any single text. Their utility resides precisely in their ideal character. But the categories are not just logical. As the names I have given them should suggest, each is intimately related to some concrete activity of colonial life; taken together, they comprise a body of what I would call "kinetic" literature, writing that often eschews the contemplative and pursues the active virtues. Their relation to colonial life is one of matter and manner alike. Furthermore, the forms and the activities after which they have been named were conditioned in complex ways by that expansive world of American space for the control of which they themselves were respectively invented. In the confrontation with various kinds of landscapes, landscapes partly shaped by the biases of perception or language or action, American travelers came to reveal their own minds as well as the cognitive character of their culture.

In a sense, I am guided throughout by the view of travel and experience implicit in Bacon's *Novum Organum*. As a crucial expression of the philosophy which would come to dominate European and American thought in the later seventeenth and the eighteenth centuries, his book provides a historically accurate guide to the psychology of travelers in the colonial period. But perhaps even
16 more germane here than Bacon's ideal of open perception is his

persistent sense of the deceits inherent in any perceptual situation. The record of the discovery of America by Europe—or, better yet, the *discovering* of America—is a long chronicle of blunted awareness, of slow recognition, of crucial facts never adequately understood. What often is most interesting is what American travelers did *not* see, either because they did not want to see it or because they were unable to do so. Though by the time of the Revolution it was becoming common to conceive of the effects of America on Europe in Lockean terms, Bacon's stress on the warping influence of "idols" in fact offers us a better key to the curiously selective response of Old World men and women to New World facts. What has been noted with regard to the inadequacies of landscape description in later American travel books—that "an honest particularity of response" comes about with lamentable slowness—is even more true of colonial records, and of many other issues besides the description of landscape in them.[23]

At times inadvertently, at times with a consciousness of what they were doing, New World travelers penetrated through some of the preconceptions with which they set out into the West. Many of them recognized, particularly under the strain of severe displacements, the need for a more adequate bearing on America and a more suitable language in which to describe it. For all their shortcomings, they were indeed "diligent writers"—not only diligent *as* writers, but also diligent in that world about which they wrote. And in putting art to use in the task of discovering America they often changed European aesthetic standards (and the values which those standards reflected) as much as they altered the perceived condition of the New World itself. Like any other part of Old World order, language and its received forms—forms of literary art, but forms of discourse and syntax as well—were affected deeply by their transportation to America. Had Europeans been almost wholly closed of mind, firmly set against any significant adaptations, it seems likely that the colonization of the West never would have succeeded.

I have chosen as my focus in the following pages an aspect of what one might call "public speech" which should provide a good means for locating the various balance points between convention and innovation, pattern and particularity, in early American prose. The concept of rhetorical *topoi* (or "commonplaces") seems especially helpful here because, as a condensed formula of language and idea, a given *topos* often allowed a writer to enclose new phenomena in the confines of a ready-made intellectual and linguistic order. Such formulas were peculiarly useful to "discoverers," for whom various conventional images from Old World myth and religion provided an effective means of domesticating America. For the "explorer" and the "settler," on the other hand, the relevant *topoi* (though related to various Old World conventions) were the result of more nearly immediate circumstances.[24] In all three cases, however, certain similarities can be recognized. As a formula of expression (and understanding), any American *topos* linked language and event, word and thing, person and place, with subtle suggestiveness. In such small plots of New World ground, landscapes of perceived or endured truth, we can trace an implicit history of Old World expansion to the West—a movement from icon to formula and then to style which recapitulates the larger movement of European culture beyond its traditional bounds. Likewise, in the portfolio of early American graphic arts which accompanies my text, we can see many of the same prefigurative devices in their more strictly visual mode—means of control and recognition which bear a particularly rich significance. As spatial ideograms and structures of moral value, the plates ought to hint at some of the connections between verbal and nonverbal approaches to the "discovering" of America.

I have placed this emphasis on convention, on the iconography of European travel in America, because in the end it is the formulaic quality of these works—and the failures of formula—which seems most rewarding for students of American culture. And it is as cultural documents, finally, that early New World travel works bear their deepest meanings. But I hope that my discussion of individual texts is attentive to the idiosyncracies of particular writers. For it would be a shame to miss the poignant sense of personality which radiates from a work written, as one author claimed, in an "unpolished and rude" style, "bearing the country's badge where it was hatched, only clothed with plainness and truth"; or to bypass the feeling of lonely endurance which emerges from another text that was composed not "with silence and leisure," as more finished texts might be, "but in forests, on rocks and mountains, amidst the hurries, disorders, and noise of war, and under that depression of spirits which is the natural consequence of exhausting fatigue."[25] Indeed, it is just at such moments, when early American style seems to offer us glimpses of a tough confrontation with reality, that the traveler acquires, as Columbus did on Jamaica or during that strange Epiphany in Veragua, a strong exemplary power. These moments constitute, finally, the real arrival of European culture in America.

One
❦ DISCOVERY NARRATIVE ❦
An Adventure
of the Eye Alone

Thus we tender to the kind reader the fruitfulness of this land, subject to his own judgment. I admit that I am incompetent to describe the beauties, the grand and sublime works, wherewith Providence has diversified this land. Our opinions are formed by the eye alone. . . .

The superabundance of this country is not equalled by any other in the world.

Adriaen van der Donck, *A Description of the New Netherlands* (1655)

THE SIMPLEST AND MOST DELIGHTFUL VARIETY OF THE NEW WORLD travel book is less narrative than declaratory, less concerned with the details of an actual endured journey than with the general design of America as a scene for potential ones. It tends whenever possible to rely on a group of presentational means in which time plays no crucial role—catalogs, tables, descriptions, discourses, expositions—forms which by their own static, even iconographic, nature convey writer and reader alike into a state of existence beyond the limits and confusions of a historical moment. Like much New World prose (the tales of conquest by the *hidalgos,* for instance), it is indebted to the chivalric romance, the medieval literary mode in which travel as an earthly deed was joined with the mysteries of religious truth, in which adventure and advent were intimately mixed. But it derives from that form a structure of spiritual meaning rather than a model of events or an ideal of action. It portrays America as a fund of vegetative symbols, a place of "superabundance" counterpointed to the implicit wasteland of Europe.[1]

The discoverer, to be sure, exists in a world of plots and actual journeys, and in this sense the discovery account has temporal and spatial implications. The loose frame of a personal survey often surrounds the discursive matter which the discoverer presents: Adriaen van der Donck's observations regarding the landforms of New Netherland, its Indian inhabitants, and its European settlers all rest in the most general way on his own accumulated experience in the colony. He asserts frequently in his catalogs that he has seen a certain species of animal, or has witnessed a certain natural event. Such personal attestations are rhetorically effective where they occur, since they establish the author as a witness, a person in touch with the facts. In a less local sense, they help the reader to imagine America not simply as a cabinet of curiosities, but also as a place of possible experience.

One never would know from the *Description*, however, that van der Donck was arrested once by Peter Stuyvesant, or that he took part in a mild rebellion against the latter's stern governmental measures. He leaves out of the *Description* all the political commentary which he included five years earlier in his *Remonstrance* (1650) to the home government. That other work opens, curiously enough, with a survey of New Netherland that reads like a rehearsal for van der Donck's later book, then passes on to a series of charges and denunciations which never surface in the *Description* itself. The relationship of these two texts tells us a good deal about van der Donck's intentions in each, but it suggests, too, a relation between those larger forms of which each book is an example.[2]

Reality in the *Description,* as in similar texts, stays conveniently distant. Experience is not a web of events and places and personalities, but rather a simple contact between mind or emotions and a generalized American scene. New Netherland becomes the implicit subject of innumerable vague predications: it is a "fine, acceptable, healthy, extensive and agreeable country."[3] Even the mass of details which van der Donck collects regarding flora and fauna, landforms, and human inhabitants serves his essentially abstract, selective purpose as a writer. His prose rests at the level of descriptive images, still shots of a world which we never see in motion. Adventure is a matter of seeing and hearing and tasting; the adventurer is less an actor than a passive receptor, a traveler poised in wonder before a world lush in vegetation and vibrant in animal life.

In another sense, however, this passivity itself becomes a deeply chivalric form of action. At the heart of the discovery narrative stands the ravished observer, fixed in awe, scanning the New World scene, noting its colors and shapes, recording its plenitude and its sensual richness. For such a traveler, no other act than this is necessary, no penetration or possession is required, no movement out
22 into the landscape. The simple timeless stare in which the dis-

coverer is wrapped, and the emotional stasis which envelops that figure's mind, together constitute a full adventure.[4]

This adventurous core of the discovery account explains many technical features of the form. The lack of a true narrative interest, for instance, can be seen as an absolute necessity rather than an anomaly. It is a fundamental principle of discovery: standing in silence before a purely present landscape, the discoverer achieves through perception alone a communion with the eternal sources of life. Viewing such a world in such a way becomes a ritualistic, even eucharistic, act. America from this standpoint is a vast emblem of rejuvenation; to see (and later to explicate) that emblem is to enter a state where time does not matter, a period of enhanced duration which gives access through the realm of history to the domain of spiritual force. Each of the discoverer's descriptions repeats for the reader this structure of spiritual ascent. Like the medieval knight who returns from his quest to tell the tale of his adventure (for part of his duty is to relate what he has seen and undergone), the discoverer relays his account of the strange world he has entered to an audience which remained at home.

In this web of spiritual purposes, the techniques of the discovery account acquire even in the simplest case a symbolic power. The catalog, a central strategy in such works, is more than a list of items. It refers to New World facts, and organizes them in terms of scientific categories. But it has a moral purpose as well as an informative one. Through the very detail of its enumeration it expresses an idea of the American God as the ultimate good provider, as a providential deity in the root sense of the term. The Lord of the New World is the creator of vegetation and game, the architect of mighty rivers and fertile grounds. Viewing those things which God has made, the discoverer comes almost into the Divine presence.

Quick gain, long-term profit, even settlement all are implicit in such lists. The idea of use, of exploitation, lurks everywhere in the discoverer's paean to American nature. Yet it lacks here that programmatic (even greedy) thrust which, as I argue in my next chapter, distinguishes the second ideal type of travel book. The keynote is wonder, rapture, and a language which comports with such emotions by its own superlative uplift, its haste of enumeration. "There is no countrey," Walter Ralegh writes of Guiana, "which yeeldeth more pleasure to the Inhabitants, either for these common delights of hunting, hawking, fishing, fowling, and the rest, then Guiana doth. It hath so many plaines, cleare rivers, abundance of Phesants, Partridges, Quailes, Rayles, Cranes, Herons, and all other fowle; Deare of all sortes, Porkes, Hares, Lyons, Tygers, Leopards, and divers other sortes of beastes, eyther for chace, or foode." To be sure, Ralegh mentions at the start of his book that lost colony of Roanoke for which, had the weather been better, he would have searched on his return voyage; and he outlines in his peroration an imperial scheme for the Queen, a quick move against Spanish domination in South America. Yet in the quoted passage he is neither the remembrancer of a tragically failed attempt, nor the promoter of an heroically presumptuous one. He is a rapt observer, a writer whose prose overflows with delight. Finally, the line of his own disaster was to lead out of another aspect of his *Guiana,* and was to force on his life a plot of delusion and failure: for it was the elusive realm of El Dorado (and its capital, "Manoa") which most fascinated Ralegh. His execution by James I after his seventh New World voyage, when he came back without the gold he had promised, linked him with the Roanoke settlers rather than the happy huntsmen of his rapturous catalog. The Guiana volume itself was the first act of his tragedy, full of those deceits and frustrations which were to be his only real portion of American wealth; but in the midst of it he was poised for an instant on the edge of a quite different future, and a quite different New World.[5]

REASON AND WONDER

At some point along a continuum, the exultant catalog as one sees it in Ralegh fades off into the truly scientific list of a naturalist. Locating that point in individual books, or in the form as a whole, is a tricky business. Rational scrutiny and wondering observation do not necessarily exclude each other, and in many instances are so mixed together that separating them is almost impossible. Furthermore, even the most avowedly rational works may feed through the rigor of their description a strong emotional need in the writer or the audience. Science becomes one means by which the true nature and extent of America are concretized in the travel book, and hence made more sensuous and more imagistically present to the reader. By organizing American facts, reason makes them available as signs of emotional possession.

Depending on the context in which they appear, even the barest listings of New World animals and plants, complete with specimen weights and biological details, may function in a symbolic, rather than simply a cognitive, way. When Thomas Jefferson attempts to answer in his *Notes on the State of Virginia* (1785) Buffon's theories about American "degeneration" (theories which, postulating that America was a wasteland, were a European response to the discoverer's sense of rapture), he takes the course most appealing to his own philosophical interests, and most appropriate to Buffon's scientific pretensions. Gathering detailed information from people in several regions of the country, he produces elaborate tables (see PLATE 2) comparing the known weights of New World animals with those of their European counterparts. The tactic justifies his prior estimate of Buffon's thesis, since with few exceptions the American creatures weigh much more than the European ones. But the tables are more than expository devices. Showing such a favorable picture of American nature (its ability to sustain animals, whether native or imported, in their most healthy condition), they argue silently for the regenerative powers of the New World scene. Setting out to disprove an uncomplimentary theory, Jefferson winds up substituting a strongly complimentary one for it. The fact that so many animals are "aboriginal" only to America likewise suggests, by the copious blank spaces thus introduced on the European side of Jefferson's table, that New World life is far more various, as well as more powerful, than that of the Old World. Jefferson's argument with Buffon uses reason in the cause of truth, but also in the cause of wonder.[6] There is a touch of American audacity in the whole performance, even a sense of frontier humor: simple Jefferson with his concrete beasts outsmarts the French dandy with his grand speculations, his civilized scheme of reality.[7]

Notes on the State of Virginia is not a travel book in the ordinary sense of that term—indeed, its attack on Buffon includes an attack on his sources as well, on those travelers in America from whom the French theorist has derived his wrong information. Yet Jefferson's book holds up as an unspoken ideal Francis Bacon's image of the traveler as a person in touch with reality. And it points toward the West of American curiosity as well as toward the East of Jefferson's audience, setting up a plot of native discovery which was to mature in the Lewis and Clark expedition twenty years later. Commenting on the presence of fossils in the inland reaches of the continent, Jefferson considers several (European) theories of their origin, then holds back from accepting any: "There is a wonder somewhere" (33), he concludes, and decides that it is better to remain in doubt than positively to err through dogmatic and uninformed assertions. By implication, knowledge will follow on the heels of 25 travel. The West of Jefferson's whole text is a fund of mysteries mediated back to the East through rumor and tale, through vague hint and even conscious imposition. ("We are told of Marble at Kentucky," he wrote in his manuscript of the book. "This may or may not be. Those countries have been explored chiefly by people of sanguine complexions of mind, eager to see in every object there whatever is most perfect in nature" [265]). Science will provide the means of rationalizing such hints, and will do so by producing a cognitive map of the West allied to that which Jefferson himself sketches in his charts and measurements of the East. The task of science in the face of terra incognita is to deny the negation of that term by making the place to which it refers known, *cognita*. Discovery becomes a process of stipulation, of turning the suggestive stories of western travelers into the natural history of a continent. Wonder is a spur to experience, not its end point. Hence Jefferson's stance toward the West (in which direction one face of Janus-like Monticello fronts) is an uncomfortable mixture of longing and design. He both desires and fears an unmediated contact. Power and size require an answering form. Like the world which it addresses, science abhors a vacuum.

Jefferson occupies a borderground of discovery as act and idea. The passage of the Potomac through the Blue Ridge, he asserts, "is worth a voyage across the Atlantic" (19), yet his own experience of that grand scene (and of the Natural Bridge) reveals how uncertain in the presence of American nature even so sophisticated a man as Jefferson can be. Like the legendary mammoth which he evokes as an elusive symbol of New World potentiality, the Potomac and the arch of stone suggest both the great scope of natural event in America and the large, possibly threatening forces at work here. We see in these details of the landscape a certain ferocious quality, a frightening dimension to abundance itself.[8] From its base, the Natural Bridge is a perfect emblem of the sublime, a cause of inexpressible delight: "the rapture of the Spectator is really indiscribable" (25). From its top, however, it affords a dizzying glimpse into "the abyss" below, a glimpse which few travelers willingly seek. Becoming for the moment a literal as well as an intellectual discoverer, Jefferson tells of his own experience: "You involuntarily fall on your hands and feet, creep to the parapet, and peep over it. Looking down from this height about a minute, gave me a violent head ach" (24-25).[9]

26   The episode is a model of European reaction to the New World,

even under the spell of innocent wonder. Jefferson's headache, like that of the contemplative discoverer (and like the heartache of so many settlers) is as much a sign of the "indiscribable" (unnameable, unordered) nature of the American scene, and of experience in it, as is the rapture of that "Spectator" who views the bridge from below. The whole passage in *Notes on the State of Virginia* shows us a man struggling to find his proper perspective, that single organizing viewpoint from which the great size of America can be reduced to proper dimension. This is the discoverer's struggle par excellence, the deep structure of psychological unease which accounts for that figure's persistent schematics. America must be diminished from a world to a list of words (and things), from a vast hemisphere to a convenient perceptual or moral formula. In Jefferson's case the reduction is highly instructive. The creeping movement out to the edge of the bridge is balanced by two countermovements: the descent to terra firma beneath, from which acclivity becomes beauty, the "parapet" (itself an architectural image) becomes "so beautiful an arch, so elevated, so light, and springing, as it were, up to heaven"; and the redefinition of the upper surface itself, the extension of a metaphor implicit in the object's name: "This bridge is in the county of Rockbridge, to which it has given name, and affords a public and commodious passage over a valley, which cannot be crossed elsewhere for a considerable distance" (25). The former stance allows the traveler to see and articulate a shape presumably immanent in this natural detail, to reconcile wilderness and art; the latter converts acrophobia into a means of moving into the agora beyond. The transfixed wanderer is allowed to retreat into design as a habit of perception, or as a plan of action. When Jefferson adds as a final word on the place that the stream passing under the arch, Cedar creek, "is a water of James river, and sufficient in the driest seasons to turn a grist-mill" (25), he is linking this landscape by another pair of lines to the known ground of the East: to the chart of explored water, to the scheme of human use.[10] His perceptions and his language function throughout as vehicles of ideal settlement, subtle devices for the assertion of control and prefigurative order.

In an early version of the passage, Jefferson goes so far as to distort topography for the sake of his aesthetic (and social) ideals. He there writes that, from the lower perspective, one looks through the arch to a "very pleasing view" beyond: "the North mountain on one side, and Blue ridge on the other, at the distance each of them of about five miles."[11] Thus the viewer is so placed that the natural object becomes an artistic frame; the eye moves out into the same realm of planar space which the traveler passing over the "bridge" enters. The vertical axis, fruitful of both exalted wonder and precipitous despair, is replaced with the horizontal. Altitude fades into latitude, and with latitude comes a greater freedom of informing sight and action. The "great convulsion" (24) which Jefferson thinks is responsible for the formation of the arch—another sign of American power and destructiveness—hence is forgotten in the traveler's ability to organize (and use) the scene. Jefferson's own geometric approach to this site of presumed geologic violence likewise shapes it into a catalog of lines without perspective: "The arch approaches the Semi-elliptical form; but the larger axis of the ellipsis, which would be the cord of the arch, is many times longer than the semi-axis which gives it's height" (24). Almost a parody of a theorem, this description urges us to see the arch as a shape on paper, not as an object in space seen from a definite spatial viewpoint. Every avenue of approach to the Natural Bridge, except that of the man who creeps out to its edge and peers into the abyss, is a means of codification, of retreat into established systems of thought and deed. In this sense, Jefferson is not so much discovering the object as he is struggling to include it in prior orders.

Jefferson's description of the Potomac and Shenandoah a few pages earlier begins with a similar, but grander, struggle. His long answer to the previous query ("A notice of its rivers, rivulets, and how far they are navigable?") catalogs those natural features by mapping a vast inner region in terms of human movement, actual and potential, through it: rivers are channels of communication and trade, much as the Natural Bridge is partly a means of passage, a link between severed cliffs. Science and commerce combine to make this section of Jefferson's text a prime example of the explorer's mood and stance. The verb tense is future, the angle of intersection between landscape and humanity is determined by the narrow arc of "use." Yet the mere abundance of water in Jefferson's catalog exerts a subtle, wondering effect. We are not surprised to find that "The *Ohio* is the most beautiful river on earth" (10), or that the "Cumberland is a very gentle stream" (12), or that "The *Great Kanhaway*" is bordered by lands of high "fertility" (13). In the end, Jefferson's way of organizing all the streams is economic (the gentleness of the Cumberland, for instance, is important because it allows "loaded batteaux" to pass along for "800

28

miles, without interruption" [12]); but we sense, too, that an
aesthetic order lies implicit in the channels of commerce. It is a
cause for wonder, in fact, that the landscape seems to unfold itself
according to the urgent human principle of navigation, that the
given world of America is appropriate to an imported means of
passage.[12]

Introducing his treatment of American rivers, Jefferson suggests
that inspecting a map of the country "will give a better idea of the
geography of its rivers, than any description in writing" (5). Beyond his modesty is a true grasp of the function which maps often
have performed in the New World. They have been primarily
charts of "idea," spatial ideograms which transcend the sequence of
a traveler's life in space and time by making the American scene
amenable to the categories of geographical science. Freezing the
New World into a set of lines and symbols, the mapmaker catalogs
the hemisphere by a sign system allied to that of the naive discoverer. From Juan de la Cosa's tentative sketch of 1500 to John C.
Frémont's detailed charts of the 1840s, one can follow the ac-
celerating movement of comprehension, the embracing of emptiness by lines which are first outlines, then transverse probings, then
finally (as though they have become organic) veins of actual white
expansion, capillaries of plantation and growth. Platting and plotting thus merge, the one art reflects (and promotes) the other.[13]
What is lost in the process is a sense of the real terrain as a place of
action rather than grand plot. St. Jean de Crèvecoeur, himself a
surveyor and mapmaker in Canada, has one of his fictional settlers
express just this point: "Nothing is so easy as to travel on a map;
our fingers smoothly glide over brooks and torrents and mountains. But actually to traverse a track of one hundred miles, accompanied with eight children, with cattle, horses, oxen, sheep, etc.—
this is to meet with a thousand unforeseen difficulties."[14]

Such contrasts inform Jefferson's passage on the Potomac and
Shenandoah. His earlier general section on the rivers of Virginia
and the West derives from mapmaking (and the art of topographic
description) both a fund of information and a hint for his own
aloof form. His stance is far above the landscape, abstract and
inclusive.[15] At the start of his fourth query ("A notice of its mountains?"), he likewise gestures toward cartography: "For the particular geography of our mountains I must refer [the reader] to Fry
and Jefferson's map of Virginia; and to Evans's analysis of his map
of America for a more philosophical view of them than is to be

found in any other work" (18).[16] But the course of his discussion is away from such categorical arts. He maps the mountains as an orderly series of ridges, and encompasses their diversity by stressing their essential unity from the Northern states almost to the Gulf of Mexico. It is the kind of survey which clearly cannot exist without prior mappings, without a graphic base from which to elaborate a "description in writing." But then he notes, in discussing the Apalachicola river, that its name derives from "the Apalachies, an Indian nation formerly residing on it." That local fact, he continues, has been extended by "European geographers" into a taxonomic label for all the mountains stretching to the North, "as may be seen in their different maps." Then comes his particularist assertion, its rhetoric allied to that which he uses in his refutation of Buffon: "But the fact I believe is, that none of these ridges were ever known by that name to the inhabitants, either native or emigrant, but as they saw them so called in European maps" (18). Cartography, which enters his text as an ideal means of discovery and comprehension, suddenly becomes an abstract and distant art, out of touch with the world which it pretends to describe.

What Jefferson substitutes for it is a momentary yet intimate sense of the American landscape not as it is "called" but as it is: three-dimensional, local, alive with force. The movement of the Potomac through "the Blue ridge" (*not* the Appalachians) is a vibrant event, "perhaps one of the most stupendous scenes in nature." His epithet, "stupendous," is crucial. It hints at stupefaction, emotional paralysis, but also at enormity and wonder. The observer balances between disorder and a feeling of organic form: as he stands "on a very high point of land," he is both safe from the tumult below and, literally, on its verge. He is involved in that world as no mapmaker would be. The drama of impulse and resistance which Jefferson imagines as an explanation of the scene is fully scientific in its terms, but kinetic and close in its origin: it seems to grow in the observer's mind as he stands viewing the landscape below him. If this is theory, it hardly resembles the geographic theories of European savants. It springs up on the spot, the urgent discovery of a traveler rather than the aloof invention of a philosopher. It is an "opinion" into which "the first glance of this scene hurries our senses," an "impression" which is corroborated by details emerging from a closer view. Spatial perception thus is an unfolding of objects and events, an organic process of sensation and thought which mirrors in its own fluidity that of the world which it addresses.[17]

The eye and the mind, to be sure, seek fixture in such a landscape. Their grasp of the forces at work in nature (time, change, "disrupture and avulsion") is one means of seeing order in disorder itself, of finding an explanation which allows one to tell the story of this landscape, and hence to comprehend it narratively. Yet nature provides on its own a further line of organization by inducing one's eye through the "cloven" mountain to a scene "as placid and delightful, as [the other] is wild and tremendous." The "distant finishing which nature has given to the picture" allows the observer not only to perceive nature as itself an artist, a personification of the human rage for ordermaking, but also to find in the merely present world (rather than in some hypothesized narrative past) a balancing explanation of violence. Hence in the interplay of an immediate world of force and a distant, mediated world of peace the observer's eye "ultimately composes itself," perception becoming (like the given space) an artwork, a dynamic movement toward completion. As in the Natural Bridge passage, verticality yields to a lateral expanse, depth to distance: "a small catch of smooth blue horizon, at an infinite distance in the plain country, inviting you, as it were, from the riot and tumult roaring around, to pass through the breach and participate of the calm below." Finding this passage for the eye, and this destination for the mind, one soon discovers that the traveler's road "happens actually to lead" toward the point of balance, the blue horizon and the plain. There remains yet the harrowing descent into the scene, the tenuous reversal of acclivity as one winds beneath "terrible precipices hanging in fragments" above the road; but the journey now has a composition of its own. Its line follows out the line of sight already established. The order discovered from above has organized the traveler's way, has insured that the "stupendous" scene will become an occasion for wonder rather than horror or immobility (18–19).[18]

By substituting, even through such active means, a distant spatial point for a vast and close arena, Jefferson has repeated a pattern typical of the discovery account. He has moved from a world of time and extent (to which a narrative form is appropriate) to a world of condensation and poise which can be rendered as a descriptive image. Though he probably intended "the State of Virginia" in his title as a political phrase, it has overtones, too, of an older American usage (as in Robert Beverley's *The History and Pres-*

ent *State of Virginia,* 1705; or Hugh Jones's *The Present State of Virginia,* 1724): the idea of a static present condition of which the writer's book is an equally static portrait. Rejecting maps at the outset of the passage, Jefferson comes back finally to a cartographic model for his prose and for the imagined journey which it records. The traveler's experience ends, in effect, with the aesthetic contemplation that overtakes him on his hill and that organizes the landscape below. The vanishing point of that world becomes the means of making all disagreeable facts vanish; the remainder of his journey is a shift of perspective which itself converts that point into a literal location as well as a moral and spatial focus for his "picture." His map of the surrounding terrain is bisected by the road which he will follow: that human line comes to dominate the natural ones which first engrossed his attention (the ridge, the converging streams, the enlarged river flowing off through the cloven landscape), and at its end lies a plain country which discovers to him an America to match his imagination.

The whole passage, like most of Jefferson's book, is marked by an effort to confine action to the eye and mind. Though he paints a titanic, heroic landscape, his traveler is a hero of order and comprehension rather than event. In his movement through the "breach" one can trace, nonetheless, the remnants of an epic-chivalric situation (Thermopylae and Roncevaux come to mind), even if the "war" in this case has been fought between the rivers and the mountains, and the traveler's own deed is abstracted, intellectualized, as linear as the road which he follows.[19] Indeed, the road itself is a chivalric sign, an indication that beyond the present rough world of history is a realm of suggestive renovation. The trials of sight and thought in the foreground are given meaning by that further range of space, much as the knight's quest is shaped by his spiritual destination, or Roland's death in the narrow valley is made significant by the larger French victory which it assures. It is no accident that Jefferson, who first saw Harper's Ferry in 1783 when bound for the Congress in Philadelphia, organizes the landscape there as a visual parable of the nation's recent struggles with Great Britain, or that he makes the Potomac, in its urge for a free passage, into an implicit symbol of similar expansive urges in the American population.[20] His scene is alive with hints of a grand future romance: his wilderness seems to open itself up, with violent rapidity, for the flood of western emigration. Like Daniel Boone, who describes the mountain passes of the Cumberland Gap region as a "wild and horrid" sight and notes that "it is impossible to behold them without terror," Jefferson also can see such "ruins, not of Persepolis or Palmyra, but of the world"—Boone's rather surprising language in John Filson's *Kentucke*—as the necessary cleavage of a resistant hemisphere for the passage of white intent.[21] The rubble of an ancient epoch thus becomes the raw material of a futuristic plot; natural signs are curiously consonant with the imported language of pastoral desire. The republic of yeomen farmers lies beyond these monuments of geologic, and emotional, upheaval.

WONDER AND WELL-BEING

Throughout its range, the discovery account delivers its reader to the threshold of such promising and revivifying locales. It offers a glimpse into strange regions where, amid wondrous beasts, unknown tribes, and incalculable powers, a traveler may encounter the proof of a further "beyond." To the extent that a discoverer does travel, he enters a stylized landscape, a world of lapidary order where disruptive facts are downplayed. Like the anonymous author of "The Wonders of Canada" (1768), he goes forward, "dashing through difficulties, over vast lakes, rivers, rapids, creeks, swamps, and deep forests"; or, like Jean-Bernard Bossu, he may pause to summarize in a sentence or two the extended burden of his new experience: "Our eyes are charmed by the beauty of nature, unadorned by art, exactly as it was fashioned by the hands of the Creator before the fall of our first ancestor."[22] The great stretch of Bossu's North America, a vast area through which he traveled for twelve years, thus becomes prime ground, strangely at the center of European myth. The natural details of this region bolster his Edenic imagery: "Louisiana has all sorts of curious and hitherto unknown animals," and is covered by "entire forests of sassafras trees, used for medicine and dyes." "Some trees," he continues, "contain copal, a gummy substance which is a balm as good as that made in Peru. Animals wounded by hunters cure themselves by rubbing against a tree from which this balm flows." For travelers who find their way growing weary or overlong there is a similarly spontaneous cure, since the sweet mockingbird "enjoys the company of man." "It is almost as though these birds were made expressly to help the traveler relax and forget his weariness" (196, 203).

Other benign alliances reveal themselves during Bossu's North

American sojourn. Adopted by one Indian tribe, he devotes a good
deal of space to a description of its customs and those of other
native groups. Though he is a candid observer, aware of imperial
policies and not hesitant to criticize Indian ways, he is notable for
his openness of mind with regard to American cultures. Initiated
into some native practices, and with a fair insight into the meaning
of Indian rituals and beliefs, Bossu emerges in his book as a European for whom American experience has bordered on the episodes
of romance. Like the glowing lists of American natural objects and
animals he presents, his inventory of Indian life evokes for his
reader a sense of some penultimate earthly terrain, a place of great
distance and difference. At its optimum, the New World in Bossu's
text seems, like the mockingbird, to have been created primarily
for the traveler's delight and refreshment.[23]

Neither Bossu's *Nouveaux Voyages* nor any other given book is a
pure idyll of balanced perception and harmonious movement. Like
Adriaen van der Donck's *Remonstrance,* Bossu's letters home attack
the maladministration of colonial officials—so effectively, in fact,
that he was to be imprisoned for six months at the instigation of Kerlérec, governor of Louisiana. He suggests that the potential of
America has been diminished by European errors, and thus im-
merses himself in a complex of Old World designs and failures
which intervenes between his wondering eye and the present
American scene. Telling of the disasters visited on earlier New
World travelers (Hernando de Soto, La Salle, Major d'Artaguiette,
General Braddock, among others), he sketches a plot of Western
experience which is far from romantic in shape and meaning.
Hence he enters the rhetorical ground of the settler, the figure of
lament who catalogs not the strange abundance of America but the
sad defeat of those who have tried to possess it. Even his own
wanderings are not free from trouble. He frequently remarks on
his extreme condition, tells of almost being drowned, of being
dragged to the bank of the Tombigbee one night by an alligator
greedy for the fish wrapped up in his bedding.

Such remarks, and the perceptions which stimulate them, are by
no means peculiar to Bossu. Even that anonymous traveler who
"dashed" through the difficulties of Canada in 1768 came to admit
that, after all, such a tour "affords greater satisfaction in the reflection than in the execution," that generally "there is more pleasure
in having seen, than in the seeing." Henry Woodward's "Westoe
voyage" of 1674 leads him finally to a "sparkling" country, but only

after he has endured constant rain for several days, has gone over "many fattigous [i.e., "fatiguing"] hills," and has acclimated himself in other ways to the new landscapes beyond which the Westoe region lies.[24]

In a larger sense, the Atlantic passage itself comes to represent in the travel book just this trial of will and endurance, this attenuation of experience between departure and arrival. Thus George Alsop writes in his *A Character of the Province of Mary-Land* (1666) of those exploited tradesmen of England who would "as live take a Bear by the tooth, as think of leaving their own Country, though they live [elsewhere] among their own National people, and are governed by the same Laws they have here, yet all this wont do with them." The only reason which such squeamish folk can offer for their reluctance, Alsop continues, is that "There's a great Sea betwixt them and Mary-Land, and in that Sea there are Fishes, and not only Fishes but great Fishes, and then should a Ship meet with such an inconsiderable encounter as a Whale, one blow with his tayle, and then *Lord have Mercy upon us.*" Let one come upon such men in their "common Exchange"—some sleazy bar—and the air will be filled with heroic boasts. But let someone "step in and interrupt their discourse, by telling them of a Sea Voyage, and the violency of storms that attends it, and that there are no back-doors to run out at"—the sort of convenient escape which such *milites gloriosi* would call "a handsom Retreat and Charge again"—then "the apprehensive danger of this is so powerful and penetrating on them, that a damp sweat immediately involves their Microcosm, so that Margery the old Matron of the Celler is fain to run for a half-peny-worth of Angelica to rub their nostrils."[25]

Often extravagant, scurrilous whenever he can manage to be, Alsop here touches lightly on an abiding Eastern fear. His Atlantic is a realm of rumored death, a vacancy filled with fantasies which warrant procrastination. His very wit suggests the strength of Old World anxiety, and his larger cure for that condition is redolent of a wide pattern in the travel book. What awaits the voyager on the western shore is a fund of revivifying images, a realm of harmony like that discovered on native ground (and beyond a native void) by Jefferson, Bossu, and others. If "Margery the old Matron of the Celler" is a condensation of English life, the answering figure in America is a young and sensual Mary-Land "drest in her green and fragrant Mantle of the Spring." Taking the metaphor in his title seriously, Alsop develops a Theophrastian "character" of his adopted province, but one entirely in its praise. Topography becomes physiognomy, and the benign face of America is a true sign of its essence. Changing his metaphor but retaining his theme, Alsop declares that "The Trees, Plants, Fruits, Flowers, and Roots that grow here . . . are the only Emblems or Hieroglyphicks of our Adamitical or Primitive situation . . . which still bear the Effigies of Innocency . . . which by their dumb vegetable Oratory, each hour [speak] to the Inhabitant[s] in silent acts, That they need not look for any other Terrestrial Paradice, to suspend or tyre their curiosity upon, while she is extant." One may find in Mary-Land the "Landskip of the Creation drawn to the life," may "read" there "Natures universal Herbal without book." All other regions once renowned "for a vegetable plentiousness, must now in silence strike and vayle all, and whisper softly in the auditual parts of Mary-Land, that None but she in this dwells singular." Without equal, Mary-Land is a womb of life which gives forth "Natures extravagancy of a superabounding plenty," a breeding organ amenable to foreign seed—but notable most of all for "the rareness and superexcellency of her own glory," that "abundancy of reserved Rarities" not known elsewhere on earth (344–45).

Not without reason, Alsop complains of the great task laid on him in writing such a "character": "For I have had so large a Journey, and so heavy a Burden to bring Mary-Land into England, that I am almost out of breath" (342). Amazonian in her proportions, his heroine exhausts his muse. A sexual play clearly is intended here, as so often in Alsop's text. His prose is foreplay to the emigrant's consummation, an act of pandering designed not to bring Mary-Land into England, but just the reverse. Verging constantly on a parodic overstatement, he both postures and impostures, and one never is quite sure at what point his delight becomes a waggish equivocation.

It remains certain, nonetheless, that Alsop's America waits eagerly for the traveler at the end of an Atlantic breach, a sign of health and arrival beyond the dangers and fears of crossing. An indentured servant, Alsop found his lot more than acceptable in his province, and his less flighty prose portrays the typical emigrant's fortune in glowing terms. More is involved in his book, however, than economics (or the economy of sexual and other appetites). He wrote the piece while recovering from an almost fatal illness, and the exuberance of his style is a record of his own rediscovery of life

in the New World which he almost lost. At the end of his text is printed a series of letters to his family and friends, documents placed after his "character" of Mary-Land but in fact prior to his more public utterance. There he records the passage of his spirit into a province of faith and renewal, a crossing of the gulf which gives his arrival an extra burden of significance. "We are only sent by God of an Errand into this World" (386), he writes on the brink of death; four months later he feels like Lazarus, amazed by the wonders of God. However bawdy his tract, however scurrilous his wit, there lies behind its exultant portrait of America a true discovery of Alsop's own, a sense of rebirth which makes his Mary-Land a second mother as well as a lover. In Freudian terms, such doubling renders his book more complex. But in terms of the prose tradition in which it was written, *A Character of the Province of Mary-Land* thus develops its plot of the Western voyage from the shape of its author's own life. Having passed through a scene of dissolution to the country of amazing health, Alsop urges upon lingering (and malingering) Europeans a similar journey of renewal.

"In a word, it's a place so every way inviting," Charles Wooley proclaimed of New York in the same period, "that our English Gentry, Merchants and Clergy (especially such as have the natural Stamina of a consumptive propogation in them; or an Hypocondriacal Consumption) would flock thither for self-preservation." Like Alsop's Mary-Land, Wooley's land of health lies across a void: "self-preservation" requires a prior exposure of the self, and there are those who are taken aback (or kept back) by fear of that prior deed. Cured himself by the voyage, Wooley mimics the hesitant much as Alsop assaults them: "but oh the passage, the passage thither, *hic labor, hoc opus est:* there is the timorous objection: the Ship may founder by springing a Leak, be wreckt by a Storm or taken by a Pickeroon."[26] Such fears enter his prose only to be dismissed, as preparation for a transcendent arrival. He goes on to portray the Atlantic crossing as itself the occasion of delight. Sea-sickness becomes possible proof that the ocean contains "an *Emetick Vomitory* vertue . . . which by the motion of the Ship operates upon the Stomach and ejects whatever is offensive." Moreover, "there is a daily curiosity in contemplating the wonders of the Deep, as to see a Whale"—not "encountering" a vessel, but rather "wallowing and spouting cataracts of water"—or "to see the Dolphin that hieroglyphick of celerity leaping above water in chase of the flying fish." Better yet, one might eat the latter fish when it chanced to land on deck in its flight, or even eat the shark (a nice retribution indulged in only "for want of other Provisions"). Far from being a void, the ocean is seen as a foretaste of the continent beyond, a world of recovered health, of wonder, of sustenance. In the end, to be sure, sharks may eat men as well as vice versa; but, Wooley asks, "what difference betwixt being eaten by fish or by worms at the Christian Resurrection?" Citing an anecdote from Bacon, he adopts in his final comment a Baconian attitude himself, an openness of mind and an experimenting mood: "'One was saying that his Great-Grand-father Grand-father and Father died at Sea. Said another that heard him, and as I were you, I would never come to Sea; why saith he, where did your Great-Grand-father and Ancestors die? he answered where but in their Beds, saith the other, and I were as you I would never go to Bed.['] But for all this," Wooley concludes, "I durst venture a knap in a Cabbin at Sea, or in a Hammock in the Woods. So Reader a good Night" (61–63). Whatever is bad in the voyage is universal; whatever is good is local, and points west. The ship's bunk prefigures the slung bed of America, and the passage, like the arrival, is a "venture."

For William Wood, mapper of the New England plantations in his tract of 1634, the "prospect" of his adopted ground was equally bright. As I noted earlier, the metaphor of his title is one version of a figure which pervades the literature of discovery. A prefatory poem by one "S. W." urges us to use the book as a vantage point for a Western survey, a *"Mount"* grounded on Wood's ample American experience *"From whence we may* New Englands Prospect *take."* Overview, picture, map (but also point of view), the "prospect" is both artifact and its fertilizing stance, end product and the process leading to it. Far from silent, and hardly on a peak in Darien, Wood nonetheless adopts for his "true, lively, and experimental descrip-tion" an attitude like that of Keats's Cortés, a prospective stare, even something of a wild surmise.[27] Though Thomas Morton three years later was to joke on Wood's name and the title of his book (a "wooden prospect" becoming for him the code word for stiff, un-sensuous prose), Wood himself is as good as the words on his title page, both lively in style and kinetic in his concerns.[28] He served Morton as a lesser but available target for shots aimed actually at the Puritan elite. Nonetheless, Morton's pun on Wood's metaphor offers an instructive hint: the latter's "prospect," like the former's figure of "Canaan," provides an aloof and prior frame for the countless details relayed in his prose.

In the case of Wood, as the prefatory poem suggests ("Sure thou

deservest then no small prayse, who, / So short cut to *New England*
here dost show" [A4r]), the movement "up" to a prospective stance
for the reader cuts short the distance intervening between England
and America. Wood himself states on his title page that the book
has two intended audiences: "the mind-travelling Reader" and "the
future Voyager." Hence his controlling metaphor is itself a pun,
the "prospect" being both a mental image and a field of action. As
his preface makes clear, the book is designed to enlarge the views of
insulated Englishmen (who, like "tub-brain'd" Diogenes, have cir-
cled themselves in the "circumference" of an enclosing truth); it
does so by laying out a contemplative *and* active New World, a
realm of expanding horizons that is imperial and intellectual at
once. Citing the proverbial charge against travelers, that "they may
lie by authority, because none can controule them," Wood gives the
lie himself to his potential critics by making the perusal of his text a
voyage of inner and outer discovery, a line of understanding which
leads west through the broken circle of accepted dogma (A3r). If
the extent of his subject requires a vertical ascent for the inscription
of that line, so, too, does the confined mentality of his double
audience.

Like the map which accompanies and is complemented by his
prose (the tenth chapter of his first part being a lengthy gloss on it),
the substance of Wood's relation is, indeed, a "short cut" out of
England to the New World. It takes its beginning in an act of
literary criticism typical of many such texts, a reaction against the
"many scandalous and false reports past upon the Country, even
from the sulphurious breath of every base ballad-monger." Countering such lies by revealing the true lay of the new-found land,
Wood uses the authority of his American journey as the foundation
of authorship. His four years of New World experience are a personal terrain of which his book is a public prospect. The voyage
over and the long period of acclimatization become for the reader
"two or three houres travaile over a few leaves." With such a modest investment of time, the reader may "see and know that, which
cost him that writ it, yeares and travaile, over Sea and Land before
he knew it" (A3v). Hence a much later sense of "prospect" is also
appropriate to Wood's book: for the text is a refined ore of long
endurance, a line of glittering richness leading through a "mount"
of ordinary earth and rock.

Rich, too, is the state of health associated by Wood with New
England. Avowedly cautious in his claims (for "death being certaine

to all, in all Nations there must be something tending to death of like certainty"), Wood nonetheless asserts that "the common diseases of *England,* they be strangers to the *English* now in that strange Land." Of the three deaths which occurred in his own American town, one was due to an ailment predating emigration and the other two resulted from miscarriage. His own case solidifies the argument: "although in *England* I was brought up tenderly under the carefull hatching of my dearest friends, yet scarce could I be acquainted with health, having beene let blood sixe times for the *Pleurisie* before I went; likewise being assailed with other weakening diseases; but being planted in that new Soyle and healthfull Ayre, which was more correspondent to my nature, (I speake it with praise to the mercifull God) though my occasions have beene to passe thorow heate and cold, wet and dry, by Sea and Land, in Winter and Summer, day by day, for foure yeares together, yet scarse did I know what belonged to a dayes sicknesse" (9–10). Not all travel, clearly enough, need be "travail" as well.

There are, of course, beasts waiting by the side of the road. Wood's penultimate chapter in the first part lists the most salient: wolves, rattlesnakes, spiders, wasps, biting flies, mosquitoes. The section is a mere breath mark in between his hopeful survey of the present plantations and his advice to future voyagers, the chapters which precede and follow it. The rattlesnake, for instance, is a far more sluggish creature than has been reported in England: if it does have a nasty habit of lying "in pathes," Wood assures his reader that it sleeps soundly in the hot sun ("I have knowne foure men stride over one of them, and never awake her"). And should the creature chance to wake, it may be killed "easily" with a "small switch." If the worst happens, any person or animal bitten by the rattler may be cured readily with an application of snakeweed (45). The true serpents in Wood's Eden, in fact, are those double-tongued settlers who have been disappointed in America (usually because they have violated Wood's law: "all new *England* must be workers in some kinde" [48]), and who therefore have given it a bad name in the Old World. In a chapter which begins with a list of natural evils, such bad-mouthers wind up dominating the author's prose. His concluding remarks praise New England outrightly; even his concessions become a eulogy on his sometime home. The real evils there are imported, not native.

Having cleared the traveler's path in America, Wood turns east toward the ocean. "Many peradventure at the looking over of these

40

relations," he begins, "may have inclinations or resolution for the Voyage." Though wanting to use "no forcive arguments to perswade any," he is quick to dismiss from his concern here that "mind-travelling Reader" who earlier was half of his supposed audience, and to adopt a fully active purpose for his book (49). One suspects, in fact, that such was his hidden intention from the start, and that the uplift of his prose throughout has aimed at converting speculative delight into concrete speculation. In the second part, treating the natives of New England, he will hint at deeper hesitations (cannibalism, for one); but even there his dominant stress on the fruitfulness of America will win out, and Indian life itself will become an invitation to white voyaging.

Wood's text is not, however, an emigration tract in the strict sense. Like the other authors examined here, Wood writes from the stance of an excited traveler for whom curiosity—and the desire to play upon it, even to share it with the uninitiated—is the primary impulse. His westward voyager does not dash through the difficulties of an ocean passage, but neither is that figure solely a practical traveler. What Wood inscribes is a pathway of implicit renovation, a mental road made concrete through the active claims of his prose. Acknowledging the common fear of the sea, he urges that his reader view a ship as a "Cradle, rocked by a carefull Mothers hand." Though it often may be shaken "too and againe upon the troublesome Sea, yet seldome doth it sinke or over-turne"—the grammatical confusion is telling—"because it is kept by that carefull hand of Providence." One sinking per ship would be enough, of course, but Wood is playing the percentages here, absorbing the uncertainties of any single crossing into the large assurance of a pattern: "It was never knowne yet, that any ship in that voyage was cast away" (50). Moreover, of the five hundred people who have passed over already, only three or four individuals have died at sea; and of those who embarked "with such foule bodies . . . as did make their dayes uncomfortable at Land," a good many "have beene so purged and clarified at Sea, that they have beene more healthfull for aftertimes" (51). In short, the landsman's fear is misplaced. The breach once again seems like a necessary episode in the brightest New World plot.

By reducing ocean and ship alike to the scale of a domestic world, Wood effectually "encircles" the void, and thus come to resemble those "tub-brain'd" provincials of England whom he accuses earlier of being blind to the wider world. He posits a single line which 41 connects Europe and America, a river that flows between them through the sea, and that is charmed by God's protecting care. A wreck may be a statistical possibility, but it is made to seem theologically improbable. Similarly schematic reductions occur throughout his text, acts of clearing which offer the reader a "clarified" perspective from England to America. By abstracting potential dangers from the traveler's way, and placing them in appropriate discursive categories, Wood dismantles New England as a realm of events. He replaces the field of experience with a series of descriptive set pieces.

The limits of such an approach can be seen most poignantly in Wood's treatment of the New England Indians. Split down its middle by an unacknowledged line of color and culture, his book deals disjunctively with the "new-come *English* Planters," as his title page promises, and then with "the old Native Inhabitants." A classic device of the discovery account, this division holds apart in discourse what would come to be joined in growing complexity by New World narrative art—especially by the tales of border warfare, the captivity accounts, the relations of missionary work, and the native autobiographies. Wood posits, in effect, two New Englands, or two states of that single region which are to be understood from separate, perhaps exclusive, viewpoints. He thus untangles the possible web of cultural interchange: each group has its proper place (geographically and textually), much as "Beasts that live on the land" and "Beasts living in the water" do (18, 24). Having described the semicircle of English settlements which rings the Bay, Wood can go on to contemplate the hinterland of Indian life. Between the two actual spaces is a verbal gap, a leap of prose. The only implicit link between the two, in Wood's reality and in his book, is a parallel enjoyment of New England profusion.

THE CORRUPTION OF WONDER

This double encircling of American conditions is Wood's grandest and most hopeful scheme. Within four years, the soldier John Underhill would force the issue in his prose, as Wood's New England (with Underhill's aid) already had forced it in a series of bloody events. Yet Underhill's *Newes from America* (1638) exhibits amid the carnage of the Pequot War a curious tenacity of wonder. The breach opened by history in Wood's cultural and literary wall becomes an outlet rather than an inlet, a means by which the sanitizing flood of white discovery can flow out over previously forbidden ground. Underhill's emotional possession of the natives' dispossessed land is a strong balance to unspoken guilt. Split between martial and peaceful impulses, his book promises both a "true narration" of the war and "a new and experimentall discoverie" of amenable places beyond the circuit of Wood's Bay. Pleading a lack of time, Underhill confesses that he has not been able to sort out these two purposes into two separate sections, and hence must offer a hasty text which will "interweave" description and narration.[29] Whatever the extenuation, the result is highly suggestive. His impacted, sometimes confused history simply breaks off at its midpoint (the action in suspense) as he surveys a group of wonderful sites for the peaceful expansion of English order. Like the wedge of force sent against the Indians, of which Underhill himself was one surface, this section of his book is a means of laying bare a farther range of inviting American land. Underhill's weapons opened that terrain by removing its cover of native life; his description likewise dis-covers it by giving it entrance into prior categories, settling it conceptually as a first step in literal plantation.

By such means Underhill defends the war and dismisses its disastrous implications. Like Wood's ocean (or Jefferson's Potomac scene), his battleground is breached by the force of logic and of future emigration. Precisely through the middle of the Pequot War, and his account of it, passes a line of sight and foresight which displaces from the center of his narration the problematic facts of violence and death. Nowhere else can one find a better example of the discoverer's desire to stop American time, to retreat into a world of categorical design which is free from the narrative implications of his real career. In the midst of a war (not between the rivers and mountains, but between two human groups), Underhill finds in the snatch of a future horizon the necessary oblivion for a historical struggle which he would rather forget. The defense of genocide by an argument from cultural imperatives lies implicit in this uncanny, almost accidental, mix of modes. As Wood pushes to one side of "the pathe" any natural evil, and crowds the traveler's way with presumed delights, so Underhill and a hundred apologists after him insure the safe passage of European culture to America by defeating the natives in deed and word. No less than Wood, Underhill offers a prospect into (and of) America, a shortcut revealed by sharper weapons but a duller wit. His own "mount" (and that of the reader) is a bloody pile of corpses, the

ruins of an opposite—and, in his biased view, an opposing—
way.

We verge in *Newes from America* on another border of discovery, a
world where the foreground of an American Roncevaux threatens
to obscure the background of a peaceful space won or defended in
"war." Underhill's central glimpse into the latter region saves his
muse while it indicts the implied aesthetic of his action. The given
plot of his experience and the hopeful plot of his static vision are at
odds, and in ways that cannot be ignored (as allied conflicts in Wood
and others can be). His wonder is forced in more senses than one.
Hence his book belongs as much to the realm of settlement accounts
as it does to the world of discovery, though Underhill himself would
not understand why. His mixture of the two terrains, and their appropriate emotions, is the exact watermark of a subgenre in American writing, a form distinguished by its radical fluctuations of mood,
its pursuit of different and opposing goals. The obverse of his account is Cabeza de Vaca's *Relation* (1542), or James Smith's *Remarkable Occurrences* (1799): the record of white captivation which finally
hints at a cultural discovery, a sense of wonder derived from a cast-
away condition among the "other." Such books, which tell of journeys away from the common white path, break down the walls of
European deed and prose.

Underhill had his own problems with the orthodox New England
way which he supposedly was defending. His troubles are a reminder of how concrete the Puritan saying ("look there be better
walking") was for the extra-vagant settler. But Underhill represents
the slightest of accommodations to New World possibility. It is important to recall that even so concerted a colonial scheme as that of
the Bay planters partook in a larger movement into America, a
movement which transcended religious as well as national boundaries, and of which Underhill (or any land-hungry settler of
Plymouth or Boston) was a coequal, if scorned, agent. The charters
of various colonial ventures, whether formal or informal, differed
widely; but the charts of expected action and perception were more
nearly consistent from group to group. Underhill's inviting prospects of American land may have seemed threatening to the Bay
elite, much as his attempt to settle in New Hampshire afterwards
did. Yet such a disagreement touched more on means than on
ends. Both parties to it (and to similar arguments elsewhere, or at
other times) were concerned with the formulation of America, with
the act of imprinting on its supposedly empty sheets the symbols
44   and legends of a European understanding.

Wonder itself was simply the vaguest of such assertions. Even the most rapt discoverer shared insidiously in the larger design, if only by suggesting that the possibility of bewilderment or loss in the New World was remote—by postulating a relation between American fact and European category which was only mildly dialectical, and in which the schematics of perception and thought held a clear advantage. "Discovery" as an act or an idea did not deliver the traveler, or the reader, to a world of utter strangeness, but to a realm of enhanced normality; the voyage, the journey, the intellectual departure, all became deeds of transitional growth rather than radical discontinuity. If at the end of such itineraries there waited something qualitatively different from European understanding, its difference often was expressed as a quantitative exuberance, a matter of larger content instead of strange form. The path of discovery thus implied a double passage: a movement of eye and mind away from old centers of order, and a return in fact and word once the new center had been glimpsed. Unlike exploratory documents or settlement narratives—both of which portend a final departure, a real commitment of the self to the distance—the discovery account keeps open a means of expected retreat. Its central situation is a poise of contemplation which leads less to further discoveries in the actual "beyond" than to an act of literary disclosure intended for, and often written in, the settled grounds. Its form is circular, enclosed.

The discoverer's most typical deed, the application of word to thing, becomes a means of covert plantation. If that deed often leads into a confession of the discoverer's inadequacy, the failure of mind to encompass American reality, the confession itself is further testimony to the unnamed but beneficent abundance of New World life. Silence is a form of contemplative hush in which words are wanting for the size and detail of American objects, but not for their evident European meaning. Imported vocabularies (or even native adaptations) fail to embrace the variety of sights and sounds because they are themselves the product of a narrower world or a mind unused to such expansive awe. Hence the Canadian traveler of 1768 confesses, as he confronts Niagara Falls, that "new expressions are wanting," that any words he can "put together" are too weak to convey that sense of confused wonder with which the imagination itself must struggle here on the spot. Crossing the Niagara above the cataract, climbing down a cliff at its base, glancing over the whole scene from a hill, the traveler is trying (like Jefferson at the Potomac breach) to locate the ideal viewpoint for himself and his language. Testing the force of nature, he balances between aesthetic composure and kinetic trial. "Indeed the risque is great," he writes of his passage across the river, "for mistaking the Land-marks, breaking a setting pole or paddle, or even missing a single stroke, and all is lost. Faith nor all her works will protect you from perdition." The traveler's saving graces are not abstractions: topographic acuity, a feel for the strength of crucial materials, a sense of muscular harmony—these are the means of passage, the almost ritual acts of composure and arrival. They allow the wanderer to dance around the chasm which both terrifies and enraptures him. Not Providence but his own good skills allow his deliverance. Hence "perdition" is avoided, the void itself annulled; the landscape finally is benign rather than satanic. Traveler and reader alike are led to a brink from which what Jefferson himself describes as a grand impediment of nature to human movement (see *Notes*, 15–16) can be passed over with the eye, and with the cautious, tentative progress of the body. If there remains an unordered, chaotic maelstrom in the middle of this traveler's account, a breach in one rumored Northwest Passage, his prose impounds it much as his body has impinged on it. Gesturing toward a future when "Seneca the tragedian's prediction will be fulfilled," he frames a close disorder with a prospect of distant beauty, a glimpse of "resurrected" empire (*Mag. Am. His.*, 1:244–45). Like his own narrative (which predicts in its structure the later course of westward emigration), the movement of American order into the wilderness presumably will bridge such horrendous natural gaps.

Though lacking in explicit words to match his experience, the traveler thus surrounds Niagara Falls with the terms of a linguistic imperialism. Anonymous as he remains, one is tempted to take him as a type, representative of that class which grew up with the sudden accession of territory to Great Britain in 1763, and then emerged after the Revolution within an avowedly American context. His private wanderings mesh with the grand schemes of Robert Rogers in his *Concise Account of North America* (1765), or with the attempt of Jonathan Carver to map out in the Northwest a set of future provinces for British development (see PLATE 5).[30] Yet even the most innocent of discoverers tends to frame his New World scenes in similarly neat formulations. The case of John Bartram, Quaker botanist and gentle farmer, is instructive in this regard. His relation to the wilderness appears from our own viewpoint like an early model of a quite different American future, that

46

conservationist movement which aimed at walling out development instead of opening up the country for it. But Bartram reveals in his writing (as in his botanizing) a curiously strong impulse toward order-making, a dread of the wilds which is balanced by his assertive spirit. Though we may want to see him as a countering force to the boosterism and exploitation about to reach new levels just after his death in 1777, he prepared for that speculative surge by his own habitual bearing toward the American landscape and its "riches." His famed garden in Philadelphia (see PLATE 6) was a *hortus conclusus* of American profusion, a construct consciously abstracted from the wilderness and there (as the explorer was so fond of saying) made to blossom as the rose. His enclosure suggests how right was the early national alliance of settlement with landscape gardening, for it postulated an America only roughly composed in itself, a fund of abundant raw materials on which the European mind had to impose a grid of understanding and spatial arrangement. It seems strangely appropriate that Bartram contributed to *Poor Richard* in 1749 an essay concerning "the improvement of estates, by raising a durable timber for fencing and other uses."[31]

Bartram's garden was an organic cabinet of curiosities, a tangible expression of the cataloging urge. And his great shipments of specimens abroad, particularly to Peter Collinson and his friends, extended eastward (as travelers from Columbus and Cortés on had done) the wondering excitement of American collectors. Like Jefferson's relations with Buffon, Bartram's with his English patrons (and customers) were strained at times, and he often adopted, or had thrust upon him, that role of a New World *realist*—the person in touch with American facts—which Jefferson exploited in his book and in his dealings with Buffon.[32] Bartram was, however, an arm of the Old World mind, a means by which theories and schemes developed in the East could be applied for verification in the West. When Linnaeus himself termed the Philadelphian the "greatest natural botanist in the world," he was stressing the uncannily active source of Bartram's knowledge. Yet both Linnaeus and his pupil Pehr Kalm, whom the Swedish Academy sent to America, at the suggestion of Linnaeus, to gather specimens and data—and who found Bartram as much a cause for wonder as the New World scene—drew on Bartram's hard-won learning, and thus underscored its essential continuity with Old World science.[33]

Crèvecoeur provides in his *Letters from an American Farmer* an alternate myth of Bartram's intellectual origins, a nativist scene in 47 which the future botanist finds his vocation in the rapture of contemplating a simple daisy in his fields. Whatever the accuracy of that account, it is worth pondering: for Crèvecoeur portrays Bartram as the floral analogue of Jefferson the ethnologist, a man wholly committed to the idea of European order and its expansion in America, but touched lightly by a melancholy sense of what he must destroy in furthering his avowed ends. Whereas Jefferson thought it regrettable that Indian tribes were destroyed *before* their languages had been understood and inventoried (*Notes,* 101), Crèvecoeur's Bartram thinks it a shame that he has been "employed so many years in tilling the earth and destroying so many flowers and plants without being acquainted with their structures and their uses!" (188). The issue is not one of understanding so much as one of intellectual preemption on the American scene; the discoverer as scientist is a pioneer of other orders, a figure whose own relation to the American landscape precedes that of the settler but does not invalidate it. Bartram's real anxiety about the spread of settlement into wilderness areas grew from his sense of prior scientific claims upon them, not from an outright objection to the destructive force of "progress."

The anonymous introducer of Bartram's *Observations* (1751) provides a series of subtle links between the author's journey to the Canadian frontier in 1743 and the hopeful progress of British order in the near future. Declaring that "knowledge must precede a settlement," he offers on his own authority a "desirable prospect" of British imperial expansion which, he admits, may seem "chimerical, because great and distant," but for which Bartram's own text provides a concretely close warrant.[34] Written in the growing heat of English rivalry with the French, the preface maps out a broad region of spatial and institutional conflict between the two powers, and sees the journey of Bartram, Conrad Weiser, and Lewis Evans—botanist, Indian negotiator, and topographer—as a penetration of that debated ground which bodes well for future events. It sketches out in a rough and hasty fashion the sort of contrast which later was to inform Francis Parkman's histories of the period: the French have been bold in their relation to the continent, cutting a line of knowledge and tenuous possession into the vast inner regions, whereas the British have clung to the coast and have planted there an extensive area of settled order. Quoting with evident glee Charlevoix's confession that France cannot view the English colonies "without Terror" (iii), the writer himself views the accomplishment of France as both a disturbing coup and an instructive model for English imitation. He clearly prefers agriculture to the kind of attenuated spatial relationship between the French and America, yet wishes to incorporate aspects of that relationship into the English system. Eminently "industrious in agriculture and commerce," the English colonists are lacking in other essential traits. They have not, as yet, proved "adventurous in inland discoveries" (iv), and in this sense have much to learn from Canadian precedent.

English penetration inland will adopt French habits in the service of English goals. Bartram himself observes that the once and future enemy holds its territory by the slimmest of expedients—a line of "small posts, inhabited by no subjects of *France* but soldiers," forts which can exercise authority only as far as their guns can shoot. The practice of his own people, on the other hand, is to ground the claim (and the actuality) of possession on a series of expanding circles, points of order from which cultivation spreads out to reclaim the wilderness (51–52). His journey of 1743, as recorded in the *Observations,* combines the two modes of relation as paradigms of literal movement and cultural possession. His book is remarkable in the period for its faithful and detailed rendering of a line of actual travel: its prose moves uphill and down, through narrow valleys, along small runs, across open bottom land or upland forest. Like the dotted trace inscribed by Evans on his 1749 map to show the route of their journey (see PLATE 7), Bartram's book draws across the wilderness from Philadelphia to Lake Ontario a passageway of experience and recognition. It opens up the intervening landscape by force of personal endurance, and thus anticipates (and justifies) the call in the preface for a more "adventurous" relation to American space.

Bartram's line of passage, however, evokes other prospects than the abstract imperial one added to his text in London. Like Robert Rogers's account of his voyage to Detroit in the *Journals* (1765)—a wondering conclusion to his record of tough wilderness warfare in the East, it ends with the literal conveyance of French authority to the English crown—the *Observations* points toward that time when the Great Lakes shall become "accustomed to *English* navigation" (50). Quoting an unnamed but "most judicious" writer, Bartram endorses his sentiments: "'He that reflects on the natural state of [the] continent must open to himself a field for traffick in the southern parts of *N. America,* and by means of this river [the Mississippi] and the lakes, the imagination takes into view such a scene of inland navigation; as cannot be paralleled in any other part of the world'" (51). Far more interesting than such grand prospects, however, is Bartram's imaginative "view" of the American scene throughout his own present journey. Strung on the line of his itinerary is a series of open landscapes which gives to his French-like penetration a markedly English cast. Empire is an object of immediate perception as well as general reflection. Always on the lookout for good farming land, Bartram specifies the potential wonder of the wilderness by expressing it in terms of definite social uses. His journey is structured by an alternation of movement and pause, penetrating deeds and reckoning "observations." Composed while he was traveling (he "regulated" his journal at several points in the forest), his book maps out both his own steps and the future course of English settlement.[35]

Challenges arise in the text, impediments to bodily and mental progress. The northern Pennsylvania hills, part of what Evans in his map tellingly calls "The Endless Mountains" (one section being "Impenetrable" as well!), give the traveler a sequence of prospective views. Once they have been breached by a single human passage, they allow a further contemplation of eye and mind. But the labor of ascent and descent, and the movement at one point through an intervening "dismal wilderness" (Evans's "Dismal Vale," probably along Lycoming creek), suggest how hard it can be to achieve such elevated viewpoints and the intellectual mastery which they seem to afford. Rattlesnakes, swampy ground, yellow wasps, flea-ridden campsites—these and other annoyances of the trail likewise slow down Bartram's literal journey and his prose. Balancing his expanding vision with a sense of enclosure, a feeling that the linear trail does not open up but rather narrows (almost stops), these details hint at the traveler's possible bewilderment, his loss of control over the world which he hopes to organize by his passage through it. Like Jefferson's Potomac scene, though on a far more subdued level, they energize the landscape of America by opposing its own forms to those of white culture and white perception.

Bartram became strangely furious whenever his designs on the New World forest were blocked. Believing without doubt in his scheme of scientific settlement, he expressed to Peter Collinson again and again the resentments which seethed inside him at the postponement of any planned journey. He was a driven man for

whom the explanation of "curiosity" is not wholly sufficient: underlying all his efforts was a paradoxical passion for order, a deep need to clear and to clarify the wilderness, as he did on his farmland along the Schuylkill, or in his garden, by his shipments to Europe or his contributions to botanical knowledge. Wonder corrupted in him until it became a militant and systematic impulse, a spur to active and organizing perception. Often enough, one finds more of that naïve emotion (and its stylistic uplift) in Collinson's letters to Bartram than in Bartram's own. It is as though the Englishman has distilled from the American's arduous travels some essence of distant enjoyment. Like the packed plants or extracted seeds which Bartram sent him, Collinson's perception of the latter's experience was abstracted and hence idealized.

But Bartram also was a distiller. By linking public history with his private fears, he came to blame the frustration of his designs on the hindering presence of Indians in his botanic storehouse of America. Writing to Collinson in February 1756, Bartram describes the "grievous distressed condition" in which Pennsylvania has been placed by the inroads of "the barbarous, inhuman, ungrateful natives weekly murdering our back inhabitants." Rumor has it, he continues, that the responsible Indians are those who have been befriended by the settlers: "such as were almost daily familiars at their houses, ate, drank, cursed and swore together—were even intimate playmates; and now, without any provocation, destroy all before them with fire, ball, and tomahawk." Demons of destruction, Bartram's Indians are notable for their covert methods and their insidious violence. If pursued, they reveal a devilish, animalistic nature as they merge with the forms of the wilderness: "in the level woods, they skip from tree to tree like monkeys; if in the mountains, like wild goats, they leap from rock to rock, or hide themselves, and attack us in flank and rear, when, but the minute before, we pursued their track, and thought they were all before us." In short, "they are like the Angel of Death—give us the mortal stroke, when we think ourselves secure from danger" (*Memorials*, 206).

This outburst and others are caused only in part by the current troubles with France: the war becomes a correlative for Bartram's inner anxieties, a means of specifying the fears aroused in him by the wilderness. If, as Crèvecoeur would have us believe, Bartram's botanizing began with a reaction against his own destructiveness—a guilt over white plantation—his myth of the Indians as a collective genius of destruction is a conveniently cleansing projection. And 51

Bartram's myth surpasses such basically social issues. A figure of "the Indian" (generic rather than individual or even tribal) haunts his mind as the sign of all resistance to white "progress"—whether of the solitary traveler or the race. More suggestively, that same figure stands in the path of Bartram's personal journey, the linear yet encompassing movement of his intellect into the oblivious, unordered forest. Writing again to Collinson at the end of the war, he praises the idea of a complete survey of England's new empire, "a noble and absolutely necessary scheme" for searching "all the country of Canada and Louisiana for all natural productions, convenient situations for manufactories, and different soils, minerals, and vegetables." Faustian in its proportions, the scheme attracts Bartram's own energies. Willing to undertake the last part of it himself, he seems already packing his equipment and preparing his route. But a customary hindrance rears up to block his way: "Before this scheme can be executed, the Indians must be subdued or drove above a thousand miles back." Though he wonders in his *Observations* about the "origin" of the Indians, he is concerned here with their disposition—and in two senses. "No treaty will make discovery safe," he adds, thus implicating science in the empire, the discoverer's language firmly in the world of time. "All the discoverers" on the proposed expeditions, he grimly predicts, "would be exposed to the greatest savage cruelty, the gun, tomahawk, torture, or revengeful devouring jaws" (254–55). Between the designing mind and its spatial goal, its realm of ordered and ordering action, lies the red shadow, bloody and racially strange.

Earlier in the same letter, Bartram offers testimony about more private schemes, a naive buildup to his venomous conclusion. A bit boastfully, he paints himself as a man of remarkable acuity and attentiveness: "I have now travelled near thirty years through our provinces, and in some, twenty times in the same provinces, and yet never, as I remember, once found one single species in all after times, that I did not observe in my first journey through the same province." Citing one instance in Virginia, Bartram emerges through this self-portrait as an innocent traveler, a hero of scientific recovery, a creature of wonder rather than wrath. "The first time I crossed the Shenandoah, I saw one or two plants, or rather stalk and seed, of the *Meadia,* on its bank. I jumped off [the horse], got the seed and brought it home, sent part to thee, and part I sowed myself; both which succeeded, and if I had not gone to that spot, perhaps it had been wholly lost to the world" (254). Out of the oblivious wilderness, against the destructive push of white settlement—for plantation is the suspected agent of plant-loss here—Bartram has retrieved an unknown token of natural profusion.

At the end of this letter, however, Bartram evokes a far different episode from the history of his travels, and hence a quite different model of the discoverer's career. "Many years past, in our most peaceable times, far beyond our mountains, as I was walking in a path with an Indian guide, hired for two dollars"—his steplike modifiers holding off the climax—"an Indian man met me and pulled off my hat in a great passion, and chawed it all round—I suppose to show me that they would eat me if I came in that country again" (255). Finally we have reached the ground of Bartram's fear, and of the imperial means which he adopts to control it. Concerned with making the American continent *produce,* and hence support colonial expansion, Bartram seems gnawed by the doubt of his own possible consumption. Cannibalism thus is the false charge which he levels at his stereotypic "Indian," as if he realizes the devouring impulse of white culture, even among its scientific pioneers.

Though he had been a party to diplomatic negotiations in 1743—it being Weiser's purpose then to resolve a dispute between the English and the Six Nations over land boundaries—Bartram consistently took as his own stance a militant position unusual among the Quakers. His letter to Collinson in September 1763 shows the coloration of Pontiac's Uprising, to be sure, as does the message of the following month, in which he urges that "the most probable and only method to establish a lasting peace with the barbarous Indians, is to bang them stoutly, and make them sensible that we are men, whom they for many years despised as women." Yet such local colorings affect only the tonal quality of a portrait long imprinted on Bartram's mind. Like the whole French War of the 1750s, they are objective facts put to highly subjective uses. A verbal Paxton Boy, Bartram reveals the sharp imbalance in white thought between actual events and proposed (or executed) reactions to them. The October letter offers a further explanation. Though it opens with what may appear to be an ideal contrast to its brutal conclusion—for Bartram tells of two expeditions to the Jersey coast, designed to show his son John "the very spot where grew a pretty *Ornithogalum*"—even Bartram's brief account of these journeys hints at the source of his racial anxiety. The star-of-

53

Bethlehem which he sought was gone (perhaps effaced by settlers), and Bartram's net gain from the tours was an "exasperated" ulcer over his left shin bone (255–56). More like the Fisher King than a questing knight capable of miraculous cures—the latter role he had played when he published a finding list for American medicinal plants, a discursive botanical "map"—Bartram has discovered a diminished world answering to his diminished self. One can trace in his concluding remarks about the natives a grasp of his implicit "impotence," and a rage striking out at its displaced "cause."

A final letter deserves consideration. Written on 11 November 1763, it opens with Bartram's sour commentary on the merely "titular" acquisitions which have fallen to the English in the war, titular because France still will push its claims to the Mississippi valley, and thus threaten the colonists. The Indians allied with them (and in Bartram's shadow chart of American politics this means, essentially, all Indians) will join in their pretense. The natives require the same rough treatment he urged earlier: "unless we bang [them] stoutly, and make them fear us, they will never love us, nor keep peace long with us." A barrier, an outrageous hindrance to white domination, the natives must be confronted and beaten into submission, literally terrified into love—and all in service of the most innocent of goals. Bartram ends his bloody program with the following rapture: "The variety of plants and flowers in our south-western continent, is beyond expression. Is it not, dear Peter, the very palace garden of old Madam *Flora?* Oh! if I could but spend six months on the Ohio, Mississippi, and [in] Florida, in health, I believe I could find more curiosities than the English, French and Spaniards have done in six score of years." Then arises the old hindrance, with a marvelous metonymy for English imperialism, a coy reduction of avowed European intent: "But the Indians, insti-gated by the French, will not let us look at so much as a plant, or tree, in this great British empire" (256). A merely curious spectator longing for wonder, Bartram's American traveler seems absolved of any guilt, either past or prospective. The letter shows how a crooked and complicitous logic might be used to straighten the discoverer's path, to clear that figure's way of any impinging difficulties, actual or moral.

In Collinson's answer of 6 December, Bartram's fellow Quaker is quick to point out the tortuous shape of his friend's logic, and the literal tortures of white practice which it seeks to avoid. "My dear John, thou does not consider the law of right," Collinson begins, "and doing to others as we would be done unto." He offers an opposite image of the European traveler in America, evoking the sad example of the infamous "Walking Purchase" to suggest that not all wanderers have sought simply to "look" at the New World scene. "We, every manner of way, trick, cheat, and abuse these Indians with impunity.... I could fill this letter with our arbitrary proceedings, all the colonies through; with our arbitrary, illegal taking their lands from them, making them drunk, and cheating them of their property." Against Bartram's Indian-hatred Collinson puts forth neither the easy scheme of "noble savagery" nor the condescension of a savagist view. "As their merciless, barbarous methods of revenge and resentment are so well known," he continues, "our people should be more careful how they provoke them." Not the Indians themselves, but their "methods," are barbarous—and, Collinson clearly implies, those methods are employed only in reaction against obvious injuries and provocations. A realist, he accuses Bartram of willful blindness to the true political state of colonial affairs. Distant from America yet strangely in touch with New World actualities, Collinson asserts that his friend "does not search into the bottom of these insurrections." Their deeper causes "are smothered up," he adds with firm psychological insight, "because we are the aggressors" (257). Though Collinson could be overbearing toward Bartram at times (telling him once, for instance, how neatly he must dress when calling on prominent colonial officials, lest his shabby appearance embarrass Collinson himself), here he strikes deeply and rightly through the shams of his friend's prose.

His reaction can provide us, in fact, with a means of proper reading, a model of our own approach to early New World texts. We need to know, more than anything else, how to draw from episodes and the language which recreates them lines of strong yet suggestive connection to the dialectics (and dialects) of American culture as a whole. Since in so many cases the individual's separate journey is presented as at least an implicit version of the national tour, the larger shape of the travel book itself is rich with cultural meaning. A single plot enacts ritualistically the grand plot of European expansion into the West. The problem, given such general connections, is to transcend them without belying their generality, to read particular passages in the light of overarching historical, moral, social, or aesthetic principles. Collinson's analysis of what Bartram says about the Indians submits the latter's opinion to the

sort of contextual scrutiny which it clearly requires. What Bartram
tries to simplify and schematize Collinson must place in its complex
historical framework. Whereas the American is attempting to clear
his path by concentrating all impediments in an adversary who is
capable, as he thinks, of a quick defeat, the Englishman raises impediments within the colonial camp itself, hesitations about the
unspoken imperative in Bartram's prose. Like William Wood's
sluggish rattlesnake, Bartram's Indian is venomous but disposable;
once that creature has been cleared from the land, Bartram
suggests, an open trail will lead from the centers of English settlement directly to the terrain of wonder beyond them. Attacking
those very centers, however, Collinson suggests that European
ideals require "better walking," that a true line of sight from established areas will lead along a far more cautious and conscious
"path."

Even when Bartram does not directly raise the issues which
called forth Collinson's attack, his prose implicates them covertly.
His Florida journal (1765), product of his desire to explore the new
English lands, asserts as does the *Observations* a simplicity which
neither text finally supports, a clear path which the author himself
never travels. One scene in the earlier book, descriptive of Bartram's passage through a thickly forested lowland along Towanda
creek, is particularly worthy of attention, for it condenses into a
single landscape the typical anxieties of this would-be discoverer.
On the previous day, Bartram and his companions pass through
the "dismal wilderness," and that night all but Bartram himself and
one of the Indians accompanying him sleep quietly in the warm air.
The native at one point performs "a solemn harmonious" song
which Bartram (who tends, significantly, to "wake with a little noise,
rarely sleeping sound abroad") takes for "a hymn to the great
spirit." A suggestive epiphany, the silent exchange between Indian
and white man is rich with other relations than that which Bartram
finally envisions for the races. Almost a dream, the episode seems
to offer Bartram a chance for insight into native cultures, an extraordinary moment which calls for more than ordinary understanding. On the following day, however, Bartram locates in the
"great white pine, spruce swamp full of roots, and abundance of
old trees lying on the ground, or leaning against live ones," ample
cause for his old mental stance—an aggression of nature against
the traveler which he quickly transforms into a paradigm of his
racial geography. So thick are the trees in this swamp, Bartram

writes, "that we concluded it almost impossible to shoot a man at 100 yards distant, let him stand never so fair. The straight bodies of these trees stood so thick, a bullet must hit one before it could fly 100 yards, in the most open part" (29–30).

It is as if the abundance of American nature, here seen as a decadent rather than regenerative force, suggests the possibility of human deceit, the need to shoot a man suddenly found lurking among the trees; or as if, more complexly, abundance itself is a kind of adversary, personified in the lurking enemy—in which case the fact that one would "wound" a tree in attempting to hit a man is nicely meaningful, a deflection of aim and intent which further links the causes of anxiety. Enormous, numberless, so closely set that they become an effective wall opposed to the wanderer, the trees are both emblems of what the botanist seeks and interpolations between him and his specific goal. Bartram is in a world vastly disproportionate to himself, a place which humbles, lessens, even threatens to annihilate him. On a piece of what travelers routinely called "waste land," he confronts the weakness of his active scheme: neither body nor eye can travel on as he would wish, and should a more explicit resistance arise even his weapon would be curiously impotent. Though Bartram in fact moved on, he painted the scene which he left—surely without conscious intent—as a miniature version of his psychological map of America. Turned aside by the wall of natural inopportunity, the rigorous drive of his "science" transmogrifies into a violent will, opposing that wall yet finally ineffectual against it. And at the shadowed edge of his thick forest lurks the supposed source of all his troubles, the man who needs only to be banged stoutly for the continent to open of itself.

NO DECEIT

Alexander Garden, the South Carolina botanist of doubly significant name, wrote to Cadwallader Colden in 1754 that Bartram's garden was "a perfect portraiture of himself," since one might meet "here . . . with a row of rare plants almost covered with weeds, here with a Beautiful Shrub even Luxuriant amongst Briars, and in another corner an Elegant and Lofty tree lost in a common thicket." Yet he also noted that Bartram's commanding eye looked out over the wilderness, the intrusion of weeds on his paradise balanced by his own intrusion on the forest. "In a word," the letter runs, "he disclaims to have a garden less than Pennsylvania, & Every den is an Arbour, Every run of water, a Canal, &

every small level Spot a Parterre, where he nurses up some of his Idol Flowers & cultivates his darling productions."[36] The palace garden of "old Madam *Flora*" also was his own. And, as the comment of Garden suggests, the proof of his possession lay in the powers of his style, his ability to rename pure nature and thus apparently transform it.

In a paper of the same period on the "troublesome" plants of his native state, Bartram himself enumerates those which, having been brought from Europe by accident or design, have "escaped out of our gardens, and taken possession of our fields and meadows, very much to our detriment." The issue is more than botanical. Bartram might be William Bradford lamenting the "escaped" settlers of Plymouth, or a ministerial official in London vexed with the problem of trans-Allegheny penetration. Yet Bartram opposes to his catalog of noxious plants an ideal list built up throughout his career, a catalog of those floral riches which, by their sad dispersion across America, have suffered an analogous "escape," a lapse from white attention. A garden in ruins, the continent is Jefferson's Potomac scene writ large; and it is Bartram's intent, by deeds and words, to round up all such languishing fragments of life and knowledge, to practice Adam's prerogative of naming in a fallen world. He deals less in wonder than in an immuring, almost passionless emotion. Extending the walls of intellect until no rare thing remains outside (for white ignorance is oblivion), he takes possession of America in the name of science, but in the service of a cultural order of which science is one compartment. For that larger purpose, he must dispossess whatever now owns the land, whether it is another culture resistant to his or a flora resistant to agricultural design. Significantly, the second part of Bartram's inventory of "troublesome" plants concerns those which are "native" to America, and which are, like the Indians, "with difficulty eradicated" (*Memorials*, 385).

That same inventory introduces another American traveler, and a quite different approach to the New World scene. Puzzled by the rapid spread of the cotton groundsel "in our new cleared land after the first ploughing," Bartram speculates about its means of dispersion. The issue is particularly knotty for him since "in old fields, or meadows, there is not one stalk to be seen," while on newly opened ground it "grows . . . all over, so close that there is no passing along without breaking it down, to walk or ride through it." The old
pattern of hindrance arises, the philosophical problem echoing in

mental terms the difficulty of a literal passage. Bartram's tentative solution presupposes an absolute distinction of American space according to European categories: the plant is, he opines, "natural to new land and not to old"—as if such classes of terrain are indigenous to America, rather than applied to the continent by white labor and by the schemes of white knowledge (including Bartram's own prose at this point). But Bartram goes on to tell, after referring to the doctrine that "every plant is produced from the seed of the same species," an evocative anecdote which brings into his text (and into our consideration here) the alternative example of his son "Billy." "One day when the sun shone bright, a little after its meridian," the anecdote begins, "my Billy was looking up at it, when he discovered an innumerable quantity of downy motes floating in the air, between him and the sun. He immediately called me out of my study, to see what they were. They rose higher and lower, as they were wafted to and fro in the air, some very high and progressive with a fine breeze, some lowered, and fell into my garden, where we observed every particular detachment of down, spread in four or five rays, with a seed of the *Groundsel* in its centre. How far these were carried by that breeze, can't be known; but I think they must have come near two miles, from a meadow, to reach my garden" (386–87).

Head turned up, eyes open to the possibilities of wonder, William Bartram stands even in this passage of his father's prose as the exemplar of a radically separate vision. Whereas John tries to fit this one detail of American natural history into the framework of political geography, his son (not yet twenty years old) exhibits an unframed viewpoint which allows him to locate the indigenous structure of that detail and the wider American scene through which it expresses itself. William's *Travels through North and South Carolina, Georgia, East and West Florida* (1791) extends with great enrichment the same basic stance, offering in its portrait of the American traveler a reborn view of that figure's original wonder, linking this purified emotion—its chivalric sources reclaimed—with the current canons of a new transatlantic romanticism. Not disabled by scientific concerns, but rather invigorated by them, his book uses rationalism itself as a means to closer union, a source of ecstasy. "Observation" becomes for him, as it does not for his father, a way of restructuring the self according to natural form. John Bartram seeks in his writings, as in his journeys, to shape the wilderness until it matches his prior chart of its ideal condition;

William, on the contrary, derives his own ideals from the very landscapes which he surveys. Order flows into him, not out: the self is settled by the world which it confronts rather than vice versa. Hence discovery becomes a real possibility, the New World a site of actual newness and renewal.

The exasperations of his father are gone from William's book, and the schematics which he retains themselves merge with a fine uplift of feeling. Full of scientific labels, his prose is latinate where it is not fully Latin, and the language functions in part as an informing medium, a means of converting the sometimes violent wilderness into a realm of bookish balance, peace, composure. Yet Bartram's fiction, so innocent that we come to share in it, is that his rapture has its true origin in hints supplied by nature. He suggests in almost every one of his descriptions that the world to which his Latin tags are applied requires for its accurate rendering some such vocal music, a sign system noteworthy less for its botanical precision than for its evocative lushness. Though imported into the New World and attached to American objects with systematic rigor, his language seems appropriate to the subtropical regions which he explores, for it is organic to their rich life.

Like the natural theologians, Bartram views science as the servant of piety. Nature is a mediate ground between humanity and God, and the scientific approach to it can reveal precisely by an attention to natural structure the grand designs of creation. The more a botanical traveler sees, and the greater his accuracy, the more he thus is likely to support a prior view of the universe; his discoveries seem bounded by the limits of a broad expectation—they confirm rather than innovate. Nature is an allegory of God's workmanship: "The pompous Palms of Florida, and glorious Magnolia, strike us with the sense of dignity and magnificence; the expansive umbrageous Live Oak with awful veneration; the Carica papaya seems supercilious with all the harmony of beauty and gracefulness," and so forth, through other large species and on to more useful but less grand ones (whose "valuable qualities and virtues excite love, gratitude, and adoration to the great Creator").[37] Architect of form and use, Bartram's God is not merely an aloof concept. The traveler sees all around him as he journeys more than the accumulating proof of divine Providence. Creation seems to be reborn in his senses, and nature becomes an animistic realm full of the very powers of divinity. Allegory yields to symbolism: what appears at the outset to be a prior scheme, less

60

political than that of Bartram's father but nonetheless imprinted on the American scene, soon emerges in the *Travels* as a lively discovery. Deductive truth must be refound in the traveler's inductive career.

By implication, nature thus exists not just as a source of information, or as an impulse to worship (the two purposes which Bartram assigns to travel at the start), but also as a fund of suggestive signs for the traveler's own inner state. Didactic intentions merge with those of self-discovery, just as the uses of nature are joined with the sheer delight which natural form produces in the wanderer. The allegorical properties of some species, and the economic virtues of others, are supplemented by the "very remarkable properties" of those plants which "excite our admiration, some for the elegance, singularity, and splendour of their vestment, . . . others . . . by their figure and their disposal of vesture, as if designed only to embellish and please the observer" (17). The "designer" of such delightful effects is, to be sure, the same deity who has shaped nature for our sustenance and our pious regard. But this third purpose, though it has obvious connections with the others, transcends them by its undefined end. The simple play of sensual fulfillment aims at the "embellishment" of the observer, at the enriching of his emotional and spiritual life. And it is this open feeling, this search for growth, which comes to dominate Bartram's book (see PLATE 8).

Details enter the *Travels* as if already composed into an echo of human order, a gentle parody of our own arts. The "vestment" and "vesture" of the plants listed by Bartram in his "Introduction" suggest not only that God has "dressed" the world, but also that the traveler can perceive his surroundings through the categories of social life. Most of Bartram's descriptions infuse nature with similar human properties. Since he argues that plants have animal traits, and that animals have human capabilities, such informing metaphors are more than possessive in intent. Interpenetrations of language suggest a shared life rather than our own control of "lesser" forms. No dialectic of ownership underlies Bartram's purposeful confusion of linguistic categories. Hence when he describes the sandhill cranes of the Alachua savanna, he tells how these "sonorous" birds, "in well-disciplined squadrons, now rising from the earth, mounted aloft in spiral circles, far above the dense atmosphere of the humid plain; they again viewed the glorious sun, and the light of day still gleaming on their polished feathers, they sung their evening hymn, then in a straight line majestically descended, and alighted on the towering Palms or lofty Pines, their secure and peaceful lodging places" (167).[38] Pious natural theologians in their own right, the cranes seem to offer the traveler a model of his own relation to the world. But there is in their military order, their geometric design, their gemlike wings, their joyous songs—as in their return at night to "lodging places"—an even subtler prefiguration of human life within the wilds. Although the savanna has not been settled in any literal sense, it already exhibits the principal arts of Bartram's homeland. The play of his language and perception in this given world organizes it into a neat emblem of the settled ground so far behind him. Though moving themselves, the cranes fly with such grace that they assume an almost static, iconographic pose.

All of this, however, is part of an innocent rhetorical strategy, a means of bringing the reader gradually into the strange new world of Florida. It aims less at ordering the landscape than at suggesting an inviting organization implicit in its own economy—an organization which urges the reader to enter this radiant place. Bartram's personal delight acts like an allied gesture of embrace and revelation, a means of initiating the audience into those wonders first seen by him and now discovered through the efforts of his pen. His prose holds nature back far enough that we want to approach it, to sense and experience it ourselves. The appeal to our senses seems to call us into a journey of our own. "Observe these green meadows how they are decorated; they seem enamelled with the beds of flowers," Bartram writes even in his "Introduction." If to travel is to observe (and to observe is to be "embellished" and "pleased"), to read the traveler's report is to share in such acts and emotions. Hence Bartram's further comments in the passage open a prospect of ravishment and wonder which leads us from the echoic similitude of nature as an artful realm to a sense of intimate involvement in the present natural scene. As argument gives way to example, concept yields to direct perception. Naming several species in his meadows, Bartram seems to be painting a general landscape; but then he narrows his focus to a single plant, the yellow trumpet-leaf, and his description of it recapitulates the shift of his rhetoric from general principle to specific observation. "Shall we analyze these beautiful plants, since they seem cheerfully to invite us?" he asks. "How greatly the flowers of the yellow Sarracenia represent a silken canopy? the yellow pendant petals are the curtains, and the hollow leaves are not unlike the cornucopia or

Amalthea's horn; what a quantity of water a leaf is capable of containing, about a pint! taste of it—how cool and animating— limpid as the morning dew" (17–18). At the start of his description, this detail of nature seems to represent a human artifact; before long, however, it has become a source of present experience, the mediating comparison no longer necessary. Like the mode of presentation, the scale also changes: we move from a broad scene to a species to an individual leaf, from the enduring categories of science to a single moment. That the water inside the leaf seems "limpid as the morning dew" heightens our sense of evanescence at the same time that it introduces a natural comparison, a simile linking the given plant to its organic surroundings. The art of description acts here like a pathway of language which discovers the American scene by penetrating one of its mysteries, and by bringing the reader into it.

Bartram's genius in such passages elaborates with great art a basic strategy of discovery accounts. It rests on his ability to filter the wilderness, and hence allow his reader only a highly controlled access to it. He becomes a provider of contrived sensations, an artist whose raw material is nothing less than the American continent. A model of intellectual settlement, the *Travels* constructs a map of the tropical world by locating within it points of stasis and order, benchmarks of human comprehension. Bartram does with language what the main character in Edgar Allan Poe's "The Domain of Arnheim" (1847) does with the sign system of landscape gardening. Using his fantastically large inheritance to construct the ultimate garden (it reaches as far as his eye can see), Poe's Ellison is a poet of concrete order and earthly rhythm. He is a philosopher as well. His efforts are not aimed, he asserts, at reclaiming "the original beauty of the country," for that first beauty was "never so great as that which may be introduced." If the world as originally conceived was to be a perfectly "finished" place, the plan was destroyed by earthquakes and other natural disasters. Such disasters are, in Ellison's view, "prognostic of *death*," and it is his purpose to remove from all his land those signs of corruption.[39] The landscape artist's task merges with that of the discoverer: both figures try to efface the deathly evidence visible in nature, to reform the world into a scene symbolic of life and order, of obedience to rule. What Ellison performs by the literal manipulation of detail Bartram (and the discoverer generally) performs by substituting the marks of verbal renovation for the signs of natural decay.

It is, of course, a widely recognized fact that early descriptions of America often are founded on an Edenic preconception. What has been recognized less widely, however, is the extent to which such Edenic images of the New World are constructed by conscious artifice, or the crucial role which language as a system plays in their construction. There is a constant tension in these images between the given chaos of American detail and the imported schema of resolved order. As we have seen in almost every text examined here, the discovery of an enhanced New World comes about in the midst of historical realities—whether those realities take the shape of Adriaen van der Donck's political troubles in New Netherland, Jefferson's sense of geologic violence in Virginia, or Captain Underhill's bloody struggle in New England. The discoverer concedes to the audience that no earthly terrain enjoys a complete exemption from historical strife—even if the concession is not always explicit or heavily stressed. Yet such facts of history as the discoverer admits into an American prospect are allowable only for the sake of a final contrast. They are the price of an imaginative entrance into some further world from which history itself seems excluded—trials adjacent to the ideal road, but held back from it so that they do not characterize that ideal passageway.

As I have suggested in the case of John Bartram, the accumulation of equivocal detail, especially when the author deals with it in such a way as to become an historical figure himself, can threaten the closure of any further perspective. To the extent that narration intrudes on the poised world of the discoverer, wonder passes away. With time comes change, and unless the writer can control the flow of events the static ideal of American space will be submitted to the criticism of reality. Hence the author of a discovery account must be a tightrope artist, and language—in which the principles of narration are so deeply implicit, are indeed the very basis of syntax—itself must be clarified in order to serve him as a means of spatial and cultural clarification. When Daniel Denton writes in *A Brief Description of New-York* (1670) of the strawberries which grow wild on Long Island (so abundant in June "that the Fields and Woods are died red"), he paints a mock-chivalric picture of the "Countrey-people" who seek such rich natural rewards: they "instantly arm themselves with bottles of Wine, Cream, and Sugar and instead of a Coat of Male, every one takes a Female upon his Horse behind him, and so rushing violently into the fields, never leave them till they have disrob'd them of their red colours, and turned them into the old habit."[40] Inverting the shape of heroic

64

action, these delightful forays do not make the green grass red with blood, but rather drain away the latter color: harvest invalidates war by adopting the language of violence for its gentle purpose. Still, one can see in the rush of the rural people a slight sense of mad desire, a prefiguration of later extinctions. If the final implication of Denton's coy language is that warfare must seek a displaced (and peaceful) outlet in the New World, the field of battle becoming a pastoral terrain of fulfillment rather than death—the natural signs here being "prognostic" of life—one finds beneath his words a certain uneasy energy. As a paradigm of the American journey, the "rush" embodies conflicting elements, an imbalance of form and intent. The passage succeeds, on the other hand, because it deflects the energies rumbling beneath it. It admits narrative as an appropriate frame for the New World, but its mocking tone suggests that heroic narration, and the historical sense inseparable from it, are vastly overbuilt for American purposes. One might even conclude here that heroic language can be employed because America is so safely distant from any real threat of violence. Denton's travelers themselves can mock the forms of Old World action (and speech) since, in their innocence, they do not understand them.

William Bartram's *Travels* characterizes with immense detail an analogously peaceful journey for the American. The author's own "sylvan pilgrimage" (140) confirms the witty comparison offered by William Byrd in his *History of the Dividing Line* (1730s) between those travelers who "some ages before" used to "saunter to the Holy Land and go upon other Quixote adventures," and those who now—afflicted with "the itch of sailing to this new world"—"take a trip to America."[41] It also suggests, as Byrd does, that the chivalric model is a consciously available one for expressing the shape of an American journey, even if, Byrd and Denton agree, it is so only by a witty negation. Bartram is, by contrast, more naively assured of the model's direct application. Yet his American wilderness, lushly tropical as it is (and the tropics are, he avers, those earthly regions where "more luxurious scenes of splendour" are to found [15]), is converted into a realm of chivalric action mainly by the expense of his own art. That action is a form of contemplative movement, a pilgrimage of which the stations are a series of "sylvan" moments frozen by Bartram's language.

Nowhere in the book does Bartram better reveal his artistic method and its cultural foundation than in his long description of a particularly beautiful "bason" of water. All here receives the painter's brush, not merely in color and composition, but even more impressively in its finish, its almost varnished appearance. "Behold . . . a vast circular expanse before you, the waters of which are so extremely clear as to be absolutely diaphanous or transparent as the ether; the margin of the bason ornamented with a great variety of fruitful and floriferous trees, shrubs, and plants, the pendant golden Orange dancing on the surface of the pellucid waters, the balmy air vibrating with the melody of the merry birds, tenants of the encircling aromatic grove." A miniature portrait of the discoverer's New World, circular, clarified, embraced by beautiful and useful vegetation, the basin seems to be literally enchanted—a place protected by the charm of Bartram's prose. Yet it is itself encircled by a threat of imminent violence, for it contains within its clarity animals which, as Bartram's epithets indicate, are known for their ferocity: "the voracious crocodile," "the devouring garfish," the "inimical trout," the "barbed catfish, dreaded sting-ray," and "ominous drum." Strangely, these creatures do not engage in open violence, staying in "their separate bands and communities, with free and unsuspicious intercourse performing their evolutions." Indeed, "the different bands seem peaceably and complaisantly to move a little aside, as it were to make room for others to pass by." Caught as they are in the perfect clarity and openness of the basin, in a world where "no covert, no ambush" exists, these creatures "absolutely alter their conduct." Elsewhere they still exhibit their typical violence; but here, among "these Elysian springs," they seem to become a "just representation of the peaceable and happy state of nature which existed before the fall." Contained, illuminated, embraced in circles and laid open to the skies, this basin without deceit, this "paradise of fish," excludes the potential disorder of the wilderness—much as Bartram's language does throughout the book. The basin becomes, in fact, a splendid symbol of Bartram's own descriptive art (150–51).

The traveler admits that the peacefulness of the pool rests on an illusion, that "in reality it is a mere representation," not an actual paradise (151). And he makes it clear elsewhere in the book that his own experience has not always been delightful. His encounter with the alligator, for instance, sorely taxes his conceptual and linguistic control over events in the wilderness: in a place where ambush *is* possible, Bartram finds himself the object of another creature's "curiosity," and his science yields to self-preservation. Wholly unmediated, nature in such situations calls forth no gentle paeans, no rapturous flights, but rather an answering violence ("I resolved he

should pay for his temerity.... I soon dispatched him by lodging
the contents of my gun in his head" [117]). Yet the encounter is a
stark episode in a softened, drifting book; it does not dominate
Bartram's prose (or his mind), as on the contrary his father's
encounter with his typical Indian does.[42] One can argue, in fact,
that William's consistent stress on the primacy of sensation almost
requires this intrusion of violence into his idyll, that its total exclusion would amount to a kind of blindness which would destroy his
aesthetic. Since that aesthetic rests on vision, on a thoroughness of
observation, to omit the alligator would be to fail in the crucial act
of discovery. A hymn to perception (which *is* discovery), a call to a
veritable busk of the senses, the *Travels* needs for its sane balance
some such disruptive, almost disastrous heightening.

Full of enamelled landscapes (see PLATE 9), the work aims at an
exuberant norm which finally excludes any sense of terminal disaster. The worst fact of Bartram's experience in Florida, his previous failure as an indigo planter there in the 1760s, receives no
notice whatsoever. Nor is there any real coloration in the *Travels*
from the emotional impact of that failure. Henry Laurens wrote to
John Bartram in August 1766 to describe the unbelievably poor
location of the young man's land ("on a low sheet of sandy pine
barrens, verging on the swamp"), and added that William "had felt
the pressure of his solitary and hopeless condition so heavily, as
almost to drive him to despondency" (*Memorials,* 439, 441). More
devastating than any alligator attack (for one thing, it verified
John's low estimate of his son's practical sense), the episode is left
out of the book, and with its exclusion a sense of history which
might have entered into Bartram's prose also is elided. The few
ruins which William surveys carry no extra freight of feeling, even
if they do complexify the text; they are other sights, noted and then
passed by.[43] Instead of a settler whose views have been soured by
disappointment, Bartram becomes a chivalric traveler, a man in an
almost timeless, always fruitful world. "I continued several miles,"
he writes at one point, "pursuing my serpentine path, through and
over the meadows and green fields, and crossing the river, which is
here incredibly increased in size, by the continual accession of
brooks flowing in from the hills on each side, dividing their green
turfy beds, forming them into parterres, vistas, and verdant swell-
ing knolls, profusely productive of flowers and fragrant strawberries, their rich juice dying my horses feet and ancles" (281). Gone is
the linear route of his father in the *Observations,* gone the need for
some future plotting—gone, most significantly, the scene of immi-

nent resistance in the given world. A saunterer in Henry Thoreau's sense (one going *"à la Sainte Terre"*), Bartram seems already to have arrived in the Holy Land of his sylvan pilgrimage.[44] When, like his father, he also meets an Indian on his trail, William comes to see him as a "humane and compassionate" man—even though, as he later learned, the "intrepid Siminole" was reputed to be "one of the greatest villains on earth," and had vowed just before coming across Bartram to "kill the first white man he met" (44–45). Almost designed as a counter to John's similar tale, the incident pits white rumor against an experienced fact rather than a white man against a red. It suggests a new eye, and a new mind-set to be created by it. A cultural discovery, it extends Bartram's wonder into the human world: the space where he and the Seminole meet is, like the basin, without deceit or the need for ambush which it creates—including the deceit of white prejudice. Neither traveler is a treacherous creature, unlike the animals in the basin; finding the right common ground (their humanity, but also their spiritual openness to each other), they can come together as brothers.

This small moral landscape merges with those larger sensuous ones painted throughout the *Travels*. Bartram offers here, as in the others, a rich example of the *topos* which energizes the discovery account across its wide range: that glimpse into an amenable place (the *locus amoenus* of classical rhetoric) where the memorials of history and death vanish under the charm of a better imagining. It is Jefferson's snatch of smooth blue horizon, Wood's innocent "prospect," van der Donck's land of "superabundance," Woodward's "Westoe" country. Whatever its local variations or its temporal shifts, the formula persists as a means of abstracting the American scene from the constraints laid on it by time and experience. A place to be cataloged, the *locus amoenus* seems as frozen in its own right as is the language used for its description. Abundant, self-revealing, even inviting to the European eye, such a New World rests always in some further range of actual space; yet it always appears to offer the promise of a glorious entrance, the chance for a journey through any hindering middle ground, the hope of an arrival at a locale where, as van der Donck writes, only the doctors "have meagre soup" (60). If there linger around its borders strange warning shapes, tales of a different American career, those shapes and those tales are consigned to an effectual oblivion as the discoverer saves the amenable New World itself from oblivious time.

Two

❧ EXPLORATORY NARRATIVE ❧

Many Goodly Tokens

All my hopes were in the riches that might lie underground, there being
many goodly tokens of mines.
> William Byrd, "A Journey to the Land of Eden" (1733)

AT THE HEART OF DISCOVERY LIES A LARGE AND INESCAPABLE irony: the poise of timeless delight cannot conceal the great histori-cal innovation which is being announced, since the moment of unveiling itself gives birth to time. In this sense the discoverer's central pretense is doomed to failure, for his idealized journey implicates the found world in history, and his act of publicity, aimed as it may be at solely contemplative responses, threatens to tangle that world even more complexly in events. The need for balance and stasis is so high precisely because such threats are so intense.

For the explorer, on the other hand, time is an openly accepted fact of American life, the desired medium of his being and prose. Since the explorer consciously anticipates, even aids, the actual settlement of wild lands, his acceptance of time is a clear necessity. A visionary of social and personal change for whom the mere discovery of a terrain is not sufficient, this figure longs to harness New World nature, to transform its details into human objects or artifacts. Often enough, the explorer views such transformations as mythic acts, as means of reclaiming America from time by erasing the signs of its evident discomposure. Yet he recognizes that his vision is one of process, and as such requires a temporal world for its realization. His intent thus is to control the direction and force of events rather than to elide them entirely from his rendering. For this purpose he admits temporality only in its positive and fulfilling form. History is a vehicle of aggrandizement, not decay, a way of expanding the moment of discovery into a new and lasting epoch.

In terms of both literary and experiential style, this contrast is reflected in a greater complexity of grammar on the explorer's part. Action is the key to this traveler's language, for he gives to the discoverer's sense of wonder (which in fact he may share) an edge of calculation and containment. The New World of such works 69 generates whole sentences rather than fragmentary lists; the explorer activates his described or imagined scene by adding to his catalogs a set of verbs and subjects. Events thus enter his American landscape, their potentially disruptive force dispersed by the presence of an actor to whom is granted the power of almost perfect control. That actor is, in essence, an allegorical figure, an embodiment of Old World culture whose ability to determine the course of events expresses the explorer's comic vision of westward travel. The invention of true sentences, by which things are subordinated to human will, provides a concise model of colonization, for the web of statement and prediction mimics the array of actual order in an ideally settled New World. The disposition of words within exploratory prose mirrors the disposition in reality of the things which those words represent.

Similar points might be made about the discoverer's use of language. William Bartram's amenable view of the Southeast, for instance, exhibits a continuing effort to illuminate and control whatever scenes it embraces, and to do so by means of verbal order. Yet Bartram's endeavor, as I have argued already, aims at a quite different end. His prose allows us to organize American space on what seem to be its own terms rather than ours. The postulated traveler of his book is less an actor than an observer, less the proper subject of narrative sentences than the passive receptor of freely given sensations. Bartram's metaphysical framework suggests that the wilds are organized already, and that his verbal structures merely copy that inherent organization. We are led to believe that what he presents has been found rather than invented, whereas what the explorer presents is obviously a scheme for founding (or imagining) a human world on the base of a natural one. Bartram tries to expunge action from his described world (as in his basin of no deceit), or to reduce it so far in scale that it effectively vanishes; the explorer, however, is committed to the mapping of incipient events, and hence is eager for historical deeds and narrative prose. Since the universe at rest is sufficient in itself for Bartram, the best style for treating it is one of gentle attribution. The copulative verbs so common in his descriptions thus have a thematic significance of their own. But for the explorer, nature is likely to seem disordered or even meaningless until human intent has been impressed on it. What shapes America (and his verbal portrait of it) is a design quite foreign to the West, a design linked to America only by his projection of it into that region. Though his primary imaginative act thus is copulative, like Bartram's, it is so strained that it requires more deeply active, even violent, verbs for its formulation. Like the industrial arts for which explorers often are spokesmen, exploratory prose is a means of processing raw American matter rather than a way of preserving or probing it. Bartram's Florida would call forth from an explorer a far less mystical gaze, a glimpse less of natural balance and beauty than of practical use. His vision of Bartram's ground would be an obviously human one, a predictive view of actual plantation.

The word "explore" itself hints at such distinctions, for its Latin root *plorare* means "to cry out," and probably is an imitation of the hunter's shout on finding game. If to discover also is to find (and this act also may issue in a "cry"), the discoverer nonetheless aims at a goal less clearly defined than the explorer's. Whereas the former rests with a sense of generalized—perhaps only anticipated— revelation, the latter seeks to attach his uplifted feelings to some actual and tangible objective. The sheer abundance of details which greets him in the New World is reduced to a convenient formula, their profusion of interest only insofar as it hints at the large profit which may be realized from the West. Exploration is the hunter's act, the locating of a desired commodity, the catch of a usable quarry. And the explorer's prose accordingly is a trap, a means of ensnaring beast, plant, or mineral, a way of confining the land itself within some social design.

Such cultural imperatives are so strong that they affect even the work of a discoverer like Bartram himself. He catalogs the "singular and surprising" qualities of Spanish moss, for instance, in a true mood of discovery, but the end of his rapture strikes a note of human use. When this moss is fresh, he writes, "cattle and deer will eat it in the winter season," nature thereby providing an easy fodder for domestic or wild animals. Moreover, the plant seems peculiarly fit for "stuffing mattresses, chairs, saddles, collars, &c; and for these purposes, nothing yet known equals it." Bartram's catalog thus is a list of producible objects rather than organic entities, and his prose appropriately becomes a recipe for further production. "The Spaniards in South America and the West-Indies," he notes, "work [the moss] into cables, that are said to be very strong and durable; but, in order to render it useful, it ought to be thrown into shallow ponds of water, and exposed to the sun, where it soon rots, and the outside furry substance is dissolved. It is then taken out of the water, and spread to dry; when, after a little beating and

71

shaking, it is sufficiently clean, nothing remaining but the interior, hard, black, elastic filament, entangled together, and greatly resembling horse-hair."[1] Abstracted in such a way from its natural setting, the moss no longer is a plant. The actual process described here is reflected, moreover, in the structure of Bartram's language, which is a means of "rendering" this one detail only in terms of its translatable qualities. What appears to be of interest economically and stylistically is the end product of a reductive act. The prose itself contracts as we proceed.

It is worth noting, nonetheless, that even here Bartram's abiding organicism controls him. The economic act is a form of busk, a movement from original beauty through decay to renewal. The crass motives revealed by his earlier term ("stuffing") and traceable in two later ones ("beating and shaking") finally disappear in the wonder of this transformation. Usefulness, as Bartram declares in his "Introduction," also can be a source of awe. Likewise, a similar sense of discovery underpins Bartram's grander explorations, those scenes where he envisions a present or future settlement embracing and enhancing natural form. Along a tributary of the St. John's river, for example, he presents a picture of the traveler's calm journey which ends with a somewhat startling, but finally appropriate prediction: "We gently descended again over sand ridges, crossed a rapid brook, rippling over the gravelly bed, hurrying the transparent waters into a vast and beautiful lake, through a fine fruitful orange grove, which magnificently adorns the banks of the lake to a great distance on each side of the capes of the creek. This is a fine situation for a capital town" (160). All the motion of the creek, like the movement of Bartram's prose, seems to point (beyond our initial surprise) toward his discursive conclusion. A human settlement appears to be the just basin of natural flow, the last flower of such abundant groves.

More complexly, Bartram elsewhere offers detailed comments on the specifically social virtues of various regions. One such place, notable for "meadows glittering with distant lakes and ponds, alive with cattle, deer, and turkeys"—though marred by the "remains of ancient Spanish plantations"—thus seems capable, "under the culture of industrious planters and mechanics," of becoming "a rich, populous, and delightful region" where "almost every desirable thing in life might be produced and made plentiful" (199).[2] Delightful in itself, this locale is the proper material of further delights, the medium of social arts. Similarly, the Alachua savanna

would support by its "exuberant green meadows" and the "fertile
hills which immediately encircle it" more than "one hundred
thousand human inhabitants, besides millions of domestic animals," and thereby would become "at some future day...one of
the most populous and delightful seats on earth" (211). A man of
sites rather than sights, Bartram is creating a quite different map of
the wilderness here from those which he sketches at other points in
his *Travels*. As his recurrent use of the adjective "delightful"
suggests, however, he is anxious to include such social visions in the
category of wondering discovery. He wants to connect the two
functions of his eye and thus to stress the continuity of natural and
cultural form.

One of his longest catalogs of social advance on the frontier, a
sketch of Fayetteville, North Carolina, suggests how powerful these
desires are, for it copies the structure of an earlier passage on the
spread of Spanish moss through the forest. Hence the means of
natural expansion, a cause for the traveler's awe, also become the
vehicle of his own possession. Conversely, the moss is seen as a
pioneering plant, its first tentative growth expanding with great
rapidity until it possesses a vast region. It thus is an advance guard
of human settlement, an implicit validation of human desire:

> *Wherever it fixes itself, on a limb, or branch, it spreads into short
> and intricate divarications; these in time collect dust, wafted by the
> wind, which, probably by the moisture it absorbs, softens the bark
> and sappy part of the tree, about the roots of the plant, and renders
> it more fit for it to establish itself; and from this small beginning, it
> increases, by sending downwards and obliquely, on all sides, long
> pendant branches, which divide and subdivide themselves ad
> infinitum. . . . Any part of the living plant, torn off and caught in
> the limbs of a tree, will presently take root, grow, and increase, in
> the same degree of perfection as if it had sprung up from the seed.*
> (92)[3]

"Small beginnings" are the very stuff of white American myth, the
starting point of every colony, the initial condition of such cele-
brated men as Benjamin Franklin. One is not surprised to find
Bartram describing Fayetteville in analogous terms, as if it also
grew from a curiously potent source:

> *The creek descends precipitately, then gently meanders near a mile,
> through lower level lands, to its confluence with the river, afford-*

ing most convenient mill-seats: these prospects induced active en-terprising men to avail themselves of such advantages pointed out to them by nature; they built mills, which drew people to the place, and these observing eligible situations for other profitable im-provements, bought lots and erected tenements, where they exercised mechanic arts, as smiths, wheelwrights, carpenters, coopers, tan-ners, &c. And at length merchants were encouraged to adventure and settle: in short, within eight or ten years from a grist-mill, saw-mill, smith-shop and a tavern, arose a flourishing commercial town, the seat of government of the county of Cumberland. (377)[4]

The shape of frontier experience here, as in Bartram's solitary wanderings, seems to unfold effortlessly from nature. In a topo-graphic sense, nature itself seems to smooth out its rough surface so as to aid the implanting of human order: at first precipitous, the creek soon grows gentle, and the lands around it become level, until stream and landscape alike can be seen (and named) in terms of human use. Facts become "prospects," the world playing a di-dactic role which anticipates, and thus authorizes, the explorer's own vision. Mill seats are transformed into actual mills, and each further step in the process of settlement appears to ramify from earlier ones: stream is to mill as mill is to an increase in population, while that increase allows other "eligible situations" to become "lots," and on those lots are built various craftshops—Bartram's catalog now a list of human agents, not of natural detail. Finally come the merchants, who link the small town with a wide outside world, thereby enhancing its local importance. From a set of sim-ple, rudimentary shops and mills has arisen as if by magic not just a larger settlement, but one different in quality as well, a true com-munity worthy of the governmental power now assigned to it.

This is history, to be sure, rather than prediction, and hence it differs noticeably from the two futuristic passages quoted earlier. Yet it is in another sense the history of a predictive mood in the culture as a whole, a contingent narration which accumulates into something more than a local tale. Each step in the process is part of a much larger undertaking; the syntax of this one experience points toward both the national action and the futuristic spirit on which that action is grounded. So interested is Bartram in this overarching pattern that he converts his narrative at the end into a contrast of two terminal states, leaving out the process of change which connects them. His last words on the city extend such a shift

74 even farther: "When I was here about twenty years ago, this town

was marking out its bounds, and there were then about twenty habitations; and now there are above a thousand houses, many wealthy merchants, and respectable public buildings, a vast resort of inhabitants and travellers, and continual brisk commerce by wagons, from the back settlements, with large trading boats, to and from Wilmington" (377). The moments of conception and realization merge as if twenty years of intervening change—and hence the need for a truly historical approach—have been forgotten, or subsumed under another kind of temporality. If he is describing in the whole passage a series of social and spatial events, he frames them at last by means of a timeless fiction. As if the city has appeared suddenly on this site, it seems to be an immediate interpolation into nature, its discovery by the traveler almost an act of visionary perception. The flux of actual time is hidden beneath Bartram's two deeds of fixed survey, and the plantation (for all its supposed organicity) is rendered as a linked pair of iconographic images. It is all "before" and "after," with no sensed transitions, no moments of doubt or false change. The sort of human similitude which Bartram subtly "finds" so often in his purely natural details here has been inserted literally into a landscape, the simile become glorious fact (see PLATES 10–12).

One might describe this iconographic approach as yet another facet of Bartram's enduring wonder, an attempt to include white history in the mysteries of natural time. But the device points, in fact, to the very center of exploratory prose. It is a solution to the anxieties of a temporal career, a check on the momentum of desired change. This *topos* of magical transformation elides from the explorer's view all the disagreeable violence of his own announced intent by submerging the process of settlement beneath a surface of easy contrasts. Indeed, the explorer is likely to displace onto the continent itself, or onto its rightful owners, those doubts which have their rise in his private ambivalence. It is here that Bartram parts company with him: the *Travels* suggests that social order is best when it takes its shape from that of its surrounding world, whereas the explorer almost uniformly views that world, beyond his tributes to its abundance, as a disordered place in need of human design. The poles of his contrast are emptiness and fulfillment, chaos and composition, nothingness and some completed whole. Unless it has been given an obviously human form, either in fact or by means of verbal fiction, American nature is almost literally incomprehensible to him.

The New World of exploratory works is a void, a silent abyss—the opposite of all human arts and sign systems, a place to be described by a series of negative participles: unmarked, unplowed, unsettled, unsung. Even the discoverer's scene of peaceful abundance becomes here an affront to European culture, as in Daniel Denton's vision of New Jersey, in his *Brief Description of New-York* (1670), as a profuse yet strangely decadent country—"full of Deer, Elks, Bear, and other Creatures," yet distressingly empty of human life (with the usual afterthought: "you shall meet with no inhabitants in this journey, but a few Indians"). New Jersey is covered with "stately Oaks, whose broad-branched-tops serve for no other use, but to keep off the Suns heat from the wilde beasts of the Wilderness," or with "grass as high as a mans middle, that serves for no other end except to maintain the Elks and Deer, who never devour a hundreth part of it, then to be burnt every Spring to make way for new."[5] Rich, yet ordered by an economy which Denton seems unable to understand, the region is a wasteland because so much of its profusion is "wasted." Unlike his earlier image of the American traveler as a chivalric hero who gently despoils the land of its innocent fruit, Denton's answering figure here is more clearly designing. "How many poor people in the world would think themselves happy had they an Acre or two of Land," Denton asserts, "whilst here is hundreds, nay thousands of Acres, that would invite inhabitants" (15–16). A moment of poised enjoyment among the strawberry fields of Long Island is balanced by an abstract view of permanent and more active possession. Direct sensual involvement yields to an intellectual relation between the traveler and New World space. Mediated by the schemes of social order, a rich landscape becomes a collection of "Acres," land reckoned in terms of its human divisors, all its profusion to be shared like a dividend among those whom it "invites" across the sea.[6]

It is Denton, of course, who does the inviting here. The pretense of his prose, and of the explorer's generally, is that it speaks for the land, that its own sentences articulate a meaning latent in the region which it describes. Bartram indulges, by his organic vision, in a similar fiction. Yet he lacks Denton's vigorously imperial impulses. Exploration for him is a second step to discovery; the hope of human possession rests firmly in the attitude of wonder. Whereas Denton is saddened by the prospect of unused abundance, Bartram stresses the continuity of delight through the stages of transformation. Hence he suggests that change really is no change, that plantation is (as the word literally implies) a perfectly natural act. Denton, on the other hand, sees unsettled ground as disordered space, and the act of settlement as a deed of mythic organization. Plants themselves thus are tools of possession for Denton: the Delaware country, he writes, "is good for all sorts of English grain" (16), giving crucial advice to any would-be emigrant—but also making literal transplantation, the introducing of "English grain" into America, a means of Anglicizing the land which sustains it. Since he is writing in the wake of an English conquest over the Dutch (who in his opinion have been sluggish in expanding European order), even this one detail of agricultural advice fits into his scheme of active settlement. Open to wonder, Denton finally imagines a New World in which the crucial deeds are those of enclosure.[7]

The explorer's time is always future, the present moment pointing by ineluctable lines of argument and vision to some instant of realized intention. Denton stresses the ease with which his own imaginations can be made concrete by referring to "several Towns of a considerable greatness" which have been "begun and setled by people out of New England" since the Dutch defeat (17). His overall strategy in the *Brief Description* is to use such known achievements as hints of a future expansion. New York is "a known unknown part of America," he asserts in his preface, placing side by side the two terms of his guiding perception. Such a binary contrast is a syntactic model of the *topos,* and the relation between its poles is one of hopeful clarification. The unknown shall be known, and in knowledge is both power and wealth. In fact, the unknown terrain of New York is double: those "places lying to the Northward yet undiscovered by any English" being the horizontal *incognita*—"the Bowels of the earth not yet opened" being the vertical. In both cases "yet" is the key term; the future moment of discovery already is contained in Denton's curious narrative structure. That he offers vague clues about what those two regions contain ("Glittering Stones, Diamonds, or Pearl" to the North; "Gold and Silver" underground) suggests that he longs to substitute current rumor for future fact, and that his seemingly prudent call for a supplement to his own book (to be prepared when "a better discovery shall make way for such a Relation") is an empty gesture. The essential truth about America already has been established, the designs of European economic order having dictated beforehand the terms of any discovery.[8]

The explorer's accepted task is to verify those terms both as a   77 deductive mapping of the New World and as the given parameter of his own report. He solves the problem of a possibly uncertain future by pretending that his ideal history of European expansion into America can be pre-scribed, written up before the fact—much as colonial schemes can be plotted beforehand. For all his asserted caution, Denton gives at the end of his book a description of New York's present state which is actually a pre-dictive vision, an icon in lieu of a history. "What shall I say more?" he asks; "you shall scarce see a house, but the South side is begirt with Hives of Bees, which increase after an incredible manner: That I must needs say, that if there be any terrestrial Canaan, 'tis surely here, where the Land floweth with milk and honey. The inhabitants are blest with Pease and plenty, blessed in their Countrey, blessed in their Fields, blessed in the Fruit of their bodies, in the fruit of their grounds, in the increase of their Cattel, Horses and Sheep, blessed in their Basket, and in their Store; In a word, blessed in whatsoever they take in hand, or go about, the Earth yielding plentiful increase to all their painful labours" (21). Couched as a benediction, the passage is not merely an ending; implied in its rhetoric—even if one grants a certain ambiguity in those "painful labours"—is an unspoken commandment delivered through Denton to an English flock: "Be fruitful, and multiply," multiply in fact by dividing the rich land and its inordinate promise.[9]

What separates such effusive prose from the discoverer's is a shift of vocabulary, and of the concepts which underpin it. The myth of renewal acquires a contingent urgency which it lacks in the more meditative texts of discovery. Though experience remains for the explorer a concept rather than a body of detailed events (since, as a Georgia tract of 1732 puts the idea, "there is no answering for Events," even in America), one can find in this figure's manipulation of New World landscape an enhanced valuation of civic history, a sense that all will be well once real voyagers depart for America.[10] The mental traveler to whom William Wood at least partly addresses his *Prospect* of 1634 has vanished altogether from the explorer's audience. Those who read (or listen) have become far more active, their speculative voyage transformed into a different kind of speculation. What is closet drama in the case of discovery accounts has changed into an actual playscript, a sketch of action which is to be performed by one's audience. The reader's journey ought to emerge at some point into the real world of space and

time, its own experienced shape providing a narrative fulfillment for the explorer's prior sketch. Hence the aptness of a label often used for such works: "promotional tracts," literature which aims at persuading the reader to move, to make a commitment and thus realize the ideal journey of the text.

The explorer's narration is visionary in its sources and nature, future-perfect in its grammar and emotions. Writing in the late 1750s, the almanac-maker Nathaniel Ames divides American time into three parts—a past sunk in oblivion, a present embroiled in war with the French, a future which far outweighs the other parts in its superlative promise. Though he is bothered by the unrecorded history of ancient America and worried deeply by the course of the war, Ames is so excited by his glimpse into the times to come that his sense of the future English memories which shall embellish the landscape completely counters his current troubles. The continent itself seems to long for English, rather than French, control, and Ames's vision of continental growth destroys any lingering doubts over the possible survival of the English way. The war is a test of his people's will, of their right to possess "the Garden of the World." Once having asserted that right, the English settlers will find that America is a fund of workable substance—as, indeed, time itself is during the war—"a vast Stock of proper Materials for the Art and Ingenuity of Man to work upon." The expected progress of secular culture to the West (like that of the Gospel, which shall "drive the long! long! Night of Heathenish Darkness from *America*") will fill the void with recognizable shape and meaning: "Arts and Sciences will change the Face of Nature in their Tour from Hence over the Appalachian Mountains to the Western Ocean; and as they march thro' the vast Desert, the Residence of Wild Beasts will be broken up, and their obscene Howl cease for ever;—instead of which, the Stones and Trees will dance together at the music of *Orpheus,*—the Rocks will disclose their hidden Gems,—and the inestimable Treasures of Gold and Silver be broken up."[11]

A collection of transformable matter, a chaos of "obscene" creatures and objects awaiting the impress of an almost divine social order, the continent is to be settled by means of a gentle dialectical process, the thesis of cultural design meeting hardly any resistance from nature, the synthesis a perfect realization of human scheme. Nature seems to desire the change, even partly to anticipate it by "disclosing" on its own where the tokens of economic value lie hidden. An Orphean figure, the personified nation embarks on a

"Tour" of the wilderness: it will endure no severe trials, no disappointments, no dead ends. And the harmony of its stride will make the stones and trees themselves "dance together." Noise yields to music, the "vast Desert" is crossed by a line of human intent, and even the reaches of space beneath the ground are opened up to the explorer's eye.[12]

Like Bartram, Ames hints at a natural warrant for these acts of human formulation. But the justification in his case hardly is organic. Like the historical imperative which he cites ("the Progress of Humane Literature . . . is from the East to the West . . . and now is arrived at the eastern Shore of America"), his argument from nature is legalistic and abstract. Abundance becomes a sign of economic imbalance: since "Nature thro' all her Works has stamp'd Authority on this Law, namely 'That all fit Matter shall be improved to its best Purposes,'" the white desire to use American "matter" seems like humble obedience to a plan that is far more than human. Settlement will rectify the New World by expressing in concrete detail this overarching rule of fit use; exploitation will not alienate humanity from nature, but rather join agent and world more closely together.

Such an argument may seem organic on its surface, since it makes the settler base his own acts on the implied principles of the world around him. Yet the means of his union with that world, and the symbols of it, finally are mechanical. Drained of wonder, Ames's American scene is inexpressible on its own terms, unapproachable except through the designs applied to it. New World matter is perceived less as a collection of formed objects (since objectivity implies a prior completion, a visible order) than as a lumpish mass discriminated into separate entities by white planters and laborers. Hence plantation *is* creation, not just a human echo of a divine act. And Ames's own prose is a mill of primary industry, a vehicle for naming matter and thus giving it entrance into the world of use. The geological formations of America become, in his narrow vocabulary, "Vast Quarries that teem with mechanic Stone," the reductive figure itself a settling device. Nor do such acts of linguistic transformation stop with simple naming. Ames invents a syntax as well as a taxonomy, model sentences in which the course of white expansion is reflected: the stone which is fit "for Structure," he writes, will be "piled into great Cities," while that which is appropriate "for Sculpture" will be worked "into Statues to perpetuate the Honor of renowned Heroes; even those who shall NOW save their Country" (32–33).

Almost before our eyes as we read, the war is won, the continent settled, the "Tour" completed. American space here seems amenable in another sense: receptive of white design, languishing from the lack of an informing vision, happy to occupy a subordinate place in reality and in European narrative statement. As the desert becomes a quarry, and then yields up the "mechanic Stone" of civic order and artistic celebration, Ames shifts his attention away from the ominous time of war and toward that much later moment when his vision shall have been realized. "O! Ye unborn Inhabitants of America," he exclaims, "Should this Page escape its destin'd Conflagration at the Year's End, and these Alphabetical Letters remain legible, when your Eyes behold the Sun after he has rolled the Seasons round for two or three Centuries more, you will know that in Anno Domini 1758, we dream'd of your Times" (33). Oblivion remains a threat (an almanac being a strange medium for such expansive, hopefully enduring predictions); yet beneath this conventional irony is the bedrock of Ames's expectation. The future lies like a seed in his own age: American time is a pair of answering instants, a projective and a realized moment linked through all the intervening years by the strength of a cultural plot, a line of idealizing sight and language.[13]

No matter how distant it is from his own day, the explorer's future always serves as the final scene of his play, the time of comic resolution. Ames might as well change his final assertion: what he means, in fact, is not "we dreamed *of* your times" but rather "we dreamed your times," we scripted them (and you yourself) by an exercise of cultural fantasy, and we bequeathed that fantasy to you as the blueprint of your identity, your contingent and actual world. It is a Columbian stance, time substituted for space, the future New World itself a realm awaiting discovery. Implicit in such a shift of plot (though Ames strives against recognizing this point) is the chance of a Columbian disappointment, a landmass of experience inserted between the place of departure and the rumored Indies of fulfillment. Having admitted time into America by making the prospect of delight a temporal concept, the explorer has allowed the later perversion of his plotted history. One even might speculate that this figure's reliance on vision as a mode of understanding, however keyed his own visions are to social purpose, has authorized a deeply antinomian strain in later times. Once endorsed as a public art, prophecy can act as a means of highly individualistic, and hence dispersing, insight. It is partly because of this threat that the explorer tries to narrow the gap between the moment of conception and that of maturity. That gulf remains, however, like a terrain of doubt between himself and his appointed heirs, a vacancy, a vast desert of potentially disruptive events. Like the creatures which impinge on the discoverer's trail in William Wood, such a doubtful intervening world becomes the locus of the traveler's anxiety, the thing to be bridged or abridged if his ideal New World (and his account of it) is to survive. In the case of Ames, this anxiety is deflected onto the American natives and the French.

Magical transformation serves the explorer as a central bridge of time. Since it allows one to mix moments freely, almost literally to see the future scene implicit in the present, it suggests an adequate control over intermediate ground, an unalterable chain of events. Though it marks the traveler's commitment to history, it elides the actual process of change. At its most mystical, it hints at the convergence of times, a holistic view of temporal life which sustains the white apprehension of America. Against the episodic sense of experience so often rendered in accounts of actual settlement, the explorer's text asserts a coalescent vision: the magical union of now and then becomes a model of coherent narrative form and of national (or regional or communal) consciousness. Every event is given its ideal relation to all others, its unchanging role in a single inclusive action.

In this sense, the future is a terrain of romance, the temporal equivalent of the discoverer's spatial "beyond." Ames's imaginary "Tour" of artful order to the West seems like a spatial act, but is in fact less a means of covering ground than of bringing America into history. It marks the beginning of white memory in the land, and thus is the prospective deed to which the reader's retrospect "two or three centuries" later will refer. Settlement, like sculpture, is an aid to perpetuation, a way of linking disparate moments through a material continuity. The projection of civic images into the American scene organizes the present world; but it maps out, too, a series of later presents, an accumulating growth.[14]

Almost everything which the explorer sees in the New World enters his text as a sign of this larger process, a token of the grand symbolic scheme. Each act of perception thus brings into European awareness both another detail and a pattern of meaning in which it is made to exist. Whereas the discoverer's prose is likely to be paratactic in form, cumulative in its bias, that of the explorer introduces into the web of American facts a principle of grammatical and philosophic subordination. The ruling muse is "Commod-

82

ity," and precisely in the sense defined by Ralph Waldo Emerson's *Nature:* "The misery of man appears like childish petulance," he writes, "when we explore the steady and prodigal provision that has been made for his support and delight on this green ball which floats him through the heavens.... Beasts, fire, water, stones, and corn serve him. The field is at once his floor, his work-yard, his play-ground, his garden, and his bed.... The wind sows the seed; the sun evaporates the sea; the wind blows the vapor to the field; the ice, on the other side of the planet, condenses rain on this; the rain feeds the plant; the plant feeds the animal; and thus the endless circulations of the divine charity nourish man."[15] Though stated broadly, Emerson's formulation echoes a particularly national rhetoric. Unlike his earlier, more mysterious catalog in the essay— "language, sleep, madness, dreams, beasts, sex" (11)—this one is both more and less than a list of nouns. He adds to that structure a ministering verb and an indirect human object, thus making it a model of the explorer's simplest syntactic change. General in tone, unlocal and unspecific, the statement nonetheless stipulates a relation between humanity and nature which is fixed in value and in the axis of allowable action.

Emerson's pretense of passivity is important here: it is the means by which "support" and "delight" are joined, the wonder of discovery fading off into an anticipation of use and profit. Whereas his first sentence might be found anywhere in William Bartram, the rest of what he writes has a certain pragmatic edge rare in the *Travels.* Even the passive role assigned to mankind is partly an evasion: under the benign dispensation of this world, half of our labor is performed for us by natural forces. Like those New Jersey "Acres" of Denton (which "would invite" settlers to possess them), the cosmos itself becomes an aid to human exploitation. Indeed, nature emerges as a human agent, co-worker in the task of transforming "the field" into a series of defined and usable spaces. Personified, it joins the farmer who divides and plants the earth—is, in fact, a farmer itself. Hence those arts by which pure nature ("space, the air, the river, the leaf") is impressed with our own "will" (and thus changed into artifacts, "a house, a canal, a statue, a picture") already are anticipated by nature acting alone (11). "Commodity" as a theory of the world rests on a commodious disposition in the cosmos.

This final point illuminates the whole course of Emerson's argument. Like the human attitudes which it describes, his language   83 becomes a tool of predication, a means of adding to things-in-themselves a set of economic specifications. He himself cautions, to be sure, that "A man is fed, not that he may be fed, but that he may work" (15)—commodity being subordinate to the higher "uses" of nature. By a good inversion, Emerson thus makes discovery posterior to exploration, beauty dependent on survival. Yet here and elsewhere in his writings Emerson endorses a less than wondering attitude, confusing values which are radically at odds. If, as he proclaims, "the eye is the best of artists" (15), he does not discriminate adequately between the kinds of vision available to his fellow citizens. He fails to see how possessive the American eye often has been, the extent to which its act of composure has mimicked (and aided) the literal expansion of economic order, frequently at the expense of other designs.[16] In the middle of "The American Scholar," in fact, he portrays the hero of his title as an active figure whose intellectual deeds copy the progress of the nation across America. Like Nathaniel Ames, he envisions nature as a statically unformed realm, a world in need of our own filling act:

> The world,—this shadow of the soul, or OTHER ME,—lies wide
> around. Its attractions are the keys which unlock my thoughts and
> make me acquainted with myself. I run eagerly into this resounding
> tumult. I grasp the hands of those next me, and take my place in the
> ring to suffer and to work, taught by an instinct that so shall the
> dumb abyss be vocal with speech. I pierce its order; I dissipate its
> fear; I dispose of it within the circuit of my expanding life. So much
> only of life as I know by experience, so much of the wilderness have
> I vanquished and planted, or so far have I extended my being, my
> dominion. (58–59)

Emerson's assumption here is that a rhetoric appropriate to the life of the mind in America must derive from the rhetoric of ordinary American affairs. Bothered by the possibility that his scholar may retreat from experience, he posits a set of metaphoric equivalencies between mental and physical exploration. "Life lies behind us as the quarry from whence we get tiles and copestones for the masonry of to-day," he asserts. "This is the way to learn grammar" (60). Instinct with the attitudes of an Orphean myth, and those of the *translatio artium* motif (which Ames also uses), such an equation urges us to see settlement itself as a paradigm of American art and thought, the historical base of an individual growth. And it hints as well at a syntactic connection between the language of art and the terms of national experience, a link of "grammar" not simply between nature and artifact but also between the particular aesthetic of the American scholar and the particular plot of New World life. Emerson's simile of the "quarry," like Ames's similar metaphor, maps out a far from passive role for the explorer, a formulative act rather than a receptive one. If what he finally means is that the scholar is to make his own web of correspondence according to suggestions in nature, he expresses this insight by a more narrow language than he intends: not nature, but nature methodized, is the source of his figure.

So, too, a comparison of Walt Whitman and Brigham Young entered by Emerson in his journal during 1863 points not only to the national status of the poet's art, but also to the artful grammar of national action itself. *"Good out of evil,"* Emerson glosses the link: "One must thank the genius of Brigham Young for the creation of Salt Lake City,—an inestimable hospitality to the Overland Emigrants, and an efficient example to all men in the vast desert, teaching how to subdue and turn it to a habitable garden. And one must thank Walt Whitman for service to American literature in the Appalachian enlargement of his outline and treatment."[17] Out of the emptiness of silence, or the empty and silent spaces of the West, the settler-poet and the poetic settler are to create a world of predicated order and meaning, an America of the imagination laid over the given New World of fact. The struggle for national expression to which Emerson was a witness—the effort to make a consciously national literature—thus took place not in a void of language or example, but rather in an atmosphere of prior ventures into literal voids, previous incursions of the mind through regions significant of the artist's private "abyss." And the syntax of those initial acts, the grammar of extraction and of informing statement, was to be a model of aesthetic expansion as well.

Whitman, for his own part, declared in 1855 that the poet "places himself where the future becomes present," a borderline of high art which copies the boundaries of the culture as a whole. His expansive catalogs finally are modeled on the discoverer's rather than the explorer's rhetoric: they are acts of naming performed in a mist of wonder, gentle and loving. Yet an undercurrent of possessiveness constantly threatens to surface in his poems, a solipsistic tendency for the namer to engross what is named, for his appellations to become deeds of title. Realizing this danger, Whitman announces in his first preface that the great American poem is *not* to be "direct or descriptive or epic"—that its bearing on the acts of

New World experience is to be oblique. Unlike Joel Barlow (though Whitman also has his own Columbian poems), he does not aim to *record* the expansion of Eastern order, but rather to imitate it—and cleanse it—by the "Appalachian enlargement" of his stance and line. This last point is essentially what Emerson, beyond his ambiguity, means in his journal passage. But Whitman has his own uncertainties, a confusion of matter and manner which leads him to present the poet as a naively exploratory figure, one "mechanic" among many: "Here comes one among the wellbeloved stone-cutters and plans with decision and science," he writes, "and sees the solid and beautiful forms of the future where there are now no solid forms."[18] Taking to himself the scheme of expansionist order, Whitman raises that scheme to mythic proportion: the conquest over a trackless, timeless world—the assertion of cultural design in space—hints at the active program which a poet struggling to fill in the blank spaces of poetic possibility must follow:

> *See, vast trackless spaces,*
> *As in a dream they change, they swiftly fill,*
> *Countless masses debouch upon them,*
> *They are now cover'd with the foremost people, arts,*
> *institutions, known.*
> "Starting from Paumanok," ll.25–28

Copying the plot of national event, the poet gives it an aesthetic warrant after the fact. His verse is one more act of "coverage," a further arrival on the once vacant ground. Starting with six syllables and ending with seventeen, his four lines suggest by their own swift expanding movement a parallel (and equally artful) movement in the nation. Like Bartram's vision of Fayetteville, Whitman's generalized contrast of emptiness and fulfillment urges us to see only the paradigm of settlement: its details dismissed, its aesthetic shape emerges as an almost pure and contemplative design. A merely quantitative change, an act of "filling," thus becomes a qualitative uplift, a substitution of "the foremost people, arts, institutions" for a vacant, implicitly meaningless world.

By such retrospective views, the flow of control to the West is validated, the informing act itself informed by later art. But the explorer works his own imaginative changes by similar means: Whitman's rhetoric copies the manner of exploratory prose, not just its matter. The syntax of the explorer's vision, even on the local level, is a vehicle of control, a way of linking the almost inex-

pressible New World with those things which cover it and discriminate it into locale. Like Whitman's "people, arts, institutions," his
own are tokens of possession, signs of the predicative (and predictive) intent of his culture. And his language is a tool of union, a
transitional weld which joins together the two halves of an innately
American conceit—the desert which is the opposite of all social
order now twined inextricably with the symbols of that order, a
marriage of opposing principles achieved by the magical harmony
of grammar. The authoritative structure of a sentence (its power
lying in its verbs, its polity expressed in its own inward subordination) comes to mirror, partly to cause, the expense of authority in
American space. Each exploratory statement condenses and
clarifies the sprawl of actual expansion. By asserting its simplified
lines of control and use, it excludes the very details which Whitman
does, leaving only the scheme of ideal transformation.

PROFIT AND LOSS

In one of the earliest surviving English promotion tracts, *A Briefe
and Summary Discourse upon the Intended Voyage to the Hithermost Parts
of America* (1583), Christopher Carleill builds for his audience—
most germanely, the Muscovy Company—a neat model of his
proposed commerce in the West which exploits a good many of the
explorer's arts. A prospectus for potential investors in his scheme,
the tract is true to its function: it is an aid to better sight (and
vision), a bringing-near of the supposedly distant New World. Yet
it aims at more than an innocent and entertaining discovery. Near-
ness implies exploitability rather than delight: the "easie kinde of
travell" that connects Europe and America is a commercial asset,
not a spiritual sign.[19] Rhetorically, Carleill's piece begins where he
himself stands, in that web of commercial lines already linking
England with foreign lands in the Eastern hemisphere. It looks in
this opposite direction, however, only so that its glimpse into
America can be the more inviting. The "forren voyages and trades
already frequented and knowen" serve as a "Touchstone" by which
the worth of his own "intended voyage" may be tested. Yet his test
also works in reverse, for as Carleill surveys each of the accustomed
trade routes and lists their difficulties, the touchstone itself seems
impure. By implication from the start, this "Goldsmith" of commercial profit—for such is his rhetorical stance—will reveal an
imposture in the established system by uncovering lead within its
gilded surface (80). By implication, too, the New World route will   87

offer up a golden opportunity of unexampled richness, if not a mountain of actual gold.

These hints materialize as Carleill starts to "lay downe" the debits of each old route. His account of the Muscovy trade, of that with Turkey, Italy, Barbary, Spain, and Portugal, becomes an accounting as well, the balance tipped by a series of natural and human impediments. A basic commercial premise lurks everywhere in his imagery: one must get something for something, a return for an outlay. The flux of money and goods is a mathematical abstraction of voyages out and back, a way of "figuring" events. And the established ventures are in this sense out of kilter, the expense of resources too high for the actual benefit gained. Beset with large initial costs, the Muscovy trade has run into countless hidden charges: gifts for the Emperor and his nobles, bribes for lesser figures at the court, the general fickleness of affairs throughout the country, all have combined to reduce the merchant's profits drastically. Add to these internal problems the presence of stiff competition from the Dutch, the bad "qualitie of the voyage" (it is "such as may not be performed but once the yeere"), the trader's expense in supporting diplomatic exchanges, and the intervening power of the Danish King—seated astride the route like a menacing presence—and the situation seems bleak indeed (81–83).

A coy writer, Carleill actually is painting here a displaced portrait of the English merchant's anxieties about American trade: a region of lost investments where much is expended for little, Russia is a stand-in for the New World of rumored disaster. The substitution is aided by his use of an almost philosophical arithmetic throughout the tract. The long and interrupted passage to Moscow, cluttered with wayside difficulties and aimed finally at the doubtful gain, becomes an expense of capital in a waste of profitless uncertainty. At its end lies an almost embodied Nothingness, a chaos of unamenable facts which resists English design—both mercantile and epistemological. The collapse of commercial economy hints at the attrition of other orders mirrored in it, "loss" being an appropriate summary of both sad events.

Having suggested that Old World commerce may invert the merchant's dream (*something for nothing* being redefined here, the something spent, the nothing taken in), Carleill turns his attention west, and almost revives in that direction the usual meaning of such an axiom. Blockage, indirection, deceit, corruption—the facts

of an Eastern voyage—disappear from the merchant's way into

America. Closure yields to disclosure: Carleill's rhetoric now is a means of opening up rather than laying bare. The new passage, he declares, "hath as many points of good moment belonging unto it, as may almost be wished for." Directed along the "latitude of fortie degrees" ("or thereaboutes," for latitude requires latitude), the projected voyage aims at the "hithermost part of America," the cusp of land that itself leans almost invitingly toward Europe. At the outer edge of European trade, England now has an inside advantage. Lying at the end of a short cruise, this near ground can be reached "all times of the yeere" by means of "one wind, . . . whereas most of your other voyages of like length, are subject to 3. or 4." Performed on the open sea, a Western voyage is free from the coastal dangers perceived by Carleill in Old World sailing, and is likewise safe from the intermeddling of Continental powers. Since, in addition, both Ireland and England "are very well stored of goodly harbours" in convenient areas, the voyage is as nicely accommodated at its near end as its far. Neither nature nor mankind can sever this line of induction: the West extending east, the East prepared, the nothing in between a reassuring sign of something yet to come (83).

Like George Alsop in the next century, Carleill thus tries to bring
America into the English mind—to make it seem like a reasonable
place for new endeavors—as well as to bring the English mind into
America. His desired link, however, will result from transportation
as a kinetic fact, not from transport as a spiritual one. Having
sketched the form of his intention, he passes on to its contents,
those things which are "the matter especially looked for" from any
commercial venture. Mathematics here assumes a new function:
the initial returns from New World trade will be smaller than those
known in other ventures, but since the effort will demand a smaller
outlay the whole scheme remains in balance. In the long run, what
is more, the art of multiplication is more nearly appropriate to
American commerce than a system of debit and credit. Against that
subtractive rhetoric which he uses for treating European trade
Carleill adduces an exponential language which seems like the re-
quisite of his New World hope. When American commerce "shall
have bene haunted and practised thirtie yeeres to an ende, as the
[Russian] hath bene," he writes, "I doubt not by Gods grace, that
for the tenne shippes that are now commonly employed once the
yeere into Moscovia, there shall in this voyage twise tenne be im-
ployed well, twise the yeere at the least" (84).

Many Goodly
Tokens

89

As he develops his catalog of future commodities, Carleill likewise uses a more than additive prose. Each new item suggests a similar multiplication of net tonnage and profit, and the sum is greater than its parts only because Carleill's ledger is open-ended, not because some spiritual implication arises. The single line of connection between England and America thus bifurcates into two laterals which lead north to a region of naval stores and pelts ("Pitch, Tarre, Hempe, and thereof cordage, Masts, Losshe hides, rich Furres"), and southwest to a place of more temperate produce—wines, olive oil, wax, and honey (84). By such triangulating arguments, Carleill maintains a verbal control over what might expand otherwise into an undesirable complexity. The first effort contains all further ones, unifying them at the same time that it is divided and expanded itself. Since multiplication as an economic fact (and a rhetorical gesture) raises the specter of multiplicity, and thus of disunity, this strategy is crucial to Carleill's eulogistic and promotional purposes. By a kind of transformation no less magical than that in Bartram or Ames, he converts the small beginning of his private speculation into a concrete sign of large future accomplishments. One man's vision becomes the base of a thousand happy careers.

That vision itself is based on a Europeanizing metaphor which converts the American voyage into a substitute for Old World trading routes. The new way is not merely easier than the older ones but will supplant them entirely. Its northern commodities will equal those which "the Easterne Countreys doe yeeld us now," Carleill argues, while the southwestern produce will deserve comparison with that of Spain, Provence, and Italy. All in prospect, such equivalencies suggest a merging of spatial grids, a convergence of economic maps. Yet Carleill envisions an even stronger link between England and America than the ones which now tie his homeland with Europe. His commercial scheme calls, in fact, for an effort at colonization, the intended settlement to be a token of abiding English interest in the West. Implicit in the first Western voyage is a set of benign social consequences for America and England alike. Trade with the natives is to be induced by the gift of "such trifling things as they desire of us," and it is "to bee assuredly hoped, that they will daily by little and little forsake their barbarous and savage living, and growe to such order and civilitie with us, as there may be well expected from thence no lesse quantitie and diversitie of merchandize then is now had out of Dutchland, Italie,

France or Spaine." Since this new Europe of the West will be under English control (for all the colonists shall be "our own kindred, and esteemed our own countrey nation"), the political troubles of Europe itself—and the threat of commercial competition—are excised from the bright scenario (84–85). By the magic of verbal prediction, a New World from which the reader expects almost nothing becomes more English than the known scenes of Old World life. A simple plot becomes a plat of vast Western regions.

Other advantages seem to grow by an allied magic from the rich soil of Carleill's prose. By "the good prospering of this action," he opines, "there must of necessitie fall out a very liberal utterance of our English Clothes into a maine Country, described to bee bigger then all Europe," and other English artifacts will fare equally well. Such commercial "utterance," in fact, is a pragmatic reflection of Carleill's own artful speech, the imagined profit of his imaginary predictions. Likewise, the good establishment of an English colony may lead to the discovery of an even farther economic possibility, a northwest passage which may be "most assuredly" found by "those who shall inhabite and first grow into familiaritie with the Inland people." If he finally demurs from making any forecast of "What Minerall matter may fall out to bee found"—this being "a thing left in suspence" (both active and narrative)—Carleill hardly is modest in proposing less outrageously rich discoveries. The "great promises" of other promoters unfortunately have created in his audience a sense of fraud and disappointment, a view that such designs "be but wordes purposely cast out for the inducing of men to bee the more ready and willing to furnish their money toward the charge of the first discoverie." Less extravagant himself, at least in the initial pages of his *Discourse,* Carleill bends all his wit to a similar task, an allied "inducement" of financial support. Merchants may be reluctant to supply the funds required for colonizing schemes, since the large expense of a first effort may imply that subsequent costs will be equally high. But, again by multiplication, he notes that "in all attempts unknowen" first investments "are commonly adventured in more desperate kinde, then those that followe upon some better knowledge." Hence, "whereas one adventureth in the first enterprise, an hundred for that one will of themselves bee willing and desirous to adventure in the next"—at least if some evidence is found that "our first presumption" was correct (85–86).

Carleill's own presumption runs high, and his suggestions about its truthfulness also are exuberant. The reluctant merchant is a victim of "frivolous scruple," a person who "will not otherwise be satisfied, then by the report of Saint Thomas." Such a trader's hope is that his "money should not be wasted to nothing in the preparations," that the line of debt will become a large line of credit. Carleill thus must balance in his prose events which he hopes will be balanced, and profitable, in reality. A "right examination" of the project, he proclaims, must lead to the "contrary sequell of the common Proverbe, . . . Nothing venture, nothing have." The contrary of such an axiom is not true, of course—indeed, is there any?—but Carleill bends logic to support the hopeful mathematics of his design. Something venture, something have (better yet, much have) is the ruling law of his imagined New World, so powerful that even the great nothings of England, the numerous poor, will get their something in America. Since "this is not an action which concerneth onely the Marchants particularly, but a great deale more the generall sort of people throughout all England," the smallest show of success will call forth broad support from the nation (87).

The peroration of the *Discourse* combines such mildly utopian visions with an even keener economic sight. Christian charity, that virtue on which John Winthrop later would found his scheme for Massachusetts Bay, enters as an appeal to those who have "forward mindes in well doing" to humanity. The relief of the poor will be a relief of "the better sort" of Englishmen as well, utopian improvement in the West becoming a means of improving Old World order. Like English cloth, the idle and poverty-stricken also will be "uttered" into America, and as a result homeland speech will be improved. The argument here is economic rather than humanitarian, the poor being seen as a kind of surplus, a drug on the English market. Like warfare (an older way of venting such surplusage), colonization can help transform "very evill and idle livers" into men "very industrious in their facultie"—and it can do so without the pain and suffering common in war. It also aims at a higher purpose, a better recompense, and can be pursued with "an assured kind of good hope" lacking in military life (88).

"Thus you see in every point that may bee wished for in a good action and voyage," Carleill asserts near the end, "there is matter and reason enough to satisfie the well disposed." Desiring to "growe somewhat neerer the quicke," he offers what becomes a long narrative exemplum, drawn from Jacques Cartier's experience in Canada and aimed (despite the disasters of that man's Western life) at the encouragement of English effort. Detailing the troubles undergone by Cartier, Carleill finally attributes them to French errors—a failure of design rather than a resistance of place. Both model and foil, Cartier embodies a correct attitude of expansive vision, along with a flawed strategy. His insult to the Canadian natives, caused by his kidnapping of their king (who later died in France), fortunately has been forgotten in the fifty years intervening, and the way once more has opened for French commerce. The new trade carried on for the past two seasons evinces the ideal form of Carleill's own intent: the first endeavor was made with "a small barke of thirtie tunnes," the results so profitable that the next year "a shippe of fourescore tunnes" was sent. The latter showed such profits that during the present year the French "have multiplyed three shippes"—a total tonnage of 360. The figures themselves tell Carleill's burden, the sense of small things leading to great, the tentative act inscribing a line which later deeds will darken into an established route of exchange. By an argument almost sophistic in its shape, making the lesser appear the greater, Carleill has turned a narrative of failure into a tale of future glory and profit. The details of Cartier's experience are admissible insofar as they are not final or tragic, their shape itself "in suspence" until it is fulfilled by more recent events. If so much has been gained by the French in such a short time (and in the North, to boot), then "it is worth the thinking on to consider what may be hoped for from the Southerne part, which in all reason may promise a great deale more." The ratio of French returns, fourteen or fifteen to one, may seem fabulous, but Carleill's intended route points toward a region more fabulous still. American trade offers one a "greater and more assured commodity" than any comparable route (88–91).

As the promoter of that trade, Carleill assures his audience that he has "passed cleare and unspotted in matters of greater importance and difficultie" (91) earlier in his career, and hence is worthy of the investor's trust. His proven character matches the asserted nature of his America; his literary style thus is his personal style as well, and both combine to render for the reader the stylistic stresses of a New World voyage: "clear passing" is the mark of all three, the man, the language, the intended act. No mere practical pamphlet, the *Discourse* maps the western scene and sketches out the track of a literal and metaphoric movement toward it. It is one episode in a large myth-making enterprise, an attempt to process America by means of the processes of language itself. Part activated catalog,

93

part dynamic gesture enacted verbally, it seeks to unite the objects of the New World with the will and power of Old World men. The economic framework within which Carleill views America is inseparable from his typical syntax. How he handles words as grammatical entities reflects an actual handling of the things to which they refer. By its own disposition of verbal power, each of his statements evokes a polity for New World attempts, an ideal relation between European traveler and American reality. Hence his prose does not merely describe his project, but anticipates it as well. Implicit everywhere is a future history of which the present text is a trial version, a narrative "germ" in which one can already trace the potential for some finished tale.

SMALL BEGINNINGS, SUDDEN ACCOMPLISHMENTS

Carleill's brief book exemplifies a broad format in New World prose. Texts written at much later periods, and concerned with quite different purposes, share with Carleill's the desire to encourage a particular American "action," and they thus exploit in their attempt to procure actors for it many of the persuasive techniques used in the *Discourse* of 1583. As a group, such works may be described as syntactic fragments, structures of language from which the proper subject of New World narrative is absent. The author's aim is to convince those who read to become more than readers, to enter both the text and the universe which it seems to describe. But not all the tracts which can be compared with Carleill's on these grounds are nearly so exuberant in tone or so forgetful of the risks involved in an American voyage.

Three pamphlets composed by William Penn between 1681 and 1685 demonstrate how cautious other promoters might be. They also suggest how, as some proposals were realized, the caution of a small beginning might be replaced with ever more hopeful claims. The first of Penn's works, *Some Account of the Province of Pennsylvania* (1681), was written before Penn actually had seen his American lands; it is, as a result, guarded in tone and strategy, heavy with arguments rather than images. Penn seems concerned with objections commonly raised against any plantation (that it may sap the strength of England), and hence he spins out a web of doubt and hopeful counterassertion, a logical dialogue between Old World and New World partisans. Even in this defensive dialogue, however, Penn's vague America becomes a simplified terrain free of the social problems which actually cause the ills ascribed to emigration.

94

America is new, England old—so much so that when Penn con-
esty and industry of Man, it may be a good and fruitful Land," he is
implying that England has passed its prime, that such statements
no longer can be applied to it, whereas they are the essence of
Pennsylvania.[20] Modest in his claims, Penn speaks well for (and of)
his American namesake, the simplicity of his language itself a
significant image of the "Country in America" which, as he says, "is
fallen to my lot" (202). Opposed to "the great Debauchery" (206) of
England, one item in Penn's list of Old World discommodities, is
the quiet peace and unobtrusive abundance of America, a place
where the industry of emigrants "is worth more than if they stay'd
at home, the Product of their Labour being in Commodities of a
superiour Nature to those of this Country" (203).

Passing from argument to the concrete scheme which he is urging, Penn describes the natural, political, and economic advantages
of emigration. He then lists those Englishmen who may undertake
the voyage with most hope: "Industrious Husbandmen and Day-
Labourers," practitioners of the basic crafts (carpentry, black-
smithing, tanning, shipbuilding, and the like), "those Ingenious
Spirits" whose worldly position impedes the expression of their
genius, "younger brothers of small Inheritances," and those "Men
of universal Spirits" whose love for "good Discipline and just Government among a plain and well intending people" will make them
helpful in the governance of Penn's new colony. Each category is
part of an ideal dramatis personae for the New World action which
Penn has in mind. But it is not enough merely to sketch that action
or to enroll its players. Penn offers a series of cautions to his cast,
stage directions designed to guarantee as good a performance as
possible. In discussing "The Journey and it's Appurtenances, and
what is to be done there at first coming," his purpose is to insure
that "such as incline to go, may not be to seek here, or brought to
any disappointments there." Part of his advice is practical ("all sorts
of Apparel and Utensils for Husbandry and Building and House-
hold Stuff" are essential stores), but more important is his spiritual
warning: crucial as props will be to the success of the venture, one
must prepare inwardly as well, must understand that—since "Imaginations are great flatterers of the minds of Men"—one is not to
expect an "Immediate Amendment" as soon as one lands (209–11).

Yet what Penn proposes as a more reasonable expectation
(people must "look for a Winter before a Summer comes; and . . .   95

be willing to be two or three years without some of the con-
veniences they enjoy at home" [211]) hardly seems like a radically different vision. It is the mildest of doubtful futures, a mere
episode of hard living in an assuredly good career. Since Pennsylvania is buffered to the north and south by well-established colonies, it will rest secure against the threats which so often arise in
utterly unsettled ground. The shape of the colonist's experience is
buffered by the same fact, earlier successes suggesting his own as
well. Advising would-be emigrants to "consider seriously the prem-
ises, as well as the present inconveniences" of his scheme, not just
their own "future ease and Plenty" (215), Penn finally hints that
such a serious consideration is merely a formal requirement, a
pause of meditation before the awaited act of commitment. Beyond
his caution lies a great expectation of renewal, a sense of the New
World as a place of fulfillment rather than asperity. His rhetorical
pose is partly a mask, a concession to Old World doubt which is
untrue to his own American hopes.

A draft of his plans, and of the colony's desired history, Penn's
tract points to further acts of draftsmanship. In detailing "the Con-
stitutions of the Country," he lists four salient principles, the first
three of which regard issues of law and governance, and hence are
"constitutional" in a technical sense. But the fourth principle concerns the means by which Pennsylvania itself is to be constituted,
made up according to the will of Penn and his emigrants: "so soon
as any are ingaged with me," he promises, "we shall begin a Scheam
or Draught together, such as shall give ample Testimony of my
sincere Inclinations to encourage Planters, and settle a free, just
and industrious Colony." The next division of his prose concerns
"The Conditions" of engagement, and though cast in a tentative
language—itself a demonstration of Penn's willingness to be joined
in such formulations by his colonists—it is a model of the settler's
designing arts, a means of schematizing American space. It begins
with an enumeration of emigrant classes—purchasers, renters, servants of absentee owners—and then suggests a "Divident" by which
the land may be parceled out to them: "if the persons concern'd
please," Penn proposes, "a Tract of Land shall be survey'd; say
Fifty thousand Acres to a hundred Adventurers; in which some of
the best shall be set out for Towns or Cities; and there shall be so
much Ground allotted to each in those Towns as may maintain
some Cattel and produce some Corn; then the remainder of the
fifty thousand Acres shall be shar'd among the said Adventurers

(casting up the Barren for Commons, and allowing for the same)
whereby every Adventurer will have a considerable quantity of
Land together; likewise every one a proportion by a Navigable
River, and then backward into the Country" (208–9). Next to this
rather grandiose scheme, Penn's literal attributions to Pennsylvania
("For Fowl, Fish, and Wild-Deer, they are reported to be plentiful
in those Parts," and so forth [207]) seem tame, even understated.
But his metaphoric settlement of such a large region reveals how
high he has set his aim, how engrossing are his predications.

Widely distributed by Penn and his agents, *Some Account* went
through several editions in English, Dutch, and German, and it
seems to have induced a good many emigrants to set sail. When
Penn himself left England in August 1682, over 600,000 acres of
his American land had been sold there, and from spring of that
year until early 1683, more than thirty ships brought over several
thousand settlers. Not all of these emigrants, to be sure, can be
viewed as the cast of his particular script: there were other tracts
and broadsides available; word of mouth probably was an effective
informal agent; and the intended colony was to be planted, after
all, on ground already settled by the Swedes and by earlier Quaker
emigrants. The great tide of migration, on the other hand, had a
clearly discernible effect on Penn's future writings. Aimed at the
inducement of even more emigration, his *Letter* of 1683 to the Free
Society of Traders and his *A Further Account of the Province of
Pennsylvania* (1685) both extend Penn's cautious rhetoric in the
1681 piece, its extension warranted by the expansion of the colony
itself. Hence the deed urged by his first tract, once accomplished,
has allowed (perhaps demanded) the more grandiose projects announced in his later ones. The mere number of willing participants
has served as a further wall against uncertainty.

Penn's pose in the two subsequent texts thus is that of a chronicler whose comments on the recent past map out an imminent
future. Magical change is the formula which explains the history
and the prospects of Pennsylvania. Having arrived in America himself, Penn joins to the accomplishments of his colony the fact of his
own more concrete knowledge, his list of natural commodities in
the *Letter* already reflecting a vastly more detailed sense of the
American scene—as well as a more clearly designing attitude toward it. Though he begins his exploratory catalog with a disarm-
ingly cautious statement—"The Country it self in its Soyl, Air,
Water, Seasons and Produce both Natural and Artificial is not to

be despised" (225)—his actual comments later on are quite exalted, even exultant. "The Waters are generally good," he writes, "for the Rivers and Brooks have mostly Gravel and Stony Bottoms, and in Number hardly credible" (226). No other aspect of New World space evokes from him a *less* wondering sense, and in every case the hope of usefulness is high, the economic outlook itself exciting. There arise, of course, certain impediments: though the natives garner from Penn a good deal of praise ("They care for little, because they want but little; and the Reason is, a little contents them: In this they are sufficiently revenged on us; if they are ignorant of our Pleasures, they are also free from our Pains" [233]), he sees in them a threat to English continence, a possible loosening of the settler's morality akin to that seen by the Pilgrims and the Puritans in New England's flirtations with an alien way. The earlier Dutch planters become signs of an undesirable waywardness, since they have been seduced away from agriculture by the natives, who have "made them the more careless, by furnishing them with the means of Profit, to wit, Skins and Furs, for Rum, and such strong Liquors" (237). If Penn means something quite innocent when he writes that the English must "out-live the Knowledge of the Natives" (236)—that is, must show their moral superiority by living up to their own laws—his very choice of words is a sign of tensions beneath his rosy surface.

When he turns to "Philadelphia, the Expectation of those that are concern'd in this Province," Penn defuses any latent explosive in his scheme. No longer a mere idea, but a place "at last laid out to the great Content of those here, that are any wayes Interested therein," the great city is an icon of success, an actual mark of Penn's foresight (239). Accompanied by a "Plat-form" which shows the names of purchasers (see PLATE 13), the pamphlet centers itself on this preeminent sign of colonial health, and Penn's comment on the aptness of its site ("of all the many Places I have seen in the World, I remember not one better seated; so that it seems to me to have been appointed for a Town" [239]) indicates the shift of his language toward more suitably concrete modes. The rather vague predications of *Some Account,* having been realized in part through the platting of Philadelphia, now become more specific—so much so that the land itself seems like the author of Penn's "sentence," the willing agent of human design. When Thomas Holme, Penn's "Surveyor General" and maker of the "Plat-form," remarks in his appendix to the *Letter* that "such a Scituation is scarce to be paral-

lel'd" (242), he is verifying the change in his employer's prose.
Caution has been replaced with hyperbole; the validation of modest hopes has justified more ambitious ones. Penn's tentative draft of a colony, now specified in the map of his draftsman (and on the ground), appears like an astounding theatrical success, and a sequel clearly is called for.

The *Further Account* of 1685 exhibits even in its somewhat conventional title the drift of Penn's imagination toward "further" things. An exuberant catalog of intervening achievements, it is based on the "freshest and fullest Advices of [Pennsylvania's] Progress and Improvement," reports sent to Penn during his sojourn back in England. The main purpose of his return voyage was to reach a settlement of his dispute with Lord Baltimore—the latter becoming a kind of minor villain in Penn's comic plot here, the technical hindrance to his fulfillment. Appropriately, the *Further Account* opens with an announcement of Penn's success in clearing up the dispute. Having been reluctant to publish any news about the colony "whilst it lay under the Discouragement and Disreputation of that Lord's claims and pretences," he now can break his silence—and just in time, since any further lack of news might "disoblige the just inclinations of any to America, and at a time too when an extraordinary Providence seems to favour its Plantation and open a door to Europeans to pass thither" (259). If Providence does open such a door, Penn himself takes on the role of a guide beyond its threshold, conductor of emigrants as well as of the colony. Written in England, as his first tract also was, this work reveals everywhere that fuller weight of transatlantic experience which one finds in the *Letter*. It combines the stance of both earlier pamphlets, linking the knowledge which Penn has gained from (and in) the distance to his actual presence in Europe. Tangibly "here," yet emotionally "there"—the *Further Account* ends with Penn's avowal that he soon will take his family and possessions to America (though in fact he did not return until 1699, and then left for good in 1701)—Penn himself combines Old World and New, and thus suggests the relative ease of an inward emigration.

But absence and presence, like Lord Baltimore's presumption, raise important problems here for Penn. His *Letter* to the traders opens with a reference to the rumor that he has died in America (and a Jesuit to boot!), a rumor which he attributes to the "Spite and Envy" of his opponents in England. Thus is begun what is a minor theme in this tract and the third one, a problem of keeping open between England and America a line of truthful reportage. "Absence being a kind of Death," Penn asserts in 1683, "ought alike to secure the Name of the Absent as the Dead" (225), but what is intended as a modest defense of his character becomes a characterization of America itself as a world of the absent-dead, the void which sets it off becoming a figure of its own true nature. The rumor of his death is like an alternate history of his attempt, his absence in the New World allowing others to re-present him in another light at home. Thus his comic script, fleshed out more fully in the *Letter,* is answered by a tragic counterplot which plays on the anxiety of departure and innovation. Christopher Carleill's fear of loss is rendered here as a dread of spiritual rather than financial disaster.

The dispute with Baltimore is a variation on the same theme. Forcing Penn into silence himself, it has cast a pall over the whole colony. Penn admits in the *Further Account* that "some [have] urged my coming back, as an argument against the place, and the probability of its improvement" (277)—his presence in England marking the absence of his spirit from America. Likewise, he notes that "many Stories have been prejudicially propagated" about the relationship of settlers and natives in Pennsylvania, tales which suggest that, "like Jobs Kindred," all the whites but "the Messenger that brought the Tidings" have been "cut off." On the contrary, he asserts, "there never was any such Messenger," and "the dead People were alive, at our last advices" (276). Furthermore, he includes within his text a kind of typical settler's report, a letter from Robert Turner which is, like Penn's own account, a glowing exploration of American possibility, a message from Canaan rather than the fields of Job. When Turner writes that "We are generally very Well and Healthy here, but abundance Dead in Maryland this Summer" (272), he is quashing the bad reports of Pennsylvania troubles at the same time that he is slyly undercutting Baltimore's domain. "Abundance Dead" is a tellingly bleak gloss for any colonial enterprise, to be sure, a link of radical opposites which threatens to whelm the benign vision of Penn's own report. But Turner attempts to deflect its force onto the enemy's country, and thus to bolster a further opposition between competing locales.

Competition, however, finally is not Penn's framework for the explication of Pennsylvania. Aside from the flanking maneuvers of Baltimore, there is little to suggest deep rivalry in his portrait of American life. Though the people of his own colony, for instance,

"are a Collection of divers Nations in Europe: As, French, Dutch,
Germans, Sweeds, Danes, Finns, Scotch, Irish and English," they all
"live like People of One Country"—such a "Civil Union" having
"had a considerable influence towards the prosperity of that place"
(260). As for the natives, affairs with them seem even more utopian, since the whites "leave not the least indignity to them un-
rebukt, nor wrong unsatisfied," and such "Justice gains and aws
them" (276). Presumably there *are* indignities and wrongs, but
Penn does not specify any; his stress is on correctness and correc-
tion rather than error. As an added proof of peace, he notes that
the natives have agreed to obey the settlers' laws, and to accept
punishment for any breach of them.

One has, against this bland social background, the immense
close-up world of American nature, painted by Penn so that his
legend of colonial "Progress" is evident in each natural icon, the
great "Encrease" of produce itself a model of social success. His
triple purposes in the tract are bound together by this rhetoric of
enlarged use and established certitude:

> *First. To Relate our Progress, especially since my last of the month
> called August, '83.*
> *Secondly. The Capacity of the Place for further Improvement, in or-
> der to Trade and Commerce.*
> *Lastly. Which way those that are Adventurers, or incline to be so,
> may imploy their Money, to a fair and secure Profit; such as shall
> equally encourage Poor and Rich, which cannot fail of Advancing
> the Country in consequence.* (259)[21]

Penn devotes the first pages of his *Further Account* to the sort of
social inventory already mentioned: the "Fourscore Houses" of
1682 have become "Three hundred and fifty-seven" even at the
time of Penn's departure for England,[22] while his list of the
tradesmen now established in Pennsylvania ("Carpenters, Joyners,
Bricklayers, Masons, Plasterers, Plumers, Smiths, Glasiers, Taylers,
Shoemakers, Butchers, Bakers, Brewers, Glovers, Tanners, Fel-
mongers, Wheelrights, Millrights, Shiprights, Boatrights, Rope-
makers, Saylmakers, Blockmakers, Turners, etc." [261]) suggests
both the success of his efforts at inducing such people to emigrate,
and the equal achievements of the colonists themselves, the very
catalog of skills hinting at their industrious nature.

The list hints at the same time that the relation of settler to world
is one of formulation: people are "makers," actors who transform
the raw material of nature into the stuff of civil use and order. This

same role likewise is implicit in everything Penn has to say about the "Capacity of the Place": "the Produce of the Earth," "the Produce of our Waters," "Provision in General." In each case the natural scene is rendered (almost literally) in terms of its use, Penn's language acting as an agent of benevolent and profitable change. "The Earth, by God's blessing," he proclaims, "has more than answered our expectation; the poorest places in our Judgment producing large Crops of Garden Stuff and Grain." Even before it has been cleared and settled, the ground proves fertile and inviting, the "Weeds" of the woodlands supporting both beef and dairy cattle, the swamps and marshes yielding winter fodder. By the same token, the waters ("*our* Waters") teem with edible or usable creatures, "Mighty Whales" that "roll upon the Coast," sturgeon that "play continually in our Rivers in Summer," alewives in plentiful number, herring which "swarm in such shoales that it is hardly Credible," and which the inhabitants "almost shovel . . . up in their tubs." Though rumor has it, Penn notes in his section on "Provision in General," that the settlers "were starv'd for want of food" (or survived only by importing rations from elsewhere), the fact is that they have found Pennsylvania to be a richly sustaining locale (264–66).

What sets Penn's catalog off from that of the discoverer is precisely the bluntness of human intrusion into the cataloged world: "they almost shovel them up in their tubs." This is a far cry from the contemplative pause of William Bartram, or even from the wondering commodity lists of William Wood. Different, too, is the reader's implied role here, for there is a shift from contemplation to action on this front as well. Penn's farewell is a "well met," an address to those "that think of going thither," in which biblical cadence is put to worldly use and modesty becomes a guarantee of large future success:

> I have this to say, by way of caution; if an hair of our heads falls not to the ground, without the providence of God, Remember, your Removal is of greater moment. Wherefore have a due reverence and regard to his good Providence, as becomes a People that profess a belief in Providence. Go clear in yourselves, and of all others. Be moderate in Expectation, Count on Labour before a Crop, and Cost before Gain, for such persons will best endure difficulties, if they come, and bear the success, as well as find the Comfort that usually follow such considerate undertakings. (278)

That labor precedes a harvest, or cost precedes a gain, is an obvious point, but in Penn's case precedence is a kind of causation as well. Like Carleill's *Discourse,* his almost Pauline epistle implies that if one works one will profit, and probably at an exponential rate. "The Improvement of the place," he writes of Philadelphia, "is best measur'd by the advance of Value upon every man's Lot. I will venture to say that the worst Lot in Town, without any Improvement upon it, is worth four times more than it was when it was lay'd out, and the best forty" (262). Though in his 1683 *Letter* Penn professes himself to be "ill at Projects" (241), he clearly understands that art of magical multiplication on which the worst of such schemes, in word or deed, must rest.[23]

HOPE AND DESPAIR

As a later English "utterance" into the New World, Penn's colony indeed did benefit from the accumulated example of other ventures, as well as from the presence of a settled population to its north and south. The void into which it was projected in the 1680s was more temporal than spatial, its test experiential rather than environmental. Compared with the *Discourse* of Christopher Carleill, as a result, Penn's writings in support of the undertaking are less conceited in their idea of America; the fact of established colonies there has made almost unnecessary those acts of metaphoric settlement which characterize the earlier work. Magical transformation seems in Penn's case to be the result of a chronicling rather than a fabulating mind, an accurate reflection of achieved change. Yet one must note the ways in which this *topos,* when used in retrospective narrations, exerts a subtly idealizing force on the matter to be recorded. If Carleill's history is all in prospect, an obvious projection, Penn's brief account of his province shapes actual events by reference to a vision of temporal life no less schematic than Carleill's. It offers us what one might call "subjunctive history," even when it pretends to give a simple record in the naive past tense. Following out this tradition of American narrative, one passes through the epic of Joel Barlow to the massively detailed, yet still "ideal," record produced by George Bancroft in the middle of the nineteenth century. That record, based on the conceit that *United States* history essentially began with Columbus (ironically, Bancroft managed to trace it only up to the adoption of the Constitution!), portrays all events as they lead into—and through—the Revolution,

103

each separate plot a part of one grand action, all of them converging in the "plat" of nationhood adopted in 1789.

This pattern of narrative was the explorer's central gift to national language, much as the discoverer bequeathed his sense of timeless awe, and his innocent eye, to those who followed him. Within exploratory prose itself, the pattern served purposes closely allied to those which it came to serve in later epic visions. Since the explorer calls so forthrightly for his readers to commit themselves to a world of action, what he writes becomes a mediation between verbal and active skills. He must balance his schemes against the events which they will cause—especially when, as in Penn's case, part of what he writes is produced as those events themselves are taking place. One borderground of exploration thus is the line between predictive and recollective arts, where the author's rhetorical stance is a mixture of vision and perception. In the settlement narratives examined in my next chapter, this mixture is particularly rich in observed and remembered facts: the settler's hold on original ideals and schemes loosens as the process of accommodation which begins with settlement becomes more complex. In exploratory texts, on the other hand, experience is filtered through the grid of initial design; a good deal of contrary evidence is inadmissible to the aesthetic universe of exploration. As the discoverer attempts to control the given world of American space by describing an ideal passage through it, the explorer tries to organize New World experience—whether actual or in prospect—by subordinating possibly corrosive events to an ideal pattern of plot.

Even at the start of a colonial enterprise, however, the problem of human (and natural) insubordination places a good deal of strain on the explorer. The void of frozen intent which followed on Carleill's promotion in 1583 thus must be read as a silence engulfing his hopeful speech, a declension of the world of action from the universe of his *Discourse*. And in other texts of Carleill's age, notably in Thomas Harriot's *A Briefe and True Report of the New Found Land of Virginia* (1588), the relationship of prediction and accomplishment seems even more thickly layered. Based on Sir Walter Ralegh's previous ventures into Carolina, in at least one of which Harriot himself was an actor, the *Report* is both reportage and ideal plan. Its presumptions about the future course of English involvement in America are rooted in a narrative understanding of the past, all predictions being (at least in Harriot's view) simple extensions from prior events. Harriot accordingly has a benefit denied to

Carleill, a body of proven accomplishments which literally fill in the void of Western experience.

Linked as his own prose is to those accomplishments, however, Harriot becomes peculiarly vulnerable to a contagion nestled in Ralegh's schemes. The *Report* opens with a defense by Ralph Lane of Harriot's authorial character, a gesture which leads us into the thick of a debate about Ralegh's undertakings in the West. Harriot himself, addressing his remarks to the "Adventurers, Favourers, and Welwillers of the enterprise," quickly passes on to a group of figures that is the foil to such supporters, a gathering of unnamed detractors from "the action." Although his basic intent throughout is to eulogize "that countrey which is now called and knowen by the name of Virginia," he is drawn from the start into a world of forensic exchange: his desire to praise the land (and Ralegh's engagements in it) necessitates the dispraise of other reporters. One is impressed, as a result, with the admitted multiplicity of views, the fact that "divers and variable" accounts have been given regarding the four voyages thither.[24]

Such a debate is the hallmark of settlement accounts. John Smith's lengthy record of his personal effacement from another Virginia, the *Generall Historie* of 1624, effectually chronicles the means by which what Smith takes to be a majority voice—his own— was forced into a minority position. It is a mark of the greater simplicity of Harriot's position, on the other hand, that all his comments on variant visions can be placed at the head of his enthusiastic catalog, their dismissal an act of sarcasm rather than historical oversight. The bad reports to which he refers have resulted from bad men: from the ill will of those who, having been punished for wrongdoings in Virginia, have tried to vent their spleen in prose; from the boasting of men little experienced in Virginia, who would "make no men so great travellers as themselves"; or from the acute sensitivity of those English voyagers who have had "a nice bringing up, only in cities or townes," and who (having not found in Virginia "any English cities, nor such faire houses, nor at their owne wish any of their old accustomed dainty food, nor any soft beds of downe or feathers") discovered that "the countrey was to them miserable, and their reports thereof according" (166–67).

Since Harriot thus implies that any view reflects the viewer as much as the thing viewed, it is worthwhile considering for a moment the biases of his own sight. This is, in fact, a very complicated question. A mathematical genius whose first entree into the world of exploration seems to have been by way of an interest in navigational science, Harriot helped to instruct Ralegh and the latter's associates in the latest of seafaring skills. Yet his own interests, at least at this early point in his career, extended as well into what we now call anthropology, and once in America himself in 1585—he stayed for a full year—he spent a good deal of time traveling around with John White for the purpose of recording in prose, as White was in water colors (see PLATE 15), the details of native experience and of New World flora and fauna. One certainly cannot accuse him, as he did others, of having had only a narrow experience of the American scene. Nor can one accuse him—though much of the evidence here has not survived—of regarding that scene only from a limited, imperial perspective. Having learned to speak the Carolina dialect of Algonquian perhaps even before the 1585 voyage (during an earlier trip, or from the natives brought back to England), Harriot displayed from the outset of his American involvement a seriousness of purpose, and a depth of energy, rare among his contemporary Englishmen. His personal trajectory pointed, in fact, into the world of wondering discovery, while his public account of 1588 placed him initially in the world of exploratory promotion.[25]

This deep conflict finally was to be resolved, as we shall see, by an agency other than Harriot's. If we look at the substance of his *Report,* and the context within which it appeared, we can understand the forces which conditioned both his own effort and that later resolution. The Carolina coast on which Harriot was landed in 1585, along with a hundred other colonists, had been visited only the year before by Philip Amadas and Arthur Barlowe, the latter having written up a glowing account of the region—declaring at one point that "the earth bringeth foorth all things in aboundance, as in the first creation, without toile or labour."[26] This vision of discovery certainly had been confirmed during Harriot's stay there with the first colony, even if Ralph Lane the governor complained of unruly colonists, and at the end, when Drake's men took off the settlers, some of Harriot and White's best specimens were ruined in the water. Harriot's prose applies to this attitude of wonder, however, a categorical scrutiny which transforms it into a more nearly economic emotion. The *Report* of 1588, unlike Barlowe's account, is a conscious attempt to subordinate American "aboundance" to English desire.

106   One key to this transformation lies in the promotional materials

which the two Richard Hakluyts prepared as a spur to Ralegh's
project. The elder Hakluyt declared in 1585, for instance, that with
respect to the "soile and climate" of Virginia the voyagers were
"with Argus eies to see what commoditie by industrie of man" the
region might be made to "yeeld."[27] "Yielding" is, in fact, the prime
act of the American continent in Harriot's text, the passive action
by which the New World signifies its amenability to European desire and design. When the younger Hakluyt in his *Discourse of
Western Planting* (1584) provided a list of European participants for
Ralegh's action (or any other), he was specifying a cast whose presence is assumed everywhere in Harriot's text: "Arrowheadmakers,
Bowstave preparers, Glewmakers . . . Makers of spades and shovells
for pyoners, trentchers, and fortemakers, Makers of basketts to
cary earthe to fortes and Rampiers . . . Grubbers and rooters upp of
Cipres, Cedars, and of all other faire trees for to be employed
in coffers deskes &c. for traffique . . . Millwrightes . . . Sawyers . . .
Carpinters . . . Joyners . . . Blacksmithes . . . Pitche makers . . . Tarr
makers . . . Burners of asshes . . . Cowpers . . . Tallowchandlers . . .
Waxechandlers . . . Diers . . . Mynerall men . . . Brickmakers . . . Tile-
makers . . . Lyme makers . . . Synkers of welles and finders of
springes," and so forth (*Writings*, 2:322–24). Hakluyt's catalog of
laborers, mixed in as he writes it with a list of appropriate tools, is an
abstract of European formulation, the agentive forms themselves
revealing the author's economic bias. Implicit in such charts of
expectation is a model of New World epistemology, a way of seeing
and understanding—finally, of encompassing—American phenomena.

The Hakluyts themselves took hints from Carleill on such topics,
their overall strategy for the West mapping out a similar vision of
English domination—a solipsistic answer to the complex of European politics. Harriot, more sympathetic at the start toward other
views, succumbed through most of the *Report* to a grammar in
which American objects serve with great docility a set of imported
intentions. His three categories of Virginia goods (for trade, for
victual, for building) all are put to a use within his text which
mirrors their presumed use in the colony. Thus he writes: "Cedar.
A very sweet wood, and fine timber, whereof if nests of chests be
there made, or timber thereof fitted for sweet and fine bedsteds,
tables, desks, lutes, virginals, and many things els (of which there
hath bene proofe made already) to make up fraight with other
principall commodities, will yeeld profit" (170). Of the same tree,

Barlowe notes more simply that those he saw were "the highest, and reddest Cedars of the world, farre bettering the Cedars of the Açores, of the Indias, or of Lybanus..." (*Roanoke*, 1:96–97). We have a sense in this case of actual trees, the wonder of beholding them, the way in which they fit into the observer's old knowledge only by bettering it—and thus become symbols for the discovery of something greater than themselves. Harriot's prose, on the other hand, is a vehicle of division, a means for reducing the strange to the ordinary: the actual living object is lost in a list of human goods, the "very sweet wood" suddenly become "fine timber," finally to become "sweet and fine bedsteds." The two attributes which Harriot applies to the cedar thus are applied in the end to artifacts manufactured from it. It is as if human language, like the industrial arts, is a closed system, all its expenditures returning at last to mankind. "Will yeeld profit" is the gloss of his long catalog, each of the several dozen commodities which it describes capable of being made into a plus in the balance sheet of English effort.[28]

Several facets of Harriot's art remove him nonetheless from the merely calculating approach of Carleill and other explorers. His parenthetical comment on the cedar ("of which there hath bene proofe made already") suggests, for instance, a certain weight of New World experience which lies behind the whole listing and gives it more dimensionality. "To prove" is another of Harriot's favorite verbs, its presence throughout the text subtly bolstering Ralph Lane's assertion at the start that Harriot, as "an actor in the Colony" (165), and an honest man to boot, is to be trusted implicitly by the reader. Likewise, a tendency toward understatement in some parts of the catalog hints at a complexity below what actually is stated. We thus can read in what seems like a mercantile abstract the traces of a rich encounter with American life. When Harriot indicates, for example, that the Carolina natives eat "their Woolves or Woolvish dogs," and adds that—having tasted the fare himself—he has "not set [it] downe for good meat," lest some reader should "understand my judgement therein to be more simple than needeth" (182), his laconic tone adds a wide margin of credibility to the comment. Furthermore, when he goes on to note that he could say something, if he wanted to, about the comparative flavor of native and English dog, the judgmentally inclined reader is wholly disarmed.[29]

Such gestures are effective rhetorically because they make the text subordinate to the man who wrote it, the argument an ethical rather than hyperbolic one. And it is precisely the man behind the Report who comes to attract our attention as we read on through it. If Harriot's approach to the American scene by means of the catalog device portrays him at first as an "Argus-eyed" traveler who perceives Virginia only through the filter of economic needs, the depth of experience which is rendered through Harriot's catalog—even perhaps in spite of it—shows us other angles of approach and less engrossing perceptions. Harriot's linguistic skill, for one thing, stretches the limits of the catalog as both a prose strategy and an intellectual framework. Though the reader presumably would be able, without Harriot's lengthy glosses, to understand a list of commodities like the following—"Silke of grasse, or Grasse silke ... Worme silke ... Flaxe and hempe ... Allum ... Sassafras ... Wine ... Furres ... Copper ... Pearle," and so forth (168–71)—the author's explanations are absolutely essential for such a list as this one: "Pagatowr ... Okindgier ... Wickonzowr ... Macocquer ... Openauk ... Okeepenauk ... Kaishucpenauk ... Tsinaw ... Cosushaw ... Habascon" (173–79). Like the "Veragua" of Columbus, these later terms become by their strange verbal shape a convincing proof of the author's literal voyage, as well as his inner movement beyond European experience.

Nor do Harriot's explanations always help bring the reader closer to New World reality. For many of those commodities which he names first in Algonquian, he offers one or more Old World labels: *pagatowr* "in the West Indies is called Mayz: English men call it Guiny-wheat or Turkey-wheat," while *macocquer* is a generic term for the melon and squash family, the individual plants "called by us [i.e., the colonists] Pompions, Melons, and Gourds, because they are of the like formes as those kinds in England" (173). In other cases, however, Harriot confesses himself unable either to translate the Indian terms—indeed, simply to list them—or to find Old World analogues. One senses a frustration in his voice, as well as an impatient longing to return to America in order to finish his ambitious survey of New World flora and fauna. His description "Of Fowle" is a good example here:

> *Turkie cocks and Turkie hennes, Stockdoves, Partridges, Cranes, Hernes, and in Winter great store of Swannes and Geese. Of all sorts of fowle I have the names in the countrey language of fourescore and sixe, of which number, besides those that be named [above], we have taken, eaten, & have pictures as they were there drawen, with the names of the inhabitants, of severall strange sorts*

of water fowle eight, and seventeene kinds more of land fowle,
although we have seene and eaten of many more, which for want of
leasure there for the purpose, could not be pictured: and after we
are better furnished and stored upon further discovery with their
strange beasts, fish, trees, plants, and herbs, they shalbe also pub-
lished. (182)

Though his overall strategy here may be economic, use being his
standard of measure, Harriot's interest transcends mere profit. We
are impressed, as we read, with a feeling of large abundance, and
with a sense of deep curiosity in the traveler who has touched it.
Since the present catalog is substantively inadequate (as Harriot
admits), we are led to consider other possible inadequacies in it as
well. His hint of a further publication suggests a manner of approach which may be different in quality, not just more inclusive.[30]

That further publication both did and did not materialize. We
enter here on a particularly knotty subject, one which is made
doubly difficult by historical complexities and by the apparent disappearance of other Harriot texts on the Roanoke venture. Harriot
himself acknowledges in the *Report* that he already had completed
one other work: "Of the Captaines and Masters of the voyages
made since for transportation, of the Governour and assistants of
those already transported, as of many persons, accidents, and
things els, I have ready in a discourse by it selfe in maner of a
Chronicle, according to the course of times: which when time shall
be thought convenient, shall be also published" (196). Like the
action it was intended to embody, and thus to explain, this
"Chronicle" did not survive—surely one of the most persuasive
instances of "significant form" in literary history. Harriot's reference to it in the *Report* points, nonetheless, to a peculiar mixing
between his own eulogistic vision and the growing shadows which,
even when the *Report* itself appeared in 1588, already were encircling Roanoke. Harriot seems to have written his surviving book
in order to promote the second colony, which departed under John
White in April 1587. For unknown reasons, however, the work did
not appear in print until the following spring—hence Harriot's
reference at its end to White's voyage the year before. To make
matters more complicated still, White already had returned to England when the *Report* came out, and during the spring and early
summer was trying to fit out a supply squadron for the colonists.
His own effort, undertaken in two small ships, proved inadequate
against the confusion of the sea in this year of the Armada, while

Grenville's effort shortly afterwards was countermanded, his larger vessels ordered to join Drake's fleet against the Spanish. It was 1590 before White was able to return to the colony, only to find the settlers gone and the settlement itself in ruins.[31]

Some of these details suggest the way in which Harriot's inducements were ringed by a world of hard realities. In a very real sense, what he was urging no longer had any existence, his promotion cut short by the quick accumulation of negating events. Hence his vision was left hanging, pure enough within the boundaries of its own text, clarified on the page as the Carolina undertaking ought to have been in fact (and was not)—yet, for all its carefully preserved optimism, carrying a circumstantial air of doom. From White he was sure to learn before the *Report* was published that Grenville's small colony of 1586 almost certainly had been destroyed, as well as that White's larger body of settlers was in need of instant help. Indeed, how could his "Chronicle" (if he had finished it, as he states) have avoided such disappointing news, the retreat of English effort against his own scheme for its grand expansion? And why, if he knew of these things, did he persist in bringing out what even then was an anachronistic prediction of a future history which most assuredly had not been realized, which had been positively frustrated?

Answers to such questions must remain speculative at best, largely because of the dispersion visited on Harriot's literary remains. One possibility is that Ralegh saw in the *Report,* which probably had been written at his direction in the first place, a means to the recouping of his American losses. Yet a reissue of the book in 1590, the very year of White's last and saddest voyage, offers an alternate explanation. As the "action" from which the *Report* grew (and the enlargement of which it initially urged) faded into a memory of half-accomplishment, Harriot's text assumed in the face of history almost a different status. Its promotional edge remained, but its drive for knowledge about American facts and customs on their own now assumed greater importance. Action was replaced with contemplation, exploration with the attitudes of wondering discovery. From the Roanoke debacle was salvaged by this shift of status a strangely older moment in the sequence of English involvement in America, Harriot's text becoming in time a companion to Barlowe's rather than Carleill's.

Crucial to this change was the 1590 reissue of Harriot's book, to which Theodor de Bry added engravings he had made from John

White's watercolors. A magnificent folio, the first of the de Bry firm's famous "America" series, the new edition extended Harriot's stress on native American life by using only the ethnographic scenes produced by White. The list of commodities still remained, but the later pages of the *Report* thus acquired an importance which mere bulk had not accorded them in the 1588 version, or in Hakluyt's reprinting the next year. The Virginia scene as rendered in de Bry became as a result a more nearly romantic locale, use balanced if not supplanted by other angles of relation. Nor, apparently, was this different emphasis foreign to Harriot's own later intent. According to David B. Quinn, Harriot well may have hoped to produce on his own with White a series of folio renderings of the New World, with a whole range of subjects minutely illustrated and described. As his comment on Virginia fowl indicates, he longed for a detailed yet sweeping knowledge of Western phenomena. If he used an economic model for the *Report,* he certainly was aware of other ones, and perhaps was anxious to employ them in the future. He may even have found de Bry's reissue of that book, lavish as it was, a mere inkling of what could be done if White and he collaborated on a truly thorough account of the region through which they had traveled together in 1585 and 1586.[32]

Five years after that time, as John White's sad letter to Hakluyt in 1593 indicates, at least one of the two men had lost all interest in such an exuberantly naive record of events now clouded over by later tragedies.[33] But the de Bry, incomplete as it may have seemed to Harriot in light of what else he knew or only suspected, was to survive for the next two centuries as a primary text of wondering contact, unmarked by those sad sequels. By this means, Harriot and White both achieved an almost unsought fame that transcended the occasion of their art. Locked by a convergence of pen and brush in an attitude of first arrival on strange ground, the two came to occupy—as if offering, at times, a warning gesture to more violent travelers like John Smith—an ideal place in the constellation of Old World bearings on the New. The natives of Harriot and White, caught in a frame of self-enclosure which is a wall against white aggression, make a stunning contrast to those illustrated in subsequent de Bry texts (see PLATE 16), where the fatal conflict of Spanish and American figures so often represents a graphically brutal stage in the history of transoceanic contact. One can only wish, from a modern perspective, that the real utopian vision of

the two Englishmen (not Roanoke itself, but a viewpoint born almost inadvertantly amid its failures) could have become more than
an embellishment, as the de Bry plates did, to later European
books about America—that it could have issued into the world of
practical action as well. Contained in the engravings of 1590 is a
quite different plot from that which finally was enacted; latent
there until obscured in the confusions of after times, it now seems
to retain its wondering potential only by the force of artistic clarity,
those strong bordering lines which set the natives off from any
outside world in the plates. This impression is particularly acute in
White's view of Secoton (PLATE 17), the native village which has no
defensive walls except those provided by White's immuring art.
How soon this ordered vision yielded to more violent ones is
suggested by Ralph Lane's report of the 1585–86 venture: even
while White was painting Secoton, Englishmen were fighting
elsewhere with the natives, the plot of encirclement and extermination which was to be prescribed for Virginia in the 1620s, and for
the nation later, already traceable here on the shores of Pamlico
and Albemarle. Juxtaposed with such brooding hints of the further
future, swallowed soon afterwards in the close gloom of the English
colony itself, Harriot's clarified assertions and White's clear renderings rest in a tenuous space between the noise of war and the
silence of loss, between the scramble of figures on a bloody field
and the retreat from view (who knows where?) of the 1587
settlers.[34]

THE UPROOTED

Harriot and White suggest our need to refer early American art to
its full historical context, and to do so with an understanding of
how complex the relation of language and event can be. By turning
to a final exploratory work from a much later period, we can locate
more precisely some of the issues involved here. The text in question, a pseudonymous emigration tract of 1773 entitled *Informations
Concerning the Province of North Carolina* (by "Scotus Americanus"),
offers a number of insights into those issues. Addressed to a very
specific audience, the Highlanders of Scotland, the pamphlet assaults the poor situation of its readers in Europe and invites them
to discover a far better one in America. Like Carleill's *Discourse,* as a
result, *Informations* sets off New World and Old; the negations of
the latter place heighten our sense of the former's attractions. In
the present instance, however, these debits and credits figure as   113

items in an account of self-preservation rather than simple profit. The author's assaults on Scotland are mostly economic, but economics itself is a measure of several other concerns. What is hindered in the author's (and reader's) home is less the desire for gain than the hope for sustenance and survival. As a consequence, his portrait of North Carolina as a land of peace and plenty is more than a crass promotional gesture. Discovering to the reader a place of inner wholeness and independence, he opens up a spiritual terrain which, detailed as it is by a catalog of economic opportunities, retains throughout a higher meaning.

"Nos Patriam Fugimus," the legend on his title page runs, and this sentiment itself indicates the historical complexities involved here. If the Highland country were indeed the homeland of the Scots—of the author himself—then his whole effort would be unnecessary. What the Highlanders know in Scotland, however, is not a sense of rooted location but rather displacement, "home oppression."[35] Due to a series of social and economic changes which began with the defeat of 1745 (and which already had sent thousands of Scots to the colonies by 1773), the traditional method of land tenure had been severely upset. So drastic was the situation that the small farmers who mostly worked but did not own the land became increasingly marginal to a system which never had served their interests in the first place. The crucial symptom was exorbitantly higher rents, raised in some places two or three hundred percent within a few years. This symptom in turn pointed to the displacement of the landlords themselves, largely as a result of laws enacted to solidify the English victory in 1745. Deprived of much traditional authority as clan leaders and as hereditary justices, the lords looked to other means of asserting their power, and found in a more demanding economic relation with their tenants a substitute for older feudal ties. Since productivity was not increased noticeably, except through the disruptive enclosure of strip fields and commons, the tenants found themselves burdened with sharply higher expenses and stable incomes. Justifiably, they saw their class, and even their individual lives, severely threatened. Faced with this bleak prospect, many moved from the Highlands, including a good number who came to American settlements.

The tract of Scotus Americanus—signed by its author at Port Askaig, Islay—emerged from the geographical heart of this disaffection and the desire to emigrate which it produced. It is both a 114 history of actions already accomplished without its aid and an attempt to increase the cast of similar future deeds. Hence *Informations* begins in the thick of historical discontent, the long winter of endured belittlement. Though its final purpose is to boost North Carolina, it is concerned with a broader philosophical problem—a problem to which North Carolina offers a conveniently concrete solution. The question might be defined as that clash of exclusive social visions which develops from the conflict between ownership and labor. The lords of Highland life are rendered by the author as a decadent and heartless group, concerned only with increasing the income from their lands without regard for the human cost. They have lost touch with the old nobility and humanity of their position. To his eulogy of New World conditions, this opening attack by Scotus Americanus forms a somber background; the value of his later assertions is determined by the scale of values in Scotland itself.

The tract opens on an ambiguously conciliatory note. Describing the large impetus of recent migrations, the author admits that "the matter is serious, and, to some, the consequences are very alarming" (429). Certainly both comments were true for a pair of travelers like Boswell and Johnson, who were in the Highlands in the same year, and in whose records one can find some evidence of alarm.[36] For the author himself, the situation raises an irony already hinted at in the legend on his title page. The Highlanders have always been remarkable, he asserts, for their attachment to their native land. Partly a matter of local feeling, partly a question of familial ties within the clans, such an attachment overcame in the past whatever doubts the Highlanders may have entertained about the meager economic resources of their terrain. Clearly, the forces which could cause them to move away at the present time must "be very cogent and powerful" (429). As his argument develops, this suggestion leads us into the heart of landlord abuse. But it serves as well to answer a possible charge that the emigrants themselves were "abandoning" their homeland—a charge motivated by the considerable concern in England and Scotland over recent losses of native talent to the colonies. Scotus Americanus anticipates such accusations by portraying the emigrants even in his first paragraph as the victims of expulsive conditions in Scotland, moved by irresistible currents of social change. Whereas Boswell reported on a dance called "America"—which began with one couple, but wound up engrossing the whole company ("It shows how emigration catches till all are set afloat," Boswell observed [242–43])—the author of 115

Informations tried to understand the mass exodus in terms of far less faddish, and more severe, "movements" in the society.

As a result, his explanation does not isolate the emigrants from Scots life (as the charge of abandonment does), but places them solidly within the texture of contemporary experience. Indeed, since so many of the landlords have become, in his view, absentee holders of their large estates, the actual or prospective absence of their tenants is merely the answer in one level of society to actions begun in another. If anyone in the situation can be accused of "dancing," it is the landlord: "Careless and unconcerned the master lives in the circle, as it is called, of the gay and the great. There, [in] a round of merriment and whim, in a vortex of airy amusements, of giddy and unsubstantial pleasures, and at the height of an expensive, though false and unnatural taste, he squanders away his fortune, and wastes his time and his health at once." The argument here, in fact, is notably similar to Penn's in his first pamphlet. "The luxury, dissipation, and extravagance of the times" chiefly are to blame for the lords' neglect of their traditional duties; the fabric of respect and concern has been torn apart by the creation of artificial tastes and wants (430).

What Scotus Americanus suggests, in essence, is that the Scots lords have become anglicized since 1745, the literal and emotional "distance" which they keep between themselves and their tenants a reflection of the distant English government. Though he does not specify this view in so many words, his portrait of the lords as alienated figures—fops of the first water, complete with a ring of "minions and sycophants" (430)—clearly stresses their removal from the universe of ordinary life in the Highlands. In effect, such men already have emigrated from Scotland in spirit—and often in body as well—leaving behind them a vacuum of authority which has destroyed the old structure of relationships. Thus abandoned as an outskirt of British life, the Highlands have become almost an America of wasteland and deserted terrain deep in the heart of Old World experience. For the subsidence of agricultural arts (and of the landlords' profit) the farmers are denounced "as an intractable, idle, and useless set of beings." They are expected, against many impediments, to transform the land into a highly productive region, but for this end they receive only the encouragement of higher rents. The vain wish arises among the lords that "another 'set of tenants more able and industrious'" may be introduced into the area, a body of farmers "'that will soon make the country put

116

on a different aspect, that, by dint of labour or magic, shall make their barren wastes, and heath grown mountains, rival, in verdure and produce, the fertile plains of Lothian, or the Carse of Falkirk'"—that shall do all this, what is more, while bearing "any load laid upon them by their tender-hearted landlords, with chearfulness, and without murmuring" (430–31).

"Labour or magic": by this phrase alone the author suggests the link of Old World and New, invoking for his sarcastic comment on the lords the very *topos* which controls so many American promotional tracts. In the case of Scotland, however, neither labor nor magic will work such quick changes—while in the case of North Carolina, we are led to believe, labor itself is a kind of magical force. Destined to remain, within the vision of the author, in a state of perpetual disintegration, the Highlands thus are held off against the fresh (and free) spaces of the Western continent, the hope of a clear title to land there merely increasing the gloom of continued struggle in Scotland. The latter place is a backwoods, while America is a frontier—the former in decay, the latter all in prospect. Whereas force is the policy of the old land (it is assumed that higher rents will force a tenant to produce more), initiative is the watchword of the new. And it is the initiative of those tenants who first chafed under higher rents that now has opened "a door for themselves and friends in a land of liberty and plenty." So wide has been this breach in the old design, in fact, that the oppressive masters in Scotland have tried to slander America, catching at "any discouraging tale, picked up from some sailor or skipper that has but touched on the coast of North Carolina." Balancing such superficial tales, fortunately enough, is a wealth of more experienced relations, those "most favourable accounts" and "most pressing invitations" which Highlanders already long settled in the colony have sent back to "their friends and acquaintance" (433–35). As in Penn's case, a presumed message from the servants of Job is countered by the actual tales of western success.

Since *Informations* itself is founded on "unquestioned evidence, as well as personal observation," its form is an elaboration of such domestic reports. Prepared himself to "risque my all, and fix my residence there for life," the author adds to his act of authorship the further, and more convincing, act of promised emigration (435). His rhetorical position thus will be validated in the future by his new geographical one, the "door" opened up by his prose becoming more than metaphoric. From this point on—with appropriate cautions about the different climate in America, and its attendant hazards to health—he opens beyond that door a deep perspective of economic and spiritual fulfillment. Like the discoverer, he thus builds in his prose a spatial prospect which is enthralling to the reader's mind. Yet he has, as most explorers do, a specific design on that reader's active self. Against the evidently tragic plot of Highland experience, in which the farmers are both used *and* useless, he asserts the availability of a world where the suffering passivity of such victims becomes an active and happy state, where nature (if not exactly paradisal) is readily amenable to honest human use. The pseudonym which he has adopted, the "American Scot," is the label of a new species of mankind. This figure is a hopeful combination of spatial and moral opposites, a character on whom the Atlantic passage will work a magical transformation. The wasted laborer in Highland economy, and thus an embodiment of the wasteland of Europe, this man shall be made fruitful again by his emigration west. In the new country, "unmolested by Egyptian taskmasters," all emigrants "may reap the produce of their own labour and industry" (434). Owning their land, they will own themselves as well.[37]

Willing agents without a proper substance on which to work, the Highlanders compose a cast which lacks its appropriate action. It is the author's intent in this pamphlet to join such actors with the scene of a pending performance. He does not have in mind any particular voyage, nor the furtherance of any actual plantation: his North Carolina landscape is notable precisely because so much of it is rendered as the available stage of a hundred different plots. He sketches in the general action, indicates the motives relevant to it, and speaks loudly about its essential themes. Unattached as all of this is to some given venture, it seems more obviously true to the reader—less an act of lying boosterism than a pious homage to the needs and opportunities of his fellow citizens. "Tradesmen, mechanics, and labourers of all sorts," he concludes, "have here an ample range before them: hither then they may repair, and no longer remain in a starving and grovelling condition at home: they may hasten across the Atlantic, and carry over with them some remains of the true old British spirit before it be totally vitiated and extinguished: thither let them import their yet generous and liberal sentiments: let them transport thither the polite arts and sciences, that they may grow up and flourish in a happier clime, and under more benign skies" (450). Since, as the author has observed earlier

in the piece, "the power of vegetation" is so great in North Carolina
that peach trees bear fruit three years after the stones are planted,
and fig trees produce two crops ("of large and luscious fruit") each
year, one hardly is to expect a less splendid result from human
plantation. Like the seeds of greater things themselves (the "small
beginning" of a later fruition), the emigrants will come to share in a
broad pattern of amazing growth and productivity. If "Plants from
Europe arrive at perfection here, beyond what they do in their
native country," then the uprooted of Scotland surely will thrive in
America (442). The closing vision of *Informations* suggests just such
a melding of human and natural growth: "Here each may sit safe,
and at ease, under his own fig-tree, indulging himself in the natural
bent of his genius, in patronizing the useful arts of life, and in
practicing the virtues of humanity" (450–51).[38]

It is difficult to connect this almost oriental, even Thoreauvian
view with the actual terrain to which it points: that region along the
Cape Fear river which William Bartram visited in the same period,
and which he came to describe in his *Travels* as the seat of a vigorous
transforming culture. Yet everywhere in the Scots pamphlet a
sense of nature as the inducing medium for active human change,
an "abundantly inviting" world (450), also is evident. The change in
an emigrant's self can occur only because the individual Scotsman
now will find himself in a realm where his inner drive is registered
adequately in the outer scene, where "in a few years, a poor man,
with a throng family, may work himself into affluence" (448). The
settlers of *Scotus Americanus* are the agentive half of an industrial
equation, the verbal element in a potential New World sentence. If
the author's text closes with what is almost a tableau from the
Cocaigne myth, its initial portrait of Scotland deep in the welter of
historical realities helps anchor the whole work in a firmly actual
world. The hyperbolic tone of its glowing passages on America is
warranted by the hyperbolically bad state of affairs across the sea.
Like the initial pieces in Crèvecoeur's *Letters from an American
Farmer,* the tract is structured on a principle of chiaroscuro, Europe
all dark and the New World all bright. What the emigrant is creating is not simply a new patrimony, or a new *patria* to replace the one
from which he has "fled"; beyond his economic success is a sense of
self-creation, an emergence from the nothingness of Scotland and
into the abundance of a new being in a new world.

In the context to which *Informations* refers, as in the wider sense
of history which Crèvecoeur developed later in his book, disastrous 119

events native to the American scene—and implicit in the very theory of America to which "Scotus" subscribes—were to intrude on such a bright formulation. Like Thomas Harriot, this Scotsman thus stands, by force of circumstance if not by virtue of his personal experience, on a distinct borderline of exploration. So strong that it keeps him from mentioning the Regulator "troubles" in Carolina, his hope aims finally beyond the endured end of those settlers whose emigration he promotes. Pointing the Highlanders into a world of renewed history, he outlines for them a glowing future plot to balance out the catastrophe accumulating around them in the Old World. Yet that charted future, when compared to the actual events which ensued, seems at best like a grand illusion. Literally outside his text, those events enter it in a larger sense because he calls so stridently for an act of commitment to the realm of action—because he urges his readers to enter the historical universe, to venture on a voyage west. To read his book properly we must place it in the environment which it helped to create, however slightly, by its own stress on an actual response from the audience.[39]

We can think of *Informations* less as an enclosed verbal act—the manner in which we are likely to regard "literary" texts—than as one scene in a much larger, historical drama: it is the contrast which we can draw between the plot line here revealed and that which emerges in later scenes, that reveals the cultural value of the work. By inviting his readers to engage themselves in the larger drama, Scotus Americanus takes on a certain responsibility for consequences beyond the ending of his text. Since his audience is to enact the ideal script which he tenders to it, and thus is to make possible a contingent narration which fulfills his own hints, the pamphlet does not close with its last words. It demands the supplement of a further report, just as Daniel Denton does more consciously in his New York tract of 1670. Prediction awaits the flood of later confirmations.

Within three years, however, the Highlander communities in North Carolina hardly were able to offer such a confirmation. If anything, their present situation would call for a quite opposite account of growing difficulties. Between the ideal vision of Scotus Americanus and the Revolution there arose an irony beyond the simple turning of his literary and historical plot. The neat harmony of his pseudonym, seamlessly wedding two locales by a conjunction 120 of grammar and action, fell apart under the pressure of colonial upheaval. Faced with a choice between the two poles of their own postulated new nature, many Highlanders chose to side with the King—by implication, with the very system which supposedly had oppressed them. Dropping off the adjective which the writer in 1773 had assumed for them, they became simply "Scots" once again, Old World figures caught in a New World conflict which was born of the very "distance" that was to be the demiurge of their new life.

Subject to retaliations supported by rebel law, to confiscation, to the marauding of patriots, to imprisonment and exile, the Highlanders once more found themselves in a marginal position. Come to the New World in search of land they might own outright, they were divested of the vision which led them toward that land—when they were not divested of the land itself. Having finally set right the effects of 1745, they were bewildered in the "peaceful" and "plentiful" West by the confusions of 1776. They supported the King in large numbers partly because they had learned the cost of unsuccessful rebellion at home. Their loyalty earned them now, at the hands of rebels who finally won, a fate as bad as that which they feared from an English Crown that twice had taught their countrymen the lessons of defeat. On the "right" side for once, they were losers once more.

Unlike those Roanoke settlers who came much earlier to this same region, the Highlanders survived the onslaught of fortune—though some did so only by emigrating again. Yet their experience was no less filled with the tragic events which have no place, according to the explorer's account of America, in the bright economy of Western life. What happened to them effectually closed the "door" of free passage by filling in the blanks of exploratory hope with the facts of endured plantation. And, ironically, their sorrows were caused by what Carleill long before termed their own "countrey nation," by the economy of colonial order rather than the competition of "native" ways. In the life of these emigrants we thus can read the tale of a quite different New World future, the beginnings of an awareness traceable throughout the colonies, an awareness from which grew a literary art aimed at the inclusion and recognition of disagreeable facts. To the wonder of a discoverer's American scene, and to the explorer's designing arts, such lives and the records born of them answer with a sense of irony and doom that converts the New World into a curiously Old World domain—in the Highlanders' case, another Scotland of disappointment (and "home oppression") akin to that from which they fled. When one Scotsman captured by patriot forces during the war described his experience as a prisoner (he and his fellows were dragged from town to town, as if on show), he was counterpointing an actual American journey to those easy ones described over and over again in more hopeful texts: "On our journey," he wrote, "no slaves were ever served as we were"—the irony which we see in this comparison is part of the difficult meaning here—"through every village, town and hamlet that we passed, the women and children, and indeed some men among them, came out and loaded us with the most rascally epithets calling us 'rascally cut-throat dogs, Murtherers, blood hounds,' etc, etc. But what vexed me most was their continually slandering of our country"—that is, Scotland—"on which they threw the most infamous invectives." Against the discoverer's stasis of language and the explorer's imperial sentences, the career of such settlers as this speaks of another New World grammar, a sentence in which the colonizing figure may be the direct object of aggressive verbs, a pawn amid large and terrifying forces, rather than the subject of a benign and idealizing transformation. In the next chapter we shall follow out the twisting line of such other statements, and the complex plot which they came to constitute in colonial America.[40]

Three

🕸 SETTLEMENT NARRATIVE 🕸
Like an Ancient Mother

I have also seen a garden on Dauphine Island which had been described to me as a bit of terrestrial paradise. It is true that there are a dozen fig-trees that are very fine and that produce black figs. I saw there three pear-trees of wild stock, three apple-trees of the same sort, a little plum-tree about three feet in height that had seven poor plums on it, about thirty feet of grape-vines with nine clusters of grapes in all, some of rotten or dry grapes and the rest somewhat ripe, about forty feet of French melons, a few pumpkins: that is the "terrestrial paradise" of Mr. Artaguette and of several others, the "Pomona" of Mr. De Remonville and the "Fortunate Isles" of Mr. De Madeville and of Mr. Phillippe; their memoranda and their relations are pure fables. They have spoken about what they have not seen at all and they have too readily believed what was told them.

Antoine de la Mothe Cadillac to Pontchartrain,
Minister of Marine and Colonies, 1713

WHEN THE AMERICAN TRAVELER STOPS IN MID CAREER AND SURVEYS the actual surrounding world—trying to break through the descriptions which have been laid over it, and to render in prose exactly what is to be seen beneath them—one is likely to sense, as in the passage quoted here, a refreshingly critical mind at work. Against the vague predications of a discoverer, or the more designing ones of an explorer, such apparently realistic comments strike the modern reader as candid and down-to-earth. For all the surprise which they may engender, they in fact are far from rare in the literature of New World travel. It is the odd book which contains none at all, though often enough they enter the texts where they do occur as passing remarks rather than elaborated, thematically important insights. Brief ironic asides, they are not always developed as they might be into a controlling focus for the account in hand, let alone into the foundation of a new aesthetic or a new view of history.

We nonetheless can isolate the mood of realism which such passages embody, much as we have isolated the moods of wonder and hope. And we can extrapolate from it, as we have from the others, a center of narrative awareness, a viewpoint sufficiently developed that it may be thought of as dominating certain actual texts. In this third case, the degree of critical pretense is far lower than it was in 123 the previous two. Since many acts of discovery, and most acts of exploration, were submitted at some point to the test of reality, there is a large amount of material which offers observations on this process, and which—given the high exuberance of European expectation—tends to adopt the very standards which we find in the comments of Cadillac. The long report quoted above, deriving its authority from things-as-they-are rather than from human language and the structures of perception which language promotes, is a concise model of a much larger form. In Cadillac's attempt to find a vocabulary (and a grammar) appropriate to his adopted perspective, we can locate the signal rhetorical task of the American settler.

A man of modest origins who rose through colonial ranks in Canada to become the founder of Detroit, Cadillac was not a person to belittle from mere aloof malice the designs of Europe on the West. We cannot understand his description of the Dauphin Island garden (or the infant colony of Louisiana) simply as the splenetic reaction of a Frenchman to a scene far less ordered than that which might have surrounded him in France. Having just arrived at Mobile Bay, current center of the colony, he is attempting in his report to Pontchartrain to specify the difficulties which lie before himself as the new governor. Critically ill for the past few months—his last comment in the report, "I do not understand how one can suffer so much without dying," suggests the extremity of his felt position—Cadillac may be viewing the Louisiana scene with a slightly jaundiced eye.[1] His sense, too, that Detroit may falter in his absense (as indeed it did for a time) perhaps is reflected in the distaste with which he describes affairs to the south. Yet, having acknowledged these strains on his personal viewpoint, we must recognize his letter from Fort Louis as something more complex than a private lament. He himself sets for it an avowedly public purpose; it is an attempt, across the "great distance" (188) which separates Louisiana and Fort Louis from the monarch after whom they were named, to inventory for officials in France the sad dissolution of French intent in America. If his whole text, like the quoted passage, seems peculiarly personal in its targets, that is because in Cadillac's opinion the failures of Louisiana can be traced to a preemption of the public good by private scheming—scheming allowed precisely by the "distance" between homeland and colony. Dauphin Island, a prime defensive position for the settlements in Mobile Bay, is now "un Salmigondi ou l'on ni connoit rien"

(165)—"a stew in which one can identify nothing at all." It is Cadillac's intent to introduce into this culinary disaster the rigor of a
more discriminating taste.

The first step in such a change is to locate the bad chefs responsible for the current bill of fare. Thus, former governor Bienville is
attacked in the person of his associate, Martin d'Artaguiette d'Iron.
Cadillac's passage on the Dauphin Island garden seems to have for
its main purpose some such impeachment of previous officials:
description becomes polemic. Fabulous prose like that attributed to
Artaguiette is viewed by Cadillac as an imposture of speech designed to hide from the home government, under a pleasant cover
of asserted public progress, the crude facts of private exploitation
and misdeeds in the colony. Having found the officials already
established in Louisiana uncooperative, Cadillac clearly feels pow-
erless in his new position. He evokes in his report an image of
corrupt practice in the past which ought to give him, if it is accepted
beyond the distance, a stronger foundation of power for effecting
desired changes. The play of his language thus mirrors the play of
political intrigue which already has engrossed his attention. His
ironic tone is a sharp commentary on the failures of older royal
appointees, not on the ultimate chances for French success in the
new region. Realism is a necessary intermediate attitude, not a final
position. Suggestive as it is of an innovative aesthetic standard,
Cadillac's stance in the end is a local rhetorical tool. Well used, it will
allow him to establish himself (and a better vision of French empire) in Louisiana.

Rejecting one enthusiastic view, Cadillac comes to substitute for it
an equally projective design on the future. In the midst of his
ironies he offers a hint of vast mineral riches in the inland region,
of commercial empire and settled order. His catalog of what we
may call "discommodities" on Dauphin Island and elsewhere inverts older patterns of New World speech without abandoning
them. Seeing disaster, he sees beyond it. What is questioned is not
vision itself but the peculiar contents (and motives) of specific visionary gestures. The settlers are rascals, the governing party hardly
better: they all can see no farther than their own quick benefit, and
the colony as a result is buried in a mess of shortsightedness passed
off to Europe as a deep concern for European plans. Against the
rumored potential of America, Cadillac reports the profligacy of
those who have been sent out to impale it. Born in the midst of such
despairing facts, his letter nonetheless maps an exploratory scheme

which he seriously promotes to Pontchartrain. Surrounded with actualities, he clings to the battered ideal. He adopts as his stylistic ground a cluttered artistic space which is the mirror image of the colony itself—old facts and new fictions juxtaposed to each other, the conflict between them unresolved. He thus suggests the changes in act and art which combine to create the New World "settler."[2]

FROM IRONY TO GLOOM

The simplest of those changes are shifts of tone, infusions of light irony into what remains an assertion of wonder or possible profit. The account of Martin Frobisher's second voyage (1577) written by Dionyse Settle, for instance, is attentive to the outward shape of the northern landscape which the expedition encountered on its way to Baffin Island, at the same time that it hints at hidden virtues beneath this inhospitable terrain. Inverting the discoverer's habitual language, Settle writes a comical description of a barren scene: "Here, in place of odoriferous and fragrant smels of sweete gums, & pleasant notes of musicall birdes, which other Countreys in more temperate Zones do yeeld, wee tasted the most boisterous Boreal blastes mixt with snow and haile, in the moneths of June and July, nothing inferior to our untemperate Winter."[3] Likewise, Settle quashes any hope for immediate uses in the North, noting that "To be briefe there is nothing fit or profitable for the use of man, which that Countrey with roote yeeldeth or bringeth forth" (152)—while, as for the natives, "Their riches are not gold, silver, or precious Drapery, but their said tents and botes, made of the skins of red Deare and Seale skins: also dogges like unto woolves, but for the most part black, with other trifles, more to be wondred at for their strangeness, then for any other commoditie needefull for our use" (145–46). Yet, against these barren observations, Settle holds out the prospect of later and better discoveries. Having read the shore as if it is an abstract of the inner regions concealed behind it, he finally is not sure that such an equivalence actually pertains. When some small birds land on the ships as the expedition is sailing along the "Boreal" coast, he takes them to be signs of a possible depth beyond the outward face of the country—indicators that, hopefully, "the Countrey is both more tollerable, and also habitable within, then the outward shore maketh shew or signification" (140).[4] Moreover, having dismissed the hope of trade with the natives ("altogether voyd of humanity" in his view, they embody the

126

spatial and economic void which surrounds them), Settle remains confident that "There is much to be sayd of the commodities of these Countreys, which are couched within the bowels of the earth"—though *he* will not say it "till more perfect triall be made thereof" (145). If the fate of the sparkling stones and glittering sand gathered by Frobisher's men on this voyage in fact suggests that such a trial may prove disappointing (the samples "verifie the old Proverb: All is not gold that glistereth" [144]), Settle himself is blithely expectant. Little known as they are, doubtful as their worth now seems, even these bleak northern regions may contain in their unexplored depths the answering sign of human desire. The tokens so far encountered are not goodly, but surely better ones must remain. Negative evidence is simply negative, not necessarily conclusive. The formulas of exploration, and of exploratory prose, remain valid beyond their particular inversion here. Frobisher's action is not terminally incomplete, only delayed.

Irony of this sort, polite, polished, contained within the framework of a larger assurance, need not detract from the furtherance of some pet project. Indeed, the candor which it suggests in the author actually may enhance the undertaking in hand. Displaying the appearance of detachment and wise caution, a writer of Settle's stamp seems far removed from those visionary schemers so engrossed in their action that they ignore obvious, sometimes fatal, problems. As a result, *his* doubts remove those of the reader: admitting difficulties, he shows himself capable of dealing with them, and thus increases our estimate of future success. Likewise, a witty attention to wayside annoyances may act within the text as a release for very real tensions developing in the traveler. In the case of a land-hungry figure like William Byrd, for instance—Byrd, that man of "goodly tokens"—irony serves to clarify rather than dismiss drives which are almost absurd in their pretension. Byrd's wit is less a means of acknowledging history than a symptom of his attempt to laugh off the confusions with which history threatens his schemes. Unable to deal directly with such threats, Byrd diminishes them by diminishing himself, by deflating intentions which he has no plan to abandon. His account of a 1733 journey to his "Land of Eden," a wilderness tract of almost twenty thousand acres along the Dan in North Carolina, shows us a traveler alternately enthusiastic and slyly doubtful about his designs on the region. His evident purpose for the journey (to resurvey the bounds and virtues of the new grant) is slightly at odds with his customary bearing on the world.

127

An ironist by temperament, Byrd has involved himself in a series of frontier endeavors which require for their success—even for their entertainment—a more naive nature than his own. The interest of his prose lies precisely in this intersection of private and public form.

Excited in 1733 by the general fertility of his lands, Byrd delights in the gifts of natural promise, and seems sincere in his wish that the settlers who eventually will occupy the grant may "live to fullness of days . . . with much content and gaiety of heart." Likewise, he remains throughout the "Journey" almost hypersensitive to rumors of mineral wealth—silver, copper, lead—on ground he already owns or may obtain in the future.[5] Yet he must note that a frontier grantee may be the victim of large impostures with regard to good soil or subterranean riches. And he realizes that, by an ironic conjunction of world and actor, fertile soil actually may produce poverty ("people live worst upon good land" [409]), while the hope of a quick profit from minerals may cause some settlers to be so "mine-mad" that, "neglecting to make corn," they in fact may "starve their families in hopes to live in great plenty hereafter" (408). Partly an explorer attracted by this same dream of quick gain (though also by more nearly utopian dreams), Byrd is a realist as well, a man who sees the serpent lying in such silken grass. Excitement and skepticism ebb and flow throughout his record of 1733, each dominant by turns, the conflict between them never quite resolved.[6]

Nor is this tension confined only to matters of economy. On a grant along the Roanoke, Byrd already had built a small house whose large name ("Bluestone Castle") signifies his intent to erect there in the future an actual castle from the bluish stones lining the bed of a nearby stream—stones that seem to exist only for such a human purpose. At one point in the "Journey," Byrd indulges in a classic act of exploration by taking his "first minister"—actually his Roanoke overseer, Harry Morris—up a hill and marking out "the place where Bluestone Castle was to stand and overlook the adjacent country" (407–8). Earlier, on his "Land of Eden," he likewise discovers "a delightful situation for the manor house" (394) which apparently is to be erected there. Landscape is perceived in terms of its human use, the structures which will dominate it almost built in the sheer imagining of their sites. Yet even in regard to these issues Byrd is aware of subtle delusions. Having been surveyed once before, the line which delimits his Eden tract has "already grown very dim" (392), the old assertion lost in a tangle of burned and storm-downed trees. We are led to imagine a conflict here between human order and natural event, as we are a few days earlier when Byrd, returned "home" to the Castle from a boat trip with Morris, indulges in a grander exploration than he has elsewhere, one which finally he undercuts himself. He writes,

> *When we got home, we laid the foundation of two large cities: one at Shacco's, to be called Richmond, and the other at the point of Appomattox River, to be named Petersburg. These Major Mayo offered to lay out into lots without fee or reward. The truth of it is, these two places, being the uppermost landing of James and Appomattox rivers, are naturally intended for marts where the traffic of the outer inhabitants must center. Thus we did not build castles only, but also cities in the air.* (388)

The "foundation" laid down at this point is simply an abstract design, an idea projected from one wilderness into another. The two Virginia "landings" are far away from the Roanoke region, Byrd's vision a desire attached to them only by its expression in his prose and in the talk recorded there. Though Byrd uses the explorer's *topos* of imaginary and rapid change, and links the scheme of settlement to the "truth" of natural order, he finally draws himself down to the world as it presently is. His irony includes even that grand unbuilt castle in the small namesake of which his plans have been hatched.[7]

A man given to acts of comic naming—an island is called "Potosi" because of its "metallic appearances" (395), while a branch of the Hyco is labeled "Jesuit's Creek because it misled us" (402)—Byrd shows himself aware of similar tensions in larger matters. Seeing both his ideal map and the actual surface of the land, he balances shrewdly between the kinds of knowledge implied by each. But it is clear from the record of his frontier activities that such a balance in his prose is at least partly a contrived effect. Having proposed in the late 1720s that the Dismal Swamp—one grand impediment to the surveying expedition of 1728—be drained and settled by a company of investors, Byrd hardly revealed by that gesture either practical sense or financial probity. And, as the record of his attempt to secure settlers for his "Land of Eden" and other tracts suggests (see PLATES 19–20), he was not above endorsing rather scandalous promotions, even if he himself did not indulge in them directly.[8] One can conclude of his ironies as a frontier writer that they are a bone of present caution lightly chewed by someone dreaming of a future feast. They are little jokes which clear the air of potentially larger doubts, and hence open the land for the author's assertion of intent.

Like Byrd's two *Histories of the Dividing Line* (written between 1728 and 1737), "A Journey to the Land of Eden" is a surveyor's document, a form of early narrative which embodies in events the first real trial of exploratory hope. Not committed as a settler necessarily is, yet clearly on the land as a designing explorer usually is not, the surveyor often adopts a Janus-like role which prefigures the doubts and clashes of later implanted attempts, but which looks back at the same time—through a channel of literal and metaphoric return—to more clarified ground. Forays to the West and back, Byrd's four recorded trips finally have a safe enclosure in their shape, an access back along their inscribed line to a world where things human, unlike the boundary markers of "Eden," supposedly do not "grow dim." The hopefulness of his literary endeavors reflects this sanguine pattern in his actual journeys.[9]

The same point holds for many surveyors. Most such figures, on the other hand, are men of measurement and technical skill who have been charged with the laying of human grids over nature, and they never remain wholly blind to the discrepancies which arise in their work. Indeed, were they blind to such things, their work never would be completed. Mediators between a realm of abstract ideals and the concrete world toward which those ideals point, they are thus peculiarly exposed to the flaws of realization. Though they may be so engrossed in some present project that, as with Byrd, their irony covers those flaws instead of probing them, such travelers often are sensitive readers of the actual, as well as the postulated, American scene. After the Revolution, for instance, the Philadelphian George Burges was one of the men engaged to survey four new settlements in northwestern Pennsylvania, and he came to see his deeds as symbolic ventures, noting the lines of fracture between his art and the realities over which it was to be asserted. His record of three days work near old Fort Le Boeuf shows us a man wittily aware of topographic ironies:

> 1ST DAY THE 21ST *All hands were employ'd in finding the center of the town and laying out the main streets.*
> 2ND DAY THE 22ND *This day was spent in staking out the streets and measuring the same about which we had like to have disagreed, our measures not proving alike.*

3RD DAY THE 23RD *Was likewise employed in staking the*
streets. This day I wrote a letter home. We have now fixed a place
for the market with many of the main streets, but yet there are no
castles nor brick houses, but on the contrary, but five or six little
dirty log huts surrounded by a great wilderness of seventy or eighty
miles with Indians hooping and halloing and begging for whiskey.
This is indeed very unlike Philadelphia but perhaps in process of
time the howling desert may be turned into pleasant fields, and
shining bricks decorate this spot of ground which now appears so
unlike a city of commerce, which should providence grant to be the
case, may pride and avarice keep far distant and not make it
appear more savage than its present state.[10]

Holding out in the midst of contrary evidence the hope that this
wild ground may become a great center in the forest—the
explorer's magical *topos* verified by history—Burges must note that
"Walnut Street" is infested with gnats (15), "Hazel Street" leads
through a swamp (16), while a marsh divided into lots is a "fine
place for mud tortoises" (18) rather than humans. The larger patterns of urban order are likewise called into question: the sequence
of qualifications ("but . . . but . . . but") suggests how the assertive act
of "fixing" is surrounded in this prose, as in fact, by a series of
encircling recognitions. Nor is the only problem a conflict of plan
and terrain. One is left finally, even if the desired transformation
should occur, with the question of urban design itself. Each "intended city" (28), as Burges calls one of them, may rival Philadelphia in the end, yet to what advantage if "pride and avarice" have
been imported into it along with the system of settled intention, the
"shining bricks" and "pleasant fields"? Imbued as his description of
the natives is with savagist prejudice, it also hints at a moral problem beyond any merely technical one; the supposed wildness of a
natural condition ("hoop, hallo") may be linked intimately with the
wild habits of "civilized" life ("beg for whiskey").[11]

Burges remains, like Byrd and Settle and even Cadillac, within
the palisades of ordered wit. That these figures can laugh at the
disappointments and ironies which they recount shows how insulated they are from any real disaster. There is something playfully
verbal about their statements, as if the true interest in each case is
less a conflict of human scheme with reality than a neat tension in
the words which describe that conflict. As we move deeper into the
records of actual settlement, the emphasis shifts away from the text
as a verbal structure and onto facts themselves. Embedded in the   131

web of events, the settler lives in a world where laughter is seldom possible, where the burden of historical awareness is so great that mere reportage is a heroic act. The feat of writing becomes in this case an attempt to recognize the shape of recalcitrant truths and to name them by their proper names. Coming as they do from an avowedly "new" country, such texts seem peculiarly old—perhaps because we can trace in their midst the ruin of wonder and hope, the wreck of enthusiastic attempts.

One example of this more implanted and problematic style is to be found in a journal kept by Bernard Diron d'Artaguiette, the younger brother of that man who supposedly described the "terrestrial paradise" on Dauphin Island, during an official tour of the Mississippi valley in 1722 and 1723.[12] Inspector of the region for the governing commissioners of Louisiana, Artaguiette reports on the disheveled state of affairs along the river with a detached anger, an aloof sense of the pettiness and confusion which seem to threaten yet another ruin for French designs in America. He is a surveyor in quite another sense, a man sent out for the express purpose of comparing the actual condition of the colony with the ideal plat imagined for it. Less a mediator between that plat and the world it concerns (as an actual surveyor would be) than a mediator of bad news to the East, an observer of failed realizations, Artaguiette composes in his "Journal" a bleak portrait of a broad discomposure, even decomposition, in the colonies strung out along an attenuated line up the river. The only wit in his work arises in a faint suggestion that the French have played a bad joke on themselves—a fatally impractical one.

Divisible into three rough parts (New Orleans; the river settlements up to Kaskaskia; New Orleans once more), the "Journal" opens with an ominously predictive entry: "SEPT. 1. New Orleans. There died here Monsieur Macée, chaplain of the ship L'Avanturier."[13] From this point on, with the exception of some more pleasant details culled from the upper country during Artaguiette's voyage there, the record returns again and again to the facts of encountered privation, warfare, natural disaster, and political intrigue. New Orleans itself, an unplanned, even unwanted settlement lately chosen as the new capital of Louisiana (the planned centers on Mobile Bay above Dauphin Island having proved inadequate), comes across in the "Journal" as the seat of corruption, disaffection, and economic instability. It is, indeed, the appropriate capital for such a colony. Artaguiette's brief description of it in his first part, punctuated with a nicely symbolic account of the devastations caused by a hurricane, contains as well ominous rumors from the river settlements above the city. The arrival of each French trader, missionary, or planter is an occasion for further lament rather than celebration, for such figures tend to bear only the saddest tidings from the North. Reunion reveals deeper disunities within French effort. Almost at the start of his record, Artaguiette quotes at length the "memoirs" of Sieur Feaucon Dumanoir, *concessionnaire* or head of a colony near Natchez—a list of twelve grievances against the "Company" which John Law had established, before the collapse of his speculative "bubble" in 1720, for the planting of Louisiana. A true settler's account, Dumanoir's text opposes to the Old World presumption of American abundance a catalog of colonial "lacks," failures within the structure of European design (or practice) which have reduced the colonists to a sorry state: "1. The lack of lodgings and store-houses.... 2. The lack of a hospital for the sick.... 3. The lack of goods to trade with.... 4. The lack of such supplies as flour, wine, meat and brandy.... 5. The lack of boats and vessels for transportation"— and so forth. From his fifth deficiency, Dumanoir opines, many inconveniences have arisen:

> That the concessionnaires have remained upon arid sand for eight months. This stay has been the cause of their consuming the whole food supply intended for their establishments, the company being in want almost continually. That all the greater part of the workmen have died in extreme wretchedness for lack of fresh provisions and lodgings, being exposed to injury from the weather and from the cold through lack of clothing and storehouses, not having the materials for making the latter. The greater part of the goods of the said concessionnaires have rotted or have been plundered, damaged or stolen. (19)

Compared with the smooth realism of Cadillac, such a record puts down in unflinching and inelidible detail the facts of a terminal suffering, a plot completed (rather than simply delayed) by its inversion. Artaguiette himself, perhaps from hints supplied by Dumanoir, offers immediately afterwards a "Memorandum of the things which are necessary for the establishment of this colony and which are absolutely indispensable"—his list an act of realistic exploration, a fact-bound design for saving the larger design itself.[14] That the colony still needs to be "established" at Natchez suggests how wide the gap has been between original schemes and the attempts born of them, how the commissioners designated by the Duc d'Orleans to save Law's company from total disaster must labor mightily even to retain the tenuous assertions made in the past few years. One is reminded here of the joke made by Artaguiette's brother years before—he wanted to insure the continuance of Mobile by renaming it "Immobile"—but the wit has evaporated amid these later, more serious ills.[15]

In the war of retention which the government now must fight, the geography of Louisiana will play a markedly negative role, the mere spread of its territory (however rich it may be) militating against the sort of focus and control necessary for success. Artaguiette's voyage up the river leads him at length to a place of ordered fertility, but one suspects that Illinois owes its more positive surface to the fact that it is far from New Orleans and near to the older settlements of New France and the commercial lines which reach out through the Great Lakes from Montreal. The larger irony of this voyage is that the traveler discovers, even during a war with the Fox, a place of general stability at the farthest reach of French control from the South. It is as if Illinois has been saved by its placement at the conclusion of Louisiana; were it closer, it would be overrun with the disasters so common downstream.

As Artaguiette's voyage turns about and heads toward New Orleans once more, the reader approaches for a second time that realm of blighted hopes from which Illinois is blissfully distant. Rumors of severe sickness work their way upstream from the capital, fever replacing now the symbolic hurricane of his earlier visit. Artaguiette's arrival is weighted down with sad recognitions: "*July* 30. Early in the morning we reached New Orleans, where we arrived about noon. One cannot enter any house here without finding sick people" (89). And, two days later: "I went to pay my respects to the Commissioners, who were all sick"—while, on 3 August, "Sickness continues to carry off many people. They bury eight or nine persons every day." Nor is fever the only problem: "Everybody complains here of famine. Everyone seems to be discontented with the new administration." Even the few attempts which are made to correct some abuses underline other ones, as when "A man called Berard" is condemned by one of the commissioners for having indulged in financial speculation, and is fined "500 livres, to be applied to building a hospital for curing venereal diseases" (89–91). The last two extended entries in Artaguiette's "Journal," covering the final days before his departure for France,

134

tell of a commissioner's visit to the house of a storekeeper who has stolen company goods (some of which he has given to his "maid"), and of two murders and an impending intertribal war upstream. The final words are simply the record of Artaguiette's intention to depart on the following day. Though he does not make the connection himself, we may extrapolate from the text a conclusion inherent throughout it: all of Louisiana remains at this point "on arid sand."[16]

Losses and Returns

The "plot" of Artaguiette's report affords the author a very different end from those which it describes for other American travelers. He is in some ways almost a tourist, his role as inspector releasing him from any terminal portion in the tale which he tells. Finally headed home, he is buoyed up in fact (if not in spirit) by the technical resolution of his journey. Yet in another sense it is just this contrast between Artaguiette's fate and that of the world he describes which binds him most closely to Louisiana. Like those messengers who have brought sad tales down the river to New Orleans, he is a man whose escape from disaster masks a large public sorrow in a single personal joy. A servant of Job, he bears home with him in his "Journal" (and in the new awareness it reflects) a memorial of all those people who cannot come back in word or deed. Like the story brought home by Melville's Ishmael (or that sent home by Poe's narrator in "MS. Found in a Bottle"), his completed narrative is concerned almost obsessively with incompletion, with a theme that is opposite to its own condition.[17]

Artaguiette's "Journal" thus raises a question of form and meaning which is central to the settlement account as a whole (and to later literary works that are indebted to it): given the benign symbolic import attached by Europe to its colonial undertakings, or by America to its own efforts beyond the horizon, how is a returned voyager to deal with failures in the "distance"? We can begin to find the answers to this question by contrasting Dionyse Settle's tale of Frobisher's second voyage to a record of that man's "third and last" venture composed by Thomas Ellis. Referring by implication to the whole Frobisher attempt, not just its final episode, the Ellis book writes with graphic skill a conclusion to the three-act tragedy which, in a literary sense, begins with Christopher Hall's sparse journal of the initial voyage and continues in Settle's record through an ironic but hopeful middle. Linked into a larger whole by the fact that

135

Hakluyt printed them together (along with other Frobisher documents), the three works represent, beyond the obvious personal differences among the authors, a maturing of narrative art that coincides with the blasting of a practical scheme. Their plot is a failure of plot in the world, a movement from grand beginnings to a small conclusion.

Hall's record, the work of a ship's master, is notably concise and observant. The author shows himself to be in touch with the realities of a sailor's world, rather than with the abstractions of a discursive universe like that evoked by Humfrey Gilbert in his learned attempt, which immediately precedes Hall's text in Hakluyt, to "prove a passage by the Northwest to Cathaia, and the East Indies" (5:92). To go from Gilbert to Hall is to leave logic for experience, proof as an act of mind for proof as an experimental attitude. Moreover, Hall's prose is void of that designing vision which is Gilbert's (and Hakluyt's) mark. A day-by-day account, it leaves out any sense of the future use to which the discovered terrain may be put. Its line of sight leads with great confidence to the things of this given world, the sea, the ice, the bare northern land. Only once, in his account of the five Englishmen captured by natives, and soon left by Frobisher for lost (136), does Hall deal with events which depart from the tangible scene around him, and which thus suggest the larger play of human forces outside the range of his close sight.

Master of a bark on the first voyage, Hall received a clear promotion for the second, sailing then as the master of a ship ten times larger. One of the men on board the latter vessel was Dionyse Settle: listed as a "gentleman," he verified that description by becoming the attendant reader of imperial signs for Frobisher, so intent on the commander's intention that his record jumps over contrary evidence and points toward a further and more satisfactory trial of the scheme. The present scene is not sufficient for Settle (as it seems to be earlier for Hall) because its own sign system does not correspond to that which Frobisher and the Company have invented. Doubly meaningful, Settle's full name suggests the frenzy of design which rumbles beneath his prose, the nervousness of his hope. His irony is a concession to a world which he finally does not consider to be "real," or as real only insofar as it matches the announced plot of English experience there. We can read in his manic humor the start of an abiding Old World reaction to the

New, a Dionysian fever born of the frustration of Apollonian desires.

Settle stayed in England during the third attempt, though Hall sailed on this one, too, listed now as the chief pilot of a much larger fleet. The advance of his personal fortunes is a lonely bright point in the record of a general decadence, a loss of fortunes more clearly economic. Thomas Ellis, apparently new to the whole venture, made his first voyage on Frobisher's last. That he did so (in the words of his original title page) as a "Sailer and one of the companie" may cause us to expect from his hand the kind of contingent record which Hall wrote earlier. This expectation is both right and wrong. In view of the harsh weather which the ships encountered—snowstorms, heavy fogs, strong currents filled with severely dangerous ice—we could not ask for a better chronicler, a man who is more directly engaged with the tangible facts of sea life. Self-effacing in his preface and in the coyly embarrassed poem which closes his tract, Ellis claims that the primary motive of his report is to satisfy the public's appetite for news about Frobisher's expedition. He would not try to do so himself, he states, if other participants who arrived home before him already had, or if men better suited to the task would accept it in his stead. Beyond his cautious tone, however, is the clear fact, in the words of Samuel E. Morison, that "his English is the most vivid of any Frobisher narrative."[18] Ellis can navigate through prose as well as through the tangled sea of a bad northern summer.

Yet his account is not simply Hall's writ large. He adds to the latter's kinetic sense a grasp of the overarching designs involved in the present action. He seems aware of the politics and economics, as well as the intellectual framework, which give shape (as in Gilbert's discourse) to the whole undertaking. Indeed, his fine descriptions of the ice floes and fog and snow, far from being mere set pieces, acquire their force by impeding the larger narration of Frobisher's purpose. When the main company of ships, after a long delay outside the mouth of Frobisher Bay, finally heads for the "wished port," the "expected desire" (161), the voyagers are trying to complete an action which has been so "incombred" (160) by natural barriers that it seems almost surely finished before it has been made whole. Aware of the projected plot (as Hall is not in his report), Ellis counterpoints to the long middle of his relation a short, hopeful beginning and a quick, even frenzied end. What 137 comes to dominate his effort as an artist is the passage west (and back east), rather than the region of supposed fulfillment which lies at its American limit, even beyond that limit and into Asia. We are left with a sense of the vast distance which severs the hemispheres: attenuation is the main fact of his New World voyage.

Unlike Settle, with whom he shares a consciousness of the larger hope, Ellis cannot dismiss the "shew or signification" of this enormous and disappointing foreground. He is a master of the contingent style. The planar surface of the northern sea, dotted everywhere with ice forms which tower over the ships or move against their sides, which advance and retreat as if animated, surrounds the author's awareness like a ring of unignorable circumstance. Full of treacherous impediments, the Atlantic cannot be passed over (in deed or word) as later writers like Carleill or William Wood would have us believe. Nor is Ellis content merely with the spectacle of oceanic force, the horrific views which a voyager may enjoy as he skirts the ice. If at one point he can recall that the bergs were "round about us . . . inclosing us, as it were, within the pales of a parke," he must show how this strangely English illusion in the western Atlantic soon was destroyed by a storm which bore down on the ships and sent "the yce comming on us so fast, [that] we were in great danger, looking every houre for death." The "parke" becomes a more wild and violent place, enclosure a terrifying spatial fact: "the yce had so invironed us, that we could see neither land nor sea, as farre as we could kenne." Amid the "great and driry strokes of the yce" against the ships—softened by cut cables hung over the side as fenders—the men "continued all that dismall and lamentable night plunged in this perplexity."

After this dark night of the squadron, by the grace of God there came a brief relent, a pause in natural rhythm which gives Ellis a good dramatic touch in his prose. The sea and air were clear, but soon the assault recommenced. It was to last, in effect, for the next month. So bad was the fog at one point that the remaining ships were dispersed (others had been lost or lost sight of already), and Ellis can write only that "we scarce knew where we were." This local comment becomes a gloss for the next long episode in Frobisher's baffled attempt. Misled into the passage through which Henry Hudson was to be led to his death some thirty years later—what Frobisher himself called the "Mistaken Strait" (taken amiss, wrongly pursued)—the main part of the fleet wandered outside the

138

track of its "purposed voyage" for many days while mutinous rumblings moved among the men (157–58).

When finally, at the start of August, the ships reached their desired port (Countess of Warwick Sound on the north shore of Frobisher Bay), the crews were put to work immediately at the main business of the expedition. This was no longer to find a China route up a bay enclosed by Baffin Island, but rather to collect ore of what had been proved at home, erroneously, to be good gold. Like Columbus and his followers far to the south, this English explorer thus was deflected from an originally far-reaching goal toward the very landscape which impeded its ready achievement. Amid further troubles with the weather, and the shrewd natives, the ships were loaded with worthless matter, more than a thousand tons of rock that was to be refined for no profit and much cost in England, and to be used at last, so William Camden wrote, to repair the highways of Frobisher's native land. Though Ellis meant by "the third and last voyage" in his title simply "the latest one" (Settle also used "last" in this sense), it is hard not to take his label as a prescient assessment by "one of the companie" of the dead end into which—geographically and economically—Frobisher had drifted.[19]

The human toll of this chimerical exploit was high, particularly during the return in 1578. About forty of the men were lost then through bad weather or disease or food shortage. Frobisher's departure from the bay had been hasty and late, delayed so long in the hope of a larger cargo that the approaching winter forced on his smaller ships far too many men, who otherwise would have been stranded in America with Frobisher himself. These ships had supplies intended, however, for much more modest crews. There were, earlier and later, other casualties. The five Englishmen who had been captured in 1576 went (as Charles Francis Hall reported on the basis of oral traditions he picked up almost three centuries later) to Kodlunarn or White Men's Island after the 1578 departure, built for themselves a boat from wood Frobisher had left there, and set out into the bay, only to perish on the water as natives watched. And the Eskimos whom Frobisher kidnapped in 1576 and 1577, two men, a woman, and her child, were to die in England soon after they arrived there. One looks in vain through the records for a single uplifting fact, and finds not even the least trace of a cultural gain, an enhanced understanding, beyond the human loss.[20]

There survive from the whole Frobisher enterprise a few graphic details to whet the appetite. An artist from the Lowlands, Lucas de Heere, was in Bristol when the three natives captured in 1577 were landed there, and he produced for a French edition of Settle's account a fictionalized composite illustrating the costumes and customs of the captives against a supposedly American background. More suggestive, in light of the artist's later New World career, are the watercolors which John White, who sailed on Hall's ship in 1577, made during his stay on Baffin Island. Finely detailed, and attentive to physiognomy as Heere's picture is not, White's separate portraits of the man and woman (PLATES 22–23) are predictive of his Roanoke style, peacefully posed and artistically isolated. Yet in a third watercolor (PLATE 24) he portrayed an action predictive of the approach which other Englishmen were to adopt in the future: in the middle of this picture is an Old World boat (blocked to the front by a seemingly decorative kayak) from which sailors are discharging their guns at four native bowmen on a small cliff to the right. Nine years before he embraced in art the Secoton settlement far to the south, White thus caught what would become the dominant mode of intercultural relations. One can see, by obscuring the upper half of the picture so that only the solitary kayakman is visible, a quite different vision of New World life. Yet White, placing that peaceful image there, will not allow such exclusive sight. History weighs down on that isolated man, much as history was to confound Frobisher's grand scheme. Even the illustrative figures in White's middle distance, too far away from the battle to participate, are ominously armed.[21]

Thomas Ellis, probably aware of this earlier conflict, chose for the single illustration in his volume what may seem at first like a much simpler subject. Facing his title page is a large foldout sheet (PLATE 25) on which are portrayed rather schematically four different views of an iceberg, one he actually encountered on 2 July 1578, the day of "great and driry strokes." A sequence of increasingly revealing pictures sketched as if by an artist who is traveling around the ice, the views convince us that the world rendered in Ellis's prose is fully dimensional, that many perspectives are required for a complete understanding of it. This suggestion is particularly strong because the iceberg here pictured was hollow on its farther side, though it first appeared to Ellis as a solid wall and he realized its true nature only after he got behind it. The deception of its initial face seems to be the main point in the woodcut, the

brief glosses attached to each view stressing an almost magical al-
teration in the object, a dynamic quality in its shape. What is pictured is a process of perception, the stages by which a voyager can
arrive at the truth of his experienced world. An epistemological
icon, the illustration has implications far beyond the literal occasion
which it reflects. We may see in it an emblem which is peculiarly
appropriate to a set of voyages like Frobisher's, voyages pursued
along a misperceived line and freighted with one kind of rock
mistaken for another. The "ore," too, proved hollow within.[22]

More obviously, the iceberg plate is a sign of the great distance
intervening between England and the site of its assumed profit, a
reminder at the start of this narrative that long delays in a middle
ground—even terminal delays—set off the Old World from the
New. Unlike the map of Frobisher's discoveries (PLATE 26) included
the same year in George Best's *True Discourse* of all three Frobisher ventures (a map which shows the dead-end bay as a strait
leading through islands to "Cathaia"), this illustration calls us to the
very facts of nature which would impede the enactment of such a
far-aiming voyage as the Best map implies. If that other icon can be
read as a symbolic projection of Frobisher's "desired port" onto the
surface of reality, a mixture of fantasy and geography, Ellis's woodcut is no less symbolic—though, crucially, it replaces prescriptive
with descriptive techniques. Its aesthetic is experiential, as is that of
the prose which it accompanies. Like White's battle painting, the
Ellis picture is a concisely narrative image of events that did not go
according to the "plaine plat" which, Best writes, Frobisher "de-
vised" for the large undertaking (Hakluyt, 5:193). It opposes to
that hopeful plat the plot of endured events, a plot which the
delusive ice-form, hard, threatening, yet strangely shifting, well
represents. Against the desire for an easy passage, Ellis asserts in
the plate a stark reminder of achieved history, the blockage of real
America to unreal designs.

Ellis praises his commander in the book as a modern man comparable to the ancient heroes, but the praise remains locked in his
closing poem on Frobisher, not really affecting the more nearly
actual stresses of his prose. The hero of his report, the active
agency, is New World nature rather than Old World man. The
voyager is a figure of endurance instead of achievement. Full of
active plans, he is forced by the "invironing" world into a markedly passive position. Whereas Frobisher gives to himself in the
plot of his attempt a clearly controlling role (he is the subject of a 141

glorious implicit sentence; the voyage is his verb; American nature is the necessary material of his completed desire), the grammar of Ellis is horrific in its structure, the actor reduced to an object at the mercy of great forces, forces through which the New World acts on *him*. The work is, in this sense, the first Gothic narrative of English America. Its plot is based on the terror of frustration, on the confusion of act and thought which results from the thwarting of European scheme by the "perplexity" of American space. Had a benign Providence not intervened, as Ellis believes it did at several points in the voyage, even this account of delay, disaster, and confusion (and the man who wrote it) might not have survived.

Like Artaguiette, though less self-consciously, Ellis is a bringer of bad news to the homeland. His sense of reality overwhelms whatever controls he tries to exert over his tale, the final irony here resulting from the failure of his delivered report to confirm the heroic themes he asserts in his poem on Frobisher—and asserts there naively, one would guess. Part of the poignancy of his text, as of Artaguiette's, comes from the fact that the writer does not really want to write what he does, that he knows the outlines of a better tale but feels constrained to tell the worse one. His reported plot acquires its human value precisely by inverting the imagined action that lies within it as a memory, a design never achieved. Ironic in their shape, not in their tone, the two works are histories in which the old desire lives on as a dreamy fiction, a collection of half-remembered words encircled now in a world of denying facts.

We approach here the condition of Columbus on Jamaica, contemplating there the final disappointment of a plan that seemed in earlier times pointed toward a better end. But Columbus writes from the New World to the Old, his words alone bearing back (as in Poe's extreme tale) what Ellis and Artaguiette bring in person. Jamaica serves in his letter as a concrete sign of his spiritual (and rhetorical) position: "Solitary in my trouble, sick, and in daily expectation of death, surrounded by millions of hostile savages full of cruelty, and thus separated from the blessed sacraments of our holy Church, how will my soul be forgotten if it be separated from the body in this foreign land? Weep for me, whoever has charity, truth, and justice!"[23] Jamaica is an analogue to Ellis's central New World symbol, the ice island that stands across the line of European intent—yet Jamaica is, at the same time, more than a thwarting fact. Occupied by the writer, not just seen or circumnavigated, the Caribbean island surrounds Columbus as an apparently permanent sign of hopes forever lost, of a personal extremity which may endure. Not possessing this farther place, but almost possessed by it, Columbus is an active figure deprived of the power to act and a proper space in which to do so. The sense of finality which one finds in Ellis or Artaguiette excludes, as that in this voyager does not, the man whose language conveys it. Those details of Artaguiette's physical world which seem to symbolize concretely the social and political troubles that he describes—the storm-ruined fields, the fever-ridden city—are not accepted facts of the self (and hence of the homeland), as on the contrary the signs of disaster in the world of Columbus emphatically are. Artaguiette's symbols, like the allied ones of Ellis and Cadillac (the ice, the blasted garden), aid in the realistic expression of what the traveler has observed, but they do not portend the close of his own career, or the closure of colonial enterprises. The condition of these three travelers acts as a buffer between European and American life, while that of Columbus or of Frobisher's dead captives and lost sailors seems final, even fatal. We have there a small beginning in another sense—a start so tragic that any future attempt seems doomed beforehand, no magic sufficient to its own mature endurance.

A Parting of the Ways

Written almost from an imagined and fugitive grave, the letter of Columbus hints at the private displacement which the most extreme New World travelers underwent. For obvious reasons, we can approach only by such suggestive links to the last awareness of the truly lost and the inarticulate dead. We must admit, to be sure, that even the last writings of Columbus embody at least a residual hope, and that they thus do not reflect as purely as we might like the terminal despair of those who did not survive in fact or in word.[24] In a very real sense, the most fully extreme records either were not composed at all, or were lost along with their authors—for in this much, at least, Poe's "MS. Found in a Bottle" (like all his texts from the grave) is a good guide to the probable and the possible. The large textual gap thus created surrounds whatever records we do have with a significant silence that is the purest expression of the settlement account as a form. Against the projected plot of an explorer, or even the contingent tale of a settler like Columbus, the untold and hence plotless fate of a lost traveler suggests a range of experience, and of potential art, far more devastatingly historical. The ruins of a scheme are reflected in this ruinous state of speech, this failure of narrative to embrace a failure in life.[25]

Articulate settlers sometimes ignore the dead and the lost, but even when they do not their bearing on such figures is complex and problematic. If the fate of unfortunate travelers is known, the simple pattern of their experience may be so subversive of a survivor's ideal action (as the life of Columbus was for Joel Barlow) that it can enter the latter's text only in a modified form. Likewise, those whose fate is *not* known weaken a narrative structure which well may be designed, given a writer's purpose, to support an undertaking sorely taxed with acknowledged disasters. If chroniclers look upon their texts as a means of retaining and reasserting some original scheme against all shortcomings, the sheer inability to tell what has happened to the most extreme actors may expose a large weak point in the attempted apology. But not all writers have such purposes. As we have seen already, the recognition of extremity is a strong theme in settlement accounts, and when a particular work embodies this effort at historical understanding the episodes of loss and death become rich moments in a process of desired, or at least accepted, reckoning.

Unlike Martin Frobisher, with whose design his own overlapped, Humfrey Gilbert did not survive the "proof" of an American voyage. A first attempt in 1578, based on a patent granted while Frobisher was off on his final try, came to nothing when Gilbert's fleet dispersed and some of his ships turned pirate. Broken in purse by this debacle, and almost in reputation, Gilbert did not gather enough capital for a second trial until 1583. He departed just in time to preserve his patent, which was to lapse soon unless he took possession of some of the lands broadly included in it. The ensuing action, wrote the participant and survivor Edward Hayes, "begun, continued, and ended adversly."[26] Yet if all its stages give evidence in Hayes's report of "difficulties, discontentments, mutinies, conspiracies, sicknesses, mortalitie, spoylings, and wracks by sea" (37)—a splendid settler's catalog—and if Hayes admits that the whole voyage finished "tragically" with Gilbert's own death, the text itself is no mere lament, no simple tragedy. Hayes frames all these sad losses in a larger comic form. The Gilbert undertaking is not seen as a single enclosed event, mysterious in the suffering which it contains—a profound symbol of history—but rather as an episode in the eventual success of English intention.[27]

In order to maintain this view, Hayes must labor mightily with the acknowledged facts, the very details which he relates. And how he struggles with them is highly suggestive. We can locate in his acts of inclusion and exclusion a quite different sense of "settlement," the historian's attempt to order events already accomplished—to order them in such a way that their rough edges disappear and their essential shape matches in art, as it did not in life, the prior outlines of an ideal. Hayes tells both the tale of Gilbert's disaster and the story of future English achievement. But his work is not, at least by intention, a starkly disjunctive one. He tries throughout to make the two tales tally, and hence to convert Gilbert's tragedy into a means of promotion. Indeed, he begins his report by rehearsing the failures of English and foreign intent which occurred before Gilbert's, and he makes these brief episodes also contribute to the furtherance of his scheme. The defeat of French and Spanish design argues, for example, that God has reserved the North American continent for English domination. The defeat of earlier English attempts there, perhaps even of Gilbert's, argues on the other hand that a domination of the temperate West must be grounded firmly on the designs of God rather than those of mankind. A providentialist, Hayes views every failure as a declension of the actor from an ideal economy—or, less probably, as a sign that the "appointed time" for converting the Americans has not arrived. Every voyage west must be an act of piety and faith, its "only cause" religious. If fame or profit follows, fine—but if "ambition or avarice" is the main motive of a voyage, the voyager "can not have confidence of Gods protection and assistance against the violence (els irresistable) both of sea, and infinite perils upon the land." Even such a misled adventurer, to be sure, will have his uses: for he may become "an instrument" of God, furthering "his cause and glory" by teaching others "not to build upon so bad a foundation" (2–3). Yet he will be, in his own right, doubly lost—lost in time and in eternity.

Hayes the writer builds on better ground, as he presumably did as an actor in Gilbert's attempt. He seems to become in his report a humble voice of the Lord, his own tonal stresses dispensing justice to the men whose fate he entombs. The sailors who man the *Delight* after Gilbert leaves St. John's, Newfoundland—earlier in the voyage, on another ship, they had reverted to open piracy—are portrayed in high "jolitie" as they sail to the south amid much "sounding of Trumpets, with Drummes, and Fifes: also winding the Cornet, Haughtboyes." But this celebration, Hayes writes, is "like the Swanne that singeth before her death," for their joy ends with the "ringing of doleful knels," and the next night the ship strikes ground and sinks, all her hundred hands apparently lost

(28–29).[28] Gilbert's private fate is not so neatly moralized by Hayes: something more than "delight" leads to his disorder. Acknowledging the sore trials already encountered, Gilbert finally declares that the survivors should "no longer strive here, where we fight against the elements" (31). In Hayes's view, however, the real fight begins with departure, for it is an inner struggle signified by Gilbert's prideful stance on the voyage home. Commanding the small frigate *Squirrel,* Gilbert holds to his intent of riding this eight-ton vessel all the way to England, even though cautious Hayes urges him to return aboard the *Golden Hinde,* his own much larger ship. That the Gilbert family crest was a squirrel is suggestive of the commander's pride here, but another impulse even closer to his heart surely influenced him. Rebuked by the queen earlier in the year as "a man of not good happ by sea," and almost kept by her from an active role in the voyage, Gilbert seems to be stating by his staunch immovability the contrary "fact" of his comic skill.[29] For Hayes, on the other hand, such behavior speaks of "rashnes," and when the end comes it is clear that Gilbert, committed to "Gods protection" by those on the *Golden Hinde,* has forfeited through his "wilful resolution" any right to divine defense against the irresistible sea (34–35). His last fight with the elements thus proves how selfish his inner purpose has been. His tragedy is Hellenic in design, not Hebraic: his flaw is precisely that of the overconfident "explorer," a confusion of will and world which is set right again by the violent activation of nature against this finally passive adventurer.

So much for Hayes's implied interpretation. The end itself goes less smoothly in his report. Shortly after the *Squirrel* has recovered from a near sinking, Hayes sees Gilbert—across the sea space that separates them like a moral distance—seated at the rear of his small ship "with a booke in his hand." Whenever the two vessels come close together, Gilbert cries out a cryptic line from this book, apparently More's *Utopia:* "We are as neere to heaven by sea as by land" (35).[30] Later that night, Hayes records, Gilbert's ship is "devoured and swallowed up of the Sea," her lights snuffed out "in a moment" and no further word heard from those on board (35–36). Within two weeks, the sole surviving vessel from Gilbert's fleet reaches Falmouth under Hayes's command, bearing home the worst tale of English losses in the West since John Cabot's second voyage ended in silence—Cabot finding, in the view of Polydore Vergil, "new lands only in the ocean's bottom."[31]

146   Chargeable as Gilbert's loss may be to his own vanity, Hayes

clearly is forced to struggle with its implications for that grand English action which he is trying to promote.[32] If he can read Gilbert's reiterated "speech" as a mark of the man's final recognition (for he is "resolute in Jesus Christ" now, not in himself [35]), and thereby can end the tragedy with a moment of acceptance in which private plot meshes with holy design, there remain unacknowledged ambiguities in what Gilbert says and how he says it. Trying to mediate the last earthly deeds of his commander through the interpretative framework which he has announced from the start, Hayes provides us with enough raw fact that we can perform our own, quite different interpretation. Gilbert's posture, both active and verbal, seems in one sense more extreme than Hayes ever would admit, even slightly deranged. Hardly absolute in its description of earthly space, Gilbert's obsessive remark masks beneath the assertion of faith which Hayes sees in it a certain skeptical opposite: "as neere," yes, but also as far. On the other hand, the very fact that his "booke" may be More's, that most ideal of verbal promotions, suggests that Gilbert's hope may have been reborn on the sea rather than abandoned to God's greater wisdom. In the *Utopia,* after all, Peter Giles describes the similar *sententiae* of Hythloday ("he that hathe no grave, is covered with the skye: and the way to heaven out of all places is of like length and distaunce") as a "fantasy" which Hythloday "had surely bought full deare" if God had not been "his better frende."[33] Was Gilbert, book in hand, mimicking the braggadocio of More's "traveler," rather than confirming ahead of time the deeply pious assertions of his literary survivor?

Such questions are unanswerable, of course, but that is exactly the point here, since Hayes's report is a long contrived answer to them. At the center of his desire to tie up such loose ends lies a trio of intertwined motives. His personal sense of an English "vocation" (4) in the West demands from his hand some kind of affirmative account, a particular narrative bolstering his general plot. Reinforcing this impulse is a more nearly aesthetic one which, given Hayes's stress on the literary shape of Gilbert's voyage, similarly requires that he make the report an act of explanation and transcendence—not simply an episode of unfathomable loss. Having returned intact to England themselves (only one man was lost on the way), Hayes and his men were "the beholders, but not partakers" of the "ruine" which engulfed Gilbert (37), and in order to explain this comic ending of his own fortune the writer must somehow contrast it to the tragic fate of his commander. Herein lies the third, and most hidden, of Hayes's motives. For if the contrast which he draws is too stark, Hayes will run the risk of seeming prideful himself. Piety will become a sanctimonious defense of his survival, an attempt to separate Gilbert's career from the one which the *Golden Hinde* has pursued. Weighed against each other in the abstract, good and bad voyages may be explicable in terms of God's economy. But when the contrast is drawn between actual fates, and the man who draws it is involved deeply in the action, such an ideal arrangement of the facts may appear to be a soothing personal fiction.

This theoretical suspicion is verified by Hayes. Praising Gilbert near the end of his report as a man "firme and resolute in a purpose by all pretence honest and godly" (that is, "to discover, possesse, and to reduce unto the service of God, and Christian pietie, those remote and heathen Countreys of America"), he finally indicts his commander for "temeritie and presumption," since he based his first frustrated attempt on "ground imagined good," and he presumed in the second voyage that a "cause pretended on Gods behalfe, would carie him to the desired ende." If, at the conclusion of his life, Gilbert is "refined, and made neerer drawing unto the image of God," the old faults remain in Hayes's account like excuses for the latter's survival, explanations for that parting of the ways which Hayes himself, we suspect as we ponder his account, does not understand fully (37–38). A beholder rather than a partaker, Hayes seems more mystified than reassured, puzzled by his private comedy rather than certain of the public one which his tragic record promotes. In these senses, his narrative is a rich model of the rhetorical "settlement" which so many similar works attempt to create as their authors survey the palpable ruin of a design.[34]

Running side by side until the fatal night, when Gilbert's vessel pulled ahead, the *Squirrel* and the *Golden Hinde* signify in Hayes's account the double plotting which one often finds in records of early American life. Loser and winner in an implicit race, the ships and the men whose philosophical positions they reflect are competing for the right to control America, to define that place and Europe's bearing toward it. At issue are two exclusive visions of the New World. The right of possession is to be decided on moral rather than legal grounds: "owning" by patent a large portion of "those maine, ample and vast countreys" to which, as Hayes notes,

148

"many voyages have bene pretended, yet hitherto never any thorowly accomplished by our nation" (1), Gilbert comes off a second best to the unpretending Hayes himself because his vocation and practice both are inadequate to the large effort in hand. Indirectly, Hayes is indulging here in an act of self-promotion which is concealed (perhaps even from himself) beneath his apparent concern with the truth of Gilbert's voyage. By the convergence of his own comedy with that larger one which he projects for English enterprise in the West, Hayes becomes—personally and symbolically—the true legatee of American potential. The hidden direction in his report, the advice it offers to future voyagers, is quite baldly this: follow my track rather than Gilbert's and thus come into the possession yourself of that "maine, ample and vast" realm that awaits your formulating power.[35]

In other settlement records, the loser's fate is put to uses which are more obviously political. Whoever controls public language in any human situation—not simply the press, but the very forms of expression—has a vast advantage over the silent and the silenced. In the New World this basic fact of political life was enhanced by that "great distance" which, as Cadillac lamented to Pontchartrain, severed the realm of action from that of final authority. Each report sent back to Europe was at least potentially a play for power in the American scene, and the "facts" which it stated often were arranged so as to increase the expected grant of power. In time, this pattern entered even those texts which were aimed at memorializing New World events within a New World context rather than reporting on American affairs to some "home" official. The pattern became in these more native works a means of solving in art conflicts which resisted solution in colonial life, or which (even though solved) remained in memory as a source of continuing doubt. Figures who threatened a settlement from within or without (malcontents and competing visionaries, slaves, foreign powers, the American natives) came to be treated, in the narratives of those centrist writers who guarded the original design, much as Hayes treats Gilbert, or as he treats those pirates whom Gilbert mistakenly took into his service because he was too anxious for a quick success. Misled, benighted, treacherous, devilish, such figures of opposition must be defeated in the writer's prose, denounced if defeat is rhetorically impossible, or—best of all—held up as warning signs if a defeat in reality has been achieved and is to be chronicled.

We have seen already, in the violent innocence of a man like

Like an Ancient Mother

149

John Bartram, how diction and jurisdiction become entangled: Bartram's attempt to clear the American "garden" of his lurking and inimical Indian is an act of verbal exorcism which makes the native a loser in the plot of white success. Confined to an essentially theoretical plane on which the play of language imitates rather than records racial violence—for Bartram is writing a myth of history, not history itself—his shadow drama is nonetheless typical of all those bloody historical works which actually report the enactment of his own desired plot. This pattern, especially sharp in cases where the opponent is an obvious "other," also penetrates into texts which record dissensions and even physical conflicts within the palisades of white intent.[36] As William Bradford, for example, narrates the doleful events of the "starving time," he contrasts to the actions of his own particular group (the healthy care selflessly for the sick and the famished) the typical bearing of the *Mayflower* crewmen, who add to the trials of disease and death a callous unconcern with the fate of their fellows. Even if grounded in fact, the contrast is a clear symbol of Bradford's hope for the colony, an implicit distinction between the unregenerate Old World man and the potentially reborn New Englander. That, in after times, selfishness was to become the main threat within Plymouth itself—abandonment Bradford's final theme—heightens a modern reader's sense of how crucial to the author's view of Pilgrim history the strangely triumphant starving time was. Verifying the ideal design of "community," the unafflicted settlers at that moment converted apparent defeat into victory, while the sailors worsened their own bad fate, and offered a warning to the faithful.[37]

This one parting of the ways, as I shall argue in discussing Bradford below, is a concrete paradigm of the structure which defines *Of Plymouth Plantation* throughout its length—a structure of counterpoint between the ideal and the real, what is striven for and what is attained. Only at the end of his text, when the "real" emerges from the very heart of Pilgrim intent, does Bradford recognize that the ideal has evaporated: and to that recognition his response is a highly meaningful silence, an abandonment of the record itself. Before that moment, however, we can observe him attempting in the very texture of his prose, governing the history as he governed the colony, to place outside the walls of ideal order any figure who represents exactly that threat of deflected purpose which later was to spread the Pilgrims across a wider space. Whereas Edward Hayes is close enough to Gilbert to see the tragedy in his fate (though, as we have observed, he pulls back from the perception lest he come to share that fate, too), Bradford can deal with such wrongly directed travelers only in a satiric mode—as he does in denouncing the selfish sailors. Thus, Thomas Morton becomes the "Lord of Misrule," fool and foil to the right ruling of Bradford and the Massachusetts Bay officials. But there are anxieties that run beneath, indeed motivate, such satiric gestures. Bradford's humor is sharp and uncertain, developed from a position of felt weakness rather than obvious strength. His attack on Morton's character in the record is a verbal equivalent of the Pilgrim and Puritan assault on Morton the man, their arrest of him, their invention of apparently false (and deadly) charges against him, his deportation back to England, even the later destruction of his house at Mount Wollaston. Bradford's approach to him in the history is an effort to exclude such a "profane" man from the verbal space of American memory (except as a dangerously negative figure), much as the governor's approach to Morton in fact was an attempt to exclude him from American space itself. To make Morton one of the losers (or even the lost, as Bradford's report about arms sales to the natives might threaten to do) is to shore up the chances of victory for Bradford's community. The clutter and dispersion, both ethical and spatial, which Morton represented to Bradford might make appropriate for the latter's book a quite different *topos* from that which he clearly wanted to demonstrate in it: no longer magical transformation, not a movement of order out into the disordered terrain of America, but rather a process of dissolution and disillusion. To defeat this insidious man with the power of government and of art is to insure a comic fate for the settlers of New England at large. His tragedy, even if rigged by fictionalized evidence, will force on his own head the very end which he threatens for Bradford's community. Perceived as a man of dire plots against that community, Morton must be ensnared in counterplottings—a legal trap, a narrative lie.[38] Like the Indian "captive" who has grown fond of an "alien" way, such a figure must be exorcised, suppressed, exiled.

Later in his text, Bradford comes face to face with a far more problematic situation. At that point, he is forced to see how blurred are the lines of inclusion and exclusion, how hard it is to attribute inner tensions solely to figures who presumably are outside the colony. Complexly political, his recognition grows out of an awareness of history, a sense of what has been immutably achieved, whether for better or worse. In this way, his own perspective—built up over more than three decades of struggle—represents that same quick perception of a frustrating reality which we have found, earlier and later, in other writers already discussed. Cadillac's first reaction to Louisiana, Artaguiette's short year of travel, the few bleak months chronicled by Ellis (even the decade of growing trouble which beset and defeated Columbus), all these seem far more brief and pointed than does the drawn-out lament of Bradford. Even in his case, however, we can identify the *topos* of his discovered form, the New World scene in which is made concrete the author's final vision of America.

THE DEAD RECALLED

Before turning to Bradford himself, I think it will be helpful to consider two much shorter texts in which an analogous sense of New World history is developed more concisely, in which it defines a more limited experience than Bradford's at Plymouth. The first of these works is a brief journal kept on the Atlantic crossing by Charles Clinton, an Irish emigrant who came over in 1729. As a voice directly from the actual sea, Clinton answers well all those speculative voices which tried to portray the Atlantic passage as a quick movement of wonder and hope, a foretaste of Western renewal on the blank ocean.[39] After having stated the details of his preparation, Clinton begins with what seems like a sanguine prediction of a voyage far different from the one he later comes to record: "June ye 2d we had a fair breeze for Our westerly Course." But immediately afterwards he must indicate the start of another plot, an assault of deadly disease: "On ye 3d ditto my Daughter Kattn. & Son James fell Sick of The measels." When, two days later (the ship still enjoying "A Strong Gale of westerly wind"), Clinton records that "James Wilson's Child died," he has begun the central narration of the emigrants' real experience, a series of losses contained within an action of supposed gain. From this point onwards, his language becomes a subtractive medium, a way of retreating rather than advancing. Throughout the rest of June, Clinton keeps up a chronological pretense. It is as if, despite the worsening disease and the bad weather, he still can follow a sequence of time which hopefully will move the emigrants closer to their desired goal. But then the growing rhythm of mortality pushes all other concerns—sea conditions, things seen, vessels passed—out of his awareness. From 5 July on, the voyage is entered only as a series of departures, a list of the lost. Open to all sorts of events at the start, and to a variety of feelings, Clinton's prose narrows its focus as it proceeds; language itself is reduced as it accumulates the facts of human reduction.[40]

More than a hundred of Clinton's fellow voyagers died during the unusually long passage of four and a half months. Clearly devastated by their suffering on the brink of a new life, Clinton writes in his journal what he calls "A Return of the persons that Died on board of ye George and Ann"—an accounting of them, but also a poignant attempt to preserve their memory, to "return" them in his prose from the final voyage they have endured in life. A stunning document, his "Return" deserves full quotation:

> *James Wilson's Child; James mcDowel's Child; a Serv't of mr. Cruise's, another Serv't of his, another Serv't of his; a Child of James Thompson's; a Child of John Brooks'; a Child of James McJore's; a Child of James Thompson's; a Child of Robt. Frazer's; a Child of Thom Delap's; a Serv't of Cruise's; a Child of John Beatty's; a Child of John Brooks'; a Girle of Robt. Frazer's; a Child of Alex Mitchell's; a Son of James majore's; Robt. Todd; a Son of James McDowel's; a Serv't of Cruises; a Child of Walter Davis; John Darbie; Thom Cowan; John McCay; a Son of Rob't Frazer's; another Son of his; a Son of Chris Beatty's; a Brother of Will Hamilton's; Will Gray; my own daughter on 2 of August at night; a Child of James Majores; a Daughter of widdow hamilton; James Majore's wife; Thom Delap's wife; Alex Mitchell; a Child of James Thompson's; Walter Davis his wife; Widdow Hamilton; Rob't Gray; a child of widdow Hamilton; Walter Davis; Jane Armstrong; a child of Jam majores; An Other Servant of Cruise's; William Gordon; Isabel mcCutchan; My Son James on ye 28th of Agust: 1729 at 7 in ye morning; a Son of James majores; a brother of And'w mcDowell's; two Daughters of James mcDowells; a Daughter of walter Davis's; Robert frazer; Patt mcCann Ser't to Tho. Armstrong; Will Hamilton; James Greer Ser't to Alex mitchell; Widdow Gordon's Daughter; James mondy died thursday 11th of 7br; a Ser't of mr. Cruise's; a Son of John Beattys; Fran. Nicholson; a Sister of andw mcDowel's; A Daughter of John Beatty's; two of mr. Cruise's men Ser'ts; Margery Armstrong; A serv't of mr. Cruise's; Two of John Beatty's Children; James Thompson's wife; James Brown; a Daughter of James McDowells; a Daughter of Thom Delaps; a Ser't of mr. Cruise's; a Child of widdow mitchell's; John oliver's wife; James majore's Eldest Daughter; John Crook a Sailor; Jos. Stafford; John McDowell; John Beatty; andw mcDowell's Sister; James wilson's wife; James*

153

*mcDowell's wife; Sarah Hamilton will Hamilton's sister; Thom
Armstrong died monday ye 29th of 7br; John Beatty's wife;
Isabella Johnston; Edw'd Norris; margt mcClaughry; widdow
Frazer's Daughter; Andw mcDowelle's Brother; Jos. mcClaughry;
a young Sister of andw McDowell's; Thom Delap and his daughter
Katherin; James Barkly—(621–22)*

Far more than a simple bill of mortality, Clinton's "Return" is the
clock of his voyage west, each epoch in that larger event marked by
the finality of another traveler's fate. Clipped as its style is, broken
as its grammar may seem, the whole piece is an eloquent evocation
of individual suffering. And it is more. Given the obvious links
among the passengers, we observe a series of smaller orders progressing through Clinton's prose, family "actions" which, by their
own growing extremity from death to death, make the entire account incremental rather than conjunctive in form. The linear
clock contains several other ways of telling time, circles of relation
which seem completed by a death that moves around them, and
which thus suggest that—regardless of the fact that the main consciousness here, Clinton's own, has survived—a number of other
potential narrative centers have not. Clinton's loss of his daughter
and his son is a severe fact, the very details added to each entry hinting at his heightened sense of these two events, the particularity
of his sorrow. Yet he, at least, has survived, whereas a sequence of
events like the following one pushes relentlessly inward toward
those adults of other families who represent to Clinton, merely by
the manner in which he describes all the deaths, the really important members of the voyage: "a Child of Thom Delap's . . . Thom
Delap's wife . . . a Daughter of Thom Delaps . . . Thom Delap and
his daughter Katherin." Or again, more complexly: "a Brother of
Will Hamilton's . . . a Daughter of widdow hamilton . . . Widdow
Hamilton . . . a child of widdow Hamilton . . . Will Hamilton . . .
Sarah Hamilton will Hamilton's Sister." The point is, finally,
that the sequence of departures is more than a single one, that the
contrast between entries like "a Brother of Will Hamilton's" and
"Will Hamilton" suggests an increasing seriousness in the situation
on board, a growing extremity. Only "Mr. Cruise" (if in fact he
sailed on the *George and Ann* himself) occupies throughout Clinton's
text a consistently insulated position—his infinite supply of servants
a verbal protection from disease. Even his name as Clinton spells it
suggests a charmed life, a passage west far different from that
endured by the other emigrants.

The catalog of human fragmentation offered by Clinton here (the voyage, the families, the bodies themselves all in ruin) ends with a common line which it is hard not to take ironically in this case: "Discover'd Land on ye Continent of america ye 4th day of 8br 1729" (622)—the only implicit subject for this act being, in fact, the inventory of the dead which immediately precedes it.[41] After all the accumulated suffering of the passage over comes a remark that, without such an intervening tragedy, might be wholly comic, a symbolic record of Columbian delight. What is particularly ironic about the line is its inversion of a usual pattern, its reminder that in this instance the would-be settler's endurance has preceded an actual landing: displacement has begun with departure from the Old World. Father of one man who was to be a Revolutionary general, of another who was to be governor of New York for two decades, as well as vice-president under Jefferson and Madison; grandfather of yet another man who was to be governor in his turn, almost president of the country, and visionary of the Erie Canal—Charles Clinton may be thought of as a "successful" emigrant. But we leave out an immense amount of life in thus glossing his career by reference to a future totally obscured in his own journal amid the losses of a bleak present, the memorials of a past cluttered with death.

The settler as a historical type points our attention back to such final memorials, such losses, and away from those bland fictions which later generations—turning the explorer's arts around—have projected into earlier times. Too often attempting to verify the call of men like the almanac-maker Nathaniel Ames for an act of retrospective idealism, a plotting of the American past which stresses the abiding realization of original design, we have elided more than is necessary for the purpose of simple narrative continuity the plain discontinuities, the terminations, of American experience. If we remember those who did not arrive, we do so as a means of asserting our arrival. They become the sacrificial victims of New World history, linked to our fate because we need to assure ourselves (afraid as we always have been that the West is synonymous with loss, with a displacement from the ancestral home) that no one in whom we might read our own great break with the past ever was truly lost. In recognizing that in fact the opposite often was true, and true even when literal survival was not an issue—as at Plymouth, where success shattered the original ideal—we may come to accept, as we should, the simple reality of where we are, of where our journey has led us.

Clinton's voyage of 1729 is in this sense a model of the one which Americans always have feared to make, yet always have boasted about having made already. The passage through a terrifying historical void, a violent middle ground which (full of death and disappointment) signifies a backward route forever closed, is a neatly realized sign of antinomies deeply laid in the white American's sense of the past.[42] Having gone through a scene of oblivion and dissolution (as a discoverer like Jefferson urges his ideal traveler to do), Clinton may have discovered beyond it a realm of fulfillment. But he bore with him beyond the end of his voyage a clear recollection, an inward "Return," of the hapless fellow voyagers left along the way. His journal was a personal testament, a pledge that any subsequent gains had to be viewed with the old despair, the old almost untellable losses, in mind. Those losses had to be possessed as something more than a closed episode: as the first events of his American career, not the last ones of his European life.

The list of the dead as Clinton writes it is a prime version of the settler's *topos,* an act of realization and memory which points us toward an empty and ruinous landscape, an America fallen into time. Implicit in Clinton's catalog is a glimpse of that American scene which has not been reached yet, a shore from which the dead are conspicuously absent. It is their absence, in fact, which makes his closing comment ("Discover'd Land on ye Continent of america") so richly meaningful, that reminds us of who did not perform such a discovery, and never would. We envision at the end of his text a vastly diminished company, the diminishment a crucial factor in how the survivors viewed their own landing. The visible gaps, the denial to so many voyagers of the sight which Clinton announces, become signs of so many subjective losses of the New World here found. And it is signs such as these which mark the mood of settlement narratives, condensing into a concrete scene— even if what makes it concrete is what it lacks (as Dumanoir's lament in the "Journal" of Artaguiette suggests)—an accumulated sense of history. An embodiment of forever arrested intentions, the absent "discoverers" are the cast of an action undertaken but never fulfilled. The space which separates them from their desired shore reminds us of less fatal separations within the plot of those who did arrive, and who lived on.

Simple arrival in any case was no guarantee of a final possession. The oceanic void of Clinton's text becomes in other instances a land-born oblivion, the same sense of space as a devouring maw—

what "swallowed" Gilbert's ship in 1583—displaced here beyond the line of first discovery. The colony at Roanoke, brainchild of Gilbert's kinsman Ralegh, provides a good example of this shift, dramatic because of the high stakes that were involved and the unsolved mystery that ensued. With fine appropriateness, it is John White who gives us our last authentic view of the venture, in a prose to match his earlier paintings. As I noted above, White was the governor of the "lost" settlers who set sail in 1587. Preserved from their fate by his quick return for supplies the same year (his purpose frustrated then by the troubles with Spain), he came back only in 1590, and in circumstances far from ideal for his intent. The commanding officer of the last voyage was John Watts, a "Marchant" of London so notorious for his tendency toward privateering that White tried to have a very large bond imposed on him to insure his compliance with the design.[43] Indignant, Watts put on shore in England all the new settlers and most of the supplies intended for them and for their fellows in America. White himself remained on board, bearing up with this "crosse and unkind dealing" (212) because, had he gone to Ralegh with a complaint, Watts surely would have left without him.

Perhaps that consequence would have been better. As it turned out, Watts verified White's suspicions by pursuing a long indirect course via the Azores and Canaries to the Caribbean, spending the whole summer on the lookout for Spanish treasure ships far to the south of Roanoke. There was some minor success, but for the most part the time was wasted—even in Watts's terms. When the English pinnace *John Evangelist* captured the *Trinidad,* for example, that Spanish vessel already had been plundered by French pirates, and what remained of her cargo ("hides, ginger, Cannafistula, Copperpanes, and Casavi" [216]) hardly was golden. Having left England in March, White did not reach Carolina until mid-August, governor of a grand enterprise on shore, but a man of dubious authority on deck. Given Watts's disconcern for Roanoke, it seems unlikely that White would have found out anything more about the colony by arriving earlier in the year, though presumably he might have had more time to conduct a search and the weather certainly would have been better. A mere codicil to the prolonged privateering of Watts, the trip to Roanoke was a hasty final scene in a drawn-out and largely profitless voyage. Staying off the coast less than a week, the two vessels were short of food and water, deprived of essential tackle, and battered with storms. They left immediately for the

Caribbean, though Watts was forced by bad winds to abandon his new scheme—wintering in the South, the ships were to have returned to Carolina in the spring—and to head home instead.

This conflict between private advantage and public conscience —the hope of a future gain and the memory of past losses— allowed White merely three days in which to look for the settlers. The first was misspent when his own boat and another accompanying it put ashore at Hatteras Island: having seen smoke rising up from that place, they unfortunately "found no man nor signe that any had bene there lately," and went back to the ships for the night, exhausted and thirsty. The next day the boats again set out through the inlet to search Roanoke Island itself. Caught between a strong following wind and a strong ebb tide coming out of the sound, both small vessels took on water. White's made it through "by the will of God and carefull styrage," but the other one was swamped and six of its rowers, along with Captain Spicer of the *Moonlight,* were lost. White's own list of the dead—"Edward Spicer, Ralph Skinner, Edward Kelley, Thomas Bevis, Hance the Surgion, Edward Kelborne, Robert Coleman"—becomes a foretaste of what he was to find the next day when he landed on Roanoke. Arriving off the island after the swamped boat was recovered and both crews convinced to go on, White spied another enticing fire in the "exceeding darke" night and rowed toward it. Dropping anchor, the men began to play music, not in "jolitie" (as those on Gilbert's *Delight* had done seven years before) but rather in an attempt to answer the fire-sign with a melody of hopeful recognition: "a Call" on a trumpet, "& afterwardes many familiar English tunes of Songs" which they hoped that those on shore would hear and, understanding, would respond to. But there came "no answere," a silence that typifies everything that White was to recover of the lost attempt (220–21).

Going ashore in the morning, the party advanced to where the fire had glowed, but found only "the grasse & sundry rotten trees burning about the place." From there they crossed to the inner shore of Roanoke, then went on to its upper end until they "came to the place," White writes, "where I left our Colony in the yeere 158[7]." This sweep northward began to repay their search for signs, since now they could read the landscape more directly than the fires—bright but finally mysterious—had allowed. Indian tracks, apparently fresh, could be seen along the shore, and then, as the men moved inland up a sandbank, they discovered "curiously carved" on a tree there "these faire Romane letters C R O." Here, at last, came the shock of recognition, at first simply because these signs were obviously English, even if their significance was unclear. Soon, White recalled the instructions he had given the colonists on his departure for England: when they left Roanoke for the mainland (as they intended to), they were to "write or carve on the trees or posts of the dores the name of the place where they should be seated," the history of their decision to be inscribed quite literally *on* America, much as White had written on his map of the region a record of his earlier reconnaissance (221–22).

But a mystery lingered in the obviously incomplete legend on the tree. And when White later came to the place where the settlers had been "left in sundry houses," only to find those dwellings "taken downe, and the place very strongly enclosed with a high palisado of great trees, with cortynes and flankers very Fort-like," his discovery there of a fuller message ("one of the chiefe trees or postes at the right side of the entrance had the barke taken off, and 5 foote from the ground in fayre Capitall letters was graven CROATOAN") hardly was more satisfactory, complete as the word he discerned was. Since the settlers were to indicate by means of a Maltese cross ("a Crosse ✠ in this forme") whether they were in distress on departing for their new ground, and the presence of a fort around their abandoned houses clearly suggested that they had been, White found the absence of such a further sign from the "graven" messages both reassuring and puzzling (222). Furthermore, the ruin of the settlement, which he went on to describe in some detail, hinted at a tragical gloss for the enterprise, a palpable end unmentioned in the "fayre" records on the trees. If he assumed that the settlers indeed were on Croatoan, the island below Hatteras which was ruled by Manteo (a friendly chief whom White had brought back from his English sojourn in 1587), and thus he believed that they were safe, what he actually saw and described on Roanoke itself was a scene of fragmentation and ruin which has become our last account of the lost colony.

The passage is, as well, a finely suggestive version of the settler's *topos* wherever encountered, an inventory of broken things which expresses a fractured venture symbolized in them, a broken spirit in the writer portraying both. White still is looking for signs consciously left by the colonists, but finds only the marks of endured history on the land. Entering the palisade, his party discovers "many barres of Iron, two pigges of Lead, foure yron fowlers, Iron sacker-shotte, and such like heavie things, throwen here and there, almost overgrowen with grasse and weedes." Along the creekside, where they seek the small vessels and the cannons left with the colonists, the men can "perceive no signe of them." When they come across a trench in which several chests were buried, but later dug up and broken open, they see the clutter of European objects there as a clear indication that the native enemies from Dasamongwepeuk, a town on the mainland opposite Roanoke, have been there and scattered the hidden goods. Particularly touching here is the fact that three of the five chests were White's own, and that he thus is describing a ruin of deeply personal significance as he lists the found objects spread chaotically across the American scene: "Many of my things [were] spoyled and broken, and my bookes torne from the covers, the frames of some of my pictures and Mappes"—his by more than possession, by creation as well?—"rotten and spoyled with rayne, and my armour almost eaten through with rust" (222–23).

White consoles himself finally with the hope that, regardless of the "spoyle of my goods," the settlers have enjoyed a less corrosive fate—the armor of their identity and purpose intact wherever they may be. As governor, he obviously feels for their welfare, but there is an additional impulse here as well, the fact that his daughter and son-in-law (Elynor and Ananias Dare), and his grandchild Virginia—first English infant born in America, though conceived (as her namesake was) in the Old World—are among the colonists whom he seeks. His further intention to follow them to Croatoan, frustrated by further disasters in the Watts fleet, can be seen as a sign of his abiding desire to confirm by experience his reading of the Roanoke remains. His hope may be renewed amid these ruins, though his prose is heavy with the stares of remorse and disbelief, and we can perceive beneath his affirmations a lingering doubt, a clutter of mind to match the clutter on Roanoke itself. Indeed, his final words on the 1590 voyage, prefixed to his narrative but providing for it a last statement of ruin, a spiritual end to match the broken end of Ralegh's venture, reveal a man who is effectually renouncing all future Western intentions. "Thus may you plainely perceive," White tells Hakluyt in the prefatory letter, "the successe of my fift & last voiage to Virginia, which was no lesse unfortunately ended then frowardly begun, and as lucklesse to many, as sinister to my selfe." Like Gilbert's fatal voyage seven years earlier, which "begun, continued, and ended adversly," White's own dis-

plays throughout a remarkable consistency, a design almost
aesthetic in nature. But White, unlike Edward Hayes, cannot contain this bleak decorum of his experience in a larger comic
framework. If he seems to do so in the narrative itself, his letter in
fact denies that earlier, more hopeful gesture. "I would to God,"
White continues of the voyage, "it had bene as prosperous to all, as
noysome to the planters; & as joyfull to me, as discomfortable to
them." But this complicated wish is vain, contradicted by the facts.
He will not assert an overarching success, a gain to balance the
human losses. He remains "contented," as he says, not because he
has survived himself (and thus has enjoyed at least a privately comic
fate), but rather because the present undertaking was "not my first
crossed voyage"—because, that is, the aesthetic pattern of his New
World experience as a whole essentially matches that of the lost
colonists' American life. Once more at home, he sees his return as a
sign of frustration instead of fulfillment. "And wanting my wishes,"
he goes on, "I leave off from prosecuting that whereunto I would
to God my wealth were answerable to my will." A tale of denied will,
of his Western ventures as still incomplete (and his longing for their
completion still strong), his letter ends with an act of resignation to
God—rather than to that righteous future voyager of Hayes, a
voyager who will be the surrogate of God in America—"Thus
committing the reliefe of my discomfortable company the planters
in Virginia, to the merciful help of the Almighty, whom I most
humbly beseech to helpe & comfort them, according to his most
holy wil & their good desire, I take my leave: from my house at
Newtowne in Kylmore the 4 of February, 1593" (212–13). It is a
"leave" taken of Hakluyt by the closing of White's language in the
letter, but a leave taken in the larger sense of America itself, of
those "discomfortable" colonists to whom the text is obliquely addressed (and undeliverable). Ever since 1577 White had been
linked with the West by act and art, but now not even his words can
reach across the sea. They are his last verbal gesture on the subject;
the rest of his life is silence.

White's report describes, as Charles Clinton's "Journal" does, a
pattern of New World travel darkly opposite to those projected by
discoverers and explorers. Its central action, a sad reconnaissance
of European purpose on an actual American landscape, reveals the
realistic drive behind all similar documents. And its main symbols
for that action—the scattered goods, the fortified but empty town,
the torn books and water-ruined pictures, the armor eaten with   161

rust—indicate by their stark contrast to the hoped-for, yet absent, signs of certain survival the settler's continuing shock of unwanted but accepted recognition. Even those meager records of their apparent new purpose which the colonists carved on the two trees, and which in one sense are the only authentic narrative of their fate, become equivalent signs of ruin. White effectively preserves for us the initial discomposure of his eye and mind when he found the first "curious" message—three "letters," printed as such by Hakluyt, not as part of a word—and he thus stresses the almost absurd status of the fragment, its lonely inarticulation in an otherwise silent world. Stifled like the colony (or abbreviated, if one prefers), the message may be taken in its discomposure and truncation as a finely abstract version of the *topos,* a ruin of language literally seen in or on the New World. Displaced from the paper of European discourse and onto an object of American space, White's "C R O" verifies, but ironically, the explorer's vision of all Old World arts as means of symbolic conversion, their "impression" on a conceptualized America the highest proof of white possession. The impression recorded here is ironic not simply because it is incomplete and therefore puzzling, but also because it is literal and as such surprises White when he first sees it—aware as he is of the arrangements made for communication, desirous as he is to find evidence that Virginia indeed has been converted.

The other message is more complete in itself, and all that it signifies makes White think that he has found in this one word a whole record of his colony. A place and a direction, perhaps a motive and a condition as well, seem implicated in the eight "fayre Capitall letters" which he immediately sees as a word, and which Hakluyt prints according to that perception. "Graven" on a tree which the colonists have made into a post, by which they have inscribed another kind of order, the message seems almost to owe its intelligibility to its more "central" location. A sign on a sign, it points nonetheless by its very completion to the abandonment within, the "houses taken downe," the heavy objects strewn around the clearing. A finished statement, it leaves the settlers' fate unfinished. It narrates only by assumption what has occurred, and thus expresses on its own terms that reduction of language seen more dramatically on the tree near the sandbank, the near oblivion of speech. Each of these messages is an icon of the lost, a fine example of "concrete" prose, form coincident with meaning.[44]

162   At their most perceptive moments, American settlers are very

astute readers of sign, not the hunter's (and explorer's) variety but rather that kind in which is condensed, as here, the legend of a baffled intent. But the settler also is a maker of signs. That any record survives in fact suggests that the fate which it describes, however inexpressible it may be or may appear, has been caught in language, immured against any further oblivion. And caught in that language, too, is a broader fact, a vision of America detailed in the minutiae of one occasion. When White writes, for instance, of an earlier discovery on Roanoke—it was in 1587, when he was landing the colony under his command, and chanced upon the ruins of the earlier one planted by Grenville—we are warranted, I think, to take his description as an evocative symbol, plotted for his prose by events (for events *do* have their logic, their design), of a more general disposition of English order in America. Intending to call on Grenville's men before heading up to Chesapeake Bay (where Ralegh's colony was to be planted this time), White found himself effectually abandoned by the ship's captain, who declared once White's pinnace was free of him that it was too late in the year for more coastal sailing, and hence that the new settlers would have to stay on Roanoke themselves. When White located on shore none of the fifteen men, "nor any signe" that they had been where Grenville left them—except for "the bones of one of those fifteene, which the Savages had slaine long before"—he clearly could not have looked on his own prospects with much enthusiasm. Furthermore, when he went the next day to Ralph Lane's old fort at the upper end of the island, and discovered there a complete disarray, he was rehearsing without knowledge his more desperate discovery three years afterwards. The scene he found there seems like a key to his later, partly hidden fear: "the fort rased downe, but all the houses standing unhurt, saving that the neather roomes of them, and also of the forte, were overgrowen with Melons of divers sortes, and Deere within them, feeding on those Melons: so we returned to our company, without hope of ever seeing any of the fifteene men living" (200–1). Suddenly we can understand the uneasiness of his survey on Roanoke in 1590, his anxious search for "signes" (and signs of *what*), his ambivalence at the sight of the later ruin.[45]

In the earlier scene there persists a different ambivalence. Though "unhurt," the houses of Grenville's men—if indeed they had come here and possessed Lane's abandoned structures—are empty and silent. Or rather what they do contain in their "neather roomes" is a sign of abundance which seems almost to mock their human emptiness. Discovery and settlement as acts and attitudes are at odds here, the latter framing the former only by means of a jarring composition that White's last remark clearly emphasizes. A man of considerable artistic talent whose greatest works are notable precisely for their careful separation of such opposing visions, White hardly can be oblivious to the mixture of modes which his verbal landscape represents. The unmentionable implication here is that the discoverer's perception is correct—Amadas and Barlowe (with whom White may have sailed) right in their wonder, even Harriot (with whom White worked) justified in his mild exploratory gestures—but that the clock of human time runs down as nature cycles on. European order here quite literally contains the abundant New World, but the European actor who ought to be in control is absent. The sentence is broken, its verb elided, too.

White tells later in his 1587 text what happened to the men who might have completed this statement. His account of their apparent destruction by natives from various Indian towns, including Secoton itself, forms a crucial background for what he tells (and cannot tell) in 1590. Like Lane's fort, the lost men suggest a narrative of outright defeat which is hidden in White's later report under the surface of his still-asserted hope. A sign of English dispersion, they convert the list of the "safely arrived" colonists which ends White's 1587 text into an inventory of the future-lost. "John White," that list begins, "Roger Baily, Ananias Dare . . . Elyoner Dare," and the other adults, until we find the "Boyes and children," and the "Children borne in Virginia"—"Virginia Dare, Harvie" (209–11). Like Clinton's "Return," though with far less conscious intent, this cast of characters becomes a census of the never-arrived, or of those who, having arrived, were too literally assimilated into America. Their first safety is a dream, a memory of a dream.

The list also becomes, as so many of White's verbal gestures do, a concise definition of the settler's aesthetic design. His most elusive gloss of that pattern, however, is to be found in his last words on the West. The letter to Hakluyt in 1593, a brief condensation of nearly two decades of American experience, is the most complete statement which White ever made. It exhibits throughout a sense of the shape which informed that long experience, and a weight of moral awareness which is more than temporary in character, which is carefully developed and hesitantly revealed. And it builds on a

literally Old World ground ("Newtowne in Kylmore") a remarkably

New World stance. Neither "here" nor "there"—and with a poignancy unmatched by William Penn one hundred years later— White describes in his own rhetorical position that peculiarly American perspective which was the result, in most colonies and at most times, in overwhelming defeat or apparent victory, of a voyage that tested every prescribed plot with the fire of actual experience. Next to the discoverer's timeless poise, the explorer's futuristic and elevated pose, White's retreating gaze in his letter ("I leave off . . .") suggests a stance of outward and inward reconnoitering which will allow no fictions. The letter itself becomes a psychological version of the *topos,* a survey of spiritual ruins which points with meaningful concreteness to the Roanoke surveys of 1587 and 1590. Those more kinetic acts are the necessary figure for White's verbal art in the last document of his American career.

AMERICA AS MEMORY, AS WORD

We can return to William Bradford by means of a final point about John White. Shaped by an irony of events, White's New World writings become in their last movements a critique of earlier visions and the texts which record them. This is the kind of literary criticism which is central to the settler's aesthetic world. In Bradford's case, the critique occurs throughout the text rather than at its end, for Bradford's beginning as a historian lies in the "end" of his colonial vision. Written largely after what he took to be the last crisis of Pilgrim ideals had occurred, *Of Plymouth Plantation* is, like White's letter to Hakluyt, a final gesture back over a long and disappointing venture. Shaped for the most part into an apparently chronological form, the work in fact is a complex interplay between Bradford's viewpoint as author and his earlier stance as actor. The record of each year's events from 1620 to 1646 is informed subtly by Bradford's initial hope and his later despair. Instead of giving us a series of discrete annals (as he seems to), he creates a full history which is unified morally and thematically in all its reaches. It is as if White, forswearing his silence, should have set down in one coherent final narrative the whole of his New World experience, as if his 1593 letter should have become the spiritual foundation of a new departure, an artistic exploration.

Bradford is not, however, simply the critic of earlier illusions. A surveyor of ruins, a figure of satire and lamentation, he also emerges in the book as a man of abiding affirmations. He has witnessed the abandonment of Pilgrim ideals by the colonists; he 165 feels that he has been abandoned himself; he adopts a stance of marginality and isolation as the hard ground of his record. Yet beyond these recognitions and Bradford's attempt to organize his art according to them, there remains a sense of devout belief in the first cause of Pilgrim emigration. If he resembles White in the honesty of his acceptance, his clear knowledge that mere wishes cannot change the past, he surpasses White in his further understanding of the power of art—the wish of recollection—to embalm the beginning hope of a New World voyage. Opposed to all his catalogs of frustration and ruin is a "Return" like Charles Clinton's, a use of language to fix in the ideal space of articulated memory a true portrait of what has since been lost. He writes his narrative as a means of "returning" himself to the original moment of expectation: it is a way of saving the author from the terminal loss which history seems to have visited on him, a way of rediscovering through art that New World which now appears so old.

Like Bradford, we must begin with the ending. In his entry for 1644, Bradford describes a crucial debate within the Plymouth congregation. That debate illuminates the whole course of his history, for it is the implicit source of his artistic viewpoint through a good portion of the text—the crystalizing moment of his memory. Ironically, the disagreement concerns what had been from the very start of the Pilgrim movement in England a central gesture of the believers' separate estate. Having defined itself by a series of "removals"—from England to Amsterdam, from Amsterdam to Leyden, from Leyden to America—the church has found that this ritual of departure, invented at first for the sake of preserving the ideal, now has become in America a primary means for its dissolution. Settled on a New World terrain notable for "straitness and barrenness," the Pilgrims have suffered again and again from the dispersion of population out onto more fertile grounds. Anxious to aid in the larger increase of European settlements in New England, they have encouraged the plantation of other groups within the limits of their own patent. But they also have watched the migration of Pilgrims themselves away from the colony's home at Plymouth, a fact which has mixed the church with those who are outside it. The debate of 1644 centers on a radical proposal for reasserting the old purity which has been threatened by such mixtures. Quite simply, the plan put forward calls for the church itself to undertake yet another removal. By resettling in a more fruitful 166 and ample region the community can avoid the sad fate which

seems to await it otherwise. If it stays at Plymouth, ignoring the
threat, the church eventually must be "weakened and as it were
insensibly dissolved." Much as the Leyden congregation earlier saw
itself faced with oblivion if it remained in the Lowlands, so now the
sanctuary which America had offered them may become profane.

The arguments for and against this proposal seem to have been
intense, even personal at times. But Bradford suggests that a
majority came to accept the plan, though many who did not favor it
very highly agreed to it in order to avert a schism in the church.
Then came the next step in the process, an exploratory survey of
the new land where they intended to replant. It introduced new
disagreements, for the tract lay "at an outside of the country remote from all society"—on the outer cape, where the soil was not so
good, nor so ample, as that around Plymouth itself. Having deeded
away much better common ground to other groups and individuals, the original settlers now found themselves deprived of any
territory adequate for their purposes. Although it seemed clear
that the Nauset tract was incommodious, some of those who most
strongly supported the removal there persisted in the project,
made a quick beginning before the church could reconsider the
plan, and were too far along for their migration to be stopped. A
scheme for preserving the Plymouth order thus became an occasion for further partings.

Unlike Christopher Carleill or even William Penn, both of whom
would be able to gloss such a splintering off of new settlements
from the old one as a sign of "multiplied" success, Bradford can
view it only as a sign of division. Because so much of his rhetoric for
describing the Pilgrim ideal is integral and unified—a means of
distinguishing it from other "ways," of justifying it by an assertion
of its separate purity—he has no real language for dealing with
departure except as a symbolic assault from within. In a rather
insidious manner, the defecting merge with those outsiders (like
Thomas Weston or Thomas Morton) who are seen by Bradford as
the villains of a competing and disorderly design. The lines of
inclusion and exclusion in his prose are sharp and heavy. And as
time passes they constrict more and more until they appear to meet
and join with the limits of Bradford's own lonely awareness. A
history thus becomes a displaced autobiography, the colony
equated with the man who tells its story. The action which Bradford is recording becomes a figure for the stages of his own inner
development.

But *Of Plymouth Plantation* also is a public narrative. All that is foreign to Bradford's intent, and hence seems excluded from the increasingly private center of his text, forms an ever larger body of "eccentric" life that comes to fill each annal, as the account of the Nauset settlers does for 1644, with ample evidence of the Pilgrims' departures from their original path into America. Bradford's center (Plymouth; the Pilgrim ideal; his own emotional ground) decreases in size both in comparison with and because of the expansion of European settlement in New England. The public record itself is double and ironic: a plot of material increase is contrasted to one of spiritual decline. The small beginning of Old World order in America has led to a great accomplishment. But the great utopian hope which ought to be fulfilled by this other success has suffered a sad diminution. Hence the explorer's *topos* is both verified and denied in Bradford's text. A grand transformation has occurred, but it has not been the vehicle of spiritual reformation. And Bradford, seeking to express this mixed state of affairs, is denied by the tangible "progress" of material culture those emblems of outward ruin which allow other settlers like John White to suggest in the fragments of literal order the fragmentation of a less literal plot. When he chooses as his figure for the result of the Nauset debate in 1644 the biblical image of an old mother whose children are gone from her in pursuit of their own youthful purposes, he is invoking in this complex version of the settler's *topos* both the success of English plantation and the attrition of Pilgrim ideals. It is a marvelous passage, rich in the conflict of Plymouth history. The "ruin" rendered in it is a strictly inward state, a void of emotional loss surrounded by other, distant gains:

> And thus was this poor church left, like an ancient mother grown old and forsaken of her children, though not in their affections yet in regard of their bodily presence and personal helpfulness; her ancient members being most of them worn away by death, and these of later time being like children translated into other families, and she like a widow left only to trust in God. Thus, she that had made many rich became herself poor.[46]

Fraught with a sense of betrayal despite the enduring "affections" of the departed young, this passage reveals the benchmark from which Bradford's most important historical measurements are run in the book. The ancient mother church is a still point of uncorrupted ideals around which circulate, in a weakening and dispersing orbit, those fugitive New World settlers whose distance from the center reflects not their actual loss in an unknown reach of American space (like the Roanoke colonists), but rather their all too certain arrival elsewhere. It is the beginning which has been lost, not the end: the very comedy of a "rich" expansion contains the tragedy of a plot that has been "forsaken."

As one of the "ancient members" himself, Bradford soon was to resume work on his history, which he had begun around 1630, but which seems to have lain by virtually untouched between that year and 1646. The verbal act which he thus sought to continue and finish, but which in fact he abandoned again when he reached the present, may be thought of as his attempt to touch back to the lost beginning. He takes on himself in performing it the voice of the almost silent "mother" church, and hence hopes to articulate exactly what had been broken in 1644. Yet his account is like a report sent from a now marginal site, Plymouth become his Jamaica. Whatever he can recover of the ideals which first moved the Pilgrim migration must remain immured in the confines of his last center of all, the wholly symbolic one of his prose. And, as if to point this very moral, he spends most of his time as a historian listing the causes of his mournful art, the forces which have denied him any other fulfillment for the original design than that which he now can afford it. The *topos* so finely developed in his 1644 annal is the concise model of his narrative practice throughout the work, even of the first passages written in 1630. Together with the last entry, an account of Edward Winslow's departure from the colony in 1646—a departure which was to remain permanent and unexplained, much to Bradford's sorrow as he wrote the tale in 1650—that earlier lament holds the key to almost every episode in the history.

This is a large claim about a large and complicated work. But the claim itself hopefully is complex, and thus will not oversimplify Bradford or his art. It is clear at numerous points in the text that the author himself wants us to read what is presently narrated by reference to later events, and by reference in particular to the declension of spirit which he describes in his last entries. When he inserts in his account of 1624 a letter from James Sherley, treasurer of the adventurers in London, and adds to it a footnote in which he answers Sherley's comment about the lack of wine in Plymouth, Bradford is revealing in a formal way the dialectic which he carries on throughout. His note is instructive:

It is worthy to be observed, how the Lord doth change times and things; for what is now more plentiful than wine? And that of the best, coming from Malaga, the Canaries, and other places, sundry ships lading in a year. So as there is now more cause to complain of the excess and the abuse of wine, through men's corruption, even to drunkenness, than of any defect or want of the same. Witness this year 1646. The good Lord lay not the sins and unthankfulness of men to their [the Pilgrims'?] charge in this particular. (373)

Rather like George Burges on the Pennsylvania frontier in the next century, Bradford here notes a lack which may be (or actually has been) supplied, but then moves beyond such a simple plot to sense a complication caused by this one fulfillment. No wine, wine, abuse of wine: small beginning, accomplishment, a worse-than-small conclusion. It is the paradigm of Bradford's Plymouth, a verifying of exploratory vision which itself undercuts what the present explorer has hoped for.

This passage represents, to be sure, a rather delicate foreshadowing. Yet its full context suggests the way in which Bradford's smallest detail points us to the heart of his greatest concerns. Sherley's whole letter is a bleak portrait of the spineless anxieties of the London partners, and the subject of wine enters it near the end because the latest gathering of these dissension-torn men has been for Sherley, with some surprise, "the lovingest and friendliest meeting that ever I knew"—and he has sent out for a "pottle" in order to celebrate this rare accord. Unfortunately, as Bradford comments in another note, this sense of peace "lasted not long; they had now provided Lyford and others to send over" (373). If we already have read through Bradford's annal for the present year, we know that John Lyford was an apparently fake minister who from the moment he came cringingly ashore displayed a genius for antagonizing the Plymouth leaders. But our own foreknowledge is not the point here; Bradford's is. Holding off against Sherley's little celebration an awareness of what that English event caused for the Pilgrims (or rather, what the celebrants caused, for Bradford is using false logic here, mixing discrete events as a means of attacking those responsible for both of them), he weaves together another tapestry of hope and recognition, a plaid of starkly varied threads. Whereas his note on wine itself contains both major strands, this earlier one is all irony, an experienced statement to answer Sherley's distant naiveté.[47]

The Bradford who received Sherley's message and the Bradford who comments on it are, in effect, two different men. Between such alternate selves is built up in his book a psychological drama which reflects the major clashes of Pilgrim history itself. The doubling or tripling of the author's viewpoint in a particular passage brings to bear on it a sense of the whole extent of Plymouth experience. Likewise, Bradford's handling of voices other than his own—voices which enter *Of Plymouth Plantation* by means of his copious inclusion of documents—tends to proceed on a similar principle of counterpoint, rather than one of mere accumulation. He often plays off one document against another, for instance, each of them representing a different stage in his own development. Quoting a letter from the London adventurers in his annal for 1623, a letter which speaks warmly of some new settlers sent out to Plymouth, Bradford clearly intends us to read this document in light of the letter from Robert Cushman (that most difficult of Pilgrims) which he has quoted just prior to it. Since Cushman notes that the Pilgrims must be on their guard against some of the arriving settlers, the London adventurers' more rosy text—the kind of document which Bradford himself might have written at the start of the Pilgrim venture—exists in an acidic medium within the history, Cushman's warning since verified in Bradford's subsequent experience. Moreover, what follows the London letter in Bradford's narrative offers a quick confirmation of Cushman's advice. Whereas the adventurers end with a hope that the "Loving Friends" in Plymouth may be able to send "joyful news" back home, and that the English and American partners may "with one shoulder" accomplish "this work" of plantation (so that glory may come to God, who "confoundeth the mighty by the weak, and maketh small things great"), Bradford reports immediately afterwards—in a figurative letter sending doleful rather than "joyful" news to England—a tale of reduction rather than aggrandizement. Great things may also be made small, particularly by small minds like those which the new settlers in large part seem to possess. Shocked by the "low and poor condition ashore," these late arrivals are "much daunted and dismayed." Some of them, Bradford reports, "wished themselves in England again," while "others fell aweeping, fancying their own misery in what they saw now in others; other some pitying the distress they saw their friends had been long in, and still were under." By way of summary: "In a word, all were full of sadness" (128–30). This common feeling inverts the spirit of the London partners' desire, and its commonality itself is ironic, since many of the new people are sad over their own envisioned despair. Where is the "one shoulder" of shared endeavor?

Bradford is led to such divisive strategies in his prose, I would argue, because his enduring viewpoint as narrator rests beyond the watershed of far more serious dissensions and disagreements. His personal sorrow makes him emphasize in the record of times which far preceded it disruptive facts that become signs of a future loss. Thus, though he goes on in the annal for 1623 to describe a severe drought which ends, and is succeeded by a rich harvest, he follows the "day of thanksgiving" which celebrates this good reversal with an account of how the old settlers and the "newcomers" are anxious to protect their private advantages. It is agreed that the grain which has been sown and harvested by the established planters "for their Particular" (that is, privately rather than in common) will not be used to feed the recent arrivals, and that the supplies brought over by the latter will not, in turn, be used for the original Plymouth colony. The evident survival of the group thus leads to a greater stress on each individual's perquisites; subtle lines of division are drawn even in the moment of celebration. Though Bradford as actor defends, or at least accepts, the new arrangement ("Their request was granted them," he writes with politic sense, "for it gave both sides good content"), we cannot avoid comparing this situation with that which he describes during the first "starving time" in 1620 and 1621 (132). In dealing with that earlier crisis, as I have re-marked, Bradford draws a line of distinction between those who share in a sense of community and those who are out for their own advantage. Now, however, this distinction must run through the center of the Plymouth group itself. As a departure from the older ideal pattern, the present agreement to disagree hints ahead at the Nauset debate.[48]

An able satirist, Bradford finds in the newcomers, as in so many peripheral groups and individuals, an effective foil for the pure Pilgrim design. Yet the rogue's gallery where they belong (along with worse figures like Weston, Morton, Allerton, Lyford, and Thomas Granger—"Horrible it is to mention," Bradford writes of Granger's "buggery," "but the truth of the history requires it" [320]) becomes in the course of his narrative a strangely corrosive model of the Pilgrims' own failings. When he writes of the 1623 emigrants that they "looked for greater matters than they found or could attain unto"—for they wanted to be "building great houses and such pleasant situations for them as themselves had fancied, as if they would be great men and rich all of a sudden" (according to the explorer's fantasy)—he seems at first to be contrasting these overhopeful (and overly materialistic) visions of the American scene with the more sober ones of his own flock. That the fancies of the newcomers soon proved to be mere "castles in the air" seems further to separate the two groups and their values (133). The quick defeat of an economic dream in this case, however, points by a subtle link to Nauset and beyond. The Pilgrims also sought to build a "great house" in New England, as John Robinson (their great leader in the Lowlands) reminded those departing on the "hopeful voyage" in 1620—his farewell to them then a call for truly communal visions. The spiritual fellowship already established ought to be joined, Robinson argued, with the tangible community yet to be planted and nurtured in the West:

> *Let every man repress in himself and the whole body in each person, as so many rebels against the common good, all private respects of men's selves, not sorting with the general conveniency. And as men are careful not to have a new house shaken with any violence before it be well settled and the parts firmly knit, so be you, I beseech you, brethren, much more careful that the house of God, which you are and are to be, be not shaken with unnecessary novelties or other oppositions at the first settling thereof.* (369–70)

If what was laughable in the schemes of the 1623 emigrants was the haste with which they supposedly were to be realized (vision and sight ultimately confused in them), what was threatening in those same schemes was their inversion of the Pilgrim design itself, their suggestion that in the very language which Robinson had used to articulate that design lay the potential for a vastly different plot. As literal houses spread over New England in later years, and the "house of God" at Plymouth appeared to be shaken to its foundation, the Pilgrim metaphor was drained of its higher meaning, while the newcomers' dream became a reality as substantial as sill, post, and shingle. Like Massachusetts Bay Colony, which saw Winthrop's glorious "Citty upon a Hill" (itself perhaps a metaphor to begin with) transformed by coastal geography and economic pressures into several cities on several hills, Plymouth became simply one settlement among many. *Its* ideal now was an airy "castle" unsubstantiated by New World fact.[49]

At this point we can turn to the most dramatic clash in the texture of Bradford's prose, the passage where the ends of his vision meet not in a recorded event but rather in the interplay of his present awareness and an earlier dream. It occurs in his 1630 section of the manuscript, where he quotes as an outline of the Pilgrim intent a 1617 letter written by Robinson and William Brewster to the Virginia Company, from which the exiles first tried to obtain a patent. Aside from Robinson's farewell letter of 1620 and some of Robert Cushman's complex writings, the piece offers us the most concrete statement of what the Pilgrim plot, both historical and spiritual, was to entail. It is the exploration to which Bradford's whole text is a settler's response, a survey far more implanted than those of Cadillac, White, or Artaguiette. But Bradford abbreviates this complex interplay by writing in what Morison judges to be an "aged hand" on the blank sheet opposite the quoted letter a lament which makes this one exchange a richly predictive paradigm of the total history. Written before the Pilgrims departed for America, the letter is answered on Bradford's facing page by a condensed report of all that has happened since they did depart, of all the subsequent departures since they arrived in the West. Brewster and Robinson adduce five reasons (32–33) why the Leyden company ought to receive a patent: they believe in God's concurrence with them; they already have suffered displacement in "a strange and hard land"; they are, as a body, "industrious and frugal"; they are united in a "sacred bond and covenant of the Lord" which will keep them joined as a community across the sea; and, finally, they are desperately serious about the venture, having almost literally no place to turn should they fail in America. Bradford's lamentation points to the fourth of these reasons, which runs in full as follows: "We are knit together as a body in a most strict and sacred bond and covenant of the Lord, of the violation whereof we make great conscience, and by virtue whereof we do hold ourselves straitly tied to all care of each other's good and of the whole, by every one and so mutually." Unlike the other four reasons (even the first one), this point concerns less the economic hopes of a colony than its very rationale as a civic venture. It has economic implications, to be sure, but at its heart lies the Pilgrim scheme in all its purified and exultant expectation. Knowing Bradford's "aged" mind, we almost can predict his response to this other prediction:

> *O sacred bond, whilst inviolably preserved! How sweet and precious were the fruits that flowed from the same! But when this fidelity decayed, then their ruin approached. O that these ancient members had not died or been dissipated (if it had been the will of*

*God) or else that this holy care and constant faithfulness had still
lived, and remained with those that survived, and were in times
afterwards added unto them. But (alas) that subtle serpent hath
slyly wound in himself under fair pretences of necessity and the
like, to untwist these sacred bonds and ties, and as it were insensibly
by degrees to dissolve, or in a great measure to weaken, the same. I
have been happy, in my first times, to see, and with much comfort to
enjoy, the blessed fruits of this sweet communion, but it is now a
part of my misery in old age, to find and feel the decay and want
thereof (in a great measure) and with grief and sorrow of heart to
lament and bewail the same. And for others' warning and admoni-
tion, and my own humiliation, do I here note the same.* (33)

Redolent of the Nauset passage, after the writing of which it clearly
was added to Bradford's fifth chapter, this sad description of the
"ruin" of Pilgrim hope (and of Bradford's own humiliated sorrow)
is the place where public and private history merge in *Of Plymouth
Plantation.* Adding to the richness of the lament is an unstated pair
of facts about the two men who penned the prospective plot to
which Bradford here offers a bleak retrospect. John Robinson,
revered and cherished minister at Leyden, never did make it to
New England. And in his farewell of 1620, the document which
develops the metaphor of the "house" as both a spiritual and a
temporal image, Robinson suggested in describing his own reasons
for failing to join the emigrants what was to become the language
that Bradford used in attacking the departed settlers of 1644.
"Loving and Christian Friends," the salutation runs, "I do heartily
and in the Lord salute you all as being they with whom I am present
in my best affection and most earnest longings after you. Though I
be constrained for a while to be bodily absent from you" (368).[50]
Though it is wrong, I think, to read the Nauset *topos* as a veiled
assault on Robinson, the mere coincidence of fact and word hints at
an unconscious convergence in Bradford's mind between the great
Leyden leader who never joined the Plymouth settlers and those
colonists who, having joined, departed in body if not in affection
from the ancient mother church. Likewise, Bradford's encomium
on Brewster in the annal for 1643 points to other hidden tensions
in both the lament quoted above and the Nauset episode. For his
praise of the elder leads him into a long aside on the longevity of
the first emigrants, and it is to these "ancient members"—himself
included—that Bradford refers in his next annal and in the note to
the Robinson-Brewster letter of 1617, and refers to them in both
these cases not as signs of God's special protection for the   175

Pilgrims—the point of his aside in the 1643 entry—but rather as men and women abandoned, types of the destitute church. Had great things followed from a small beginning, long life would be a blessing. But we must view it, as Bradford does in his last comment on Plymouth in the history ("O sacred bond . . ."), as a syncopation of ends, a survival beyond something worse than death. Like his list of *Mayflower* passengers which finishes out the manuscript volume (and which stresses their endurance, becoming a "Return" to match that of Charles Clinton in 1729 or that of John White in his 1587 report), Bradford's recollection of the aged settlers marks his final equation of the Pilgrim ideal with the Pilgrims themselves. Hence if the beginning of his text always points us to the end of his experience, the ending of his manuscript leads us back to the start, to "those which came over first, in the year 1620, and were by the blessing of God the first beginners and in a sort the foundation of all the Plantations and Colonies in New England" (441). And if this description of the first settlers seems to revive for one last time the benign *topos* of amazing growth, we must recognize that Bradford's catalog of them soon becomes a record of earthly departures after the great arrival in America. It is the bill of mortality for Pilgrim hopes; the beginning which these original emigrants represented now has ended with their existence. With high appropriateness, two other people later filled out the record after Bradford himself died in 1657, the hundred three first voyagers reduced in the last line to a single name: "And Mary Cushman is still living this present year, 1698" (448): The last survivor of the *Mayflower* company, Mary Cushman died in the following year.

Bradford's inventory of the departed lists as well the "increasings" of each family. But no arithmetic can weigh the lost (and their lost ideal) against the gains of a second or third generation. Indeed, his purpose in detailing these deaths and births is veiled in an interesting evasion. It is not simply a matter of recording facts for future reference, but something more guardedly personal as well: "It may be of some use to such as come after," Bradford notes; "but however I shall rest in my own benefit" (443). What that "benefit" might be Bradford does not indicate. His gloss of the whole endeavor at the end ("Let the Lord have the praise, who is the High Preserver of men" [447]) suggests that it is a means of giving thanks to God. But his own calculations impress us with the small gains accomplished in thirty years (from a hundred to a hundred ninety souls, including the thirty original emigrants who still survive in

1650), rather than any sense of obvious multiplication. The announced moral and the matter which it should govern seem to be at
odds. Perhaps the real benefit to be derived from his effort is the
quite modest satisfaction of recalling the old company, of recon-
stituting them now in language alone.[51]

If this interpretation is at least partly correct, it sheds light as well
on one of the last of Bradford's entries in his manuscript. For at the
start of the volume are several leaves that contain the Hebrew
"exercises" which he wrote there while he was trying to learn that
language in his final years. And his explanation of this studious
venture, also inscribed on those leaves, hints in a tantalizing way at
Bradford's ultimate view of the history itself as a symbolic gesture,
an attempt not only to detail the frustrations of Plymouth as a
historical entity, but also to restate in language those timeless ideals
of which the colony itself was to have been an assertion. A typologi-
cal thinker for whom the Israelite experience always should have
been present in that of his own group, Bradford at last saw that the
Canaan for which the Pilgrims had searched in the New World was
a perfectly inner terrain equatable with the words which first described it—much as, by a similarly pure nominalism, the Pilgrim
striving was equatable with the first settlers themselves. Detached
from history, both the biblical place (or name) and the longed-for
home of the Leyden exiles now became signs of a spiritual direction
rather than an earthly arrival. Describing the Hebrew tongue as a
promised land, Bradford thought of his new studies as a means of
discovering by inward discipline quite a different New World from
that in which he pursued them. It was to be an America of the mind
and heart, his return to the original language of revelation a way of
getting back, much as was his Pilgrim catalog at the end of the
history, to a time when ideals were articulate and whole. Hence the
historical design, formulated in words, pointed him back to words
once again. Never having stated the sentence toward which the
Pilgrims aimed their fate, the sentence of arrival and success, Bradford turned toward the field of language itself. In doing so, he
recognized the fallacies of an exploratory prose, the wrong assumption that a word either was an event in its own right, or could
plot out in advance a chain of contingent realities. But he did not
for that reason alone subside into silence. If he left his final two
annals in the history blank, mere headings which seem to announce
the victory of time ("Anno 1647. And Anno 1648." [347]), their
blankness can be seen, too, as a positive insight. It is the record of

his confession that history will always be history, and hence always an account of loss. And it thus points (as does the *Mayflower* list) to an art that is more than historical, a use of the word to find and possess the only abiding terrain of wonder, the human spirit. His study of Hebrew might be described from our viewpoint as the saddest of his returns, a complete renunciation of his American fate. But he was not only going back to the most central of Old World texts. He was defining how one could continue to live in an America which was not the image of one's desired vision, and could do so without abandoning vision altogether. As a timeless record of the spirit, the Bible was more than history. Or it was a history of human longing, and hence applicable to any place or time. Thus Bradford plotted his last voyage:[52]

> Though I am grown aged, yet I have had a longing
> desire, to see with my owne eyes, somthing of that most
> ancient language, and holy tongue, in which the Law,
> and oracles of God were write; and in which God,
> and angels, spake to the holy patriarks of old
> time; and what names were given to things
> from the creation. And though I cannot
> attaine to much herein, yet I am refresh-
> ed, to have seen some glimpse hereof;
> (as Moyses saw the land of Ca-
> nan a farr off) My aime and
> desire is, to see how the words
> and phrases lye in the
> holy texte; and to
> discerne somewhat
> of the same,
> for my owne
> contente.

❦ CONCLUSION ❦

IT WOULD BE GOOD TO REST CONTENT WITH WILLIAM BRADFORD'S own contentment in 1650, and hence to let the trailing off of his words speak for other things left unsaid here. But several reasons prompt me to carry on the present discourse a bit longer. The first, and perhaps most important, involves a rather simple point which ought to be almost self-evident by now: it is that the kind of recognition which we have seen in Bradford, though sharpened in his case by the high articulation of Pilgrim ideals, was in no essential way confined to the New England experience. If the preceding chapters share any continuing assumption about the nature of an "Americanizing" process, that assumption is an inclusive one. I cannot support the arguments of various recent writers who would see the Pilgrim and Puritan plots (both announced and endured) as the definitive, or even predominant, means by which American identity and nationhood were achieved.[1] This kind of argument is the latest in a chain of mythologizing efforts which I mentioned in my introduction. It attempts to unify American life by locating *the* beginning point of a single converging action, and then by interpreting subsequent experience (or rather those parts of it which may be made to fit the assumed plot) in light of that presumably central action. On the contrary, I would urge far more caution in such matters, in part because we traditionally leave out far too much in asserting our own schemes over the past. People and events that depart from the center (or never were there in the first place) are made to seem less important by our exclusionary rhetoric.

Still, I do not think that we should abandon the effort to delineate larger unities in national life—for though history and culture are neither wholly determined nor wholly determinative, they are obviously patterned, plotted, even designed. To persevere in such an effort, however, we must find new ways of organizing the diverse materials and facts of New World experience. We might look at Bradford, for instance, not as one of the "Pilgrim Fathers" or "New England Worthies" in whom can be located the successful rise of communal vision in the West, but rather as a figure of loss whose own isolation—perceived and actual—is far more suggestive

179

of the multiplicity of American life, the difficulty of its order. His marginal stance thus can be seen as a link between him and those very individuals and groups that threatened him and his ideal: the native tribes, the secular settlers like Morton or Weston, the presumed schismatics like Roger Williams, Anne Hutchinson, and the early Quakers.[2] A record of dissension and dissent, *Of Plymouth Plantation* suggests by its own thicket of argumentation that the center of American social existence is more often a point of departure than convergence. If we believe Bradford, who struggles to make his particular vision the "right" one, we may think that public life in Plymouth colony was organized by a split between the faithful and the faithless. Yet even Bradford, whose humanity overcomes his sectarianism, recognizes that the latter often were organized by a separate, exclusive faith, that the New World history which he was writing was bound to become an account of competing views so diverse in its texture that the mere mention of outsiders might give them a certain verbal legitimacy. Like Edward Hayes, he would like to counterpoint the desired comedy of his own view to the deserved tragedy which has overtaken its opposite. In fact, however, these aesthetic designs are reversed in his book. And the larger aesthetic unity which *Of Plymouth Plantation* creates is born from an inadvertant principle of opposition that is much less neat and soothing: for opposition itself is what organizes Bradford's prose. By dealing at such length with those people and forces that he would prefer to leave out altogether (as he would prefer to see them left out of Plymouth), Bradford suggests the typical untidiness of both early American writing and the life that writing reflects.

But what is untidy from one perspective is richly ordered from another. Bradford reveals this order unintentionally, for his text delivers us (as does Winthrop's *Journal*) into the heart of a literature of controversy which thrived in New England and the other colonial regions. *Of Plymouth Plantation* thus reminds us that the New World library often has been a place of Swiftian warfare. And Bradford's book urges us in this sense to review the texts with which it competes, which in some cases (such as Thomas Weston's) it actually includes within its pages. Even the alternate vision of New England expressed by Thomas Morton is given a prominent status, which it otherwise might lack, by the fact that both Bradford and Winthrop recognize its existence in their texts. And Roger 180 Williams's thorny attacks on John Cotton and the Bay orthodoxy gain importance from the answers which the centrist writers of Cotton's colony bestowed on them. If praise can be damning, damnation also can be a form of praise, a kind of recognition. What Bradford finally records, beyond his conscious laments and exclusions, is the building of an American community that is defined precisely by such verbal and historical tensions. If this inductive order does not match his own envisioned plot, and hence seems to him a chaos, it nonetheless is an order. It is an order, moreover, that by its attenuation in space and its great rhetorical isolations suggests the given map of early America.

These points become clear when we follow Bradford's own unintended hints and investigate, across the lines of his exclusions, the contrary side of his debates. It is obvious, for instance, that the Nauset settlers of 1644, like those who planted elsewhere on the outlying Plymouth colony lands, had designs of their own which Bradford either omits or distorts in his text so that he can keep their tales marginal to his own. Presumably they would not have characterized their departure as an abandonment, but rather as a fresh discovery—fresh even if ambivalent. By placing his characterization next to their hypothetical one, we might come to see Bradford's endeavor in Plymouth as equally marginal to theirs, as an attempt which seems central largely because of his rhetorical efforts to make it seem so.[3] That Bradford "survives" in such ample and compelling form, while so many other New Englanders do not, indicates how difficult it is to make such comparisons. But we may hope to construct, finally, a literary model which reflects the abundance of centers in New World experience and art, both public and private, rather than any old scheme of cultural dominance.

This new model will point us into the very heart of early New World prose. We must start with a simple premise of multiplicity that makes us skeptical of the tales which survive and respectful of those which do not: for we must recognize the great extent to which American narrative art has been a deeply political endeavor from the beginning, and has used language to enforce a given settlement over others. That black slaves largely were denied access to the means of public statement is an extreme proof of this point.[4] We can locate in the records of less obviously excluded figures, however, some hint of how we are to proceed here. Thus the assaults of Morton and Williams on New England orthodoxy tell us something about the attempt of the orthodox to clear their ground by means of expulsion, as well as something about the attempt of the expelled to answer with their own vision of American potential. It will not do, in other words, to treat these two men solely as incidents in Winthrop's or Bradford's story—as, indeed, few modern readers would be tempted to do. Nor is this relatively simple caution the final one here. When Williams and Morton are understood on their own terms, their art and the worldly position which it encompasses tell us a good deal about those of more orthodox figures like Bradford. Their marginality becomes an indictment of the centers against which they write, but it also becomes a positive sign of what is shared by *both* parties in such disputes. To the extent that Williams and Morton also have imagined a New World, they subvert the exclusive claims of Winthrop and Bradford to the possession of American space, both actual and verbal. All four men thus suggest that one abiding endeavor in our early writing is to constitute the whole of America as a viewpoint. Deeply solipsistic in its later implications, this effort arose from the quite simple fact that at the outset Europe knew about the West only by means of individual experience there, that the letters of a figure like Columbus, for instance, were conflatable with the new lands he had located. "Discovery" was a double concept, since it referred both to the act of finding and to the later act of revealing what had been found.[5] That places and people and events entered the European consciousness largely through language hinted that language might be equivalent to what it signified—a means of controlling whatever reality it contained, even a medium for discoveries detached from any actual world.

Columbus himself, when he wrote his later reports, recognized one corollary of this complex issue: that the multiplication of European viewpoints in America also entailed a multiplying of verbal codifications—each new text an ideal settlement—and hence a vying for grants of Old World power which was rooted in the power of language itself. His last writings accordingly attempt to banish the worthless doers and sayers from his rendered America, as well as to refurbish his own original vision. Like Bradford, he makes us aware even in these attempts that a vast penumbral region lies beyond his personal control, a terrain filled with other travelers with whom his only possible relationship is a competitive one. His loneliness results as much from this fact as from any actual isolation. And his retreat into the verbal realm of Old World "authorities"—when he attempts to prove that Paradise lies some-

where up the Orinoco river—becomes a poignant redefinition of
America, as does Bradford's retreat into the promised land of Hebrew, in wholly inward terms. It is an attempt to clear his verbal
ground of intrusive people and events, to regain his first possession. But it is, at the same time, a radical shift of direction, a pointing of the voyage away from reality. His language in the Jamaica
letter becomes an "alter America," a way of discovering the self as a
world unto itself. If what he has wished for in his historical career
has been denied—and Jamaica is the abiding symbol of its
denial—there remains the possibility of detaching desire from the
places to which it first was attached, and of using the literary forms
invented for describing those actual locales as a metaphor for the
pursuit of desire itself. The final recognition thus emerges: that
one real center in American experience has been the isolated self,
which is given some connection to presumed communities (and
thereby an identity) by its engrossment of America as an elaborate,
even arcane, sign of where it stands and what it means. The most
compelling American literature has at its verbal center figures
whose prime act is a departure (whether actual or rhetorical),
but whose departure is rendered as a deeply resonant and ritualistic
reenactment of the first voyage west. It is precisely by leaving that
our literary heroes and heroines arrive.[6]

Such a literary scheme reflects deeply ambivalent tensions in the
culture which nourishes it. In order to found his own settlement,
Henry Thoreau first must assault the achieved settlement of
America, which "Concord" (actually "Discord") represents. His
positive reenactment of the New World past thus begins with a
lamentation on the lacks of an American present. "Economy" is
both an act of conscious self-exclusion and a suggestion that the
society at large has excluded *itself* from the real promise of a New
World. By becoming an outsider in at least two senses, Thoreau
allows us to see the outsided quality of most American lives that
pass inside the traditional order, the fact that we barely have
reached "the shores of America."[7] Our coastwise condition is a
sad sign of failed imagination, but *Walden* itself does far more than
lament the outlines of a communal failure. It sets out beyond its
opening jeremiad a clear model of discovery as an external and
internal act: an attentiveness to nature, but also a conversion which
makes the self of Thoreau in the book both America and an
explorer of that enriched "terrain." Moreover, by urging in his
"Conclusion" that each of his readers "be a Columbus to whole new   183

continents and worlds within you," he suggests how a new community is to be constituted out of each of our metaphoric departures. Such a community cannot result from common endeavors like the Wilkes exploring expedition, for that grand action "through cold and storm and cannibals" was merely an extension, "in a government ship," of the homeland and home assumptions. Imperial efforts of that sort must be replaced with a turning in toward "the private sea, the Atlantic and Pacific Ocean of one's being alone" (321). For in aloneness, in the fronting of it (which is discovery), lies the only source of a reborn aggregation.

Thoreau himself points us back to the beginning by his rich convocation of older travelers as guides for the present journey. He points us back, too, by the microcosmic strategy announced in his title: America as Walden Pond (as *Walden*), this one small place and the book which explores it the signs of continental possibility. Literal pond, diminutive sea, large "eye" of wonder, reflecting medium of the self, Walden Pond also is a concrete reminder of Thoreau's distant stance as actor and writer, a figure for his rhetorical ground. So, too, the positions of earlier travelers like Williams and Morton indicate how curiously central to the act of imaginative discovery some actual displacement has been in America: Williams making for Narragansett Bay in the dead of winter, going to London in 1643 (seeking and securing a charter, blasting the Bay orthodoxy in *The Bloudy Tenent*), even at sea on his voyage over then, drafting *A Key into the Language of America* "in a rude lumpe" lest he should *"lightly lose"* by his "present absence" from the West the knowledge he had so *"dearely bought"* through his labors there—or Morton, in jail at Boston, in exile on the Isle of Shoals, playing "Jonas" in the "Whales belly" during his forced return to England, writing once he was there his reminder that "hee was a Seperatist amongst the Seperatists" of New England (exile but also dissenter), his book "but a widowes mite" because the "wrong and rapine" he had suffered in New England left him only memories, words, "to bring from thence."[8]

Even more telling are their final positions: for when Thomas Morton returned to New England in 1643, he was forced to leave Plymouth, went to Rhode Island (as so many others who had differences with the orthodox did); then to the Bay, where he spent a full winter in jail, only to be exiled at last to Maine—dying there in 1647 amid the ruins of a grand colony envisioned by Ferdinando 184 Gorges, who died the same year in England amid the ruins of the

English state. "Gorgeana," the intended colony in Maine, marked by its elaborate design, and its failure, Morton's own vision of America: when first founded, the colony had assigned to it forty-three municipal offices to be shared among the mere eighty colonists.[9] Williams, on the other hand, clearly found in Rhode Island a place adequate to his shifting desires, a literal ground which gave strength to his literary battles. But his actual power there never was large, dissent within the plantation ran high, and he himself retreated in his later years, solitary, weak, poor, into the limits of a private ground. Like Peter Stuyvesant in New Netherland, who substituted for that lost colony his quiet farm, the "Bouwerie," Williams exchanged a small and private America—essentially, his own awareness—for an older public one. In a 1670 letter to John Mason of Connecticut, Williams assailed "one of the gods of New England" ("a depraved appetite after the great vanities, dreams and shadows of this vanishing life, great portions of land, land in this wilderness"), and he signified his lasting withdrawal from such a debased worship by recounting his first trials on the way from Salem to Narragansett Bay three decades earlier ("When I was unkindly and unchristianly . . . driven from my house and land and wife and children"), then by hinting at his cure for the New England disease, a cure which surely would not please everyone—but pleasing hardly was his intent in the letter, for if land struggles should destroy his new design for peace or even his old colony, he would remain content that "that which must perish must perish." His contentment would include even the author: "As to myself, in endeavoring after your temporal and spiritual peace"—Mason's, Connecticut's, New England's—"I humbly desire to say, if I perish, I perish. It is but a shadow vanished, a bubble broke, a dream finished. Eternity will pay for all." Clearly, his "land" at this point is wholly inner, discovered as a result of deep inward explorations.[10]

That Williams has a cure in mind, even if he keeps it *there*, suggests that beyond his displaced lament we can find some trace of his old ideals. Like Stuyvesant, he retained in his private retirement the outline of a European dream for public well-being in the West, retained even the language by which that dream first was expressed: "the matter with us," he writes to Mason, "is not about these children's toys of land, meadows, cattle government: but here, all over this colony a great number of weak and distressed souls, scattered, are flying hither from old and New England; the most high and only wise hath in His infinite wisdom provided this country and this corner as a shelter for the poor and persecuted, according to their several persuasions" (232–33). Threatened with a dispossession, he can take unto himself the terms of an original possession, terms verified precisely by the "scattered" state of more recent emigrants. Similarly, Morton reveals in his exiled visions of 1637, if not at the sad end of his New World career, a resilience of hope beyond expulsion. Satirists of Boston and Plymouth, he and Williams both use satire as a means of excluding those other places. And then follows their counterdiscovery, presented in a voice which pretends to speak for America itself (as Winthrop's and Bradford's also do), which by its own energetic, excited conviction buries old schemes while resurrecting their larger designs for a new purpose. It is beside the point that Morton's imagination remained largely literary (his New English Canaan being merely that "modell of a Rich hopefull and very beautifull Country" which his book presents [3]), while Williams already had enacted many of his insights before writing *The Bloudy Tenent* and its sequel. What is crucial is that both writers see satire as a kind of catharsis, a way of making the New World a *tabula rasa* on which some new scripture may be engraved.[11] So, too, Thoreau assails Concord before he leaves for the pond, that latter place close in fact but far in spirit from the village. Like the older reprobates of Puritan design, Thoreau is a debater from the start. And his debate, like theirs, also is necessary only because other travelers have threatened his rights by leaving his vision out of their official American settlement. Those other travelers come to resemble for all three the "snakes" of William Wood, the geological forces of Jefferson, or the "Indian" of John Bartram: impediments across a just and justified path, such outrageously preemptive people must be "banged stoutly" (but now in words) if a farther range of American space and possibility is to be opened up. And it is highly significant here that these white exiles define their stance by engrossing native American life, in varying degrees, into their own viewpoints: the lasses in beaver coats, the language of America, the red face of man. Hence what they fight is not some archetypally New World opponent, but rather an "alien" figure from the heart of European design. For it is often by such a paradoxical inversion of orthodox rhetoric, some alliance between a disaffected white and a stereotypic other, that the solitary Euro-American signifies his or her alienation. Nor does this alliance always remain rhetorical or stereotyped, difficult as 186 true "contact" surely is. The exclusion of one white from the center

of white order converts the marginal fate of nonwhites into the
source of a newly envisioned community, a congregation of the
dispersed and lost. Hence Henry Thoreau surveys the ruins of that
old town near Walden Pond, which housed the slaves of Concord
"gentlemen," and he finds there an adequate sign of his own effort
at conscious (and "free") separation.[12]

A region of high vocability from its start, New England obviously
can provide many examples of these patterns in life and art. But, as
I have stated already, they are by no means peculiar to the extreme
Northeast. John Smith's *Generall Historie,* for instance, records less
the actual events of Virginia (its main subject, though it also deals
with New England and the Bermudas) than a clash of views and
language about that difficult topic. An anthology of writings by
various hands, the book is larger than Smith's vision of it, even
though he attempts to make the collection of documents present
his personal understanding. Like Bradford's text, which also
gathers the scripts of other colonial figures, Smith's *Historie* reminds us that United States society—if we insist on tracing it that
far back—began when two people of different views were placed so
close to one another that their variant perspectives issued into a
public debate. The form of Smith's book thus reflects and codifies
one important form of New World experience. Captain Smith cannot tell the story he might like to, a tale of Virginian growth and
promise, because too many other voices intrude on his. Those
other voices not only have their own tales to tell, thus interrupting
the flow of Smith's prose—they also undercut, with some subtlety,
Smith's apparent assumption that the unity of English endeavor
(should it ever be achieved) ought to be embodied in a unified
account. If his book as he presents it seems to sprawl, that very
quality of its shape is significant of its meaning.

Important, too, is the fact that Smith now can operate on Virginia, either as an actual place or a literary subject, only from the
distance of his private exile. Excluded from "the Stage" on which
English intentions with regard to America must be "acted," he occupies throughout an extreme ground which, ironically enough, is
England itself.[13] He still longs to direct the ongoing (if farcical)
American play, and his history thus attempts to show how poorly
others have done there, as well as how well he might do if given
another chance. Aimed at the powers in London, the book thus
turns Smith's position there into an asset, exiled as he is. It is close   187

and chatty, a confidential report which seems to lessen the distance between author and audience in order to gain Smith more power over the distance itself. But when we reverse the polarities, thinking of power less as an Old World grant than a New World fact, Smith's great separation from America becomes a sign of his powerlessness there. His stance is allied to Bradford's at the "end," even though Bradford actually is in America. This is not to say that Smith's "Virginia" also is an "ancient mother," for Smith's familial rhetoric (like his imperial vision) is conjugal rather than generational: his America is more like a jilted fiancée, left at the altar of a future settlement by his own forced eviction. Yet there is in Smith, as in Bradford, a sense of impotence that transcends such important differences. That feeling in both of them is complexly personal and public at once. Unable to make history, as Bradford is unable to change it, Smith is the Fisher King of an American domain who embodies in his own condition the ruin of a colonial ideal.[14] That the world over which each man's ideal was asserted still survives (and, despite the problems, still is a place of abundant promise for others if not for them) suggests that the wasteland is more truly inner than outer: a feeling of wasted effort and skill and vision on the actor-authors' part, a perception that they have been elbowed out of their history, both actual and literary, by usurping "others."

This syncopation between private and public fate increases the irony of each man's condition. Smith tries very hard, of course, to implicate Virginia's downfall in his own, and hence to make private tragedy public as well. He does so not only by displaying the varied disasters which ensued on his departure in 1609, but also by linking himself in a more positive manner with the true destiny of English settlement in the colony. When he prints as the last section of his Virginia text a set of seven questions addressed to him by the King's "Commissioners for the Reformation of Virginia," he is implying that he is the one person to answer those questions—that he is a Virginia voice, or rather *the* Virginia voice, in England. To re-form the colony will be to form it once again in Smith's image: "Idlenesse and carelesnesse," he opines in his first answer, "brought all I did in three yeeres in six moneths to nothing," and the present task is to reverse this reversal, to regain and extend his own earlier transformations (165). Something-to-nothing hardly is the right gloss for a New World history, or an Old World heroical attempt.

Like the official charge of Diron d'Artaguiette for the survey of
Louisiana, or even the French queries passed on to Jefferson dur-

ing the Revolution, the seven questions given to Smith help
establish his New World status by suggesting that America is an
entity encompassed by his own awareness. Smith himself extends
this hint. His very last words on the colony portray the writing of its
history as itself a kinetic act, a means of repossession: "Thus far I
have travelled in this Wildernesse of *Virginia,*" he states, undercutting the nostalgic quality of his metaphor by making the text as
subject to future troubles as Virginia itself has been to past ones:
"Thus far I have travelled in this Wildernesse of *Virginia,* not being
ignorant for all my paines this discourse will be wrested, tossed and
turned as many waies as there is leaves; that I have writ too much of
some, too little of others, and many such like objections." As for the
possible (or rather certain) objectors, "Ah! were these my accusers
but to change cases and places with me but 2. yeeres, or till they had
done but so much as I, it may be they would judge more charitably
of my imperfections." And, as for Smith himself, the end is like a
real farewell rather than a fresh start: "But here I must leave all to
the triall of time, both my selfe, Virginia's preparations, proceedings and good events, praying to that great God the protector of all
goodnesse to send them as good successe as the goodnesse of the
action and Country deserveth, and my heart desireth" (168).
Linked inextricably even in these last words, man and country ("my
selfe, Virginia"; "deserveth . . . desireth") become versions of each
other. The great distance which actually severs them is less important than the inward need for continuing intimacy—a need fulfilled
by the *Historie* itself, with all its jars and dissensions. Like John
White, whose 1590 account of Roanoke he quotes extensively at the
start of his book, Smith adopts the position of a banished voyager
whose will still points west, who might wish to renew his Western
attempt—indeed, he includes a plan for doing so earlier in the
book—but who must rest content with the recognition of his parting, his merely figurative presence "there."

And, like Bradford, Smith at the last can inventory only his lacks,
the little tangible evidence he has that so much of his life and
energy has gone into Virginia (and into New England): "Thus
these nineteene years I have here and there"—that is, in England
and America—"not spared any thing according to my abilitie, nor
the best advice I could, to perswade how those strange miracles of
misery might have been prevented, which lamentable experience
plainly taught me of necessity must insue, but few would beleeve
me till now too deerely they have paid for it. Wherefore hitherto I   189

have rather left all then undertake impossibilities, or any more such costly taskes at such chargeable rates: for in neither of those two Countries have I one foot of Land, nor the very house I builded, nor the ground I digged with my owne hands, nor ever any content or satisfaction at all, and though I see ordinarily those two Countries shared before me by them that neither have them nor knowes them, but by my descriptions: Yet that doth not so much trouble me, as to heare and see those contentions and divisions which will hazard if not ruine the prosperitie of *Virginia,* if present remedy bee not found, as they have hindred many hundreds, who would have beene there ere now, and makes them yet that are willing to stand in a demurre" (164). If he can go on from this, can offer in his next paragraph to assume once more the labor of setting the colony right, he has reached here in another sense the true end of his American career: a displaced discoverer, unhoused and unlanded in the land he first helped to plant for England (and by his words as well as his deeds), he has remaining to himself now simply the resources of language, and the community of those other willing travelers who, like him, stand back in the Old World to marvel at New World disorder. Virginia is left to him only as a literary topic (indeed, as a book), and a sign of his now uncontingent desire.

If Smith's work is not a full-fledged New England jeremiad replete with a sense of redemptive history, neither is it simply a "dystopian satire."[15] Like a good many texts from the South and the middle colonies, it can be linked to the settlement records of New England without fear of violating literary categories. Regardless of the different sources from which disillusionment may have come in Massachusetts or Virginia, in New York or South Carolina, what endures as a striking fact of our earliest writings is this very presence of so much letdown and disagreement and isolation, as well as a tendency for any offered corrective (and the visionary who proposes it) to be identified with that hopeful New World which, obscured as it may be at present, may yet be rediscovered. Deeply communal in their concerns and claims, such lamenting schemes suggest the degree to which a strong social theme permeates colonial prose, that theme making it colonial in purpose as well as in period. At the same time, however, we can trace in these documents a recurring paradox, an apprehension sometimes conscious and sometimes hidden that any social vision developed in a colonizing culture spread over such wide terrain is likely to be personal in origin if not in intent. Like the voices of Smith or Bradford,

each voice in these works is a center struggling for power, excluded in its own right but willing to exclude others, if need be, to
fortify its own transcendent claims. The final source of authority
here is the self as a vehicle of discovery and exploration, as a means
by which is revealed some better New World beyond the current
clutter of debate and disaffection. Personal utterance is justified, in
other words, by the pretense that it is not personal at all, that it has
been displaced onto the speaker from some actual or conceptual
New World. The text is a call for return to an old American plot—a
return that, like the old plot itself, points into the future. The
individual writer can assault some American situation because he
or she has compared it to the ideal order of Western life, and hence
can view the present as a devolution, a potential or actual ruin of
original design.

Such a pattern touches most issues and all locales. Whether we
look at Patrick Tailfer's shrewd assault on James Oglethorpe and the
Georgia trustees in 1741 (and at Benjamin Martyn's counterassault
on Tailfer's catalog of ruins); or at Samuel Sewall's impassioned
Caveat Emptor! to slaveholders in 1700 (at John Saffin's self-
serving response, too, and Cotton Mather's outrageously pious defenses of slavery)—or at a hundred similar pairs of documents, and
a hundred singular texts—we can define a common ground of
argument within each case, and within the general literary situation.[16] That ground is the rhetorical image of a literal space in
which some American "action" takes shape, the verbal reflection of
a point at which Old World hopes or designs and New World
realities meet. Surrounded by isolated viewpoints and voices, that
verbal ground also reflects a more figurative but still actual American place—a community which is made up of separate declama-
tions and exhortations that have their center in a shared sense of
the need for some consensus about the proper script of a Western
action. But, more suggestively, the debates which occur across this
verbal space themselves compose a script of actual experience. A
desire for communal agreement, for a scheme that will bind together countless smaller visions and thus achieve a settlement of all
competing views—a return to the explorer's universe, where word
is deed, where the grammar of statement also is the order of
events—is the motive force behind even some of the most disil-
lusioned American lamentations. When an old plot has failed, its
postulated community unrealized or lost, those who describe its
failure indicate by their posture and purpose both the reason for   191

defeat and the originally high expectation of success. Settlers and explorers at once, these figures combine in their own awareness the recognition of a tragic or ironic reality with the hope for Western comedy. For to admit defeat without hesitation would be to undermine not simply a single enterprise but a whole pattern of understanding as well, a long and difficult movement of the European mind away from its cushioning and inherently "significant" world. It would be an acceptance of the old "void," an embrace of silence, a seemingly perverse welcome to oblivion. If doom is an appropriate American emotion, it belongs to those who have belied (or who now threaten) the dream—and thus must be viewed as inadequate to the place they have betrayed. Any remaining hope, on the other hand, is to be attached to the speaker's present scheme for reformation. Whether it is inclusive or exclusive, that scheme opens up beyond the current disorder a farther New World amenable to those who are proper to its discovery, who can remake discovery itself out of an old discontent.[17]

The voices of debate in early America help us to evoke the tangle of different interests and understandings which characterizes—as modern nostalgia will not often admit—the history of so many settled regions. Yet the survival of earlier styles in these documents suggests a certain accumulating force in New World prose, an endurance of wonder beyond any disappointment. This accumulation is part of a larger sophisticating process by which the methods of literal description or narration were transformed into more widely usable prose strategies.[18] At the end of this process, in a literary sense, lies a book like *Walden.* But literature was not the sole beneficiary here, though the concern of writers like Thoreau with patterns of language (and with America as place and topic) makes the impact on literature more readily apparent.[19] Equally important, if also harder to define, is the effect which such a transformation had on the very texture of American language, and particularly on those structures of social speech which are prime vehicles of community. Whereas an actual traveler might use the devices examined in this study to articulate feelings and plans connected with some given terrain, the devices also developed into an elaborate body of native techniques for talking about the metaphoric landscape of American life. Likewise, since the literal modes involved a view of experience, not just of language, their sophistication can be traced in later ideas and institutions and cultural forms,

as well as in the patterns of national expression.

We have already seen in the case of exploratory rhetoric how a language invented for dealing with quite specific projects gradually emerged as a medium for dispersed and generalized sentiments about the whole land or the society which pretended (in part through these very verbal means) to its possession. When Benjamin Franklin wrote in *The Internal State of America* that "the great business of the Continent is Agriculture," he was demonstrating a simple version of this shift, as Calvin Coolidge was when he unknowingly imitated Franklin by asserting that "the chief business of the American people is business"—which appears to be a tautology, but was intended as a pun.[20] Attributing to a large region and a large population a coherently single plot, both men were defining an America in which everybody supposedly could participate. Through participation individuals would become a nation—or perhaps would signalize, in Coolidge's case, their prior community. The actual content of each definition, to be sure, suggests the tremendous shifts in economic life and social structure which came about in the years intervening between Franklin's era and that of Coolidge. But we must note, too, that a formal pattern endured throughout that long period, that it still seemed possible in the 1920s to make some such encompassing comment. Whether as place or as nation, America seemed capable of an engrossing and formulaic predication: both men could entail in one sentence millions of lives which were thought to repeat it and hence give it validity. Even F. J. Turner's theory of cultural-economic stages, from the preagricultural to the industrial, was based on a similar conception: each discrete phase of American settlement fed into later ones, and thus gave them validity. What bound those phases together in Turner's theory was a supposedly common effort at exploring the potential uses of America.

This expansion of exploratory language from a local to a continental level partly resulted from the accumulation of locales into larger geographical, social, and intellectual entities. The thin line of Dutch settlement up the Hudson had become, by 1800, a series of English counties and then an American "state." Farther west, the vast area first included in Tryon county was being cut up into several new units, each of them extending the bounds of government and law away from the Hudson and giving real substance to the old, largely verbal, claims of white possession. Likewise, though John Smith named New England before the Pilgrims landed at Plymouth, that region did not exist as an actual narrative or descriptive "subject" until after about 1650, by which time the pattern

193

of settlement had been established over a wide terrain.[21] The first histories of that postulated region, written almost exclusively by members of orthodox minorities, took "New England" as their subject only by means of a patent fiction. If William Bradford was more honest in this regard, choosing as a title for his work a modest phrase accurate to his subject, Nathaniel Morton pretended to narrate in his *New England's Memorial* (1669)—based in large part on Bradford's manuscript—a more inclusive subject than he actually did. His pretense was rooted in the explorer's central theme, the notion that small beginnings lead by a process of magical change into a grand achievement, and that the name is essentially determinative of the thing: for at Plymouth, Morton declares, God planted "a vine" which since 1620 has taken "deep root, and ... filled the land; so that it hath sent forth its boughs to the sea and its branches to the river."[22] Hence the record of one small plantation implicates the history of a far larger area; the center of Morton's affection becomes the center of a regional life which Bradford himself came to understand as a more problematic and dispersed entity—the very spread of settlement a sign of weakness, a reminder that the original center has been lost.

To the extent that the explorer's language allowed such writers as Morton to elevate smaller facts into transcendent wholes, it became the foundation for a centralizing and optimistic structure in American historiography and American thought. The Revolutionary period made this structure truly national for the first time. Political pamphleteers and journalists evoked by a series of simplified narrative models a sense of American experience as a converging action, a single plot which included all the phases of separate colonial endeavors and thus pointed to the present moment as the crisis of New World history. The perception of a shared threat in the 1760s and 1770s led colonial apologists to invent a common past which bridged the obvious differences of regional life. When the break with England seemed inevitable, past and present merged into a vision of future-history which was straight from the explorer's rhetorical universe: Thomas Paine's assertion in *Common Sense* (1776), "Now is the seedtime of continental union, faith, and honor," clearly suggested, for instance, that a defense of the achieved order also was an extension of that order into the spatial-temporal domain which was to be created and defined by resistance to England.[23]

194   As Paine's own title indicates, much of the effort of the apologists

was directed at the creation of a common viewpoint among the dispersed colonists. And to this purpose a shared sense of America's past and future was crucial. Paine's most unequivocal call in *Common Sense* was less for action than deliberation, or rather for deliberation itself as a kind of action. The real challenge delivered by the pamphlet to each reader was to envision America as a separate and unified entity of which the reader was an organic part, and hence to understand that the smallest act of the present would lead to enormous consequences for posterity. His own plot of the American past ("This new world hath been the asylum for the persecuted lovers of civil and religious liberty from *every part* of Europe" [21]) was designed to demonstrate that the unnatural dominance of a small island over a vast continent was historically wrong as well as logically absurd—since to the denial of geographical reality was added a denial of the mixed sources of American immigration. But that neat formula of the colonial past also served another purpose, for it suggested that America had been the scene of a single continental action, one which was unified in plot and motive throughout its reaches. The whole weight of Paine's forensic assault on monarchy, and on English government and its pretensions over America in particular, thus pushed onward to his real concern, the creation of "continental minds" (22) which now had the power to plot out a grand future for America.[24]

That plot would continue the best meaning of the New World into an era which even now was beginning: "expelled" from Asia and Africa, become a "stranger" in Europe, freedom itself was a wanderer for whom America could provide a home—"O receive the fugitive," Paine urged, "and prepare in time an asylum for mankind" (34). To resist England, in other words, was not to depart from the past but rather to uphold America's most ancient role in the world: for had not "the design of heaven" so arranged human history that "the Reformation was preceded by the discovery of America, as if the Almighty graciously meant to open a sanctuary to the persecuted in future years, when home should afford neither friendship nor safety" (23)? A recent immigrant himself, Paine was writing his own story here; the American past, his private experience, and the present crisis all were conflated into one simple tale. But he was writing as well an orthodox record of the colonial effort, an exploration of history which also mapped out the time to come. The beginning point of Old World involvement in the West thus was implicit in the current disorder. Indeed, it was   195 more than implicit, since from the start God's plot had been working toward this moment. Resistance to the counterplot of English tyranny was obedience to God; it also was an act which would insure the continued existence of America, and thus would reaffirm the glorious Discovery and what it meant. Paine's geographical argument ("England and America ... belong to different systems. England to Europe: America to itself" [26]) was an attempt to sever the two countries, but it was not in essence an isolationist gesture. America's "system" was more than self-reflexive, since it included an abiding connection to all of the Old World, to the long drift of European intention to the West. The true constituency of America thus was the community of the oppressed wherever its members were located. And that community was spread across time as well as space, both of its components intimately involved in the present debate. The current possessors of America had to act for a cast far larger than themselves; they had to verify the burden of history and thereby set the pattern of a new order. Displaced by Paine's rhetoric (as well as by recent events) from the world of strictly English identity, the colonists were delivered by such expansive and visionary arguments into a new being which was the psychological analogue of their first literal departure. Deliberation was so necessary because the present was a center to vast outlying regions, the starting point of a metaphoric but still venturesome journey. If the colonists did not understand the extent of their ideal nation, Paine argued by a shrewd inversion of the "small beginnings" theme, each tiny flaw in their behavior would expand enormously in future times: "The least fracture now will be like a name engraved with the point of a pin on the tender rind of a young oak; the word would enlarge with the tree, and posterity read it in full grown characters" (19). Though it was an organic whole, the plot of American life was only now being articulated. Those who doubted its almost mystical continuity might place themselves in the future, and thereby look back to their own crucial moment: "In order to discover the line of our duty rightly, we should take our children in our hand, and fix our station a few years farther into life; that eminence will present a prospect which a few present fears and prejudices conceal from our sight" (23–24). Providing both a prospect and a retrospect, for the two directions merge here, this aloof survey of America would make clear the "line" of an enduring New World action, and thus would allow

those taking part in it to map out exactly what needed to be done.

By implication, Paine occupied throughout *Common Sense* some such eminence. It was his rhetorical and emotional position. And his advice to his audience, an audience which his own words in large part created, was to possess the New World which he had imagined, which others might imagine by sharing his assumptions. "'TIS TIME TO PART," he stated (23), indicating by his metaphor of departure that the troubles with England might be solved by a political reenactment of the oldest American ritual. Indeed, the task was to accept the consequences of that first parting long before—the social effect of spatial truths. Reconciliation was geographically, as well as morally, impossible: to seek a rapprochement with England was to reverse the inevitable progress of New World action, and therefore to abandon America. "Reconciliation and ruin are nearly related" (29), he asserted in a telling paradox: for ruin was not now, as it had been throughout the colonial period, a product of attenuation across the sea. On the contrary, the structure of community now was implanted here, and to submit to foreign power by reforming the old lines of connection would undermine what had been built with such difficulty in the settlement of the West—would unsettle, rend and deracinate, the cleared ground of American identity.[25] The continental mind was self-sufficient; power was an American fact which awaited only "an open and determined DECLARATION FOR INDEPENDENCE" (43). That the document produced soon afterwards by the Continental Congress eventually came to be known as the *Declaration of Independence* (not "for") suggests that Paine's call was answered, in this most famous letter ever sent from the New World to the Old, by a recognition of evident spatial and political realities, rather than an argument in defense of American belief. For future generations, "independence" (not the rhetorical assertion of it) became the prime fact of Paine's "seedtime."

Paine's tract illuminates a central feature of the Revolutionary debate. Nothing reveals the contemporary political atmosphere better than his own form of address, the very evident sense that the colonists were speaking to and of themselves as they never before had done. Everything then said, to be sure, was said with the clear recognition that England was listening. But the crucial question taken up in pamphlet after pamphlet was the issue of American identity—the English connection being only one aspect of this larger question. And in the process of dealing with such an issue there was constituted a New World audience of a size which had   197 not existed earlier. Moreover, that audience was manipulated (in the best sense) by tropes and themes drawn from something more than the body of Whig opinion to which frequent recourse was had by the apologists. If America by its distance from London (as "Scotus Americanus" opined in 1773) was a refuge for old British liberties, it also was to be defined in more truly native terms. The *translatio* theme allowed for a conciliation between conservative and native arguments which was often exploited. Yet what seems most striking in Revolutionary debates is the attempt to discover a way of speaking, a language and an occasion for its use, which itself marks the growing split between Old World and New. For that purpose, on the patriot side at least, nothing proved more effective than the strategies exploited by Paine's *Common Sense*, strategies of definition adopted from the older and less consciously American reports on the prospects of a New World career. Instead of organizing America in the light of European categories, as it first had done, Old World language now became a means for setting the hemispheres apart, for closing the West to Eastern intent.

The imagination of American nationhood thus was itself an exploratory act. And we might trace in later times the surprisingly broad legacy of the explorer's habitual speech in the United States. Topics as diverse as American communalism and utopianism, real-estate speculation, the "success" syndrome and its various narrative reflections, industrial development and the industrial ethos, urban planning (and urban renewal), the voluntary association movement, even the idea that an individual American life, like the continent itself, is a thing of infinite capability—all these diverse strands of national life show the strong marks of the explorer's prospective gaze. More abstractly, we might note that this figure's portrayal of a literal New World scene as the stuff of a thousand imagined attributions has become the basis of an American tendency to view reality as largely passive to its beholder, as something given shape by our own will. And, recalling that an optimism like Paine's in 1776 was born in the midst of considerable uncertainty, even despair, we might want to follow out the indirect connections between his own "seedtime" and various later epochs of national reform, discontentment, and reevaluation. That the *Declaration of Independence* itself has become a model for American dissent suggests the directions to be pursued here.[26]

This last topic verges, however, on another tradition in American

life, one more clearly indebted to the difficult speech of the settler.
Paine's own life should remind us of how tenuous the new community of 1776 proved, how exclusionary it had been even in the time
of its formulation. A letter he wrote to George Washington in July
1796, sent from Paris while Paine was recovering there from imprisonment and near-death, provides a sober balance to his high
hopes twenty years earlier. Acridly personal in its attack on
Washington—whom Paine had supported staunchly in his *Crisis*
papers during the war, but who he thought had abandoned him,
and American principles, later—Paine's letter is a complex document full of disillusionment, self-pity, and lamentation over the
nation from which he himself was absent. It incorporates, apropos
of this last topic, part of another letter which Paine had written to
"a female literary correspondent (a native of New York)" around
1790. In the earlier letter, Paine tells Washington, he had recorded
the result of his attempt at that moment "to ramble into the wilderness of imagination, and to anticipate what might hereafter be the
condition of America." But that exploration, so redolent of *Common
Sense*, hardly is cheering. Founded on the *translatio* figure, it pushes
far beyond that moment of apotheosis which supposedly lay in the
American future, envisioning instead a New World which has lost
its bright promise. The "rise" of empires implicates their fall,
wherever they may be located:

> *A thousand years hence (for I must indulge a few thoughts),
> perhaps in less, America may be what Europe now is. The inno-
> cence of her character, that won the hearts of all nations in her
> favor, may sound like a romance and her inimitable virtue as if it
> had never been. The ruin of that liberty which thousands bled for
> or struggled to obtain may just furnish materials for a village tale or
> extort a sigh from rustic sensibility, whilst the fashionable of that
> day, enveloped in dissipation, shall deride the principle and deny
> the fact.*
>
> *When we contemplate the fall of empires and the extinction of
> the nations of the Ancient World, we see but little to excite our
> regret than the mouldering ruins of pompous palaces, magnificent
> museums, lofty pyramids and walls and towers of the most costly
> workmanship; but when the empire of America shall fall, the sub-
> ject for contemplative sorrow will be infinitely greater than
> crumbling brass and marble can inspire. It will not then be said,
> here stood a temple of vast antiquity; here rose a babel of invisible
> height; or there a palace of sumptuous extravagance; but here, Ah,
> painful thought! the noblest work of human wisdom, the grandest*

scene of human glory, the fair cause of Freedom rose and fell. Read this, and then ask if I forget America. (390–91)

Freed by the Revolution from transatlantic connections, America had become a world unto itself. But to be such an entity was to enter into a process of human history which was sadly uniform in all its multiple enactments—which was especially poignant in the American instance because of the high original hopes attached to America's fate, hopes which seemed to set it apart in time as in space. Paine's rhetoric in this sense is dead-center on an abiding New World melancholy, a feeling of premature ruin dictated by the very futurism of exploratory arts. To imagine one future was to invoke a line of speculation which every Old World example pushed to an extreme conclusion, which the ruins of Amerindian culture, both human and monumental, brought uncomfortably close to home.[27] As an act of temporal surveying, exploration thus could lead beyond the magic of transformation to a scene of imagined defeat, a "wilderness" rather than an "eminence." The arc of transcendent expectation finally pointed back to the historical world from which it had at first departed. "Romance" would become a category of dim remembrances, no longer a quality of projected national experience. The glorious retrospect called for by Nathaniel Ames from those who would live in the times of which he could only dream would become an inventory of lost messages, bewildered intents, waylaid travelers.

Paine's curiously personal note—"Read this, and then ask if I forget America"—suggests the future fate of this one great imaginer, whose return to the United States during the presidency of Jefferson was punctuated by raucous public assaults and, in Jefferson's case at least, warmly private reception. That Paine afterwards was denied the vote in Westchester—denied even in death a resting place in sacred ground—indicates how much internal dissension had been aroused in the nation since this architect of its future departed for Europe, the other revolution there, and, eventually, the Bastille. Nor were these exclusions the last. For when Paine's old opponent William Cobbett had the pamphleteer's body dug up from its American grave (he wanted to signify his own change of political heart by returning the man of *Common Sense* to England), the bones were disinterred only to be lost at some later time, their unknown fate an apt reminder of Paine's earthly displacements. Paine's closing comment in the 1790 text, an attestation of his internalized America, in fact points back to the start of that letter, where he apparently sought to answer his "female corre-

spondent's" report that his friends in the New World could not "be
reconciled to the idea," as Paine repeated it, "of my abandoning
America." Indeed he had not abandoned it: "I had rather see my
horse Button eating the grass of Bordentown or Morrisania than
see all the pomp and show of Europe," he countered, the very
concreteness of his imagery suggesting the intense feeling behind
the comment (390).

In fact, America had abandoned Paine and the vision for which
he spoke so eloquently. But his last loneliness should be seen less as
a personal tragedy than as a sign of those multiple exclusions by
which, almost from the start, any envisioned or described New
World community has been maintained. His case seems particularly touching because his labors in the cause of the Revolution
were so obvious and public. Yet his own settlement narrative (for
what else is the story of his life?) can recall to us those of countless
other marginal figures, men and women whose hidden labors
either supported communities and individuals more vocal than
themselves, or sought an articulation of New World life too sharply
digressive from the main lines of narrative recollection for inclusion in centrist memory. Theirs were the traveler's tales that never
did get told, or were told in such a garbled and self-serving form by
others that a sensible reconstruction of them is almost impossible.
Servants of a comic fate (and a comic story) bequeathed by raw
power to their opponents, these figures of loss remain as a permanent reminder of the ruin which contemporary America entailed
—a ruin which no far-future of the imagination needed to
suggest even in Paine's day, since it was visible all around the landscape of Revolution and national projection.

We must think particularly of the slaves in this regard, though
also of victims who suffered from less physical and less conscious
subordination—the poor, the women, the Loyalists of 1776, the
bond-servants, the lesser breeds within the law of centrist superiority. And we must think, too, of the American natives, who more
than any other group were so clearly excluded in act and word
from the start. Yet to think of these dispersed and separate groups,
or of individuals within them, should not become an exercise of
pity or sentiment over their own lamentations. Lament and protest
they certainly did, and rise in rebellion as well. But we can locate in
their heroic endurance, where that trait could be expressed
through the multiple schemes of extermination or silence invented for their control, a certain gift for discovery—for taking
on amid the troubles caused them by others the task of ar-

ticulating—as slave society did within slaveholder order, or as Indian cultures did within the humiliation of accumulating defeats—another imagination of what the New World might offer or mean. Calling those in control on their own most cherished assumption—that America finally signified what any person seeing it wished it to signify—such groups and individuals have maintained almost from the beginning a distant stance which shifts our own attention, hopefully at least, away from the centers of vocalized memory and toward the center of a large, diverse, and complex order. Down that difficult road, finally, lies the New World which still awaits discovery.

The model of understanding which might lead us there is provided, appropriately enough, by Benjamin Franklin—for we enter here a terrain of peculiar difficulty, an America of layered ideas and speech. Franklin's *Remarks Concerning the Savages of America* (1784) opens with a Montaignesque renunciation of its own title, a quarrel with the very language of Euro-American understanding: "Savages we call them, because their Manners differ from ours, which we think the Perfection of Civility; they think the same of theirs." And it goes on to detail, in its account of "A Swedish Minister" who visited "the Susquehanah Indians" and "made a Sermon to them, acquainting them with the principal historical Facts on which our Religion is founded," a model of other historical facts—as well as a more hopeful paradigm of future relations between the races and their respective points of departure. The minister's facts ("such as the Fall of our first Parents by eating an Apple, the coming of Christ to repair the Mischief, his Miracles and Suffering, &c.") were listened to with more respectful attention by the natives than Franklin himself accords them in his own summary. "When he had finished," Franklin notes,

> an Indian Orator stood up to thank him. "What you have told us," says he, "is all very good. It is indeed bad to eat Apples. It is better to make them all into Cyder. We are much oblig'd by your kindness in coming so far, to tell us these Things which you have heard from your Mothers. In return, I will tell you some of those we have heard from ours. In the Beginning, our Fathers had only the Flesh of Animals to subsist on; and if their Hunting was unsuccessful, they were starving. Two of our young Hunters, having kill'd a Deer, made a Fire in the Woods to broil some Part of it. When they were about to satisfy their Hunger, they beheld a beautiful young Woman descend from the Clouds, and seat herself on that Hill,

which you see yonder among the Blue Mountains. They said to each other, it is a Spirit that has smelt our broiling Venison, and wishes to eat of it; let us offer some to her. They presented her with the Tongue; she was pleas'd with the Taste of it, and said, 'Your kindness shall be rewarded; come to this Place after thirteen Moons, and you shall find something that will be of great Benefit in nourishing you and your Children to the latest Generation.' They did so, and, to their Surprise, found Plants they had never seen before; but which, from that ancient time, have been constantly cultivated among us, to our great Advantage. Where her right Hand had touched the Ground, they found Maize; where her left hand had touch'd it, they found Kidney-Beans; and where her Backside had sat on it, they found Tobacco." The good Missionary, disgusted with this idle Tale, said, "What I delivered to you were sacred Truths; but what you tell me is mere Fable, Fiction, and Falshood." The Indian, offended, reply'd, "My brother, it seems your Friends have not done you Justice in your Education; they have not well instructed you in the Rules of Common Civility. You saw that we, who understand and practise those Rules, believ'd all your stories; why do you refuse to believe ours?"[28]

Almost an allegorical traveler, Franklin's missionary reveals at this frontier of separate faiths the persistent inattention of his cultural world to what might be learned, or at least observed, beyond the boundaries of familiar Old World order. Perhaps as a sign of the difficulties endemic to any exchange across such well-defended boundaries, the Indian speaker himself has missed the "point" of his visitor. Yet he at least has listened, and has replaced judgment with a curiosity which allows him to make some sense, however partial, of what he has heard. We may suspect, in fact, that the sense he has made of the missionary's stories makes too much sense to the missionary himself—that it points out absurdities in Christian dogma, and hence causes the latter's vitriolic reaction. Indeed, that the Indian views his own message as a "story" suggests some final stance of undefensive relativity—a ground of "Common Civility"—which Old World religionists, and Europeans generally, well might emulate. For, in the end, America has been a series of competing stories told by figures who ought to have seen their community precisely in their parallel efforts at narrative persuasion, in their exuberance of faith, their diligence of speech.

✥ EPILOGUE ✥
A Wilderness of Books

The Library a wilderness of books. Looking over books on Canada written within the last three hundred years, could see how one had been built upon another, each author consulting and referring to his predecessors. . . . I saw that while we are clearing the forest in our westward progress, we are accumulating a forest of books in our rear, as wild and unexplored as any of nature's primitive wildernesses. The volumes of the Fifteenth, Sixteenth, and Seventeenth Centuries, which lie so near on the shelf, are rarely opened, are effectually forgotten and not implied by our literature and newspapers. When I looked into Purchas's Pilgrims, it affected me like looking into an impassable swamp, ten feet deep with sphagnum, where the monarchs of the forest, covered with mosses and stretched along the ground, were making haste to become peat. Those old books suggested a certain fertility, an Ohio soil, as if they were making a humus for new literatures to spring in. I heard the bellowing of bullfrogs and the hum of mosquitoes reverberating through the thick embossed covers when I had closed the book. Decayed literature makes the richest of all soils.

Thoreau's Journal, 16 March 1852

To approach early American prose is, indeed, to enter a rich ground full of "decayed literature"—forgotten or half-forgotten books, fugitive texts, fragments, dim memories of the now-lost. Thoreau himself liked swamps, both actual and metaphoric, for the sense of life which they exuded, but those who prefer drier and more ordered space will be grateful for the many guides which, having appeared since Thoreau's day, make our earliest writing far more accessible than it was then. Admirable bibliographies are available for certain regions, topics, or periods—the outstanding example being Thomas D. Clark's *Travels in the Old South*, 3 vols. (Norman: University of Oklahoma Press, 1956–59), its very bulk suggesting the breadth and depth of such materials, their spatial and temporal range, and the multitude of viewpoints from which they first emerged. Yet no truly comprehensive guide to the whole colonial period, and its various areas, exists at this time, and one often is made aware of individual items by coming across them in a library catalog, on a bookstore shelf, or in the list of a publisher who has ventured on a new edition. And one must remember that a good deal of relevant matter, often less than book length, remains buried in archives and special collections on three continents, while a number of texts which have little apparent connection to the topic contain brief passages or large excerpts that in fact are quite interesting. Published gatherings of shorter texts such as the *Mississippi Provincial Archives* (source for the Cadillac report to Pontchartrain) or Mills Lane's *General Oglethorpe's Georgia: Colonial Letters, 1733–1743*, 2 vols. (Savannah: Beehive Press, 1975), ought to remind us that the field is truly vast, the way through it long and meandering—but also that it is full of pleasant diversions.

Thoreau's figure of speech in his *Journal* thus is more than suggestive: for our experience of the early travel book itself is an adventure, alternately plagued and advanced by wayside accidents. As with any other journey, one needs a starting point. Perhaps the best is that provided by R. W. G. Vail's *The Voice of the Old Frontier* (Philadelphia: University of Pennsylvania Press, 1949). The collaborative efforts of several scholars went into the *Bibliography* volume of the *Literary History of the United States* (New York: Macmillan, 1948; and later supplements), which is likewise quite helpful. Justin Winsor's earlier collaborative project, the *Narrative and Critical History of America*, 8 vols. (Boston: Houghton Mifflin, 1884–89), is rich in its comments on both documentary and graphic sources for both continents. And the *Bibliotheca Americana* (New York: var. pub., 1868–1936), begun by Joseph Sabin and completed in 29 vols. by Wilberforce Eames and R. W. G. Vail, is a source of infinite advice and guidance.

The travelogues of early America are imaginative records of life, but they also are physical objects, and it is good to remember how they have descended to our possession today. Thoreau's gesture toward the library at Harvard in 1852 is illuminating here, for his own age was the great period of American book collecting, with dealers like Joseph Sabin, Obadiah Rich, and Henry Stevens avidly scouring America and Europe for copies of the rarest New World texts. Such men made their own large libraries as well as supplying other individuals, and institutions such as the Library of Congress and the British Museum, with impressive quantities of Americana. Thoreau himself benefited from the efforts of such people—and in the most direct way, since his work at Harvard for the concluding section of what came to be *Cape Cod* (1865) probably led him to books on early America which Colonel Israel Thorndike bought from a German collector in 1818, and subsequently gave to the college. Things were not so "swamplike" as he thought when he   205 viewed and touched the mossy volumes, for in fact his own interests were part of a wide and active undertaking on both sides of the Atlantic—an undertaking to which English and American, French, Dutch, German, Italian, and Spanish scholars and bibliophiles all contributed.

Nor was the mere collection of such texts, difficult and important as it was, the only significant activity on this front. From the founding of the first American historical society in the 1790s up to the Civil War, when over a hundred had been formed, local groups of people sought out and made public—either for the first time or in new form—hundreds of early American works, long and short, well-known or obscure, important or trivial. Thoreau used the *Collections* of the Massachusetts Historical Society in great detail for a number of his writings, as well as for his "Indian" project. Moreover, individual publishers in many areas of the country were busy obtaining and reprinting rare Americana, or collecting unpublished works to make them available to a reading public whose interest in history was notably high. William Gowans in New York and Joel Munsell in Albany were simply two of these men; most encyclopedic and ambitious of all was Peter Force, whose *Tracts* of the colonial period (4 vols., 1836–46) and *American Archives* of the Revolutionary era (9 vols., 1837–53) disseminated and preserved countless early documents and books.

The historians of mid-nineteenth-century America, themselves prodigious collectors of books, manuscripts, and archival materials, profited immensely from such efforts. Parkman, Prescott, Bancroft, and Sparks assiduously gathered items from the "wilderness," as Irving had done beforehand during his studies in Obadiah Rich's collection at Madrid, that "labyrinth of books" which depressed but also delighted him. The American magazines and journals of the period both supported and aided this large biblio-cultural endeavor—from the *North American Review* (which ran a "Books Relating to America" series for the first years of its publication) to the *Knickerbocker* (which included a significant number of early and contemporary travel materials—Parkman's *Oregon Trail* was one—and gave notice to many others). Most importantly, the critics who wrote about American literature in such organs gave the lie to Thoreau's contention of 1852 that the earliest American writings were not "implied" by modern New World literary art, for these people clearly thought of literature as a very

broad undertaking, encompassing all fields of experience and

knowledge. An "American book" for them was defined by its diligent concern with the New World scene—from flora and fauna to
Indian history to the most recent occurrence or idea. If "belles
lettres" was a recognized separate entity, not to be confused with
travel books and records of the old or new settlements, "literature"
was a far more comprehensive rubric. The continuities between
our earliest writing and the most recent efforts were understood,
valued, even held up as proof of one more American "departure"
from Old World standards. "Americana" itself was far from an-
tiquarian as a category of understanding: it was as fresh as Oregon,
as broad as the high plains, as exultant as the latest promotional
gesture. When Moses Coit Tyler produced the first serious history
of early American writing at the end of the century, he was building on this complex understanding—not, as has been claimed, replacing an old and narrowly aesthetic standard with a new one.

Indeed, modern readers have lost touch with our earliest writings through an opposite replacement which took place after
Tyler's era. The concept of "literary art" has narrowed appreciably
during the first half of our century, so much so that William Char-
vat failed to perceive, in his study of *The Origins of American Critical
Thought, 1810–1835* (Philadelphia: University of Pennsylvania
Press, 1936)—astute and insightful as that book remains—exactly
how broad the early national view of literature was. From the "art-
for-art's-sake" movement to the rise of New Criticism in our own
period, and with significant aid from the New Humanists and
figures like Van Wyck Brooks, we have come to regard the colonial
period as an artistic wasteland illuminated here and there (and
especially, as Perry Miller has argued, in New England) by lights
cast aslant across a dark and ignorant field. That colonial literature
has been synonymous with "Puritan" art suggests both the cogency
of Miller's studies and the relative unfamiliarity of modern readers
with texts from other regions. And that we have not sensed fully
how indebted nineteenth-century writers like Irving, Cooper,
Thoreau, Simms, and Melville were to colonial prototypes—
particularly the records of discovery, exploration, and settlement—hints at our failure to regard as seriously as they did
the literary remains of early America. As I have stressed at a
number of points in this study, the continuity of form from John
Smith and William Bradford into the national period was substantial and complex. In many senses, we have not discovered even yet
the true drift of American writing.

Yet the signs of what we might discover have been abundant. If our sense of the "wilderness of books" is essential to a fresh contact with such documents, so also is our sense of exactly how much of this matter has been made freshly available in the modern era. Winsor's great effort at surveying the history (and documents) of both continents, like Tyler's astute studies of early writing in North America, was the foundation of new endeavors as well as the culmination of old ones. Within twenty years the most important and influential collection of American writing to its time began to appear: the *Original Narratives of Early American History* series (19 vols.), published by Scribner's under the general editorship of J. Franklin Jameson. The reprints of Hakluyt and Purchas which appeared in the same period (in the Glasgow editions of each, and the Everyman's Library edition of Hakluyt) are likewise essential here, though both of the original works are far more limited in the time they cover than Jameson's collection. Also more limited, though in other ways, are the monumental series of Reuben G. Thwaites: *The Jesuit Relations* (73 vols.) and *Early Western Travels* (32 vols.), issued by the Arthur H. Clark Co. in Cleveland. More recent additions are those in the "Lakeside Classics" series of the Lakeside Press, Chicago, and such projects as the "American Exploration and Travel Series" (Oklahoma), the "Western Americana Series" (Yale and Lippincott), the "Pioneer Heritage Series" (Nebraska), "Pioneer Books" (Macmillan of Canada), the "John Harvard Library" (Harvard), many Dover reprints, various Spanish texts issued by the Fondo de Cultura Economica in Mexico City, and the "March of America" facsimiles of Xerox. Crucial here as well are the less publicized efforts of smaller presses such as Beehive in Savannah, and the various microfilm and microform reprints of English, American, and Continental materials. The reader also should turn to the many texts published by local or state historical societies, and to their journals. And, by all means, the splendid publications of the Prince, Hakluyt, and Champlain societies should be investigated and used. But it should be remembered, too, that much remains unpublished or unreprinted, and that for such material the best resource is any one of a large number of special libraries throughout the country—ranging from the Library of Congress and the major university libraries of East and West to the archives and collections of many smaller institutions. It is the rare state historical society or state library or state university which has

208 no substantial gathering of local travel records and settlement ac-

counts. For the student who wants to understand something of this most American act, and its artful record, the opportunities are very great indeed. So, too, are the things to be learned in the process: for, as countless observers and travelers and historians in the past were fond of noting, what was lost in the mists of saga or myth in Europe—the beginnings of a nation's life—occurred in the West in the full light of recorded history. If much in fact also was lost here, and lost on purpose often enough, much still remains: and it tells a great deal more than those who recorded it intended it to. It tells a tale which is still being told, a history still being lived.

❦ PLATES ❦

THE MAPS, ENGRAVINGS, PAINTINGS, SKETCHES, AND CHARTS REPRODUCED
here have a common theme that makes them more than mere illus-
trations for my main argument. Each of them organizes the New World
scene, whether concrete or abstract, by means of techniques allied to the
prose strategies examined in the bulk of this study. How an artist or
illustrator controls visual space in these plates can be compared, I think, to
the manner in which a writer controls the verbal space of a New World
report or promotion: visual design, like the grammar of Old World language, is used to give American facts a composure they seem to lack on
their own. Since most of the plates, in addition, are more or less explicit
records of travel in America, they are related by context as well as
technique to the early narratives of New World discovery. My comments
on each of the plates attempt to point out such ties between the visual and
the verbal; they also offer, where it seems relevant, some account of the
historical circumstances which called forth the item in question.

Plate 1   English sportsmen in the New World; J. T. de Bry, *Americae pars decima,* 1618.

This imaginary American scene portrays the ideal subordination of New World abundance to Old World desire: it is an icon of easy control, so easy that the happy huntsmen are all attired in courtly costume and all absorbed in their pleasant pastimes. Nothing in the landscape offers an explicit rebuff to what they are about, and there is no obvious suggestion that America is at odds with their European customs, or that those customs must be adapted to radically new circumstances. Though John Smith already had made it clear that hard work was necessary for survival in America, and within two years the Plymouth Pilgrims would find the American shore a bleak wilderness where starvation rather than ready sustenance was the rule, this little dream is crowded with the imagery of nurturance. (By way of further contrast, consider the tough circumstances Columbus encountered in Veragua or on Jamaica; the ineptitude of European chivalry as Cabeza de Vaca paints it in his *Relación* of 1542; or the eerie silence which was all that John White heard during his final visit to Roanoke in 1590.) Yet in all this brightness of the de Bry plate, one may find certain hidden hesitations: the cleared ground where the sportsmen gambol is no natural space, as the stumps spread through it suggest; and the great semicircle of open space is edged by a darker forest toward which all of the huntsmen but one have turned their backs.

Plate 2   Thomas Jefferson, "A comparative View of the Quadrupeds of Europe and of America," from *Notes on the State of Virginia,* 1788. Courtesy of the University of Michigan Library.

The first question raised by charts or tables like this one (or the one reproduced in PLATE 4) is whether they are anything more than a convenient means of organizing and presenting data. They indeed do organize and present facts, and in a manner that is immediately clear to the reader. Yet I think that other suggestions are put forth in Jefferson's comparative "View" of Old World and New World fauna. For one thing, the great blank space under "Europe" is a coyly graphic reminder of Jefferson's conclusion that America is far more lavish in its forms of life than the Old World. Though a simple listing of all the facts within Jefferson's prose might make the same point, a prose catalog would not have as great an impact as the table does. Similarly, the presentation of these data in a spatial form (rather than just in Jefferson's text) reminds the reader of the spatial poles between which Jefferson acts as mediator throughout his book. The table, in other words, is like an abstract map of the two continents—an icon of transatlantic tensions and arguments. For all its departures from the stingy European norm in this chart, however, America is Europeanized merely by its reduction to the terms of Old World science. The very fact that a comparison can be made, regardless of its results, suggests how much of America has been absorbed into Old World categories, how much of it has been "discovered" already. One thus may note in closing that even the originally exotic Tupi Indian word for the marmoset is present in Jefferson's table only as the Frenchified "Sagoin." Blank as America was to the European mind at first, it now has become crowded with knowledge and names, so filled-in that Europe itself seems blank by comparison.

11. Aboriginals of one only.

EUROPE	lb.	AMERICA	lb.
Sanglier. Wild boar	280.	Tapir	534.
Mouflon. Wild sheep	56.	Elk, round horned	†450.
Bouquetin. Wild goat		Puma	218.
Lievre. Hare	7.6	Jaguar	109.
Lapin. Rabbit	3.4	Cabiai	109.
Putois. Polecat	3.3	Tamanoir	65.4
Genette	3.1	Tamandua	75.
Defman. Muskrat	oz.	Cougar of N. America	59.4
Ecureuil. Squirrel	12.	Cougar of S. America	
Hermine. Ermin	8.2	Ocelot	
Rat. Rat	7.5	Pecari	46.3
Loirs	3.1	Jaguaret	43.6
Lerot. Dormouse	1.8	Ako	
Taupe. Mole	1.2	Lama	
Hamster		Paco	32.7
Zifel	.9	Serval	27¼
Leming		Sloth. Unau	
Souris. Mouse	.6	Saricovienne	
		Kincajou	21.8
		Tatou Kabassou	
		Urfon. Urchin	16.5
		Raccoon. Raton	
		Coati	16.3
		Coendou	13.
		Sloth. Ai	
		Sapajou Ouarini	
		Sapajou Coaita	9.8
		Tatou Encubert	
		Tatou Apar	
		Tatou Cachica	7.
		Little Coendou	6.5
		Opossum. Sarigue	

EUROPE	AMERICA	lb.
	Tapeti	
	Margay	4.2
	Cabier	3.5
	Agouti	
	Sapajou Sai	
	Tatou Cirquinçon	3.3
	Tatou Tatouate	
	Mouffette Squash	
	Mouffette Chinche	
	Mouffette . Conepate.	
	Scunk	
	Mouffette. Zorilla	
	Whabus. Hare. Rabbit	
	Apera	
	Akouchi	
	Oudatra. Muskrat	
	Pilori	†2.7
	Great grey squirrel	†2.625
	Fox squirrel of Virginia	2.
	Surikate	†2.
	Mink	1.8
	Sapajou. Sajou	
	Indian. pig. Cochon d'	1.6
	Inde	
	Sapajou Saimiri	1.5
	Phalanger	
	Coquallin	
	Lesser grey squirrel	†1.5
	Black squirrel	†1.5
	Red squirrel	10. oz.
	Sagoin Saki	

Plate 3 Thomas Jefferson, manuscript map (detail) to accompany the "Plan for Western Government," 1783–84. Courtesy of the William L. Clements Library, the University of Michigan.

Like Jonathan Carver's more finished map of 1778 (PLATE 5), Jefferson's rough sketch records the turning of Eastern attention toward the West in the later eighteenth century. The attention in this case is notably schematic: the vast West is reduced to a set of smaller units marked off largely by reference to longitude and latitude rather than the sinuous lines of the wild landscape itself. And it is from this deductive gridwork that Jefferson's troubles arise. His design for "Polypotamia" (state no. 9) would have left that "many-rivered" place bisected by the broad Ohio, while "Saratoga" (state no. 7) actually would have touched that river only at one small point (the sketch map is wrong in this regard)—and "Assenisipia" (state no. 4) in fact would have run north along the eastern shore of Lake Michigan in a narrow strip, thereby denying to "Metropotamia" (state no. 5) a port on that body of water. Though none of Jefferson's specific boundaries was accepted by Congress, his general point—that new territories should be surveyed before land grants were made—was adopted. Hence the gridwork principle won out over more haphazard (and perhaps more attentive) methods of division, though crucial concessions were made for the actual lay of the land, and certain attempts of the government to control the West (such as the intent to reserve "federal" lots in each surveyed township, and the order that mines, salt licks, salt springs, and mill seats be held for the United States) proved unenforceable and were abandoned. (See Malcolm J. Rohrbough, *The Land Office Business* [New York: Oxford University Press, 1968]). For an example of the older methods of land division in the colonies, see the eastern and northern portions of the foldout map in *Conquering the Wilderness. History of the State of New York*, vol. 5 (New York: Columbia University Press, 1934), after p. 381.

Plate 4   Thomas Jefferson, chart of the Virginia Indians, from *Notes on the State of Virginia*, 1788. Courtesy of the University of Michigan Library.

This discursive map of Virginia Indians reflects Jefferson's schematic curiosity (and his typical aesthetic) throughout *Notes on the State of Virginia*—that mixture of grand sweep and minute detail which characterizes his inquiry and his style. But as a graphic device the chart has other purposes: for it neatly encloses the named Indian groups within firm lines which represent both the white attempt to "understand" native life and the allied attempt to include that life inside the quite literal boundaries of Euro-American control. If we might say similar things about *any* chart .or table, what in the present case seems like a static arrangement of facts actually is a dynamic vision of them, a vision specifically tied to the spatial and temporal conditions of America. The knowledge stated here is tentative and incomplete, as Jefferson notes several times in his text; and excluded entirely, beyond the sparsely filled-in "West" half of the chart, is any comment on those tribes which live, unnamed and unknown, in the hinterland of Jefferson's vast Virginia (a domain that stretches, according to the old notion, as far as the Mississippi). Hence the tension which places "West" and "East" in intellectual opposition to each other also sets this whole chart off from an enormous realm that transcends its own spatial limits. But the effective oblivion to which the unknown tribes are consigned here invades the chart itself in a temporal guise: the decrease of "Warriors" between "1607" and "1669" in fact inverts the very increase of white settlement which allows such a detailed comparison, and the decrease is severe enough that the tribes most thoroughly known have become almost linguistic ruins by the later year—victims of another kind of oblivion. "What would be the melancholy sequel of their history," Jefferson writes, "may...be augured from the census of 1669, by which we discover that the tribes therein enumerated were, in the space of 62 years, reduced to about one-third of their former numbers" (see Peden's edition, pp. 95–96, and p. 281, for the full and complex statement). Thus Jefferson must work against, and acknowledge, a number of final limits in his attempt to organize this intellectual map of Indian life. The whole effort becomes, one may say without too much exaggeration, a graphic and mental analogue for Jefferson's story in the *Notes* about how he once excavated an Indian burial mound by cutting through its middle a long straight trench—the perfect act of a rationalist!—laying bare in the process, he estimates, about "a thousand skeletons" (see Peden's edition, pp. 97–100).

N O R T H.

MANNAHOACS.   **MONACANS.**   **POWHATANS.**

MANNAHOACS and MONACANS

	Tribes.	Country.	Chief Town.	Warriors 1607	1669
Between PATOWMAC and RAPPAHANOC.	Whonkenties	Fauquier			
	Tegninaties	Culpeper			
	Ontponies	Orange			
	Tauxitanians	Fauquier			
	Hassinungaes	Culpeper			
Between RAPPAHANOC and YORK.	Stegarakies	Orange			
	Shackaconies	Spottsylvania			
	Mannahoacs	Stafford. Spottsylvania			
Between YORK and JAMES.	Monacans	James R. above the falls	Fork of James R.	30	
	Monasiccapanoes	Louisa. Fluvanna			
Between JAMES and CAROLINA.	Monasiffanoes	Bedford. Buckingham			
	Mastinacaes	Cumberland			
	Mohemenchoes	Powhatan			

POWHATANS

	Tribes.	Country.	Chief Town.	Warriors 1607	1669	
Between PATOWMAC and RAPPAHANOC.	Tauxenents	Fairfax	About General Washington's	40		
	Patowomekes	Stafford. King George	Patowmac creek	200	60	By the name of Matchatica, U. Matchadic, Nanzatico, Nantico, Appamatox, Mator.
	Cuttatawomans	King George	About Lamb creek	20		
	Pissasecs	King Geo. Richmond	Above Leeds town	100		
	Onaumanients	Westmoreland	Nomony river	100	30	
	Rappahanocs	Richmond county.	Rappahanoc creek	80	40	
	Moraughtacunds	Lancaster. Richmond	Moratico river	130	70	
	Secacanies	Northumberland	Coan river	30		
	Wighcocomicoes	Northumberland	Wicocomico river	30		
	Cuttatawomans	Lancaster	Corotoman			
Between RAPPAHANOC and YORK.	Nantaughtacunds	Alex. Caroline	Port tobacco creek	150	60	
	Mattaponients	Mattapony river	- - -	30	20	
	Pamunkies	King William	Romuncock	300	50	
	Werowocomicoes	Gloucester	About Rosewell	40		
	Payankatanks	Piankatank river	Turk's Ferry. Grimesby	55		
Between YORK and JAMES.	Youghtanunds	Pamunkey river	- - -	60	60	
	Chickahominies	Chickahominy river	Orapaks	250	10	
	Powhatans	Henrico	Powhatan. Mayo's	40		
	Arrowhatocs	Henrico	Arrohatocs	30	15	
	Weanocs	Charles city	Weynoke	100		
	Passyunghs	Charles city. Jamescity	Sandy point	40		
	Chiskiacs	York	Chiskiac	45	15	
	Kecoughtans	Elizabeth city	Roscows	20		
Between JAMES and CAROLINA.	Appamattocs	Chesterfield	Bermuda hundred	60	50 Pohics	
	Quiocohanocs	Surry	About Upper Chipoak	15	3 Pohics	
	Warraskoyacks	Isle of Wight	Warraskoyac			
	Nansamonds	Nansamond	About the mouth of West. branch	200	45	
	Chesapeaks	Princess Anne	About Lynhaven river	100		
EASTERN SHORE.	Accohanocs	Accom. Northampton	Accohanoc river	40		
	Accomacks	Northampton	About Cheriton's	80		

	1669
Nottoways	90
Meherrics	50
Tuteloes	

by the name of Tosukeys

S O U T H.

This Table to be placed between Pages 100 and 101.

Plate 5 Jonathan Carver, "A New Map of North America from the Latest Discoveries" (detail), from *Travels through the Interior Parts of North America, 1778.* Courtesy of the William L. Clements Library, the University of Michigan.

When the French and Indian War ended with a great accession of territory to the English crown, Jonathan Carver gave up soldiering and became a surveyor. His change of profession was a sign of larger changes which he thought would come about as England explored and then opened to settlement its newfound empire. Like Robert Rogers, who tried to convince the home government that expansion should be actively encouraged (and who lost that campaign, though he succeeded in getting Carver to join him in the upper Midwest), Carver tried to measure the new lands by his deeds and his art. Though he was not immune to wonder, Carver was as schematic in his approach to the West as Jefferson was to be after the next American war. He cataloged the "provinces" into which he thought the upper Mississippi valley ought to be divided (a total of eleven, numbered much as Jefferson's would be), and asserted the lines of division over a frontier terrain which he knew only in part from experience. Interested in the old transcendent plots of the continent ("Here ends this attempt to find out a northwest passage," his journal of western travel ends), Carver nonetheless gave a domestic turn to his imagination. He introduced the word "Oregon" to the language, and thus pointed ahead to the grand sweep of Lewis and Clark across the West; but he also looked toward those farmers for whom his own prose and maps opened up an intervening paradise. Province "No 3," he wrote in his journal, contained "many fine ilands, large meadows, and plains"—"Many of the rivers which enter [the Mississippi] in this space have fine intervals on one or other of their banks, it frequently happening that there is found a mountain on one side and interval on the opposite. These intervals often terminate in large plains covered with grass and herbage on which are seen vast droves of wild cattle, deer, elk, and other game, besides fowl in plenty. This might well contain sixty or eighty thousand settlers" (*The Journals of Jonathan Carver and Related Documents,* ed. John Parker [St. Paul: Minnesota Historical Society, 1976], pp. 136, 140). Unlike Jefferson, who had not seen the region, Carver was more attentive to the actual twistings of the rivers there and sought to ensure every one of his provinces an adequate access to water routes (compare his "No 9" with Jefferson's). Yet Carver obtained a doubtful Indian land grant while on his travels, and thus set in motion the chimerical plot of his own descendents—who sought, even into the present century, to regain their title to a vast and rich country.

Plate 6   John Bartram, "A Draught of John Bartram's House and Garden as it appears from the River," 1758. By kind permission of the earl of Derby.

John Bartram began his botanical garden in 1729 or 1730, long before he drew this sketch of it for his friend Peter Collinson. Laid out on gently sloping land that led down to the Schuylkill, some seven hundred feet behind his house, the garden was Bartram's prime abstract of American nature—a miniature continent packed with rarities drawn from many regions and there arranged within the many enclosures visible in this almost barren, perhaps autumnal, "draught." The last enclosure was Bartram's study, the small building at the head of his walk where Bartram performed his important experiments on plant reproduction and where he probably prepared his shipments of American flora for his overseas correspondents and customers. There are three essential spaces here—the land outside Bartram's fence, the subdivided and rectified garden, the almost windowless study—and together they suggest an increasing condensation of discovery, an economy of experience which finally points us toward some categorical knowledge. The linear garden walks (keyed as "5" and "6") likewise recall, but in a simplified way, Bartram's many wearisome travels in the American wilderness: for the itinerary here is constricted and finally controlled by the study which lies at the far end of the passageway. The little traveler with his staff seems safe from all intrusions on his innocent occupation.

A Draught of John Bartram's House and Garden as it appears from the River 1758   Sent to P. Collinson

1. my Study
2. Common Flower Garden
3. upper Kitchen Garden
4. the Lower Kitchen Garden
5.6. Walks 180 yards long
of a moderate descent

A new flower
Garden
25 yards long
& 10 Broad

A
Pond for
Spring fish   conveyd under ground
to the Engine
on mill House Side

the Length of this fence is Northwest & south east

Schuilkiln River 200 Yards wide

Plate 7 Lewis Evans, *A Map of Pensilvania, New-Jersey, New-York and the Three Delaware Counties* (detail), 1749. Courtesy of the John Carter Brown Library, Brown University.

This portion of Evans's map, about half of the whole sheet, indicates the route which Evans, John Bartram, and Conrad Weiser traveled in 1743 from Philadelphia to the Iroquois settlement at Onondaga. The dotted line tracing their journey begins southwest of center, at the effectual end of "Pensilvania" and the start of "St Anthony's Wilderness." Passing northwest and west to join the Susquehanna, the trail then heads north to and through the "Dismal Vale" (skirting the "Impenetrable Mountains"), and finally goes off to the northeast and north toward the travelers' destination. Like Bartram's verbal record of the trip (or Evans's own fragmentary "Journal," partially preserved in Thomas Pownall's *Topographic Description* [1776]), this fragile line traces the halting progress of Eastern knowledge through a relatively unknown wilderness beyond those "Blue Mountains" which wall off the settled ground. But Evans has filled up the Western vacancy of his map with more than one tentative, perambulating line. His ample prose "Remarks" cover the empty conceptual space as if suggesting that the literal emptiness soon will be in balance with the already "completed" lands nearer to Philadelphia. One feels that spatial vacancy and verbal silence are equivalent for Evans, and that the first can be controlled by breaking the second. As Jefferson suggested in his comments on William Dunbar's Red River expedition of 1805, travel could be a kind of art, a means of specifying blankness: "We shall delineate with correctness the great arteries of this great country: those who come after us will extend the ramifications as they become acquainted with them, and fill up the canvas we begin" (quoted in Merrill D. Peterson, *Thomas Jefferson and the New Nation* [New York: Oxford University Press, 1970], p. 765).

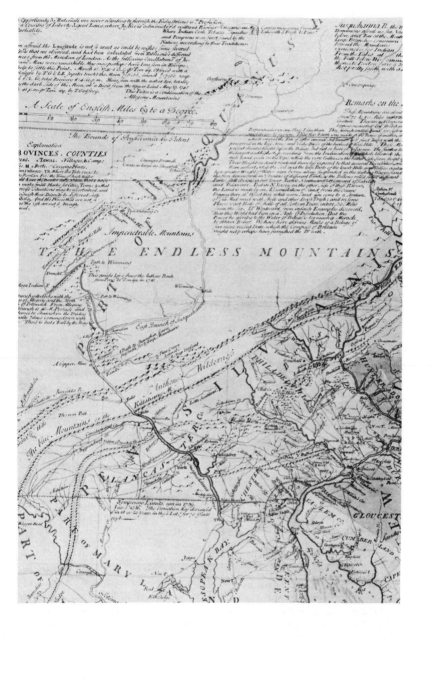

Plate 8 William Bartram, *"Franklinia Alatamaha.* A beautiful flowering Tree. discovered growing near the banks of the R. Alatamaha in Georgia," 1788. Courtesy of the Trustees of the British Museum (Natural History).

We have in this watercolor by William Bartram (dated 1788 but perhaps based on earlier sketches) a fine example of his skill as an artist and his attentiveness as a traveler. Confined to a very small spatial range, the *Franklinia* was first discovered by William and his father John in October 1765, when it was not in flower and hence would have been hard to distinguish from related genera found in the same geographical region. William describes in the *Travels* his own separate encounter some ten years afterwards: "After my return from the Creek nation, I employed myself during the spring and fore part of summer, in revisiting the several districts in Georgia and the East borders of Florida, where I had noted the most curious subjects; collecting them together, and shipping them off to England. In the course of these excursions and researches, I had the opportunity of observing the new flowering shrub, resembling the Gordonia, in perfect bloom, as well as bearing ripe fruit. It is a flowering tree, of the first order for beauty and fragrance of blossoms: the tree grows fifteen or twenty feet high, branching alternately; the leaves are oblong, broadest towards their extremities, and terminate with an acute point, which is generally a little reflexed; they are lightly serrated, attenuate downwards, and sessile, or have very short petioles; they are placed in alternate order, and towards the extremities of the twigs are crouded together, but stand more sparsedly below; the flowers are very large, expand themselves perfectly, are of a snow white colour, and ornamented with a crown or tassel of gold coloured refulgent staminae in their centre, the inferior petal or segment of the corolla is hollow, formed like a cap or helmet, and entirely includes the other four, until the moment of expansion; its exterior surface is covered with a short silky hair; the borders of the petals are crisped or plicated: these large white flowers stand single and sessile in the bosom of the leaves, and being near together towards the extremities of the twigs, and usually many expanded at the same time, make a gay appearance: the fruit is a large, round, dry, woody apple or pericarp, opening at each end oppositely by five alternate fissures, containing ten cells, each replete with dry woody cuneiform seed. This very curious tree was first taken notice of about ten or twelve years ago, at this place, when I attended my father (John Bartram) on a botanical excursion; but, it being then late in the autumn, we could form no opinion to what class or tribe it belonged" (Van Doren's edition, pp. 369–70). In 1832, the energetic and eccentric Constantine Rafinesque noted that the *Franklinia* nurtured by the Bartrams in their garden on the Schuylkill grew there "with the utmost perfection," having reached a height of forty feet. But the tree had disappeared from its natural habitat long before, and all other domesticated examples of it could be traced to the single plant reclaimed by William and his father. See Joseph Ewan, ed., *William Bartram: Botanical and Zoological Drawings, 1756–1788* (Philadelphia: American Philosophical Society, 1968), p. 63.

Plate 9 William Bartram, "View of Alatchua Savanah," 1775. Courtesy of the Trustees of the British Museum (Natural History).

Covering an area of some twenty square miles, these "Elysian fields and green plains of Alachua" (*Travels,* ed. Van Doren, p. 165) struck Bartram when he first saw them with a sense of enraptured discovery: "wholly engaged in the contemplation of the unlimited, varied, and truly astonishing native wild scenes of landscape and perspective, there exhibited: how is the mind agitated and bewildered, at being thus, as it were, placed on the borders of a new world! On the first view of such an amazing display of the wisdom and power of the supreme author of nature, the mind for a moment seems suspended, and impressed with awe" (pp. 166–67). Like his smaller "bason," this space is a manageable and comprehensible "America," a "new world" contained visually and verbally within a series of clarifying circles and orders. The trees, the shoreline, the grasslands, the wetlands, finally the drainage system itself—each of these topographic facts is made to serve a purpose in the aloof map allied to those served by the metaphors of his prose, giving the viewer-reader a sense of control even in the experience of "bewildering" awe. Note, too, the path that crosses over the savanna ("f–f"), and the single crane that here stands in for the ordered "squadrons" which Bartram describes in his text. He and his fellow travelers camped at the edge of the scene: "this situation was open and airy, and gave us an unbounded prospect over the adjacent plains. . . . All around being still and silent, we repaired to rest" (p. 167). Hence the literal action of his journey copied and explained the dynamic movements of his double art.

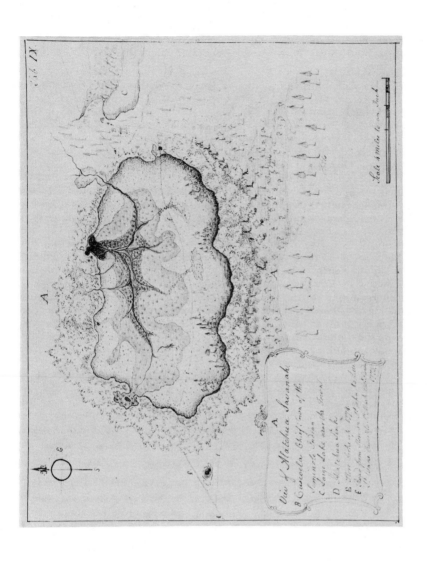

Tab. IX

A   View of Alachua Savanah.
B   Cuscowilla Chief-town of W.
C   Large Lake near the Town.
D   Sinkhole &c.
E   River where it was 1774 mile to sea.
F   Run from the river 28 to sea.
1774

Scale 6 miles to an Inch

Plate 10   Shipwreck and survival in Veragua; Theodor de Bry, *Americae pars quinta*, 1595. Courtesy of the Edward E. Ayer Collection, the Newberry Library, Chicago.

For this plate in his 1595 edition of Girolamo Benzoni's *Historia del Mondo Nuovo* (1565), Theodor de Bry borrowed a good deal from an earlier engraving by Jean Sadeler. Itself derived from a Marten de Vos painting, Sadeler's piece showed Noah at work on his ark as dark clouds approached over a tall turreted building behind him. The central action in Sadeler was definitely appropriate for de Bry's purpose—since Benzoni told how Lope de Olano and his men, having run their two small brigs on the Veragua beach, realized that they could not depend on the land itself for their survival, and hence set about building a new ship from the wreckage of the old ones. Yet de Bry changed Sadeler's design and meaning even as he copied its main event. True to the biblical story, Sadeler (and de Vos) stressed the contrast between Noah and his three sons and those other people who carried on their normal life as the Flood approached. Though there *were* tensions in Olano's company (he had beached the brigs, in fact, to keep the men from running off), de Bry's composite picture of their activities in Veragua—building shelter, planting crops, gathering and using materials for the ship—suggests a sense of concert and cooperation that makes the engraving an ideal vision of European life in America. Having removed, for obvious reasons, the superstructure which rises up from the center of Sadeler's ark, de Bry has added in the background thus opened to him a little romance of Old World industry—an unambiguous portrait of European man converting the available matter of America into the material of his own artifacts. Pushed off to a corner at the back of the plate, the old disaster which brought Olano's voyage to an intentional end has been upstaged by the energy of these new constructive acts: the "Flood" in this case is over, and the world is being made anew.

Plate 11 "A Map of the County of Savannah" (detail), from Samuel Urlsperger, *Ausführliche Nachricht von den Salzburgischen Emigranten,* 1735 (vol. 1, pt. 4). Courtesy of the John Carter Brown Library, Brown University.

This finely detailed map of northeast Georgia is a vision of the ideal progress of European order. Its mood is symphonic and futuristic, its rhetoric a visual image of expansion, multiplication, and undeniable success. From Savannah itself (the small six-part rectangle on the river opposite "Hutchinson's Island") the lines and divisions of civil space extend southward through the garden plots and the larger farm tracts to Highgate and Hempstead, two other villages, and then to the five-hundred-acre enclosures which separate the forest into neatly marked-off partitions. No tension between such divisions and the landscape seems possible. Indeed, even the larger forest outside their bounds is a polite collection of separate trees, a short of civil wilderness rather than a great dark expanse. Surrounded and magnified by these echoes of itself, the tiny city already seems assured of the bright future predicted for it by the preacher George Whitefield in 1738: "Their Beginnings as yet are but small, but I cannot help thinking there are Foundations laying for great temporal and spiritual Blessings in *Georgia,* when the Inhabitants are found worthy" (*Our First Visit in America: Early Reports from the Colony of Georgia, 1732–1740,* ed. Trevor R. Reese [Savannah: Beehive Press, 1974], p. 292). The talent for envisioning such great alterations before they took place was essential to those involved in settlement. In 1733, the promoter Benjamin Martyn urged those who might wish to lend Oglethorpe support to indulge their "Imagination," and thereby "pass over a few Years of . . . Life" until they might see "Flocks and Herds in the . . . Pastures, and adjoining to them Plantations of regular Rows of Mulberry-Trees, entwin'd with Vines, the Branches of which are loaded with Grapes; . . . Orchards of Oranges, Pomegranates, and Olives; in other Places extended Fields of Corn, or Flax and Hemp. In Short, the whole Face of the Country chang'd by Agriculture, and Plenty in every Part of it" (*The Most Delightful Country of the Universe: Promotional Literature of the Colony of Georgia, 1717–1734,* ed. Trevor R. Reese [Savannah: Beehive Press, 1972], p. 188). Yet in practice those who actually became settlers in Georgia or elsewhere often were forced to adopt a far less imaginary prose than Martyn's in order to express what they had seen and felt; see the detailed litany of errors and abandonments sent to the Trustees in 1740 by a sorely disaffected group of Georgia planters (*General Oglethorpe's Georgia: Colonial Letters, 1733–1743,* ed. Mills Lane, 2 vols. [Savannah: Beehive Press, 1975], 2:485–91). And witness the fate of Oglethorpe's other town, Frederica, described by Trevor R. Reese in *Frederica: Colonial Fort and Town* (St. Simons Island: Fort Frederica Association, 1969).

Plate 12 Peter Gordon, "A View of Savanah as it stood on the 29th of March, 1734." Reproduced by permission of the British Library.

An upholsterer by trade, Peter Gordon was appointed a bailiff and conservator of the peace for Georgia, sailed with Oglethorpe in 1732, and helped with the platting of Savannah. Taken ill on the voyage, and then again in Georgia, he was forced to seek medical aid in England in 1733, but then returned to the colony again the following year. Aware of the high impulse behind Oglethorpe's American enterprise, Gordon began his own New World journal with a gesture toward the example of Rome and the "prudent, and praise worthy undertaking" of colonization throughout history (*Our First Visit in America*, p. 3). His "View" of Savannah, commissioned by the Georgia Trustees and published by their order, was a kind of graphic fantasy bolstering such high themes. Based on a quick sketch Gordon had made while on his first visit to the colony (for he could not have been at Savannah in March of 1734), the "View" stresses the elegance and orderliness of Oglethorpe's scheme for the city: the cleared ground has been divided into four wards, each centered on an open public area reserved for churches, stores, and the like, and each flanked on its north and south sides by two rows of house lots. A three-dimensional map rather than a perspective view of any actual scene, the piece tries to convince us that America, once cleared of its heavy forest (a process in which Gordon himself took part), is almost a blank sheet on which, as with the lines of division inscribed on Gordon's engraving, the colonist can write what he wants. Yet when Gordon came back to the colony late in 1734, he found its affairs "in the utmost confusion" (*First Visit*, p. 37), and quickly returned to London so that he might lay before the Trustees his bleak report. Having left his own American affairs "in some disorder," Gordon urged the English overseers "to prevent the evil with which this colony is threatened" (*General Oglethorpe's Georgia*, 1:167), but he himself never returned to America again, his ideal map repudiated by his later abandonments.

A View of Savannah as it stood the 29th of March 1734

To the Hon.ble the Trustees for establishing the Colony of Georgia in America
This View of the Town of Savannah is humbly dedicated by their Honours
Obliged and most Obedient Servant
Peter Gordon

VÛE de Savannah dans la Georgie

1. The Stairs going up
2. A.ff Oglethorpes Tent
3. A Tent
4. The Crane and Bell Tent
5. The publick Mill
6. The House for Strangers
7. The Publick Oven
8. The Draw Well

9. B. Leding the Church
10. A. Do ⟨⟩ to
11. The Fort
12. Do. Messrs. Bryans
13. Do. Whitaker's Row
14. The Guard House and Battery of Cannon
15. Warehouses ab⟨⟩d
Peter Gordon

Plate 13   Thomas Holme, "A Portraiture of the City Philadelphia in the Province of PENNSYLVANIA in America," from William Penn, *A Letter . . . to the Committee of the Free Society of Traders*, 1683. Courtesy of the William L. Clements Library, the University of Michigan.

This very ample city plan, copied across America well into the nineteenth century, is a primary document of the American civic imagination. In its large claims for the importance of prior visions, it seems to ignore the curving landscape that surrounds it most clearly in the miniature overview placed by Holme, as if to balance his elliptical title cartouche, beneath the whole design. Yet the most serious problem in realizing this two-faced plan developed from the competition between its two faces, not directly from any topographic difficulty. As one can see even in this early plat, the greatest building in Philadelphia was to take place along the Delaware shore rather than along the "High Street" which led west from there to the Schuylkill. By 1800 the city had spread far beyond the north and south boundaries along the larger river, and Penn's intent to provide ample open spaces in the city was abandoned in these unplanned extensions. The Schuylkill end of the town remained relatively rural and undeveloped, and the middle of the city filled in only gradually. And as Holme's "Portraiture" suggests, a further street along the Delaware, crowded with shops and warehouses, quickly cut the main design off from the water. Hence the balance of Penn's first imagining was lost in the very process of success; the rather insulated, self-repeating design of Philadelphia was broken by the imperatives of a commercial growth which, centered along the Delaware, pulled the city toward England and the other colonies and away from its intended form. If Penn's gesture of control was notable for its articulate sense of what a city ought to be, it nonetheless was at odds with the site to which Penn attached it, at odds, too, with the developing facts of colonial economy.

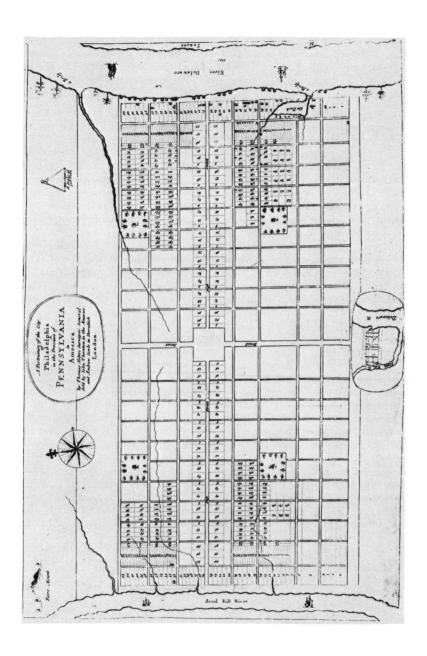

Plate 14   "A Plan Representing the Form of Setling the Districts, or County Divisions in the Margravate of Azilia," from Robert Mountgomery, *A Discourse Concerning the design'd Establishment of a New Colony to the South of Carolina, in the Most delightful Country of the Universe*, 1717. Courtesy of the John Carter Brown Library, Brown University.

At first glance, this "Plan" of Robert Mountgomery's "Form" for his Georgia settlement seems like a squared-off version of William Penn's elongated "Plat-form" of Philadelphia (PLATE 13). As in that earlier urban design, the space here is organized around five open areas, its center defined by the intersection of two main streets at a public square. Yet the total plan in this case would cover more than two hundred times the ground occupied by Philadelphia—each of the large open areas, for instance, would encompass sixteen square miles, whereas Penn's city was to cover only about two square miles *in toto!* Beyond the gargantuan presumptuousness in Mountgomery's distant scheme—which for this very disproportion was to remain unenacted and distant—one notes how the social pretentions expressed by the spatial design in this "Margravate" fragment the whole into a set of rigidly partitioned special areas. Politically as well as literally central, the Margrave's great hall pushes off toward the margins the homes of the lesser nobility and the cottages of those laborers who will support the grand enterprise—and support it not just by their hard work. Since one purpose which Mountgomery cites for his colony is the English desire to place a buffer between the Spanish in Florida and the already established colony in Carolina, it is clear that the rather absurd fortifications which surround Azilia in the "Plan" are aimed out towards something more than the vacant border of the design. And the laborers who will live near the eighty-mile-long stone wall or the cannon which surmount it will be, in a sense, hostages to the fortune which Spain can manipulate if it desires. At the many-framed center will live the insulated Margrave, his rationale a sort of feudal prerogative. But the rigidity of the whole design, the firm insistence of its dividing lines and the almost Byzantine complexity (and introspection) of its overall order, suggest a need to reassert the angularity of English intent so frequently that the plan verges on a self-parody which underscores an essential weakness of Old World imagination. It is as if the presumed blankness of America has been too amply filled in here, as if the anxiety caused by that blankness is too evident in the nervousness of the design itself.

A Plan representing the Form of Setling the Districts, or County Divisions in the Margravate of Azilia.

Plate 15 John White, watercolor of a terrapin, 1585. Courtesy of the Trustees of the British Museum.

Though the topic of natural history painting may seem like a simple one—the artist's attention and accuracy being the main issues—many of the painters who first portrayed the flora and fauna (and the people) of America in fact struggled with a number of other problems. The Italian Jacopo Ligozzi, a sixteenth-century artist who did not visit the New World, produced exquisitely detailed renderings of the agouti, the agave plant, the parrot, the pineapple, and the marvel of Peru from specimens he saw in Italy in the 1580s (see Hugh Honour, *The New Golden Land: European Images of America from the Discoveries to the Present Time* [New York: Pantheon Books, 1975], pp. 36, 41, 45, 46, 49), while the Dutchman Frans Post, part of an official expedition in Brazil in the mid-seventeenth century, embellished his fine Brazilian landscapes with accurate floral and faunal details which he had seen and sketched on the spot, and another of the official artists, Albert Eckhout, portrayed with great vigor the natives and the native products of South America (Honour, pp. 50–52, 78–81). John White represents a stage in the development of this practical aesthetic in between Ligozzi and the two Dutch artists. Like the latter, he knew the ground firsthand; yet, like the Italian, he had difficulty creating a full background for what he saw and rendered. His "Terrapin" is the record of an act of attention: note its wrinkled neck skin, the minute patterning of its shell, the finely alert eye, and the tensely active energy of its posture. White has gone so far as to throw a shadow beneath the terrapin, thereby adding a further sense of depth and activity to the whole. Yet the shadow falls only on the paper itself, for the creature has been abstracted from its habitat—much as Ligozzi's brilliant parrot has curved its talons but has no perch to grasp with them. One might explain this enduring problem of figure and ground (which emerges even in the bird paintings of Audubon, who often left his watercolors without full backgrounds, these being added by other hands) as the result of a conflict in the artist's goals, a conflict between the cataloging urge and the sense of a complex, enveloping "world." Like the prose catalogs of his friend and fellow worker Thomas Harriot, White's watercolors push toward some categorical contact with America, away from experience and toward the science which comes only from experience itself. By virtue of its abstraction, White's "Terrapin" becomes an icon of Old World curiosity clarified and frozen in art; but its very particularity, its existence in this one moment as a "lively" specimen, reminds us of the vast world for which it speaks.

Plate 16   Spanish justice in Terra Florida; Theodor de Bry, *Americae pars quinta,* 1595. Courtesy of the Edward E. Ayer Collection, the Newberry Library, Chicago.

This classic visualization of Spanish cruelties in America owes some of its force to the fact that Theodor de Bry, a Belgian protestant who left his home for religious reasons, had little love for catholic Spain. Yet the "black legend" of Spanish misrule in America, surely indebted to the partial arguments of people like de Bry, had its factual basis, as the devastations visited on the Caribbean tribes, recorded and lamented by the Spanish priest Bartolomé de las Casas, ought to remind ùs. (It was this eloquent Spaniard, in fact, who inadvertently gave the opponents of Spain their most powerful ammunition against Spanish colonial rule.) De Bry's engravings on the theme are notable artistically for their cluttered physical and cultural space, their suggestion that America has become the scene of violent clashes between opposing figures and their opposite viewpoints. In contrast, his engraving of John White's "Secota". (PLATE 17) is all balance and gentleness. Our horror in the present case, to be sure, derives not from any obvious conflict but rather from the eerie passivity of the natives, who are being maimed by de Soto's troops as punishment for having misled the Spanish gold-seekers. (For a parallel here, see Garcilaso de la Vega's *The Florida of the Inca* [1605], ed. and trans. John Grier Varner and Jeanette Johnson Varner [Austin: University of Texas Press, 1951], p. 564.) As iconographic embodiments of the New World—for this was the natives' role in Old World art almost from the start—the passive Indians in de Bry's engraving suggest, but with an ironic insistence, that the West clearly is at the disposition of its European possessors. The plate thus becomes an inverted exploratory vision, a realization of how Old World power might destroy the American Eden which lay so meekly open to its exercise. Pointing the inversion is the prayerful posture of the native who awaits his punishment with a sort of Christian piety while two Spanish weapons cross behind him as if in suggestion of the torture visited on Christ himself. The dramatic focus here is that chopping block which cuts itself into the foreground: but note, in the far distance, the native dwellings reminiscent of those in White's "Secota" (PLATE 17), and the lone Indian afloat in a tiny canoe, as it seems, on the nearest bend of the river. Framed by the destroying fire and the dark Spanish wall, which together define and confine the foreground, that bright distant world is violated by the upthrust weapons and the mangled arms of the victims. Yet it survives as a memory of some older New World since dissolved by such urgent realities, some discovery now almost lost in history.

Plate 17   John White, "The Town of Secota" (ca. 1585), as engraved by Theodor de Bry for Thomas Harriot's *A Briefe and True Report of the new found land of Virginia,* 1590. Courtesy of the Edward E. Ayer Collection, the Newberry Library, Chicago.

This view of a native village on the Pamlico river (White called the village "Secoton") is an anthology of many ethnological details. Like the three cornfields at the right here (seedling, green, ripe), the townspeople's various activities are a composite of separate moments condensed by the artist in his attempt to catalog native experience visually. Yet White's composition merely emphasizes the composure of native life itself; it reveals rather than creates order. Perhaps most important here is the hierarchy of space in the village, for it hints at a subtle design in the values of those who control it. Thus the foreground is a devotional area, a place for religious celebration at the right, for pious memory at the left (the fire ring is for prayer, while the house keyed "A" is the tomb of former werowances or leaders). The middle distance, in contrast, is a place of habitation and food production (in addition to the cornfields, note the pumpkins at the right, the tobacco at the back, the sunflowers and more tobacco at the left—as well as the hunters and the deer at the left rear), while the social concourse up the middle is suggestive of a certain openness in the whole unwalled settlement. All built on the same model, the buildings exhibit nonetheless an interesting variety of size, orientation, and location; and those at the left rear, extending into the trees, suggest that the clearing is defined in such a way that the village center can fade off without anxiety into the forest. Altogether, these details portray native life as a spacious economy, an intimate mixture of place and art. Though Indian culture (like the foreign one represented here in the very fact of White's attentive skill) also is an assertion over the physical world of America—for the profusion of artfully smooth lines in White's painting, strengthened by de Bry, itself makes this point—there is a sense of balanced prior achievement in "Secota" that is lacking in comparable views of European settlement in the New World. Rather than mimic an ideal aesthetic design which is to be realized in the future of America, as the "Portraiture" of Philadelphia (PLATE 13) or Gordon's "Savanah" (PLATE 12) do, European art in this case copies with quiet passivity an almost perfect prior wedding of cultural form and topographic fact. The subject of White's painting is not change or transformation, but rather stasis, the ongoing repetition of ritual and structure which signifies some communal realization. If White's own artistic stance outside the village hints at a quite different kind of change that right now (even through his brush) threatens native life, no figure in the settlement seems aware of his presence there. And if the obvious success of Indian plantation in "Ralegh's Virginia" appears to bode well for English endeavors there, White's careful bearing on the village projects for other Europeans a poised and unintrusive position to match his own.

TB   20

Plate 18   Jean Baptiste Michel le Buteaux, "Veuë du Camp de la Concession de Monseigneur Law au Nouveau Biloxy," 1720. Courtesy of the Edward E. Ayer Collection, the Newberry Library, Chicago.

This black-and-white wash drawing of exquisite detail, commissioned by the head of John Law's concession at Biloxi, represents the renewed energies of French intention in early Louisiana. "Old" Biloxi itself was an infant settlement at this time, but it was found to be inadequate on many counts: "It is situated in a place surrounded by marshes," runs a 1720 comparison between the two sites, "from which come out fogs that corrupt the air, which cause illnesses and deaths, which have carried off in the last six months nearly five hundred persons, which continue at present, through the large number of sick" (*Mississippi Provincial Archives,* ed. and trans. Dunbar Rowland and Albert Godfrey Sanders [Jackson, Miss.: Mississippi Department of Archives and History, 1926–32], 3:299). The second location, on the other hand, was thought to be more advantageous: Buteaux illustrates the hope that its "elevated, dry and healthy site and very good air," as well as the "space sufficient to establish there warehouses, hospitals and everything that will be necessary for a good establishment" (*Archives,* 3:300), would prove as promising in fact as they had in the first comparative survey. The new site thus was suggestive of activity, and Buteaux reflects in his drawing this almost frenzied rebirth of French interest. The large number of temporary dwellings (field shelters and tents, for the most part) carries just this meaning here, while the joint effort on the rather impressive "Magazin" left of center (some sort of *collombage* structure, it seems) points toward more permanent intentions for the future. With a few exceptions, every figure in the view is involved in the labor of a new settlement—even the man in the small barge at the front who is an artist, like Buteaux himself, engaged in delineating the rapid progress of more practical arts on the land before him. In point of fact, however, the fort projected for this new settlement never was built, and the capital of Louisiana was moved to New Orleans (itself an "accidental" settlement) within two years of the time that Buteaux portrayed this active scene farther east.

William Byrd, "My Plat of 20,000 Acres in N. Carolina," ca. 1733. Courtesy of the Virginia Historical Society.

Byrd first saw his "20,000 Acres" while he and his fellow commissioners finished drawing the line between Virginia and North Carolina late in 1728. At that point the tract was of no particular importance to him; in the *Secret History of the Line* it is simply one more area passed through, perceived as it hinders or promotes the task in hand. Not until Byrd retold the whole story in his later "public" *History* did he linger over the virtues of this "Land of Eden." By that time he had come into possession of the tract, and what had once been a marginal piece of ground far from the settled regions now became a central piece of alluring real estate. "I question not but there are thirty thousand acres at least," Byrd wrote in the *History,* "lying all together, as fertile as the lands were said to be about Babylon, which yielded, if Herodotus tells us right, an increase of no less than two or three hundred for one. But this [land] hath the advantage of being a higher, and consequently a much healthier, situation than that. So that a colony of one thousand families might, with the help of moderate industry, pass their time very happily there" (*The Prose Works of William Byrd,* ed. Louis B. Wright [Cambridge: Harvard University Press, 1966], pp. 289–90). Listing the crops which might be raised on the land and describing the advantages of its climate, even remarking—in a witty inversion of the usual exploratory comment—that "everything will grow plentifully here to supply the wants or wantonness of man" (p. 290), Byrd pauses from the push of his linear, expeditionary prose so that his eye can survey the wilderness in a different sense, losing the difficulties of 1728 in a vision of future happiness. Byrd's "Plat," drawn up after he returned to the tract in 1733 in order to pin down its exact boundaries, reveals a similar expansiveness: projected south from "The Dividing Line," Eden is a tangential extension of that straight symbolic mark, a deflection of Eastern interest into a more fully dimensional world. Yet the boundaries of Eden, like the great Line itself, are applied to a scene which has its own lines and organizing principles. Hence the Dan River, curving south, passes outside Byrd's little future empire, leaving that place overdivided, fractured, and arbitrarily uncohesive. It is the conflict of sinuous natural facts and the assertive regularity of a distant government which gives this map, and much of Byrd's frontier prose, its peculiarly suggestive quality. Seeking to confine the landscape, such human inscriptions are ridiculed by the actual text of an elusive world.

Virginia

The Dan

Sugar Tree

White Oak

N. Carolina

Cascade Creek

The Dividing line

The Irvin

The Dan

White Oak

My Plat of 20,000 Acres in N Carolina. Survey'd in September 1733, by Mr Mayo, being 15 Miles long, 3 Broad: at the W End & one at the E End

Plate 20 "Eden in Virginia" (detail), from Samuel Jenner, *Neu-gefundenes Eden,* 1737. Courtesy of the John Carter Brown Library, Brown University.

William Byrd's "Land of Eden" was named for Charles Eden (1673–1722), governor of North Carolina until his death, the last of the "Landgraves" there under John Locke's Carolina constitution, and prime mover of the great Line which Byrd helped to draw. But Byrd, always alert to the easy pun, clearly recognized the promotional power in his little obeisance to Eden's memory. His Swiss agent Samuel Jenner was less subtle: taking Byrd's own name at face value, he translated it as "Wilhelm Vogel" in his promotional tract of 1737, and he likewise took "Eden" as a literal tag for the lands which he hoped to populate with his countrymen. Lying some twenty miles east of the "Land of Eden," this large tract was another of Byrd's holdings along the Roanoke and Dan rivers, and Byrd himself may well have supplied Jenner with hints on how to sell it, both literally and metaphorically, to the Swiss. Jenner's design for the intended colony on the present map is, however, far more detailed than any Byrd himself drew for his own Eden. A variation on the Savannah model just then being enacted in Georgia (which Jenner may have known through Samuel Urlsperger's German reports—see PLATE 11), the large town plan in the upper left corner of the map dominates by its very size the rather sparse portrait of Virginia offered here—for Jenner's details are, for the most part, related to his civic imaginings rather than to the facts of the American landscape itself. Conveniently enlarged for the prospective emigrant's inspection, the plan is big for other reasons as well: big because the three actual versions of it which sit rather rigidly on the landscape are too small in the scale of the whole, too reduced by the realities of Eden. Like a Platonic ideal, the detached scheme hovers over the terrain where it is hopefully to be fleshed out, an icon of foresight and control akin to that "E/D/E/N" device which so neatly interleaves the tributaries of the "Roanock." Multiplying the ideal, the three little towns bolster by their number if not their size this same theme of control; they suggest a future of untold repetitions, a time of infinite enlargements and secured possession. But the great villain in Jenner's plot, the sea where his emigrants foundered as they approached America's Eden, is absent from the map—implicit only in the converging streams that point toward its inevitable presence somewhere to the unpictured East.

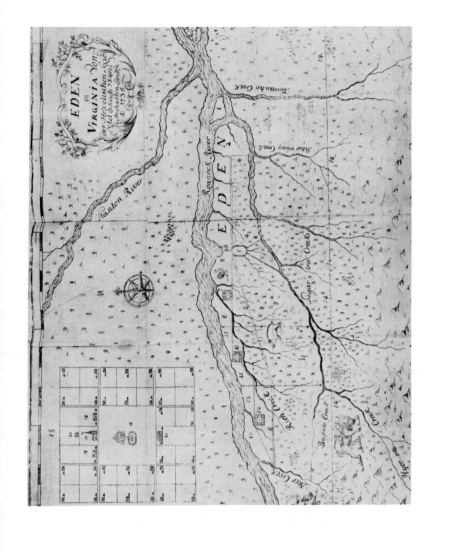

EDEN
in
VIRGINIA von
Der Nordindischen Geo...
...del Erkaufte 33400...
Nohactten Landes
A: 1736

Plate 21   Raphaelle Peale. *A Deception,* 1802. Courtesy of a private collection.

An ingenious and very early American work in the *trompe l'oeil* style, this pencil and ink drawing teases the viewer by its sharp imitation of paper and print, handwriting and engraving. Beyond the virtuosity of its illusion, however, there is a clear cultural message in the arrangement of the copied items and what they individually say. The piece asserts the real arrival of America after the Revolution (which Peale's father Charles Willson Peale served as both actor and artist)—for the arts and crafts and activities cataloged here add up to a crowded image of national action and interests, while Peale's own act of creation builds on (much as it includes) these other ones. But the mood of celebration is broken by various hesitations: the suggestively uneven margins of the copied items, and the ephemeral quality of them all—the sense that what they record has little real depth or endurance. The newspaper with its quotation of prices or list of imports, the various theater tickets, the lottery slip, the seal from a sugar package, the folded note with its scribblings, the "President's Birth Night" invitation for 1796 (three years before Washington's death), even the "Proposals" for Matthew Carey's energetically "complete" *System of Biography*—that sure-to-be-lost announcement of a formal effort at remembrance—all are suggestive of the melancholy which may be found in the later "illusions" of John F. Peto, where a certain violent sense of history is the ruling muse. If our perception of what is poignant in Peale's piece stems from this same fleeting quality in what it so faithfully records, we must note nonetheless how the items themselves are assertively decorative, oblivious to their own short lifespan. And when we look at that partly covered little newspaper clipping at the right (which recounts the demoralization of an Indian at the hands of those who have come to control his America), the hints of a "Deception" other than Peale's own begin to emerge. For this small and obscured narrative reminds us of a different American drama from those signified by the theater tickets strewn on Peale's board:

> [O]RIGINAL HUMOUR.—*Some years since, Mr.*
> *[C]——, a respectable clergyman in Litch-*
> *[field] county, was reproving an old Indian*
> *[for his] cruel and revengeful conduct towards*
> *[those] who had offended him: "You should*
> *[love yo]ur enemies," concluded the parson,*
> *[and pre]serve an affection for those that*
> *[hurt you]"—"I do love my enemies," retor-*
> *[ted the so]n of Nature, "and have a great*
> *[regard] for them that hurt me."—"No*
> *such thing," returned Mr. C——: ["]you*
> *dont love your enemies.["]—"I d[o]"—*
> *"Who are the enemies you love[?"]*
> *"Rum and Cyder."*

Plates 22 and 23   John White, Eskimo woman and child; Eskimo man, both ca. 1577. Courtesy of the Trustees of the British Museum.

Like John White's later portraits of Virginia natives (see PLATE 30 for Robert Vaughan's copies of them) or his view of "Secota" (PLATE 17), these paired watercolors are attentive to New World life and its departures from that of Europe. White's direct address to his three "sitters" is answered by their own slightly amused openness to his art. (How "foreign" these figures are can be sensed by a contrast to that long series of "Indian" portraits in European dress which was begun by the famous "Pocahontas" painting, completed sometime after 1616, and now displayed in the National Portrait Gallery in Washington.) Though the subjects here are obviously striking (or at least accepting) a rather formal pose that domesticates them to White's painterly traditions, they also reveal a certain artfulness of their own. White's interest in their clothing, for instance, focuses our attention on the ingenuity with which Eskimo culture has adapted to its bleak setting in the North: note the parka hoods, the woman's high boots and their fur lining, the drawstrings around the man's boots, the neat cut and trim of both coats. Perhaps more interesting, though, are the elongated dorsal flaps on the parkas—essential gear for sitting on the cold subarctic ground. White's composition of the two portraits stresses the self-sufficiency of his subjects in other ways, too—in their large bulk and the circular effect of their shape and posture. There is a feeling of ampleness and contentment in each: even if these fur-clad natives may seem rather wild to the European eye, the lines which delineate them are seductively civil and calm.

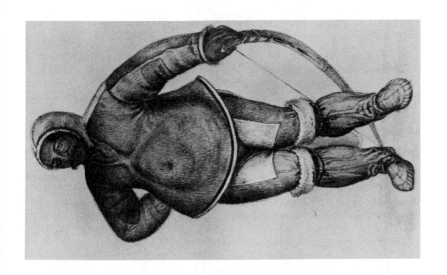

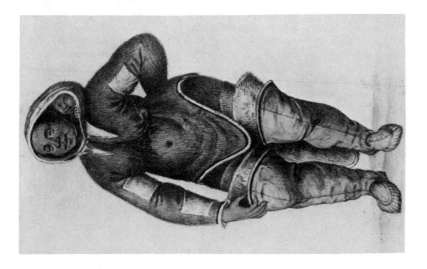

Plate 24 John White, Martin Frobisher's fight with the Eskimos at "Bloody Point," ca. 1577. Courtesy of the Trustees of the British Museum.

As I suggest in my text, there is a curious doubleness in this most active of John White's New World scenes. The single kayakman in the front is like an icon of America gently caught by European curiosity, brought up from the far background (where other tiny kayaks can be seen) so that the details of his craft and costume can be inspected by an inquisitive viewer. The heavy boat of Frobisher's men and this slim native vessel exist in part as elements in an ethnographic contrast outside the particular clash of the narrated battle. Yet White's whole composition of the piece involves that lone Eskimo in what is taking place, apparently without his knowledge, right behind him. The inverted triangle of the battle in fact balances near that man's head, its uneasy force dispersed across the neat curving lines of his kayak. And his own physical composure, similar to that of Frobisher's steersman but without the strain, likewise disperses the aggression of what would come to be called, by William Bradford among others, the "first encounter" between European and American peoples. White had his own sad encounters, and finally was bested by them far to the south at Roanoke. Yet here, as in his Virginia paintings, he reveals an artistic bearing on the New World which is deeply attentive in mood, which seeks to preserve native ways rather than confront, convert, or destroy them. The single kayakman at the front, pressed down as he is by the history taking fierce shape at his back, upstages the English soldier-explorers whose "superior" culture in this case is nothing more than their superior firepower. But Frobisher's several encounters hardly were epical in proportion or detail, for they were shabby, awkward affairs. "We disposed our selves, contrary to our inclination," Dionyse Settle comments at one point, "something to be cruel, returned to their tents and made a spoyle of the same" (Hakluyt, *Voyages*, 5:145). Or there is George Best's account of how Frobisher and one of his men seized two natives ("upon a watchword"—that is, with prior intent) during a peaceable exchange of goods, but lost the captives when, struggling with them on an icy hill, the Englishmen fell down and "their prey ranne away." Recovering their bows, the Eskimos began firing at Frobisher "and hurt the Generall in the buttocke with an arrow" (Hakluyt, *Voyages*, 5:207). If that last image is a concise portrait of the whole Frobisher enterprise, White's peaceful and graceful kayakman remains as a suggestion of a far different possibility, a glimpse of native skill and, in White's own attitude, of European attention to it.

Plate 25   Iceberg plate, from Thomas Ellis, *A True Report of the Third and Last Voyage into Meta Incognita,* 1578. Courtesy of the Huntington Library, San Marino, California.

Ellis's own comments on each section of this woodcut suggest the dynamism which is its main theme:

1. *At the first sight of this great and monstruous peece of yce, it appeared in this shape.*
2. *In comming neere unto it, it shewed after this shape.*
3. *In approching right against it, it opened in shape like unto this, shewing hollow within.*
4. *In departing from it, it appeared in this shape.*

Note the hints of hollowness in the first and second views, then the full revelation—then, quite suggestively, its disappearance from the final one. Likewise, note the artist's apparent lack of uniformity in line from view to view, which becomes an added confusion here—a further modulation in form that enhances the "inner" truth of the berg. This is a kind of magical transformation absent from the explorer's New World voyage or journey, a narrative of surprising changes inherent in the natural economy of America which leaves the traveler only a passive, circulating role. Perhaps we already can read here that theme of "deceit" which so many Europeans suggested as the real truth of Amerindian character—that hidden violence which became the defense of European "extinguishments" in dealing with the rights and the life of New World natives.

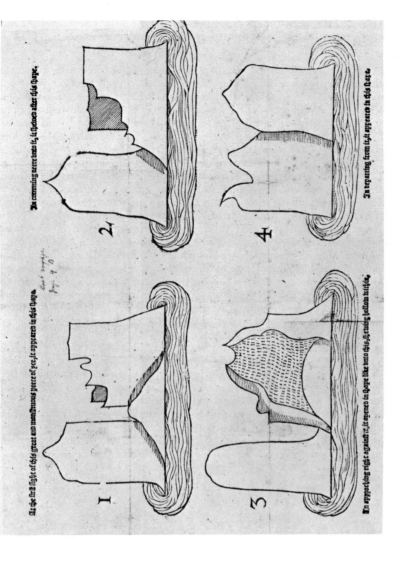

At the first sight of this great and monstrous peece of yce, it appeared in this shape.

1

In comming neere unto it, it shewed after this shape.

2

In approching right against it, it seemed in shape like unto this, streight bottom within.

3

In departing from it, it appeared in this forme.

4

Plate 26 James Beare, world map, from George Best, *A True Discourse of the Late Voyages of Discoverie*, 1578. Courtesy of the Huntington Library, San Marino, California.

Probably prepared by Frobisher's chief surveyor, this map illustrates George Best's vision of the whole Frobisher attempt rather than his narrative of what Frobisher actually achieved. As such, it suggests the degree to which any vacant space on Old World charts of New World reality almost seems to invite projective fantasies. What in fact was Baffin Island thus has become in Beare's map an orderly collection of smaller isles, each of them conveniently large enough to carry one syllable of "Me=ta In=cog=ni=ta" ("Unknown Destination"), the European name applied to this region by Queen Elizabeth herself. Like Samuel Jenner's "E/D/E/N" (see PLATE 20), this other blending of graphic and textual order is a device for the symbolic control of what it touches—not just an innocent decorative flourish. The act of naming acquires here, as so often in the records of New World travel, a deeply active purpose; it seeks to constitute and interpret, not merely refer to, the ground over which it is asserted. Yet the greatest fantasy in Beare's map is its very constitution of geography itself according to European desire. The almost straight "Straightes" that lead from left to right verbally, but from East to West toward the Orient in an active sense, are the hopeful sign of accommodation—a "naming" of the whole New World which seeks to subordinate a vast area to a single and simpleminded plan for its use. Though Beare concedes, by the dotted lines so evident in this part of his map, that the Northwest Passage (like the whole shore of America) is a pure conjecture—a possible "reading" offered in lieu of the not yet discovered "text"—his hopeful words certainly suggest that some such opening *ought* to exist. That one can name "Frobishers Straightes" means that experience in the future should verify the word, that things thus named almost will be created by their articulation. Unlike the iceberg plate of Thomas Ellis (PLATE 25), the present piece hints that reality is "hollow" exactly where Europeans want it to be. The unexplored depths of America are like a whisper which strong words can drown, a vague shape dissolved by the manipulations of our own art.

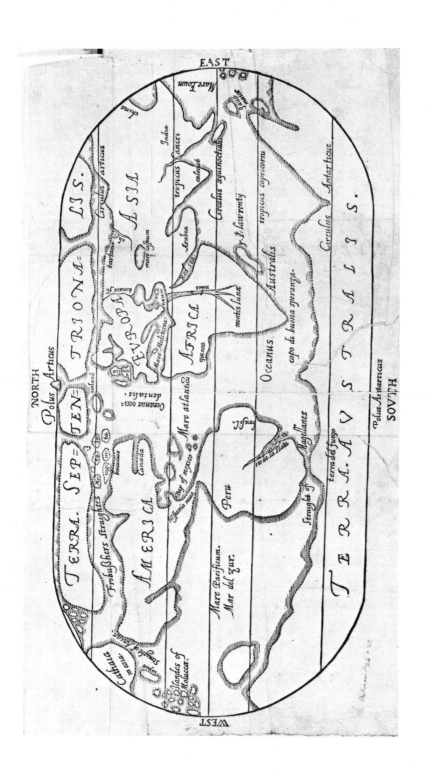

Plate 27 John Vanderlyn, *The Death of Jane McCrea*, 1804. Courtesy of the Wadsworth Atheneum, Hartford; purchased by subscription.

A visual image of the captivity myth, this oil painting depicts the tragic end of a famous American journey. McCrea, member of a New Jersey family divided by the conflicting loyalties of the Revolution, was living with her brother John, a patriot colonel, near Ft. Edward in upper New York as Burgoyne began his invasion in 1777. John McCrea moved with many of his neighbors toward the security of Albany, but he could not convince Jane to join him; engaged to a local Tory who was with Burgoyne, she apparently hoped that the British advance would reunite her with her lover and perhaps even result in their marriage. On the morning of July 27, she went to visit a friend who was just preparing to flee south with the other inhabitants. The two women soon were captured by a party of Indians in Burgoyne's service; the friend was later delivered to the British and freed, but McCrea's shot and scalped body was found on the next day near Ft. Edward. Her murder, full of so many of the ironies generated by the great war, quickly became a focal point for political and military debates and for the enduring anxieties of America's transplanted culture. Philip Freneau used the story in his poem, *America Independent* (1778), as proof of British cruelties, while Edmund Burke employed it in a House of Commons speech against the British habit of using Indian mercenaries. (See Edward T. James, et al., *Notable American Women, 1607–1950: A Biographical Dictionary* [Cambridge: Harvard University Press, 1971], 2:456–57). John Vanderlyn's painting, commissioned for a new edition of Joel Barlow's epic, *The Columbiad,* which also retold the McCrea tale, stresses the racial conflict evidenced in her fate rather than the political argument which developed from it. We have here a shadowy image of New World space and experience, a dream-like vision which displaces onto an innocent (and intensely white) woman the supposedly innocent imperatives of her culture, imperatives victimized in her own torture by a foreground of darkly active wilderness and wildness. Edmund Burke is relevant to the work as a theorist of the sublime, not as a spokesman for "humane" warfare, for Vanderlyn has conceived of his subject as a conflict between the domestic and the wild—his Indians are icons of the American forest which rises behind them like an explanation of their nature. But note the hidden currents which ripple Vanderlyn's sanitized dream: the classically ideal forms of the two grim-visaged Indians remind one of Rome rather than the Iroquois domain of John Bartram and Lewis Evans (see PLATE 7), and this very classicism seems to mock the beauty of McCrea herself—whose posture (one bent and one straight arm, for instance) is so strangely like that of her murderers, and whose left hand firmly grasps the left wrist of the Indian who has grabbed her hair almost at the center of the painting. Even the helpless little white man in the clearing at the back enters into this hidden theme: he copies and magnifies McCrea's impotence, but also copies in reverse the stance of the Indian nearest to him. The racial contrast, in other words, is subtly obscured by the mingling of its own opposite terms.

Plate 28 Pocahontas and the aggressions of Samuel Argall; J. T. de Bry, *Americae pars decima*, 1618. Courtesy of the Edward E. Ayer Collection, the Newberry Library, Chicago.

Violating the unities of space and time according to contemporary practice, de Bry illustrates in this engraving a set of loosely related events in early Virginia. The ships at the right front are those of Samuel Argall during his food-seeking voyage on the Potomac in 1613, when the Jamestown colony was once again short of supplies. As the man who helped to establish a direct sailing route between England and North America, Argall might well be represented by an allegorical ship, but the real intent of this complicated engraving points to his other actions within the colony itself. Whereas John Smith let it be known that he had served Pocahontas by allowing her to save him in 1608 (see PLATE 30), Argall arranged for her virtual kidnapping in 1613—the event prefigured in the foreground here, where an Indian priest tries to convince her to go on board Argall's vessel. Taken to Jamestown, the daughter of Powhatan married John Rolfe in 1614, sailed with him for England two years later, was received there by James I, but died at Gravesend in 1617. Her passing was like an ominous hint of later events in the difficult diplomacy between red and white (see PLATE 29). The middle ground of de Bry's engraving illustrates another facet of that diplomacy: the bargains being struck on the nearest ship and on the shore nearby are more nearly practical, linked to an exchange of commodities rather than people. But behind all of this verbal commerce is the record of Thomas Dale's punitive expedition (as we are trained to call it) against an Indian settlement on the York river, an effort motivated by the anger of Powhatan over the seduction of his young daughter. In a dramatic and historical sense, the most important events related by this engraving thus have been upstaged by a ritual of persuasion and trade which obscures the violence inevitably born of its own deceit. Even if de Bry's purpose here has been determined by some rule of artistic economy (three plates conflated into one), the unlikely juxtaposition of violence and conversation has its own subtle justice. Like Vanderlyn's simplified portrait of racial conflict, this vision of early Virginia conjoins things which it would prefer to keep separate, and by the conjunction suggests the underlying links of history (see PLATE 27).

Plate 29 The massacre at Jamestown in 1622; Matthew Merian, *Decima tertia pars historiae Americanae* (de Bry's *America*, pt. 13), 1634. Courtesy of the Edward E. Ayer Collection, the Newberry Library, Chicago.

Like John Vanderlyn's much later vision of racial conflict (see PLATE 27), this more cluttered one portrays white intentions in the New World as simple and just, a pious purpose on which alien forces have unaccountably intruded. Every settler in this "massacre" seems to have been surprised while pursuing some peaceful goal—the feasters at the left front, the carpenter to the right (his adze being a tool rather than a weapon), the men, women, and children laid low across the middle. The conceit is absurdly developed, for its development is determined by an absurd premise about English involvements in America. The settlers are figures of benevolent form, as the buildings embracing the disaster suggest, and even their defensive reaction is relegated to a far background where the gory details of white violence can be lost in an epical vision. The foreground scene, as one suspects, is an ideal view of the dire reality enacted there—ideal in its values if not its own gory details. (Note the pile of fish, abandoned on the ground like a mark of some now-outmoded abundance.) But the very attempt at persuasion persuades us of meanings other than those intended: of the settlers' inattention to the world which is destroying them, but also of their hidden complicity in the destruction. Every activated figure is native, every passive one an emigrant, yet one senses that the very uprightness of the European buildings is itself a sign of what is amiss here, that the eruption of native passion has something to do with the firm lines of Old World power. So obviously propagandistic, the engraving defeats itself by omitting the facts which abetted the destruction it focuses on. The ruined New World imagined here is too clarified in its legend, too melodramatic in its plot and theme; it covers rather than reveals the real marrow of Virginia politics.

Plate 30 Robert Vaughan, "Ould Virginia" plate, from John Smith, *The Generall Historie of Virginia, New-England, and the Summer Isles,* 1624. Courtesy of the Newberry Library, Chicago.

Most interesting among the details in this complex engraving is the fact that John Smith, the first martial hero of early America, has been inserted graphically and historically into the more peaceful visions of his predecessor John White. Hence the dance in the upper left, similar to that rendered in White's "Secota" (PLATE 17) and elsewhere, has become a warlike gesture here, a means of confining Smith, while the "conjuration" to its right, combining several of White's pictures, is a pagan rite centered on the European soldier thrust into the native ritual, rather than a simple fact of Indian practice. Though the London engraver Robert Vaughan thus relied on the best graphic models he could find in embellishing Smith's career in America, his rather slavish imitations of White give his own plate an eerie resonance, a feeling of presumptuous revision rather than plagiarism. The White paintings are copied in fact but ignored in spirit. But since presumption was one of Smith's best arts as colonist and historian, there is something uncannily right about Vaughan's insertion of him into White's universe. Note, however, the schematic nature of Smith's American deeds, the contrast between his passivity at the lower right (where he is about to be beheaded) and his almost ritualized activity at the upper right and lower left, which repeat each other and not just White. Tit for tat, the natives mistreat Smith elsewhere on the sheet. Yet the erroneous depiction of White's "Secota" as a walled town near the left border of Vaughan's map of "Ould Virginia" (that is, Carolina) is a fitting repudiation of the art which has been so much copied from White throughout the engraving, and so much changed in meaning.

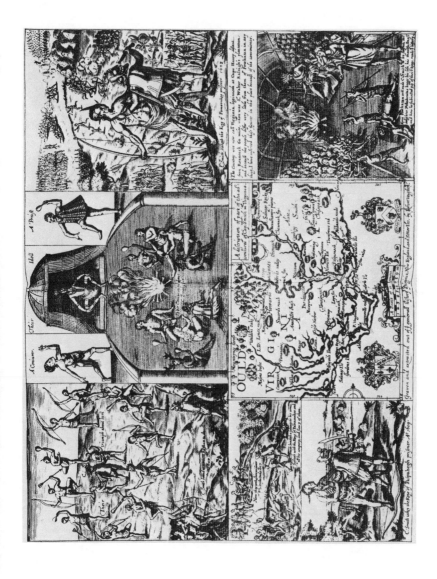

❧ NOTES ❧

PROLOGUE

1. I quote from J. M. Cohen's edition of Columbus materials, *The Four Voyages of Christopher Columbus* (Baltimore: Penguin Books, 1969), p. 291. In his next statement, Columbus goes on to thank God for having given him on this holy day a good river and a safe harbor; but then he lists for half a page a series of further frustrations and disasters, to conclude: "I know of no one who has suffered greater trials."

2. J. H. Elliott has presented a concise summary of the conqueror's political broils in his introduction to Hernán Cortés, *Letters from Mexico,* ed. and trans. A. R. Pagden (New York: Grossman Pub., 1971).

3. Thoreau, *Walden,* ed. J. Lyndon Shanley (Princeton: Princeton University Press, 1971), p. 3; Cohen, p. 304.

4. Cohen, *Four Voyages,* p. 295; as Cohen points out, the letter actually was carried (and delivered) by Spaniards.

INTRODUCTION

1. For the record, his Spanish is: *Dia de la Epifania llegué á Veragua, ya sin aliento.* I quote from R. H. Major, ed. and trans., *Select Letters of Christopher Columbus* (New York: Corinth Books, 1961 [1847]), p. 181; Major renders *ya sin aliento* as "in a state of exhaustion."

2. Arthur C. Danto, *Analytical Philosophy of History* (Cambridge: Cambridge University Press, 1968), is a suggestive study of narrative language—and particularly of the problems entailed in historical narration. I have relied on its formulations throughout the present book.

3. That is to say, Epiphany was a European fact which was irrelevant to Veragua. Columbus, of course, would not have accepted such a premise outrightly; but see his comment later in this letter: "Here in the Indies I am cut off from the prescribed forms of religion, alone in my troubles, sick, in daily expectation of death and surrounded by a million hostile savages full of cruelty, and so far from the Holy Sacraments of the Blessed Church that my soul will be forgotten if it leaves my body" (J. M. Cohen, ed. and trans., *The Four Voyages of Christopher Columbus* [Baltimore: Penguin Books, 1969], pp. 303–4).

4. Columbus heard of Veragua while he was working his way to the East along the Caribbean coast of Central America. Before actually stopping to investigate the reports of gold and goldfields at Veragua, however, he went past it, then turned around and slowly went back to the place, encountering severe bad weather en route. Ironically, the grandson of Columbus (Luis Colón) was granted in 1536, for renouncing his hereditary claims over all of the West Indies, the title of "Duke of Veragua," along with substantial tracts of land in Central America. See Samuel Eliot Morison, *Admiral of the Ocean Sea* (Boston: Little, Brown, 1942), p. 609.

5. Lee Eldridge Huddleston, *Origins of the American Indians: European Concepts, 1492–1729* (Austin: University of Texas Press, 1967), describes the sometimes absurd speculations of Old World thinkers about the number and nature of American languages; Margaret T. Hodgen, *Early Anthropology in the Sixteenth and Seventeenth Centuries* (Philadelphia: Univer-

211

sity of Pennsylvania Press, 1964), offers rich comments on allied topics—
particularly on the canons of cultural observation and description which
hampered the accurate perception of non-European life (see esp. chap. 5,
"Collections of Customs: Modes of Classification and Description," pp.
162–206).

6. Cortés, *Letters from Mexico,* ed. and trans. A. R. Pagden (New York:
Grossman Pub., 1971), p. 109.

7. The political background of the Cortés expedition was complex.
Technically, Cortés was the subordinate of Diego Velázquez (governor of
Cuba), who dispatched him in 1518 to locate the Grivalja fleet which had
been sent out the previous year, and to round up Christian captives in
Yucatan. But Cortés looked upon the Spanish record in the Caribbean as a
sad accumulation of selfish acts, and upon Velázquez himself as a prime
example of what was wrong with colonial government. Hence he exploited
his literal distance from Cuba, converting it into a base of power which he
shored up by claiming that, according to ancient Spanish custom, his followers had rejected the corrupt authority of Velázquez and had chosen
Cortés as their lawful leader. The expedition went so far as to found the
"city" of Vera Cruz as a sign that it constituted a true community, and
therefore had the right to elect a commander other than the one provided
by colonial hierarchy. Complicating matters was the fact that Velázquez,
who opposed the actions of Cortés, himself chafed under the authority of
Diego Colón, the son of Columbus and hereditary Admiral of the Indies,
and petitioned Charles V (as Cortés did) for a grant of direct power. That
Cortés did not receive approval from Charles until 1522 was a crucial fact
which influenced all he did and said up to that date. See Elliott's essay in
Letters from Mexico.

8. Harry Elmer Barnes, *A History of Historical Writing* (2d rev. ed.; New
York: Dover Pub., 1962), discusses the changes caused by the "era of
discovery" in the practice of European historiography—changes which
upset the "special languages" that I mention (see esp. pp. 136–47). His
basic point, with which I agree, is that the need to report on countless
topics about which little had been written previously caused a sudden,
dramatic expansion of historiographical practice. On the other hand, I
share with Hodgen and others a sense of the subtle ways in which old
prejudices and biases affected the white apprehension of nonwhite cultures, and hence survived in the very texture of the "new" histories. Roy
Harvey Pearce's study of *The Savages of America* (rev. ed.; Baltimore: Johns
Hopkins Press, 1965), is a reminder of how closed European minds, and
Old World languages, were when it came to confronting native life—of
how old biases might actually be extended by those works which on their
surface seemed to mark the departure of Europe from its medieval pro-
vincialism.

9. J. H. Elliott, *The Old World and the New: 1492–1650* (Cambridge: Cambridge University Press, 1970), is particularly good on the difficult intellectual reaction of Europe to America.

10. Edmundo O'Gorman, *The Invention of America* (Bloomington: Indiana
University Press, 1961), demonstrates superbly the process by which this
accommodation was achieved.

11. Federico Chabod's essay on "The Concept of the Renaissance,"
trans. David Moore in *Machiavelli and the Renaissance* (New York: Harper
& Row, 1965), discusses briefly but brilliantly the effect of the discovery on
modern views of ancient knowledge.

212   12. Bacon, *The New Organon and Related Writings,* ed. Fulton H. Ander-

son (Indianapolis: Bobbs-Merrill, 1960), pp. 13, 91. In trying to answer the
opinion that the ancients knew far more than the moderns, Bacon writes: "Nor must it go for nothing that by the distant voyages and travels which have become frequent in our times many things in nature have been laid open and discovered which may let in new light upon philosophy. And surely it would be disgraceful if, while the regions of the material globe— that is, of the earth, of the sea, and of the stars—have been in our times laid widely open and revealed, the intellectual globe should remain shut up within the narrow limits of old discoveries" (p. 81).

13. Of the "library" as a symbolic locale, Bacon wrote, "If a man turn ...to the library, and wonder at the immense variety of books he sees there, let him but examine and diligently inspect their matter and contents, and his wonder will assuredly be turned the other way. For after observing their endless repetitions, and how men are ever saying and doing what has been said and done before, he will pass from admiration of the variety to astonishment at the poverty and scantiness of the subjects which till now have occupied and possessed the minds of men" (pp. 82–83). The real task now was "the opening and laying out of a road for the human understanding direct from the sense" (p. 79).

14. On the issue of a scientific literary style, see also Bacon's comment that "experience has not yet learned her letters" (p. 97), and those many places where he assaults the "foolish and apish images of worlds" so common in older philosophy (p. 113 and *passim*).

15. I quote Ames from Merrill D. Peterson, *Thomas Jefferson and the New Nation* (New York: Oxford University Press, 1970), p. 772; for Jefferson himself, see below, chap. 1.

16. *Travels in the United States in 1847,* trans. and ed. Michael Aaron Rockland (Princeton: Princeton University Press, 1970), pp. 133, 149.

17. *The Vision of Columbus; A Poem in Nine Books* (Hartford: Hudson and Goodwin, 1787), "Dedication" (to Louis XVI). Barlow's involvement in the Scioto land frauds in France shortly after the poem appeared suggests how mixed the "blessings" of America might be, how closely linked panegyrics and promotional imposture often were in New World history; see Durand Echeverria, *Mirage in the West: A History of the French Image of American Society to 1815* (Princeton: Princeton University Press, 1968), pp. 116–74, for the various western frauds perpetrated in France during Barlow's period.

18. The 1930s leftist Josephine Herbst rendered the kind of arrogation I am thinking of here when she had a character deliver an unctuous speech on "Capital" to a Chamber of Commerce meeting in Deadwood, S. D. "I do not intend to speak lightly of the prospector," the speaker remarks. "Rather I would pay him tribute. He is the Columbus in civilization, tracking the wilderness as Columbus did the sea to discover a new world. He finds and tells the public, others come in and possess the land. They who bought the Comstock mines and manipulated their stocks have grown rich and gained seats in the Senate Chamber while the discoverer died poor, alone and friendless. Such lives have not been a failure"—*Pity is Not Enough* (New York: Harcourt, Brace, 1932), p. 345.

19. Quoted by Justin Winsor, *Christopher Columbus,* (Boston: Houghton, Mifflin, 1891), p. 57.

20. "Problems in American History," in Ray Allen Billington, ed., *Frontier and Section* (Englewood Cliffs, N.J.: Prentice-Hall, 1961), p. 29.

21. Among the frontier studies which I have found most helpful, the following deserve mention here: Earl Pomeroy, *In Search of the Golden West*

and *The Pacific Slope* (New York: Knopf, 1957 and 1965); Walker D. Wyman and Clifton B. Kroeber, eds., *The Frontier in Perspective* (Madison: University of Wisconsin Press, 1957); Edwin Fussell, *Frontier: American Literature and the American West* (Princeton: Princeton University Press, 1965); Roderick Nash, *Wilderness and the American Mind* (New Haven: Yale University Press, 1967); John W. Reps, *Urban Planning in Frontier America* (Princeton: Princeton University Press, 1969); and Charles E. Clark, *The Eastern Frontier: The Settlement of Northern New England, 1610–1763* (New York: Knopf, 1970).

22. Louis Gottschalk's "The Historian and the Historical Document," in *The Use of Personal Documents in History, Anthropology and Sociology* (New York: Social Science Research Council, n.d.), offers a number of useful comments about how historians can and do employ the kind of texts discussed here. For the critic's approach, perhaps no better example can be found than the still-standard volumes of Moses Coit Tyler, *A History of American Literature, 1607–1765* (New York: Putnam's, 1878), and *The Literary History of the American Revolution, 1763–1783* (New York: Putnam's, 1897), in both of which Tyler's method—though informed throughout by historical data (Tyler was a history professor for part of his career)— amounts to the singling out of the "better" books, and of the "best" passages within them. Of more recent attempts to combine critical and historical methods, none is more ambitious than Richard Slotkin's *Regeneration Through Violence: The Mythology of the American Frontier, 1600–1860* (Middletown, Conn.: Wesleyan University Press, 1973); unfortunately, Slotkin's stimulating thesis is reductive in its application, and his discussion of particular texts often is inattentive to what they say and how they say it.

23. Robert C. Bredeson, "Landscape Description in Nineteenth-Century American Travel Literature," *American Quarterly*, 20 (1968): 94. I recognize, of course, that we cannot ask the seventeenth-century writer to be modern in his tastes. But the point is that travelers in that period (and the adjoining centuries) often ground their claims to the reader's attention on an empirical approach which in fact they frequently abandon.

24. The term *topoi* is a metaphor for the "places" where a speaker or writer may "locate" arguments appropriate to a given subject. "Commonplaces" (*koinoi topoi* in Aristotle's *Rhetoric*) are those aids to persuasion which, like the principle of "more or less," are applicable to a wide range of subjects. Less general *topoi* (*idioi topoi* or "private places") are aids relevant to a specialized subject or a local case, such as the principles of law or of physics. Though the *topoi* which characterize each variety of American travel book have a certain general force, their relation to the facts of New World space, and experience in it, makes them in many ways a set of specialized devices, resonantly concrete figures for the traveler's journey away from the "common place" of Europe itself. Like the spatial *topoi* discussed by Ernst Robert Curtius in *European Literature and the Latin Middle Ages,* trans. Willard R. Trask (Princeton: Princeton University Press, 1953), pp. 183–202, they are verbal formulations which project onto the physical world various human ideals, values, or feelings that have a broad currency. But in many cases the act of projection performed by New World travelers is seen as a distinctively American event—a "discovery" rather than an imitation of prior formulas.

25. Louis B. Wright quotes the first comment from the sea captain John Mason in his "Introduction" to Richard Eburne, *A Plain Pathway to Planta-*

tions (Ithaca: Cornell University Press, 1962 [1624]), p. xx; the second is   *Notes to*
from Robert Rogers, *Journals* (New York: Corinth Books, 1961 [1765]), pp.   *Pages 18–25*
iii–iv.

CHAPTER ONE

1. Howard Mumford Jones discusses the link between the chivalric romance and early America, *O Strange New World* (New York: Viking Press, 1964), pp. 20–27; John Seelye argues in *Prophetic Waters: The River in Early American Life and Literature* (New York: Oxford University Press, 1977) for the importance of Spenser's *Faerie Queene* to English undertakings in the New World (see esp. pp. 26–27).

2. The *Remonstrance (Vertoogh van Nieu-Neder-land,* 1650) is translated in J. Franklin Jameson, ed., *Narratives of New Netherland, 1609–1664* (New York: Scribner's, 1909) pp. 293–354, where it is followed by Cornelis van Tienhoven's "Answer" (1650); though the *Vertoogh* was signed by several settlers, Jameson concludes (p. 288) that van der Donck was the main, perhaps the sole, author. In any event, its mixture of the perception that New Netherland is notable for its *vruchbaerheydt* (fruitfulness) with the sense that it now is languishing in a *soberen staet* (poor state) sets it off sharply from the relatively enthusiastic *Description* which van der Donck later wrote on his own.

3. I quote from the Jeremiah Johnson translation, as presented in Thomas F. O'Donnell, ed., *A Description of the New Netherlands* (Syracuse: Syracuse University Press, 1968), p. 2.

4. One of the more startling instances of this timeless feeling is to be found in Henry Woodward's "A faithful relation of my Westoe voyage" (1674): "[The Westoe Indians] are seated uppon a most fruitfull soyl. The earth is intermingled wth a sparkling substance like Antimony, finding several flakes of Isinglass in the paths. The soales of my Indian shooes in which I travelled glistened like silver"—Alexander S. Salley, Jr., ed., *Narratives of Early Carolina, 1650–1708* (New York: Scribner's, 1911), p. 133.

5. *The Discoverie of the Large, Rich, and Bewtiful Empyre of Guiana, with a Relation of the Great and Golden Citie of Manoa* (London, 1596), pp. 94, 5, 100–1; I have regularized Ralegh's use of "u" and "v" (as I shall do in similar cases throughout my text). For a 1618 engraving of America as a hunter's paradise, see PLATE 1.

6. The outright structure of Jefferson's book, a series of European questions answered by a set of American responses, makes explicit a shape which often organizes the New World report. A similar polarity between Old World ignorance and American experience enlivens van der Donck's "Dialogue between a Patriot and a New Netherlander upon the Advantages which the Country Presents to Settlers" (at the end of his *Description*), while the whole of Richard Eburne's *A Plain Pathway to Plantations,* a lively Newfoundland promotion tract of 1624, is based on an allied design— Eburne's "pathway" being, in fact, the inducing line of his own authorial stance "between" England and the New World.

7. In his edition of *Notes on the State of Virginia* (Chapel Hill: University of North Carolina Press for the Institute of Early American History and Culture, 1954), William Peden writes: "Before he sailed for France [Jefferson] purchased a large panther skin which the Marquis de Chastellux later delivered to Buffon along with a copy of *Notes on Virginia.* Still later, after having met but not convinced Buffon, Jefferson prevailed upon his old   215

acquaintance, Governor John Sullivan of New Hampshire, to obtain the 'skin, the skeleton, and the horns of a moose.' The result was ultimately complied with, although it took a 'regular campaign' of twenty men on a winter's hunting expedition in the White Mountains—and a considerable amount of money—to do it!" (p. 268, n. 28). Jefferson had told Buffon that "our deer had horns two feet long," and that "the reindeer could walk under the belly of our moose"—both of which claims the scientist rejected, calling for evidence. Sullivan's expedition, which cost Jefferson forty-five pounds, was an attempt to provide such proof; but, despite the governor's great effort and Jefferson's great expense, the specimen had very small horns. See Merrill D. Peterson, *Thomas Jefferson and the New Nation* (New York: Oxford University Press, 1970), pp. 338–39.

8. William Hilton's *A Relation of a Discovery Lately Made on the Coast of Florida* (1664), which tells of a bewitching voyage up the Cape Fear river, suggests how the delighted traveler might be "amazed" in the other sense: for, sending their boat back down the river, Hilton and his companions traveled on foot, and "were so much taken with the pleasantnesse of the Land, that travelling into the woods so far, [they] could not recover [their] Boat and company that night"—Salley, *Carolina Narratives*, p. 48.

9. Jefferson suffered from severe headaches at various points in his life, usually at times of great emotional stress; see Peterson, p. 84, and Fawn Brodie, *Thomas Jefferson: An Intimate Portrait* (New York: Bantam Books, 1975), pp. 136–37, 226–27, 314–15.

10. The "mill stream" figure occurs commonly throughout the early American travel book. It is both a means of rough measurement and a way of suggesting, as here, a future settlement on ground not yet literally settled. As I argue in my next chapter, such figures are primary devices of the exploratory account.

11. This comes from the 1787 text, quoted by Peden (pp. 263–64, n. 5); Jefferson later noted: "This description was written after a lapse of several years from the time of my visit to the bridge, and under an error of recollection which requires apology. For it is from the bridge itself that the mountains are visible both ways, and not from the bottom of the fissure as my impression then was" (ibid.). The revised description runs as follows: "This painful sensation [i.e., the "violent head ach"] is relieved by a short, but pleasing view of the Blue ridge along the fissure downwards, and upwards by that of the Short hills, which, with the Purgatory mountain is a divergence from the North ridge" (p. 25).

12. The query given to Jefferson stressed navigation; but the stress was not foreign to his own interests—see his "Instructions to Captain Lewis," in Merrill D. Peterson, ed., *The Portable Jefferson* (New York: Viking Press, 1975), pp. 308–15. Rivers, and a good deal besides, are of particular interest for Seelye in *Prophetic Waters*.

13. Maps can function as exploratory vehicles, as Jefferson's ideal scheme for Western plantations suggests (see his map of "Polypotamia," reproduced in PLATE 3; and his "Report of a Plan of Government for the Western Territory," *Portable Jefferson*, pp. 254–58). But maps also can serve the purposes of wonder when imperial scheming gives way to a simple, graphically expressed delight.

14. "History of Mrs. B. An Epitome of All the Misfortunes Which Can Possibly Overtake a New Settler, As Related by Herself," in Albert E. Stone, Jr., ed., *Letters from an American Farmer and Sketches of Eighteenth-Century America* (New York: New American Library, 1963), p. 366.

15. Jefferson prepared a map for the Morellet edition of the *Notes* (1787); he thought so highly of it that he added it to the remaining copies of the private edition of 1785 and to the Stockdale printing of 1787. Peden writes (p. xviii, n. 24) that "Jefferson frequently declared that his map was of more value than the book in which it appeared." The relation of map and text in early American works often is, as Jefferson's comment suggests, competitive. Yet it is safe to say that maps do not simply illustrate the texts, and that the prose does not merely gloss the chart accompanying it. The two arts are more often complementary, two different views of a single subject or region, and each of them can provide the other with a metaphoric heightening—as is the case in John Smith's *A Map of Virginia* (1612) or William Wood's *New Englands Prospect* (1634). Thomas Ashe thus offers in *Carolina, or A Description of the Present State of That Country* (1682) a "Draught of this excellent Country" (Salley, *Carolina Narratives*, p. 158)—a prose account organized on cartographic principles. See also Jefferson's chart of the Virginia Indians (PLATE 4), which is a geographical model, presented in prose, of the distribution of native tribes.

16. The first map referred to was prepared by Jefferson's father and Joshua Fry, William and Mary mathematician, in 1751; Jefferson based his own map on it. The second reference is to the *General Map* published four years later by Lewis Evans, and particularly to his "Analysis" of it in his *Essays* (1755), both of which Lawrence Henry Gibson reproduces in *Lewis Evans* (Philadelphia: Historical Society of Pennsylvania, 1939).

17. Howard Mumford Jones, *O Strange New World*, p. 358, praises the Potomac passage in *Notes* as the first "full panoramic landscape organized [by] aesthetic principles."

18. Jefferson's viewpoint is on the hill west of the confluence. Richard Slotkin's discussion of this scene and of the Natural Bridge passage in *Regeneration through Violence: The Mythology of the American Frontier* (Middletown, Conn.: Wesleyan University Press, 1973), pp. 245–47, links Jefferson's meditation on natural violence to the themes of the captivity accounts; I prefer to connect it with a more general sense of "history."

19. Other American texts, particularly war narratives like Robert Rogers's *Journals* (1765), make good use of the epic "breach" in more literal ways.

20. The rivers, like American settlers, have "ranged along the foot of the mountains an hundred miles to seek a vent," and the mountain seems justly "rent asunder" by their combined longing for a passage (p. 19). Though American expansion moved in an opposite direction, it did so along such opened passageways: the Potomac, Jefferson writes earlier, is blocked for navigation at the falls, but may be corrected "at no great expence" (p. 7), and thus will provide a convenient way into the hinterland. In a less economic sense, the battle of water and rock which produces a glimpse into the "plain country" is a clear allegory of the Revolution; the British have hindered the natural desire of the colonists for a freer movement and a more ample ground.

21. John Filson, *The Discovery, Settlement and Present State of Kentucke* (New York: Corinth Books, 1962 [1784]), p. 58. Boone's almost melancholic record of his early travels in Kentucky, full of a resignation which allows the traveler to find "pleasure in a path strewed with briars and thorns" (p. 54), opens up at one point to a sense of wondering ravishment as the hunter surveys from a "commanding ridge" both "the ample plains, the beauteous tracts" of Kentucky, and "the famous river Ohio" rolling "in

217

silent dignity," and with "inconceivable grandeur," below him (p. 55). Finally, however, Boone's "astonishing delight" (p. 55) and his perception that "Nature [is] . . . a series of wonders, and a fund of delight" (pp. 51–52) are destroyed by his involvement in the bloody history of this region.

22. "The Wonders of Canada: A Letter from a Gentleman to the Antigua Gazette," reprinted in *Magazine of American History*, 1 (1877): 244; Jean-Bernard Bossu, *Travels in the Interior of North America*, trans. and ed. Seymour Feiler (Norman: University of Oklahoma Press, 1962), p. 203 (based on Bossu's *Nouveaux Voyages aux Indes Occidentales*, 1768).

23. Bossu tells of his Indian adoption, and of his tribe's customs, in "Letter V," pp. 60–67. A postscript to this letter tells of a certain "half-Indian" who was the son of a Breton sailor named "Rutel." Like his father, who was adopted by the Caddo Indians after he got lost during La Salle's expedition in 1682, and who lived among the natives in harmony, this young man offers a quite different example of a European's fate in America from that provided in the horrific account of Monsieur de Belle-Isle's captivity among the Attacapas, related by Bossu in "Letter XX."

24. "The Wonders of Canada," *Magazine of American History*, 1 (1877): 244; Salley, *Carolina Narratives*, p. 131.

25. Clayton Colman Hall, ed., *Narratives of Early Maryland, 1633–1684* (New York: Scribner's, 1910), pp. 359–60.

26. *A Two Years Journal in New-York: and Part of its Territories in America*, ed. E. B. O'Callaghan, reprinted in Cornell Jaray, ed., *Historic Chronicles of New Amsterdam, Colonial New York and Early Long Island* (Port Washington, N. Y.: Ira J. Friedman, 1968), 1st ser., p. 60. Wooley's work deals with the period 1678–80, but was not published until 1701.

27. *New Englands Prospect* (London: Tho. Coates for John Bellamie, 1634), A4r and title page.

28. *New English Canaan, or New Canaan. Containing an Abstract of New England, Composed in Three Bookes* (Amsterdam: Jacob Frederick Stam, 1637), pp. 27, 28, 53, 64, 84; Morton's own chap. 9 offers a "Perspective to view the Country by," a "prospect" much larger than Wood's.

29. *Newes from America; or, A New and Experimental Discoverie of New England* (London: Peter Cole, 1638), p. 1 and title page. "Newes" is to be taken not simply as "information," but also as "new things," a Saxon version of "discovery."

30. Rogers's *Journals* gives the itinerary of his experience; the *Concise Account*, on the other hand, offers a discursive map of a vast region extending from the Floridas to Newfoundland, from Virginia to the Mississippi and beyond. The author's attempt in the latter is to organize such an expansive world—as when he trisects the whole Northwest by locating above Lake Superior "the Head of the Country" (an Indian concept), from which flow out three great rivers that divide "the continent . . . into so many departments, as it were, from a center." Though the northernmost of these departments, lying near Hudson's Bay, is unsuitable for settlement, the others lack "nothing but that culture and improvement, which can only be the effect of time and industry, to render [them] equal, if not superior, to any in the world" (see the London ed. of 1765, printed for Rogers, pp. 153–54, 264). Carver's *Travels* (1778) presents in its map of the Northwest an even more definite scheme, for it shows the region "partitioned . . . into plantations or subordinate colonies"—Carver's purpose being to insure

218 "that future adventurers may readily, by referring to the map, chuse a

commodious and advantageous situation"; see the third ed. (London, 1781; Minneapolis: Ross & Haines, 1956), p. 531.

31. Ernest Earnest, *John and William Bartram: Botanists and Explorers* (Philadelphia: University of Pennsylvania Press, 1940), p. 181.

32. To take one example from the voluminous Bartram-Collinson correspondence: "I really believe my honest John is a *great wag*, and has sent seven hard, stony seeds, something shaped like an acorn, to puzzle us; for there is no name to them. I have a vast collection of seeds, but none like them. I do laugh at Gordon, for he guesses them to be a species of Hickory. Perhaps I may be laughed at in turn, for I think they may be, what I wish, seeds of the Bonduc tree, which thou picked up in thy rambles on the Ohio" (1 April 1762). And Bartram's later response: "The hard nuts I sent"— surely punning on "seed" and "puzzle"—"were given me at Pittsburg by Col. Bouquet. He called them Hickory nuts. He had them from the country of the Illinois. Their kernel was very sweet. I am afraid they won't sprout, as being a year old." See William Darlington, *Memorials of John Bartram and Humphry Marshall* (Philadelphia: Lindsay & Blakiston, 1849), p. 233.

33. Earnest cites the opinion of Linnaeus, p. v.

34. *Observations on the Inhabitants, Climate, Soil, Rivers, Productions, Animals, and Other Matters Worthy of Notice* . . . (London: J. Whiston and B. White, 1751), p. iii; the preface probably was written by someone connected with the publishers.

35. See *Observations*, p. 34: "A little before sun-set I walked out of town to regulate my journal; but the gnats were so troublesome I could not rest a minute"—a good image of the unregulated journey itself interrupting the traveler's attempt at composition. See also the earlier misprint: "Here we regulated our journey" (p. 16).

36. Quoted by Earnest, p. 21.

37. *Travels of William Bartram*, ed. Mark Van Doren (New York: Dover Pub., 1955 [1928]), p. 17.

38. Compare this passage with the original in Bartram's journal, in *Travels in Georgia and Florida, 1773–74: A Report to Dr. John Fothergill*, ed. Francis Harper. American Philosophical Society *Transactions*, n. s., 33 (1943) pt. 2, p. 148.

39. *The Complete Works of Edgar Allan Poe*, ed. James A. Harrison, 17 vols., (New York: Thomas Y. Crowell, 1902), 6:186, 184.

40. *A Brief Description of New York*, ed. Gabriel Furman (New York: William Gowans, 1845), p. 4.

41. *The Prose Works of William Byrd of Westover*, ed. Louis B. Wright (Cambridge: Harvard University Press, 1966), pp. 158–59.

42. But see p. 120, where Bartram writes that the prospect of passing by boat through the alligator-infested water near "Battle Lagoon" "appeared to me as perilous as running the gauntlet betwixt two rows of Indians armed with knives and firebrands."

43. Bartram does describe some ruined plantations (see pp. 74, 97, 198, 212), but his descriptions generally lack the sort of private resonance which one might expect to find in them.

44. Thoreau's definition (based on false etymology) occurs at the beginning of his essay "Walking" (ca. 1850), which develops a transcendental theory of travel—especially in the New World. I quote from *Excursions* (Boston: Ticknor and Fields, 1863), p. 161.

CHAPTER TWO

1. *Travels of William Bartram,* ed. Mark Van Doren (New York: Dover Pub., 1955 [1928]), pp. 92–93.

2. This transformation can take place, Bartram notes, only if "the Siminoles who are sovereigns of these realms" cede them to the whites (p. 199); but his own prose is almost an act of taking possession, regardless of native rights.

3. One of the more insidious implications of this passage (if we read the whole as an unacknowledged paradigm of human plantation) is the fact that Spanish moss is epiphytic, living on the surface of other plants and never rooted in the ground itself. The vigor with which it spreads and takes possession of the trees that support it makes it a good image for restless colonial energies.

4. On the "small beginnings" theme, see William Bradford, *Of Plymouth Plantation,* ed. Samuel E. Morison (New York: Knopf, 1952), p. 236: "Thus out of small beginnings greater things have been produced by His hand that made all things of nothing." Also, Franklin's *Autobiography,* ed. Leonard W. Labaree (New Haven: Yale University Press, 1964), especially pp. 75 (Franklin's own "unlikely Beginnings" as a youth in Philadelphia) and 141–42 (his account of how the Library Company rose "from a small beginning" to become a cultural model for all the colonies); the opening of Crèvecoeur's "What is an American?" in Albert E. Stone, Jr., ed., *Letters from an American Farmer and Sketches of Eighteenth-Century America* (New York: New American Library, 1963), p. 60, his fine description of Nantucket as a settled region ("barren spots fertilized, grass growing where none grew before, grain gathered from fields which had hitherto produced nothing better than brambles, dwellings raised where no building materials were to be found, wealth acquired by the most uncommon means" [102]), and the long, complex rendering of Farmer James's private *locus amoenus,* his small bower built by industry out of a seemingly vacant world (pp. 177–80); and, from an abundance of later materials, Melville's description of New Bedford in *Moby-Dick,* ed. Luther S. Mansfield and Howard P. Vincent (New York: Hendricks House, 1962), pp. 32–33: "So omnipotent is art," Melville concludes of this town planted on the "once scraggy scoria of a country"—for art has "superinduced bright terraces of flowers upon the barren refuse rocks thrown aside at creation's final day."

5. *A Brief Description of New York,* ed. Gabriel Furman (New York: William Gowans, 1845), p. 15. Denton's stress falls on the negative (if rich) emptiness described by Crèvecoeur. A more conceptualized version of the motif is to be found in Robert Cushman's "Reasons & Considerations Touching the Lawfulnesse of Remouving out of *England* into Parts of *America,*" appended to "Mourt's Relation" of 1622. Since New England is "a vast and emptie *Chaos,*" full of "common . . . or unused, & undressed" land, Cushman argues, the English have every right to go there and work for "the conversion of the heathens": "to us they cannot come, our land is full"—"to them we may goe, their land is emptie." See *Mourt's Relation,* ed. Henry Martyn Dexter (Boston: John Kimball Wiggin, 1865), pp. 150, 148, 147, 148.

6. Compare Denton's portrait of New Jersey to the benign portrayal of Canada offered by Anne MacVicar Grant in her *Memoirs of an American Lady* (1808), which begins as a fond recollection of the American colonies but ends as a bitter assault on those who forced her own family from the West during the Revolutionary period. Still in British hands, Canada pro-

vides Grant with an obvious contrast to the politically hostile United States: though the Northern region is "barren" along its coasts, "It becomes more fertile as it recedes further from the sea. Thus holding out an inducement to pursue nature into her favorite retreats, where on the banks of mighty waters, calculated to promote all the purposes of social traffic among the inhabitants, the richest soil, the happiest climate, and the most complete detachment from the world, promises a safe asylum to those who carry the arts and the literature of Europe, hereafter to grace and enlighten scenes where agriculture has already made rapid advances." See *Memoirs of an American Lady,* ed. James Grant Wilson (New York: Dodd, Mead, 1909), 2:229–30; compare also Grant's description of her father's "lost" New York patent, 2:128–29—which is full of amenable "signs" and tokens.

7. John Bartram's curt phrase for one piece of ground reported on in his *Observations*—"good corn land" (p. 30)—is a fine example of the explorer's "enclosing" language, the use of futuristic terms (for what Bartram means is this: "If one plants corn on this land, one *will* reap a good harvest") for an apparently present description.

8. *A Brief Description,* "To the Reader," n.p. This is William Byrd's strategy in "A Journey to the Land of Eden" as well, "rumors" displaced there by the "tokens" of future wealth. See also the discussion of Dionyse Settle below.

9. Denton's bees are animate signs of New World abundance, as well as the pioneers of European success. Likewise, Anne Grant sees the beaver colony established on her father's land in New York as a hopeful sign of human enjoyment, for these "old settlers" had saved her family "much trouble" by clearing "above thirty acres of excellent hay-land" (*Memoirs of an American Lady,* 2:129).

10. Benjamin Martyn, *Some Account of the Designs of the Trustees for Establishing the Colony of Georgia in America* (1732), in Trevor Reese, ed., *The Most Delightful Country of the Universe: Promotional Literature of the Colony of Georgia* (Savannah: Beehive Press, 1972), p. 72. Reese's book is one of a series of important works published by Beehive.

11. "America, Past, Present, and Future," in Ola Elizabeth Winslow, ed., *Harper's Literary Museum* (New York: Harper & Brothers, 1927), pp. 31–33. In his account of Humfrey Gilbert's death on the return voyage from Newfoundland in 1583, Edward Hayes is hopeful enough that he can offer the following comment: "We could not observe the hundreth part of creatures in those unhabited lands"—and his mere one percent is enough to make him urge his countrymen to "obtaine an habitation in those remote lands, in which Nature very prodigally doth minister unto mens endevours," in which it provides, too, ample substance "for art to worke upon." See Richard Hakluyt, *Voyages,* 8 vols., (London: Everyman's Library, 1907), 6:23. Compare also Hayes's account of the feast given to Gilbert's men by the fishermen moored in St. John's Bay (p. 17).

12. The "dance" of the rocks and trees to the music of Orpheus is, of course, a motif of classical myth. Note, though, that Ames chooses this pleasant detail for his own purposes, and not the tale of Eurydice or the story of the dismemberment of Orpheus himself.

13. Ames's shift from a spatial to a temporal axis is implicit, of course, in any exploratory gesture—the basic pattern being contained in John Bartram's "good corn land." Yet we can find in Ames one of the first "grand" temporal visions of American history, an application of local verbal strategies to the whole of New World time. His almanac piece points ahead

(particularly in its own longing for some future recollection) to such poetic explorations as that of John Trumbull in "Prospect of the Future Glory of America" (1770), or that of Philip Freneau and Hugh Henry Brackenridge in *The Rising Glory of America* (1771)—and especially to that which is developed in *The Golden Age: or Future Glory of North America* (1785), a dream vision in which "Celadon" is led by an angel to a peak in the middle of the continent and is allowed to see from that eminence the future transformation of a vast spatial arena. Freneau's later poem "On the Emigration to America and Peopling the Western Country" (1785) embodies most of the themes discussed so far in this chapter.

14. In his *Eulogium of the Brave Men who have Fallen in the Contest with Great Britain* (Philadelphia: F. Bailey, [1779]), H. H. Brackenridge links those who have died in the war with the great heroes of all times and places, but "more especially" with "the early navigators and the first discoverers of America" and "the early settlers" of the thirteen colonies. In Brackenridge's simple, single plot of American life are included not only these actors but also those later artists who will "recollect and set in order every circumstance" of the present war, and who will thus will "give them bright and unsullied to the coming" generations (see pp. 18–20, 24).

15. *Ralph Waldo Emerson: Representative Selections,* ed. Frederic I. Carpenter (New York: American Book Co., 1934), pp. 14–15.

16. On Emerson's (and Thoreau's) lack of "discrimination," see Sherman Paul, *Emerson's Angle of Vision* (Cambridge: Harvard University Press, 1952), p. 228: the "most suggestive correspondence" of both men, Paul writes, lay in the "fusion of Western destiny with the moral destiny of man," a fusion which might seem to justify, by recourse to their spiritual potential as exemplary acts, the most "extravagant, rapacious, or unrestrained" deeds in American expansion.

17. *The Heart of Emerson's Journals,* ed. Bliss Perry (Boston: Houghton Mifflin, 1926), p. 299. When Emerson visited Salt Lake City on his return from California eight years later, he called on Brigham Young. For the humorous consequences, see the report of J. M. Forbes (Emerson's son-in-law) in Oliver Wendell Holmes, *Ralph Waldo Emerson* (Boston: Houghton Mifflin, 1885), p. 265.

18. *Leaves of Grass: Comprehensive Reader's Edition,* ed. Harold W. Blodgett and Sculley Bradley (New York: Norton, 1968), pp. 716, 712.

19. Hakluyt, *Voyages,* 6:85. Carleill was a man of some talent in mathematics—as will be clear in my discussion below. (See *DNB*). His voyage apparently was aimed at Nova Scotia or Maine, and he may have hoped to settle there a Protestant colony to balance out the Catholic one which Humfrey Gilbert was thinking of planting in Newfoundland. In any event, his ships got no farther than Ireland in the summer of 1584—as David B. Quinn notes in *England and the Discovery of America, 1481–1620* (New York: Knopf, 1974), p. 340.

20. Albert Cook Myers, ed., *Narratives of Early Pennsylvania, West New Jersey, and Delaware, 1630–1707* (New York: Scribner's, 1912), p. 207.

21. Thus we have the pattern: old accomplishments, new potential, future design, further accomplishments. The structure of Penn's intent as a writer copies that of his intention as a leader.

22. Robert Turner, who notes that he has had a brick house built for himself as an encouragement to other settlers in Philadelphia (brick being more permanent and also more appealing), adds in his letter another

increment to the rising glory of Penn's city: "Now as to the Town of Philadelphia it goeth on in Planting and Building to admiration, both in the front and backward, and there are about 600 houses in 3 years time" (p. 269).

23. One fact never mentioned by Penn (perhaps because, as a dissenter with very high political connections, he felt ambivalent about his personal power) is that he returned to England not merely to settle the Baltimore dispute, but also to aid more than a thousand Quakers who were being held in British prisons. He succeeded in getting many of them released.

It is worth comparing the sequence of Penn works examined here with Robert Mountgomery's grandiose plan for a colony in Georgia, described in *A Discourse Concerning the Design'd Establishment of a New Colony to the South of Carolina, in the Most Delightful Country of the Universe* (1717). A fantasy completely out of touch with New World realities (and hence a good reflection of the explorer's most extreme mood), Mountgomery's plan calls for enclosing the four-hundred square mile "Margravate of Azilia" within stout defensive walls: at its center will be the margrave's house and grounds (sixteen square miles), bordered in each direction by an area set aside for the lesser nobility (one hundred twenty estates, each of one square mile), with four large parks for hunting (each equal to the margrave's grounds in size), and then a perimeter of two hundred square miles, in which the agricultural lands and the workers tending them will be contained. But this is only a beginning: once this first colony has succeeded, others modeled exactly on it will be built! Overzealous for his "Form" (PLATE 14), which is both his plat and the idea reflected in it, Mountgomery shows that the shrewdness exhibited by Penn in his first *Account* was an absolute requirement for colonial success. The Georgia scheme admits no awareness of intervening troubles, no sense of the stages of achievement: "now" is the moment for articulating the "then" of one's desire, complete on paper if not in fact. For Mountgomery's *Discourse,* see Reese, *The Most Delightful Country,* pp. 3–31.

24. Hakluyt, *Voyages,* 6:164–65.

25. Much new information about Harriot and his varied talents has been discovered recently. See *Thomas Harriot, Renaissance Scientist,* ed. John W. Shirley (Oxford: Oxford University Press, 1974), particularly Shirley's own essay, "Sir Walter Ralegh and Thomas Harriot" (pp. 16–35), and that of David B. Quinn, "Thomas Harriot and the New World" (pp. 36–53). Also, Quinn's chapter, "Thomas Harriot and the Virginia Voyages of 1602," in *England and the Discovery of America,* pp. 405–18.

26. *The Roanoke Voyages, 1584–1590,* ed. David B. Quinn, Hakluyt Society, 2d ser., nos. 104–5 (1955), 1:108. Quinn notes that Hakluyt himself "omitted this sentence in 1600, apparently as not contributing to the narrative"—one may wonder, on the other hand, whether the subsequently bleak failures at Roanoke weren't behind this omission. Barlowe's exuberance was simply out of keeping with what occurred afterwards on the ground which he first described in such innocent terms.

27. *The Original Writings and Correspondence of the Two Richard Hakluyts,* ed. E. G. R. Taylor, Hakluyt Society, 2d ser., nos. 76–77 (1935), 2:333. This passage is from the elder Hakluyt's "Inducements to the Liking of the Voyage Intended towards Virginia," which begins with a list of thirty-one such "inducements," including many of Carleill's, then goes on to describe, as follows, the overall design:

The ends of ⎧ 1. To plant Christian religion. ⎫
this voyage ⎨ 2. To trafficke. ⎬ Or, to doe all
are these: ⎩ 3. To conquer. ⎭ three.

A delightfully ironic paradigm, especially by virtue of that right-hand comment, Hakluyt's outline leads him immediately into a thicket of cross-purposes reflected in the style of his own gloss on it: "To plant Christian religion without conquest, will bee hard. Trafficke easily followeth conquest: conquest is not easie. Trafficke without conquest seemeth possible, and not uneasie. What is to be done, is the question" (2:332). Indeed!

Like his younger cousin, Hakluyt offers a list of the "Sorts of men which are to be passed in this voyage," a cast of "Salt-makers," "Lime-makers," "Coopers," "Fletchers," "Bowyers," and so forth—as well as a few exotics, like those "Men bred in the Shroffe in South Spaine, for discerning how Olive trees may be planted there." With more prescience than he intended, Hakluyt predicted the general fate of Roanoke, if not exactly the detailed end of that colony, when he wrote: "But if seeking revenge on every injurie of the Salvages we seeke blood & raise war, our Vines, our Olives, our Figge trees, our Sugar-canes, our Orenges and Limons, Corne, Cattell, & c. will be destroyed, and trade of merchandise in all things overthrowen; and so the English nation there planted and to be planted, shalbe rooted out with sword and hunger" (2:336–38). Hakluyt's catalog of "our" plants would serve in normal exploratory works as a hopeful verbal fiction, a means of "transplanting" such signs of possession and success into an imaginary New World. Here, however, the realization of this innocently fruitful design serves only as an intermediate step in a doleful Jeremiah-like vision of that further future in which, unless "revenge" is eschewed, what the English will achieve shall have been destroyed. The passage is Hakluyt's effectual answer to his earlier question ("What is to be done?"), since it opposes one of his "ends" to another, and shows that in fact they must be set far apart if the larger action is to succeed: the English *cannot* "doe all three."

28. Harriot has another passage on the cedar: "a sweete wood good for seelings [i.e., ceilings], chests, boxes, bedsteads, lutes, virginals, and many things els, as I have also said before" (6:184). The reductive vision embodied in such formulas (trees = timber = lumber = formed objects) is seen at its worst in Samuel Jenner's *Neu-gefundenes Eden* (1737), a tract designed to encourage Swiss emigration to William Byrd's lands on the Virginia frontier. Jenner's prose is an unabashed recipe of European consumption, each detail of New World nature entering it only by means of its potential service to Jenner as a sign of human use.

29. Harriot could offer a comparative report because Ralph Lane had had occasion to taste both native and English dog (see *Roanoke Voyages*, 1:387, nn. 3 and 4).

30. Consider, too, this passage on the fish of the region: "There are also Trouts, Porpoises, Rayes, Oldwives, Mullets, Plaice, and very many other sorts of excellent good fish, which we have taken and eaten, whose names I know not but in the countrey language: we have the pictures of twelve sorts more, as they were drawen in the countrey, with their names" (6:183).

31. Quinn's "The Failure of Ralegh's American Colonies" and "The Lost Colony in Myth and Reality, 1586–1625," *England and the Discovery of America*, pp. 282–306, 432–81, are helpful in straightening out the details of Roanoke; I also have used Samuel Eliot Morison, *The European Discovery of America: The Northern Voyages, A.D. 500–1600* (New York: Oxford Uni-

versity Press, 1971), pp. 617–84. On White and his relationship with Har-
riot, see Paul Hulton's introduction to his facsimile reprint of the 1590 de
Bry edition of Harriot's *Report* (New York: Dover Pub., 1972), and Quinn,
"Thomas Harriot and the New World," in *Thomas Harriot, Renaissance Sci-entist* (n. 29 above). White himself is discussed at length in my next chapter.

32. "Thomas Harriot and the New World," p. 42.

33. For White's letter, see Hakluyt, 6:211–13.

34. Lane's report to Ralegh, printed by Hakluyt (6:152–59), tells of his clashes with the natives. White himself in 1587, seeking revenge for the murder of one of Grenville's men, moved against an enemy town on the mainland—discovering just in time that the natives there were friendly interlopers stealing supplies left behind by the departed inhabitants.

35. The tract is reprinted, with an outdated introduction, in William K. Boyd, ed., *Some Eighteenth-Century Tracts Concerning North Carolina* (Raleigh, N.C.: Edwards & Broughton, 1927), pp. 419–51; for "home op-pression," see p. 436. Background on Scots emigration is provided in Duane Meyer, *The Highland Scots of North Carolina, 1732–1776* (Chapel Hill: University of North Carolina Press, 1961), and Ian C. C. Graham, *Colonists from Scotland: Emigration to North America* (Ithaca: Cornell Univer-sity Press, 1956).

36. See Frederick A. Pottle and Charles H. Bennett, eds., *Boswell's Jour-nal of a Tour to the Hebrides* (New York: Literary Guild, 1936), pp. 54, 104, 132, 156, 199, 242–43.

37. "Scotus Americanus" does mention the fact that some emigrants find it necessary to pay their way by becoming bound servants. He avers that a good many such people, however, will find it possible to work their way out of indentures before their time is up.

38. The "fig tree" figure is biblical—see 1 Kings 4:25, Zech. 3:10, Mic. 4:4; also Jer. 5:17, where the destruction of Israel is rendered as a laying waste of the "vines" and "fig trees" (a passage which would seem to lie behind the elder Hakluyt's sad prediction in his "Inducements"—see n. 27 above). For another use of the figure in roughly the same period, see Charles Woodmason, *The Carolina Backcountry on the Eve of the Revolution*, ed. Richard J. Hooker (Chapel Hill: University of North Carolina Press for the Institute of Early American History and Culture, 1953), p. 214.

39. We might formulate this point as an axiom for wider application: since early American texts often record episodes of a larger "real" action which itself is conceived as an almost literary whole, they must be read in light of this transcendent aesthetic design, not just as the isolated frag-ments which they may appear to be. "New Criticism" simply will not work as a means of approach to such texts, unless its concern with artistic shape can be directed away from the literary work and onto the broader cultural undertaking of which it is one part.

40. Meyer quotes the prisoner's statement, *Highland Scots*, p. 150. It should be remembered, as Meyer notes, that some Highlanders were prominent in the patriot camp throughout the Revolution, and that there was considerable uncertainty among the emigrants as a whole in the first years of trouble. On the other hand, Meyer's explanation of why so many of the Scots finally sided with the King—essentially because the English government had succeeded in attracting the Highlanders' loyalty after Culloden—seems to me oversimplified. Indeed, a text dated from Wil-liamsburg (Va.) in 1775, addressed to a group of Highlanders recently arrived, urging them to join with the colonists in resisting English tyranny,

and signed—with high appropriateness—"Scotius Americanus," suggests that the Scots could read in colonial unrest precisely the record of their own treatment by the English at home. "It was not to become slaves you forsook your native shores," the author writes with an orthodox Whig bias. "Nothing could have buoyed you up against the prepossessions of nature and of custom, but a desire to fly from tyranny and oppression." Rehearsing the arguments we already have examined against the lords and their "favourites and dependents," he concludes that "No people are better qualified than you, to ascertain the value of freedom. They only can know its intrinsick worth who have had the misery of being deprived of it." Though he urges that the emigrants disavow any potential drive within the colonies for independence, he thinks it their higher loyalty as heirs to the British Constitution and "limited monarchy" to openly support "the war" of the Americans against the corrupt home government. "As you participate of the blessings of the soil, it is but reasonable that you should bear a proportionate part of the disadvantages attending it."

This last comment constitutes a great act of accommodation on the author's part—for the writer, we can assume with some assurance, was the same man who wrote *Informations* two years before. His closing vision here, as in that work, is of an oriental realm of peace and meditation: "Let us view this Continent as a country marked out by the great *God* of nature as a receptacle for distress, and where the industrious and virtuous may range in the fields of freedom, happy under their own fig-trees, freed from a swarm of petty tyrants, who disgrace countries the most polished and civilized, and who more particularly infest that region from whence you came." That the vision here, however, is an acknowledged fiction, a wish ("Let us view . . ."), while in the earlier text it is a bald assertion of possibility ("Here each may sit safe, and at ease, under his own fig-tree . . .") suggests the great distance, literally and rhetorically, which Scotus/Scotius Americanus has come. True to his pledge that he himself will emigrate, he has been true enough to the observed reality of America that he no longer can balance New World against Old along the simple scale he used in 1773. "Blessings" and "disadvantages" both must be accepted in the West, history recognized. Unfortunately, his later promotion did not succeed as his earlier one may be thought to have done: for the majority of Scots emigrants sided with the world from which they came, not the one to which they had ventured. If the name "Scotius Americanus" is not a mistake on the part of Peter Force, who gives the Williamsburg text in his *American Archives*, we can see in the writer's subtle change of name (from *American Scot* to *Scots American*) an act of domestication which his countrymen for the most part did not match—and did not, I would argue, because the mere displacement of their voyage was great enough without the added dispossession of political identity that he urged on them in 1775. His earlier assignment of "blessings" and "disadvantages" to separate geographical realms was a good indication of the balance which they probably desired to maintain, which they had little wish to upset by becoming rebels. See *American Archives*, 4th ser., vol. 2 (Washington: Force and Clarke, 1840), pp. 1650–51.

CHAPTER THREE

1. *Mississippi Provincial Archives*, ed. and trans. Dunbar Rowland and Albert Godfrey Sanders, 3 vols. (Jackson, Miss.: Mississippi Department of Archives and History, 1926–32), 2:204. Dauphine (now Dauphin) Island, part of the barrier to Mobile Bay, first was seen by the French in 1699; a

settlement established there in 1707 was attacked by the English three years later, after which it languished. Cadillac, who found only a few settlers on the island in 1713, wanted to revive the undertaking there. I have not located writings by the four men derided by Cadillac which describe the "garden" on Dauphin Island—though François de Mandeville's "Memoir on the Colony of Louisiana" (1709) may be in Cadillac's mind in the passage quoted at the head of this chapter (see *Archives*, esp. 2:50).

2. For Cadillac's new schemes, see *Archives*, 2:175–78. Even these hopes, however, are conditioned by the governor's sense that, contrary to the usual pattern of American experience, "Nothing has been done in this colony" (2:189): "It is not to be doubted that we are in a country of gold and silver mines, but the problem is to find them, and how can we find them if we do not seek them, and how shall we seek them if we do not have the experience and the knowledge of them, and how in short can we succeed in this if nobody is willing to bear the expense of it?" (2:177). For a hopeful French view of the nearby colony of "New Biloxi," see PLATE 18.

3. Hakluyt, *Voyages*, 5:139.

4. Settle's willingness to "read" the shore or the lands behind it is aided by that Renaissance theory of "signatures" which Michel Foucault discusses in *The Order of Things* (New York: Random House, Vintage Books, 1973), esp. pp. 17–45; indeed, it is worthwhile comparing any explorer's search for "tokens" or "signs" in the New World to the elaborate system of perception examined in Foucault's book. The underlying assumption of exploratory texts is that the American scene itself is a text, that the writer's task is to discover those signs of nature which comport with his own intent and understanding. Certain facts are in a quite literal sense symbolic, and thus have a higher importance than others, which are like noise rather than speech (signs only of the "void") and hence must be filtered out of any narrative. The settler, on the other hand, becomes more and more concerned with those facts which symbolize an actual rather than desired American experience, and which suggest a much different order in New World space. Cadillac's concern with the "noisy" distractions of colonial life in his comments on the potential mineral wealth of Louisiana (see n. 2 above) is a good example of how a would-be explorer, sensing the presence of the "right" signs in nature, nonetheless becomes entangled in the discordant "text" of human wrongs. The "nothing" in his case is what the French have failed to do, not what America is on its own.

5. *The Prose Works of William Byrd*, ed. Louis B. Wright (Cambridge: Harvard University Press, 1966), p. 399. On Byrd's concern with minerals, see p. 385: "We rode two miles farther to a stony place where there were some tokens of a copper mine, but not hopeful enough to lay me under temptation"—that is, to make him "enter" for the tract in question. There are signs of sign-seeking, too, like all those large stones which have been "knocked to pieces" by "curious inquirers" after easy wealth (p. 408). In other cases, a traveler's own hints about mineral riches become something like a sign themselves: "Mettals or Minerals I know not of any," Thomas Ashe writes in his *Carolina; or a Description of the Present State of that Country* (1682), then goes on to tell about those "running searches" made by the Spanish in earlier times—the presence of such famous gold-seekers in Carolina vouching for his own reported rumor that "the Apalatean Mountains which lie far up within the Land yields Ore both of Gold and Silver" (Alexander S. Salley, Jr., ed., *Narratives of Early Carolina* [New York: Scribner's, 1911], pp. 155–56). Ashe's rumor is to a tale of accomplished

proof what Byrd's tokens are to achieved wealth. Similarly, William Hilton's brief comment on the mineral promise of New England—"Mines we find to our thinking, but neither the goodnesse nor qualitie we know"—is a suggestive narrative clue which stresses the complexity of colonial "thinking" and "knowing" on such topics (quoted by John Smith in *New Englands Trials,* in *Chronicles of the Pilgrim Fathers* [London: Everyman's Library, 1910], p. 254). See also Edward Hayes's comment on the "shew of minerall substance" discovered in Newfoundland on Humfrey Gilbert's expedition (Hakluyt, *Voyages,* 6:23).

6. The subject of land fraud figures in Byrd's comments about Major Mayo's previously unseen grant on the Dan, pp. 400–1—most of the land proving "below the character the discoverers had given him of it."

7. An added irony arises when Byrd must rebuke Harry Morris (and, through Morris, his wife) for having disobeyed their employer's orders on a number of occasions (see p. 408). It is not just Byrd's manorial dream that is threatened by the attenuation of space—his authority is questioned on other fronts as well.

8. Byrd's piece on the Dismal first was printed as "A Description of the Dismal Swamp, in Virginia; with Proposals for and Observations on the Advantages of Draining it," *Columbian Magazine,* April 1789. He supplied for Samuel Jenner, who was endeavoring to interest Swiss settlers in some of his Virginia lands, various notes on the natural history and the promise of that region. Jenner's outrageously hyperbolic *Neu-gefundenes Eden* (1737) was, however, his own work. For the sad outcome of Jenner's promotion (the settlers suffered shipwreck off the American coast), see Byrd's letter to John Bartram, in William C. Darlington, *Memorials of John Bartram and Humphry Marshall* (Philadelphia: Lindsay & Blakiston, 1849), pp. 314–15.

9. Byrd's *Histories,* despite their important differences—they are written from frontier and tidewater perspectives, for one thing—both are concerned with the humorous attenuation of settled expectation in the journey west. The basic irony is that the men entrusted with laying down the "line" for Virginia and North Carolina themselves overstep the unseen lines of conduct and propriety throughout the undertaking. For an interestingly concrete surveyor's journal, see John W. Wayland, ed., *The Fairfax Line: Thomas Lewis's Journal of 1743* (New Market, Va.: Henkel Press, 1925).

10. *A Journal of a Surveying Trip into Western Pennsylvania in 1795* (Mount Pleasant, Mich.: John Cumming, 1965), p. 10.

11. For a visual analogue to "hoop, hallo, beg for whiskey," see PLATE 21. The sequence "but . . . but . . . but" is a nice linguistic model of the settler's habitual realism. William Bradford's style in *Of Plymouth Plantation* is infected with similar ironic structures throughout (see n. 47 below); Robert Beverley's *The History and Present State of Virginia* (1705; rev. 1722) is built on a narrative model that is even more binary in form (his essential statement being *this, but then not-this*). Crèvecoeur's *Letters from an American Farmer* more subtly substitutes for its early, largely rhetorical, questions ("What, then, is the American, this new man?"—answered as soon as it is asked) a set of insoluble queries which reflect the Farmer's growing confusion in the midst of the Revolution ("I wish for a change of place," his last letter begins; "the hour is come at last that I must fly from my house and abandon my farm! But what course shall I steer, inclosed as I am?"). *Letters from an American Farmer and Sketches of Eighteenth-Century America,* ed. Albert E. Stone, Jr. (New York: New American Library, 1963), pp. 63, 194.

12. Though Newton Mereness, editor of the journal discussed for the next few pages of my text, asserts that its author was the same "D'Artaguette" to whom Cadillac referred in 1713, it has become clear since he wrote that the earlier writer and colonial official (Jean-Baptiste Martin d'Artaguiette d'Iron) was the brother of the man who actually composed that record in 1722 and 1723. See Marcel Giraud, *Histoire de La Louisiane Française,* vol. 3, *L'Époque de John Law (1717–1720)* (Paris: Presses Universitaires de France, 1966), p. 384; also, vol. 1, *Le Règne de Louis XIV* (1953), p. 117 and n. 1.

13. Translated in Newton D. Mereness, ed., *Travels in the American Colonies* (New York: Macmillan, 1916), p. 17. Artaguiette tells a story on 5 September which is paradigmatic of the whole "Journal," of French frustrations as well: "A man named Traverse, living in New Orleans, was today let out of prison. The cause for which he was imprisoned was this. This man had built a house in New Orleans. This house was not set in accord with the alignment of the streets, as he had built it before the plan had been proposed. M. Peauger [the engineer] had it torn down. Traverse being not well pleased about this, presented a petition to the council, asking them to recompense him for his house in order that he might have the means to build another. M. Peauger had him sent for, and, after having regaled him with a volley of blows with his stick, had him thrown into prison with irons about his feet, and today this man came out of prison almost blind" (pp. 17–18).

14. The "Memorandum" runs from p. 21 to p. 23. Though it begins with a call for the importation of "great numbers of negroes (there being no French) to clear the land," it ends with a demand "that justice should be rendered equally to all without prejudice, revenge or distinction." And, though the very presence of this inventory of needed correctives in the "Journal" suggests Artaguiette's sober view of French progress to date, he concludes: "The company being sure of the success of this colony, as we show by the proofs we send to it, it ought not to hesitate one moment to procure the necessities above specified, if it wishes to see the colony in a little while rise to a flourishing condition" (p. 23). The *topos* still may be appropriate.

15. Peter J. Hamilton, *Colonial Mobile* (rev. & enlrgd. ed.; Mobile: First National Bank, 1952 [1910]), p. 74.

16. In its overwhelmingly bleak portrait of the colony, Artaguiette's work provides a good contrast to Jean-Bernard Bossu's *Nouveaux Voyages* of some forty years later—though one must recall that Bossu, like Cadillac, was imprisoned for his acerbic comments on colonial government. Artaguiette's record also may be counterpointed to Cadillac's earlier *Memoir* (ca. 1700), which is generally serene and curious in tone, hopeful for the future of French endeavor in the upper Midwest. For this last work, see Milo Milton Quaife's edition in the fine Lakeside Classics series, *The Western Country in the 17th Century: The Memoirs of Lamothe Cadillac and Pierre Liette* (Chicago: Lakeside Press, 1947).

17. Artaguiette's inclusion of Dumanoir's lament, the Traverse story, and many other similar tales suggests that his own role, like that of Ishmael in Melville's novel, is to gather home the narratives of suffering and dispersion. That role is opposite to William Penn's in his *Further Account,* where the quotation of Robert Turner's letter converts an Old World expectation that American stories belong to the universe of Job—which is, of course, precisely the ambience of Ishmael—into a recognition of New World survival and achievement. Between them, Artaguiette and Penn

define the limits of "relation" as an American literary act. To raise the example of Melville or Poe in this context (or, one might add, those of Irving, Cooper, and Thoreau) is not really to confuse belles lettres with "subliterary" or simple "documentary" works, for the five writers just named in fact were quite familiar with such writings, and in many cases strove to model their own on them. It is clear that such a sequence of texts as the following—Irving's *A History of New-York* (1809), Cooper's *The Pioneers* (1823), Poe's *The Narrative of Arthur Gordon Pym* (1838), Melville's *Moby-Dick* (1851) or *Israel Potter* (1855), and Thoreau's *Walden* (1854)—is American as much by formal criteria as by substantive ones, that each is in quite subtle ways a "sophistication" of prior, largely "naive," New World literary modes.

18. *The European Discovery of America: The Northern Voyages, A.D. 500–1600* (New York: Oxford University Press, 1971), p. 551. I have relied on Morison's account of the Frobisher ventures as my main historical source here.

19. Morison refers to Camden, p. 545; in a note on the same page he discusses the cost of refining Frobisher's "ore."

20. Morison, pp. 543, 526, 510, 530.

21. Morison reproduces the Lucas de Heere plate, p. 530. W. P. Cumming, R. A. Skelton, and D. B. Quinn, *The Discovery of North America* (New York: American Heritage Press, 1972), give a German version of Heere's work which they trace, incorrectly it would seem, to a John White original (p. 221, pl. 265). Hugh Honour, on the other hand, prints another "Heere" work which is more nearly in White's style—see *The New Golden Land* (New York: Pantheon, 1975), p. 67, pl. 56a.

22. The woodcut in Ellis is by no means an accomplished work of art. What is interesting about it, I think, is its suggestion that some American "signs" must be read with great care—that they are deceitful, multidimensional, capable of false interpretation. Moreover, as a detail excerpted from the sea passage (rather than the New World proper), it hints that the voyager will encounter even before reaching America a particularly complex spatial world in which he can survive only by close attention to its actual design. Probably the best version of this whole theme is Mark Twain's in *Life on the Mississippi* (1883), where the river—symbol for countless orators of the manifest progress of Eastern intent—becomes for Twain an elaborate sign system, arcane and subtle in its structure, deceptive on its surface, often fatal in its force.

23. R. H. Major, ed. and trans., *Select Letters of Christopher Columbus* (New York: Corinth Books, 1961 [1847]), p. 203. J. M. Cohen, *Four Voyages of Christopher Columbus* (Baltimore: Penguin Books, 1969), renders *apartado de los Santos Sacramentos* as "so far from the Holy Sacraments"—which is particularly suggestive, since it implies that the "Sacraments" are spatially conditioned.

24. One persistent theme in the Jamaica letter of Columbus is the hope that the king and queen will right all the wrongs which he has endured at the hands of various Spaniards in the new lands.

25. When Columbus was returning from his first voyage, he encountered a severe storm which he thought might wreck the ships. Hence he wanted to preserve the record of what he had achieved, even if he himself might perish: "I wrote on a parchment with the brevity that the time demanded how I had discovered the lands that I had promised to, and in how many days; and the route I had followed; and the goodness of the

countries, and the quality of their inhabitants and how they were the
vassals of your Highnesses who had possession of all that had been found by me. This writing folded and sealed I directed to your Highnesses. . . . And I straightway had a large cask brought and having wrapped the writing in a waxed cloth and put it into a kind of tart or cake of wax I placed it in the barrel which, stoutly hooped, I then threw into the sea. All believed that it was some act of devotion. Then because I thought it might not arrive safely and the ships were all the while approaching Castile I made another package like that and placed it on the upper part of the poop in order that if the ship should sink the barrel might float at the will of fate"—Julius E. Olson and Edward Gaylord Bourne, eds., *The Northmen, Columbus and Cabot, 985–1503* (New York: Scribner's, 1906), pp. 242–43. Thus the European history of America began quite literally with a fugitive text, a pair of records themselves held against the boisterous sea as an extreme gesture toward salvation in the word. And, ironically, neither of these documents survived—as, indeed, the very journal quoted here (from the biography written by Ferdinand Columbus, which includes a fragment of the original) also did not. This was the Poe-like act par excellence, the final limit of New World speech. For an intriguing analogue, see David B. Quinn, ed., *The Last Voyage of Thomas Cavendish* (Chicago: University of Chicago Press, 1975), which reproduces, and transcribes, the final record of this circumnavigator, finished just before his death at sea on the way back to England. And, for a more figurative and psychological loss of language, see the anecdote related by Hugh Henry Brackenridge about Dr. Knight, an Indian captive from western Pennsylvania: "I saw Knight on his being brought into the garrison at Pittsburg; he was weak and scarcely able to articulate. When he began to be able to speak a little, his Scottish dialect was much broader than it had been when I knew him before. This I remarked as usual with persons in a fever, or sick, they return to the vernacular tongue of their early years. It was three weeks before he was able to give anything like a continued account of his sufferings"—Archibald Loudon, *A Selection of Some of the Most Interesting Narratives of Outrages Committed by the Indians in Their Wars with the White People* (1808–11; rpt. of 1888 ed., New York: Arno Press, 1971), p. vi. Loudon's work is not so simple as its title indicates, as his inclusion of James Smith's captivity (1799) easily proves.

26. Hakluyt, *Voyages,* 6:6.

27. Gilbert's bad first voyage was preceded by other speculative losses of an allied nature: he had invested in an alchemical endeavor to turn iron into copper and lead into quicksilver (Morison, p. 566). But Gilbert's Western effort was not merely a get-rich-quick scheme, since he intended (as Frobisher did) to settle a colony in America.

28. Actually, there were twelve survivors of the wreck (see Hakluyt, 6:30; Morison, p. 576). Among the lost were Stephanus Parmenius, Hungarian humanist who intended to describe the voyage in a learned poem akin to his earlier work (see David B. Quinn and Neil M. Chesire, eds., *The New Found Land of Stephen Parmenius* [Toronto: University of Toronto Press, 1972]); and "Daniel," the mineral-man who supposedly had found gold ore in Newfoundland. Gilbert himself lost ore samples and some writings (of an unspecified sort)—for which he beat his cabin boy, whom he had instructed to retrieve these things earlier, but who had failed to do so. Hayes's account of this beating makes concrete Gilbert's flaws of passion: "Whatsoever it was [that Gilbert lost], the remembrance touched him so

deepe, as not able to containe himselfe, he beat his boy in great rage"
(6:33). Richard Clarke, master of the *Delight* and one of the survivors, tells
in his own brief narrative of the wreck (6:38–42) a tale which attacks
Gilbert in even more direct terms. He blames the commander, in fact, for
the loss of the ship.

29. Morison mentions the Gilbert crest (p. 568), and quotes the comment
of Elizabeth (p. 572).

30. Morison identifies the book as More's (p. 577). It is possible, however, that Gilbert's reiterated line came instead from some collection of
adages.

31. Morison quotes the sardonic comment of Polydore Vergil, p. 191.

32. Hayes remained a promoter long after his involvement in Gilbert's
scheme. David B. Quinn discusses his many later "American" writings in
England and the Discovery of America, 1481–1620 (New York: Knopf, 1974),
pp. 227–45. One of these pieces, a Newfoundland tract of 1592–93, appears to have been written with the help, appropriately enough, of Christopher Carleill (Quinn, p. 334).

33. I quote the Robynson translation of 1551, as given in Burton A.
Milligan, ed., *Three Renaissance Classics* (New York: Scribner's, 1953), p.
114. Giles, who introduces More to Hythloday, basically sees the latter as a
reckless man: his rather flippant "saiynges" and his desire to be left in the
land of "Gulike" by Vespucci suggest that he takes "more thoughte and
care for travailyng than dyenge"—hardly the pious attitude attributed to
Gilbert by Hayes.

34. John Smith's *Generall Historie*, which I discuss briefly in my conclusion, is one of the most famous examples of the settlement account as itself
a rhetorical settlement of American affairs. No longer a "partaker" in
Virginia, but a mere "beholder" of the colony's seeming ruin—and hence
apparently saved from ruin himself—Smith is also the victim of a fate
worse than that which has engulfed his settlement. In exile in England
(certainly a paradoxical condition), he is a marginal figure whose separation from the New World links him with Gilbert rather than Hayes. His
denunciation of those responsible for Virginia's sorry condition remains
impotently verbal, but he nonetheless tries through it to rearrange the
order of colonial life. For a much later example of similar strategies,
consider Jefferson's attempt to draw sharp lines of distinction between
human groups—whites and blacks—in whose future, and present, relationship he sees only a threat of ruin for the state and nation. Thus in
Notes on the State of Virginia Jefferson attacks the blacks, his assault a
sorting-out of good and bad, an act of communal imagination motivated by
deep anxieties—yet one which, by its own exclusionary tactics, undercuts
the asserted ideals of Jefferson himself. Though Jefferson personally
favored (and publically supported) the enactment of a manumission law in
Virginia, and foresaw with increasing apprehension the results of formal
slavery, he replicated in the rhetoric of *Notes* the very inequality on which
slavery was based. On the other hand, his concern there with the murder
of Logan's family—a concern which was to cause him considerable political
trouble in the future—might be seen as a balancing attempt to extend the
boundaries of white law to include more positively another marginal
group. Yet perhaps the final point to be made here is that Jefferson's
understanding consistently places the fate of black and red at the disposition of the white majority: the lines of community need not be resurveyed
in order to solve these "problems," since both of them are made to seem
like matters of "foreign" policy.

35. David B. Quinn's characterization of Hayes as a "projector" throughout his life, and in his multifarious interests (*England and the Discovery of America,* p. 232), fits well with Hayes's rhetoric in the Gilbert narrative. It is suggestive to compare Hayes on these issues with the typical rhetorical strategies of Benjamin Franklin, far-fetched as the comparison may seem initially. Franklin's *Autobiography* is much more than one man's life story: it is in many ways the record of an archetypal American settlement refracted (or "specified") by the narrative of a single "citizen's" experience, and Franklin's other civic writings lend strong support to this link (see his 1743 "Proposal for Promoting Useful Knowledge among the British Plantations in America"; his 1754 "Plan for Settling Two Western Colonies"; and his 1756 letter to George Whitefield, which suggests that the two of them settle a godly colony on the Ohio). Most illuminating here, however, is Franklin's series of "partings" in the *Autobiography,* from that with Collins on the Delaware to that with General Braddock over the issue of frontier warfare in the 1750s. And the most suggestive criticism of this feature in Franklin's conception of his life—and of life in general—is provided by Melville in *Israel Potter,* in which the solitary hero of the most American war is made to ponder the suggestion of Franklin that fate is the result of personal will.

36. In the first class of works I would include the documents of missionary work, the records of white warfare against the Indians, and the captivity narratives. All three of these forms are organized by a spatial-cultural diagram which values the center of white life and alternately fears or assaults its edges. This rhetorical diagram is a verbal image of European settlement itself, a stylistic reflection of active styles. Records of internal dissent, on the other hand, are likely to be built on an assumption that the proper order of action and speech has been inverted, that a center has come to resemble its edges. Smith's *Historie* thus is structured, in its Virginia section, by an ironically hidden equivalency between Jamestown (scene of factionalism and disagreement among the settlers) and the hinterland (scene of mutual deceptions between whites and Indians). What ought to be a geography of contrasts is a landscape of subtle and disarming uniformity. For a disaffected white like Cabeza de Vaca, on the contrary, the "center" is at least part of the time beyond the presumed "edge": Indian rather than European order is the source of identity and purpose. I treat such issues in more detail in my conclusion.

37. Since Bradford probably did not write the "starving time" passage until twenty-four or more years after the fact, he was well aware of later failures of community within Plymouth itself. I discuss these complexities later in this chapter.

38. Again, the Morton episode was written down much later; for Bradford's epithet ("Lord of Misrule") and his sense of the "profane" quality of Morton's example, see *Of Plymouth Plantation,* ed. Samuel E. Morison (New York: Knopf, 1952), pp. 205, 206.

39. See my discussion of William Wood, George Alsop, and Charles Wooley in the first chapter above. Interesting here, too, are the various voyage records of Benjamin Franklin, the most complete being that of his return from London in 1726 and the most suggestive being the document he composed on his way back to England in 1757, "The Way to Wealth."

40. "Journal of the Voyage of Charles Clinton from Ireland to America," *Magazine of American History,* 1 (1877): 620.

41. A certain mystery attaches to Clinton's record of this voyage—for the ship's captain seems to have been responsible quite directly for much of the

suffering on board, and some of the deaths were owing to poor food supplies rather than disease. For more light on this issue, and on the motives for Clinton's emigration, see Dorothie Bobbé, *De Witt Clinton* (Port Washington, N.Y.: Friedman, 1962 [1933]), and Joseph Young's narrative, as given in David Hosack, *Memoir of De Witt Clinton* (New York: J. Seymour, 1829), pp. 137–41. Franklin's voyage records in 1726 and 1762 confirm the anxiety of Clinton's crossing—for in the days of sail power the "discovery" of America was no sure or simple thing. For a suggestive literary use of such emotions, see Edward Everett Hale's "The Man Without a Country" (1862), in which Philip Nolan's perpetual exile from America on naval vessels ends only at the moment of his death, when he is allowed an imaginative discovery of the land whose shores he had been forbidden to touch.

42. I certainly agree with Richard Slotkin that the early settlers were afflicted with an "emigration trauma" (*Regeneration through Violence: The Mythology of the American Frontier* [Middletown, Conn.: Wesleyan University Press, 1973], esp. pp. 107–9), but I would not limit its effects—as he does for most of the seventeenth century—to New England alone (John Smith is mentioned in Slotkin's book only once, for instance, and then only because Samuel Sewall makes mention of him in the *Phaenomena*, the text under discussion). The Jamaica letter of Columbus already offers us an apt prefiguration of these problems, as does Cadillac's 1713 report, particularly in its concern over the "distance" through which all Europeans and all European designs must pass in order to reach (and affect) America.

Orthodox history tells us that the Revolution was won in part because of that same distance: if geography reflected the white colonists' sense of exclusion, guilt, marginality, it also became a more hopeful sign of native power and resources. The patriot apologists of the Revolution thus asserted the "continental" rights of the colonies in one breath, and added in the next that their resistance to crown and parliament was in the best interest of "English" liberty itself. America was both far removed from the centers of European power and at the same time closer than any Old World nation to the center of European belief. Nor was politics the only area of life affected by this spatial-cultural tension, since, for those who "came over," the Atlantic served as an enduring sign of many things left behind—but neither wholly lost nor wholly recoverable. Hence the American desire to "play" for a foreign audience, to alternately defer to and attack foreign opinions of homeland affairs, to import with absurd flourish the words and things of European culture, or to be as absurdly assertive of homemade commodities. Hence, too, the nativist movement, the fear of alien hordes, or the alternate idealism of a welcoming stance and a supposedly civilizing imperialism.

But all of this concerns *white* American life, as I suggest in my text. For Afro-Americans, the paradigms of transatlantic space were intensely different, the "emigration trauma" less hyperbolic and more literally apt as a term for what they endured. Absent here was the mythology voiced by "Scotius Americanus," the view that the West contained "fields of freedom" for the active emigrant (who knew an effective "slavery" in the East)—since the ghastly voyage from Africa to America was designedly the first step in a process of lasting captivity and legalized exclusion. Thus, through the alembic of Bible religion, the fugitive slave narrative (prime document of black travel in the New World) came to assume the very form into which whites had poured the tales of their experience among the

Indians. But unlike the white captive, whose account was aimed most often at the reassertion of some old identity, the black fugitive had no "home" to recover by fleeing from slavery: the escape was an entrance into fugitivity rather than a loss of such a negative state. To be a "fugitive slave" was to negate the negation of slavery, whereas the white "redeemed captive" set the laws of the universe right by his or her "return" (see PLATE 27). In this sense, the slave narratives form a rich commentary on the white experience of temporary captivity, much as the whole slave experience undergulfs with far worse sufferings such a document as Clinton's "Journal" or the record of Benjamin Franklin's "confinement" (as he called it) during his 1726 voyage to Philadelphia. Or rather, the white captivities (like the white patriots' claim in the 1770s that they were being "enslaved" by English usurpations) form a flat backdrop to the fully dimensional tale of black endurance at sea and on land. We even may speculate that the captivity accounts, though they predate the earliest fugitive narratives by a century, in fact reflect the growing formalization of black slavery in North and South during the later seventeenth century, that one of their purposes is to assuage white guilt over the permanent captivity of Indians and blacks within the economy of Euro-American life. Certainly the use of a rhetoric of enslavement in the captivities is not merely biblical in resonance, as it is not merely "English" in the patriot documents of the Revolution.

As a final note, we should recognize that the Atlantic perspective has served a quite different purpose for Afro-Americans in the past century from that which it has served for whites. Not only in the "Back to Africa" movement, but also in more recent attempts to assess in detail the multiple relationships between African cultures and black American life, one can sense a feeling of desired continuity which is largely absent from white gestures east—which lacks precisely that tone of "guilt" traceable in Euro-American myth. More violent and hence more "traumatic," the black departure was also less consciously sought and thus less final.

43. Hakluyt, *Voyages*, 6:211. Morison tells of the "bond," p. 671.

44. The signs of altered intention, if not distress, which White found are suggestive of a long tradition in American history (and travel)—a theme of messages carved on the landscape itself, marks of possession and passage. The records of Oñate's expedition in the Southwest; the carvings of Oregon pioneers on Monument Rock; the "Boone" trees; the various lead plates dug up by later settlers, coats of arms first left by explorers—these and a hundred other such fugitive markers constitute a genre of American "writing" which pushes almost to the limit of silence. Interesting in this connection, too, are those "Roanoke rocks" which supposedly were discovered in this century along an old path in the South, and which purportedly explained what had happened to the settlers whom White sought in 1590 (Morison, p. 684).

45. This passage alone suggests how wrong was that conventional argument of the nineteenth century that America had no "ruins." The argument was correct in the sense that American ruins, where they existed, were far from grandiose in appearance or ancient in age. But in another sense, it reflected an anxiety peculiar to the colonial world: where every new settlement was conceived as an assertion against (and an insertion into) the "nothingness" of American space, the contemplation of ruin might prove strangely unnerving. If the "magic" had not worked in other projects, what proof was there that it would work in one's own? It is appropriate that one of the first American historical novels, *The First* 235

Settlers of Virginia by John Davis (himself a disappointed emigrant), opens with a "Preliminary Discourse" by Louis Hue Girardin on the ruins of Jamestown which is reminiscent of John White's 1587 report: "The contrast between the ravages of time and the fecundity of nature is here peculiarly striking. Where the one destroys the other creates. Love nestles, life teems, among these desolate fragments" (2d ed.; New York: I. Riley, 1806, p. xi). For two early American "ruins," see PLATES 28–29.

46. The Nauset debate is found in Morison's edition, from which I quote, on pp. 333–34. Morison notes the biblical echoes in the "ancient mother" passage.

47. Sherley's style throughout his letter, and particularly in its last two paragraphs, is riddled with contradictions which mirror the contentious state of affairs within the Company:

> *But that night they [some of the partners who were making trouble for the Plymouth settlers] were so followed and crossed of their perverse courses, as they were even wearied and offered to sell their adventures and some were willing to buy. But I, doubting they would raise more scandal and false reports, and so divers ways do us more hurt by going off in such a fury than they could or can by continuing Adventurers amongst us, would not suffer them.*
>
> *But on the 12th of January we had another meeting; but in the interim divers of us had talked with most of them privately, and had great combats and reasoning, pro and con. But at night when we met to read the general letter, we had the lovingest and friendliest meeting that ever I knew, and our greatest enemies offered to lend us £50.*
> (372–73)

Hence Bradford's note to this last sentence (which runs in full: "But this lasted not long; they had now provided Lyford and others to send over") undercuts Sherley's mood, and does so by mimicking his own impacted style.

48. One might trace out an interesting relationship between the two economic models of the colony (generalism and particularism) and the moral struggle (selfishness vs. community-mindedness) which concerns Bradford throughout the history. And one might add to this relationship Bradford's own problems as narrator, his desire to tell the "general" tale of Pilgrim success versus his need to deal with so many depressing "particulars."

49. Winthrop's "A Modell of Christian Charity" (1630) is a complex exploration of the Puritan design, a model of a model settlement. It is worth comparing it to those promotional tracts which Winthrop wrote before embarking on the *Arbella,* one of which was aimed at convincing the writer himself to emigrate! For my quotation from the "Modell," see the *Winthrop Papers,* ed. Stewart Mitchell, vol. 2 (n.p.: Massachusetts Historical Society, 1931), p. 295; for the promotional tracts by Winthrop and others, see pp. 106–49. On the dispersion of settlement in Massachusetts Bay, see Darrett B. Rutman, *Winthrop's Boston* (Chapel Hill: University of North Carolina Press for the Institute of Early American History and Culture, 1965).

50. Robinson's gesture is Pauline; see, for instance, Rom. 1:7–15.

51. Bradford's personal retrospect—indeed, the whole complex interplay of his different viewpoints in the history—is a good commentary on Nathaniel Ames's blithe call in 1758 for a future history which will fill in the blanks of his own hope.

52. I have transcribed this "concrete" text from the facsimile given in Isidore S. Meyer, "The Hebrew Preface to Bradford's History of the Plymouth Plantation," American Jewish Historical Society *Publications,* 38 (1949): 296.

CONCLUSION

1. In different ways, and with varying intensity, all of the following books make such an argument: Sacvan Bercovitch, *The Puritan Origins of the American Self* (New Haven: Yale University Press, 1975); David L. Minter, *The Interpreted Design as a Structural Principle in American Prose* (New Haven: Yale University Press, 1969); and Richard Slotkin, *Regeneration through Violence: The Mythology of the American Frontier* (Middletown, Conn.: Wesleyan University Press, 1973).

2. Roger Williams himself became a "hero" of toleration and liberty during the nineteenth century—that is, the starting point of another New World plot. But attempts to portray him as such obviously simplify his own complexities and uncertainties.

3. Bradford's own figure of the "ancient mother"—who has been "left"—is itself rich in the suggestion of marginality.

4. Eugene D. Genovese, *Roll, Jordan, Roll: The World the Slaves Made* (New York: Pantheon, 1974), traces in great detail the ingenuity with which blacks constructed a world within a world—how they built new cultures and retained old ones even in the midst of such denials. For a minor analogue, see James Deetz, *In Small Things Forgotten* (Garden City, N.Y.: Doubleday, Anchor Books, 1977), chap. 7, "Parting Ways"—an account of black vernacular architecture in a small settlement near Plymouth. One persistent problem in this complicated area is that the majority of black slaves lived in small groups, not in large communities on the plantations— yet the surviving records, especially the fullest ones, derive from the latter places. Deetz suggests one means, relatively unexploited so far, by which we can come to understand the cultural adjustments of dispersed blacks in North and South alike. And, though it is concerned with the house designs of rural whites in one specific area, Henry Glassie's splendid *Folk Housing in Middle Virginia* (Knoxville: University of Tennessee Press, 1975) offers a wealth of methodological directives on how to study such "evidence"— reminding us that we must "read" all artifacts, decoding the assumptions and values encoded in them, for though the people who made and used them "left no writing . . . they did leave all those houses" (p. 178). Glassie's stress on "grammar," adopted and adapted by Deetz, is particularly suggestive. So, too, is Henry Thoreau's attention in *Walden* ("Former Inhabitants; and Winter Visitors") to the architectural remains of that failed "village" near his pond—which predates the "earliest example of historic archaeology" cited by Deetz, James Hall's excavation of the Miles Standish house in 1856 (Deetz, p. 29). See also Robert Frost's evident use of Thoreau in his poem "Directive."

5. The perpetual charge leveled against travelers—that they are crea- tures of invention rather than reportage—verifies the ambiguity of this doubleness. It also suggests that the distance is an abiding sign for private imagination, that separation from the "center" often is viewed as a mark of antisocial behavior, even of madness. On an allied effort of "invention," see Edmundo O'Gorman's fine study, *The Invention of America* (Bloomington: Indiana University Press, 1961).

6. This is a large topic with which William Spengemann deals in *The Adventurous Muse: The Poetics of American Fiction, 1789–1900* (New Haven:

Yale University Press, 1977). I would note myself here that the long-standing debate about whether American fiction is in the tradition of the novel or the romance has failed to assess the differences between New World society and Old World order, and hence has not been able to entertain the possibility that an American character's "departures" can be deeply social in intent and meaning. "Realism" is to be defined, in other words, according to the realities of the world which it touches.

7. "If Columbus was the first to discover the islands, Americus Vespucius, and Cabot, and the Puritans, and we their descendants, have discovered only the shores of America"—"Ktaadn," in *The Maine Woods*, ed. Joseph Moldenhauer (Princeton: Princeton University Press, 1972), p. 81.

8. Williams, *A Key into the Language of America*, ed. John J. Teunissen and Evelyn J. Hinz (Detroit: Wayne State University Press, 1973), p. 83; Morton, *New English Canaan, or New Canaan* (Amsterdam: Jacob Frederick Stam, 1637), pp. 188, 3–4.

9. Charles E. Clark, *The Eastern Frontier: The Settlement of Northern New England, 1610–1763* (New York: Knopf, 1970), pp. 20, 47. Clark's book is a good model for the kind of "recentering" which we need.

10. Perry Miller, *Roger Williams: His Contribution to the American Tradition* (New York: Atheneum, 1962 [1953]), pp. 230–31, 228, 235. Miller discusses the context of this letter on pp. 226–27.

11. Even when Jefferson attacks the impermanence and inelegance of American architecture in *Notes on the State of Virginia*, ed. William Peden (Chapel Hill: University of North Carolina Press for the Institute of Early American History and Culture, 1954)—"Every half century then our country becomes a tabula rasa" (p. 154)—he is trying to "erase" the bad examples of the past himself, so that new models like Monticello can replace them. Note the satire in his attack on the "rude, mis-shapen piles" (p. 153) of William and Mary.

12. Thoreau's "Former Inhabitants; and Winter Visitors" is an elaborate explication of the abandoned houses around Walden; in it is to be found almost every *topos* and theme which I have discussed in this study. Of particular interest in the present context, however, is the alliance which he builds up carefully and suggestively between himself and the black outcasts of Concord propriety. From the same rhetorical universe but a quite different galaxy is the mock advertisement which Charles Woodmason, a sprightly Anglican minister, drew up in support of the "abused" frontier inhabitants of Carolina in 1769. See *The Carolina Backcountry on the Eve of the Revolution*, ed. Richard J. Hooker (Chapel Hill: University of North Carolina Press for the Institute of Early American History and Culture, 1953), pp. 258–59.

13. Smith uses the "stage" figure in talking about Bermuda, but it clearly is appropriate to any English endeavor overseas—see *The Generall Historie of Virginia, New-England, and the Summer Isles* (London: Michael Sparkes, 1624), p. 169.

14. Smith's return to England was impelled by a double "impotence": threats that he would be assassinated, as well as a severe wound in the lower body which was caused by a gunpowder explosion that perhaps was not accidental. For a visual parallel, see the portrayal of Smith's "beheading," PLATE 30.

15. Though he does not apply this second term to Smith's book, Sacvan Bercovitch states quite baldly that Southern settlers were uniformly uto-

pian and secular in their outlook, and that "when their expectations failed
they recorded their disillusionment not in jeremiads but in dystopian
satires, deriding the local Yahoos, mocking the vanity of human wishes and
the pitfalls of Candide-like innocence, and in general warning prospective
emigrants that America was not, after all, 'such a Lubber-land as the
Fiction of the Land of Ease, is reported to be, nor such a *Utopia* as *Sr.
Thomas More* hath related to be found out'" (*Puritan Origins*, p. 138; the
quotation is from John Hammond's *Leah and Rachel* of 1656—which is
anything but dystopian, one might add).

16. I offer these two pairings from a wealth of others that might be cited.
Tailfer's *A True and Historical Narrative of the Colony of Georgia* and Benjamin Martyn's *An Account Shewing the Progress of the Colony of Georgia* both are
reprinted in Trevor Reese, ed., *The Clamorous Malcontents: Criticisms &
Defenses of the Colony of Georgia, 1741–1743* (Savannah: Beehive Press,
1973). Samuel Sewall's *The Selling of Joseph: A Memorial* has been reprinted
with very fine apparatus by Sidney Kaplan (Amherst: University of Massachusetts Press, 1969). In particular, Kaplan places the text very well
vis-à-vis the response of Saffin (*A Brief and Candid Answer*, 1701) and
various of Mather's relevant writings. Of the latter, none is more telling
than the "Rules for the Society of Negroes," which he drew up (he says) at
the request of a group of blacks in Boston. The seventh of these rules,
quoted by Kaplan (p. 56), is a beautiful model of the problem of "centers"
and "edges": "We will, as we have Opportunity, set our selves to do all the
Good we can, to the other *Negro-Servants* in the Town; and if any of them
should, at unfit Hours, be *Abroad*, much more, if any of them should *Run
away* from their Masters, we will afford them *no Shelter:* But we will do what
in us lies, that they may be discovered, and punished. And if any *of us*, are
found Faulty, in this Matter, they shall be no longer *of us*." On the other
hand, Sewall clearly has problems in formulating his own quite opposite
"Rules" for the place of blacks inside white order: "There is such a dispar-
ity in their Conditions, Colour & Hair, that they can never embody with us,
and grow up into orderly Families, to the Peopling of the Land: but still
remain in our Body Politick as a kind of extravasat Blood. As many Negro
men as there are among us, so many empty places there are in our Train
Bands, and the places taken up of Men that might make Husbands for our
Daughters" (p. 10). If the fact of slavery disrupts the Christian scheme of
things—or, as in Jefferson, creates a very untidy hole in the system of white
jurisprudence—the presence of actual slaves in New England thus disrupts
the white mission of most importance, the charge to "people the land."

17. In theological, if not in social, terms, Sewall's proposal for the aboli-
tion of slavery was inclusive; Mather's attempt to retain and justify the
institution likewise extended onto theological ground, since an enslaved
black (he explained unctuously in *The Negro Christianized*, published in
1707) might be *"the Lords Free-man*, tho' he continues a Slave" (Kaplan, p.
49)—an argument which was exclusive even in its inclusions.

18. The earlier styles continued to be used in the nineteenth century, of
course, as means for describing literal ground: thus Emerson's reference
to Brigham Young in his comments about Whitman in 1863.

19. One might link William Carlos Williams's *Paterson* (1946–63) with
Walden here, for that epic also is rich in the sense of place, and in its
exploitation of New World forms for the expression of a modern sensibil-
ity, forms with which Williams had dealt intimately in his earlier book, *In
the American Grain* (1925). Also of interest here is Paul Metcalf's *Apalache*   239

(1977), a prose poem composed from the records of early New World travel.

20. *The Writings of Benjamin Franklin,* ed. Albert H. Smyth, 10 vols. (New York: Macmillan, 1905–7), 10:117; Coolidge, as quoted in *Encyclopedia of American Biography,* s.v. "Calvin Coolidge."

21. Arthur C. Danto, *Analytical Philosophy of History* (Cambridge: Cambridge University Press, 1968), is suggestive on the issue of narrative "subjects."

22. *New England's Memorial* (Boston: Congregational Board of Publication, 1855), p. 5; the figure, of course, is biblical.

23. *Thomas Paine: Representative Selections,* ed. Harry Hayden Clark (New York: Hill and Wang, 1961), p. 19.

24. Other neat summaries of colonial history can be found in Jefferson's *A Summary View of the Rights of British America* (1774), Stephen Hopkins's *The Rights of Colonies Examined* (1764), and Samuel Adams's (?) *A State of the Rights of the Colonists* (1772)—see *Tracts of the American Revolution, 1763–1776,* ed. Merrill Jensen (Indianapolis: Bobbs-Merrill, 1967), pp. 258–59, 43, 58–59, 250.

25. On this theme, see Trumbull's "An Elegy on the Times" (1774), which describes Boston under the strains of English occupation; also, Jefferson's words on that city in *A Summary View.*

26. See Philip S. Foner's important collection, *We, the Other People: Alternative Declarations of Independence by Labor Groups, Farmers, Woman's Rights Advocates, Socialists, and Blacks, 1829–1975* (Urbana: University of Illinois Press, 1976), especially the position paper issued on 4 July 1970, by the National Committee of Black Churchmen: "When in the course of Human Events, it becomes necessary for a People who were stolen from the lands of their Fathers, transported under the most ruthless and brutal circumstances 5,000 miles to a strange land, sold into dehumanizing slavery, emasculated, subjugated, exploited and discriminated against for 351 years, to call, with finality, a halt to such indignities and genocidal practices..." (p. 164). Note, however, that this is largely a "male" document.

27. I am referring here to the so-called Indian mounds, which some whites viewed as signs of future white decay—see, for example, Gouverneur Morris, *Discourse Delivered before the New-York Historical Society* (New York: James Eastburn, 1813).

28. *Representative Selections,* ed. Frank Luther Mott and Chester E. Jorgenson (New York: American Book Co., 1936), pp. 513, 516. It should be noted that this small pamphlet of Franklin's old age is no mere exercise of wit, witty as it is in parts. He had published some twenty years before a sharp assault on those whites who had attacked and killed several Susquehannahs at Conestoga settlement, Pennsylvania (*A Narrative of the Late Massacres, in Lancaster County,* 1764)—his use of the term "massacres" being a sign of his "distant" emotional and rhetorical position. And the simple attentiveness of his own ear to the "Indian" who answers the Swede in *Savages* suggests that he, at least, "believes." For a far more complex intercultural exchange, see John G. Neihardt, *Black Elk Speaks* (Lincoln: University of Nebraska Press, 1961), p. x.

❁ INDEX ❁

Abandonment: of American design by settlers, 175–76; of Europe by emigrants, 115; of settlers by Europe, 163; of William Bradford by Plymouth, 166

Abundance: as affront to explorer, 76, 80; as American theme, 21, 34; and profit, 71, 76, 102, 110; and ruin, 163–64; and scarcity, 128; subordination of, 106; as threat, 24, 57

Adventure: and advent, 21; passivity of, in discovery narratives, 22–23

Agriculture: as English relation to America, 48–49; ruin of, in Scotland, 116–17

Alachua savanna (Fla.), 72–73

Alienation: and discovery, 44, 182–87; and distance, 124; of Indian captives, 151, 186; of Thomas Paine, 198–201; of Scots emigrants, 120–21; of John Smith, 187–90

Allerton, Isaac, 172

Alsop, George, *A Character of the Province of Mary-Land* (1666), 35–37, 89

Amadas, Philip, 106, 164

Ames, Fisher, 11

Ames, Nathaniel, *Almanac* (1758), 79–82, 84–85, 155, 200

Animals: as embellishment of traveler's way, 33; as emblem of order, 61–62, 78; as sign of American abundance, 23–24, 109–10; supposed degeneration of, in America, 26; as threat, 37–38, 40, 66–67

Apalachicola river, 30

Arrival, as symbolic act, 35–38, 156–57, 161, 183

Artaguiette, Bernard Diron d', "Journal" (1722–23), 132–35, 142–43, 152, 156, 174, 188

Artaguiette, Martin d'Iron d', 125

Atlantic ocean: as breach or void, 36, 156; as hindrance, 138; as sign of death, 100, 144–52, 152–56; as sign of European fear, 35–36, 37–38, 40–42; as sign of renewal, 37–38, 40–42, 118

Audience: relation of traveler to, 23, 35, 37–38, 105, 120; creation of, in America, 197–98. *See also* Reader

Bacon, Francis: on Columbus, 7–9; on fear of travel, 38; on "idols," 17; on knowledge and discovery, 7–10; on language, 9–10; legacy of, in America, 16–17, 25–26; *Novum Organum*, 7–10; uncertainty of, 8

Baffin Island, 126, 139, 140

Baltimore, Charles Calvert, Lord, 99–101

Bancroft, George, 103–4

Barbary coast, 88

Barlow, Joel, *The Vision of Columbus*, 12–13, 86, 103, 104

Barlowe, Arthur, "Discourse" (1584–85), 106–8, 111, 164

Bartram, John: anxiety of, over plant loss, 48, 52; correspondence of, with Peter Collinson, 50–56; corruption of wonder in, 51; essay of, on timber (1749), 47; Florida *Journal* (1765), 56; garden of, 47, 57–58; on hindrances to travel in America, 50–51; on Indians as nemesis, 51–57, 150, 186; list of troublesome plants (1758) by, 58–59; medicinal finding list (1751) by, 54; *Observations* (1751), 48–50, 56–57; as observer and preserver of plants, 52–53; relation of, to son William, 58–60, 67–68

Bartram, John, Jr., 53

Bartram, William, 102, 119; on "bason" of water, 65–67, 70; as

241

explorer, 70–75, 76–77, 86; failure of, as Florida planter, 67; language of, 63, 83; nature humanized by, 61; perceptivity of, 59; "pilgrimage" of, 65; relation of, to father, 58–60, 67–68; on settlement, 73–75; on theme of growth, 61; *Travels* (1791), 59–68

Best, George, *A True Discourse* (1578), 141

Beverley, Robert, *The History and Present State of Virginia* (1705), 31–32

Bewilderment: vs. imaginative control of landscape, 50; possibility of, downplayed by discoverer, 44. *See also* Extremity; Loss

Bienville, Jean Baptiste Le Moyne, Sieur de, 125

Boone, Daniel: on Cumberland gap, 32–33; as solitary traveler, 12

Bossu, Jean-Bernard, *Travels in the Interior of North America* (1768), 33–34, 35

Boston, 184, 186

Boswell, James, 115–16

Braddock, Gen. Edward, 34

Bradford, William: as annalist, 165; as autobiographer, 167; composition of history by, 169; design in prose of, 151, 169–70, 180; Hebrew "exercises" of, 177–78, 179, 183; integral rhetoric of, 167; *Of Plymouth Plantation* (1630–50), 150–52, 165–78, 180, 190, 194; as public historian, 168; silence of, 177–78; viewpoint of, in his history, 172, 182

Brewster, William, 174–76

Buffon, Georges Louis Leclerc, Comte de, 30, 47; on degeneration of animals in America, 25

Burges, George, *A Journal of a Surveying Trip* (1795), 130–31, 170

Byrd, William: *Histories of the Dividing Line* (1728–37), 65, 130; ironies of, 129–30; "A Journey to the Land of Eden" (1733), 127–30, 131; on minerals, 128; as visionary, 128–29

Cabeza de Vaca, Alvar Nuñez, *Relation* (1542), 44

Cabot, John, 146

Cadillac, Antoine de la Mothe, "Report" to Pontchartrain (1713), 124–26, 131, 133, 149, 152, 174

Camden, William, 139

Canada, 48, 52, 92; "The Wonders of Canada" (1768), 33, 34, 45–46

Cannibalism, fear of, 41, 53

Cape Fear river, 119

Carleill, Christopher: *A Briefe and Summary Discourse* (1583), 87–94, 100, 103, 104–5, 107, 111, 113, 121, 138, 167; comparison of European and American trade by, 87–89; explanation of Cartier's failure by, 92–93; on "multiplication" of profit in America, 89–94; utopian concerns of, 92

Cartier, Jacques, 92–93

Carver, Jonathan, "A New Map of North America" (1778), 46

Charles V, 3

Charlevoix, Pierre François-Xavier, 48

Chesapeake Bay, 163

Clinton, Charles, "Journal" (1729), 152–56, 161, 166, 176

Clinton, De Witt, 155

Clinton, George, 155

Clinton, James, 155

Cobbett, William, 200

Cocaigne, Land of, 119

Colden, Cadwallader, 57

Collinson, Peter: and American plants, 47; correspondence of, with John Bartram, 50–56; on injustice to Indians, 54–56

Colonization: anomie incident to, 11; broad pattern of, 44; as replication of old forms, 4. *See also* Settlement

Columbian stance: and death, 155; as icon of American experience, 12; as temporal viewpoint, 81

Columbus, Christopher: change in goals of, 139; discovery and language in letters of, 182; on Jamaica, 6, 18–19, 142–43, 169, 183; loneliness of, 182–83; on Orinoco and paradise, 183; researches on, by Washington Irving, 13; as symbol of hope for Francis Bacon, 7–9; as symbol of venturesomeness for Henry Thoreau, 183–84; as symbol of victory for Joel Barlow, 12–13, 144; in Veragua, 1–2, 18–19, 109; view of F. J. Turner on, 14

Comedy: of future, 81–82; as shape of American journey, 70; and tragedy, 144–52, 169

Commerce: as goal of American voyage, 87–94; penetration of, into America, 49–50. *See also* Profit

Commodity: vs. discommodity, 95; as view of America, 82–87

Community: of the "dispersed," 186–87; and exclusion, 149, 151–52, 172–73, 181–87, 199, 201; ideal of, in America, 173, 179, 193; and isolation, 183–84; 190–91, 203; and language, 192; vs. mobility, 12; as point of departure, 180–81, 187; vs. selfishness, 150, 171–72; sense of, in Revolutionary period, 194, 196

Concord, Mass., 183, 186, 187

Connecticut, 185

Coolidge, Calvin, 193

Cortés, Hernán, *Letters from Mexico* (1520–26), 3–5

Cotton, John, 180–81

Countess of Warwick Sound, 139

Crèvecoeur, (Michel-Guillaume Jean) St. Jean de: on John Bartram, 47–48, 51; *Letters from an American Farmer* (1782), 119–20; on maps, 29

Croatoan Island, 159, 160

Cumberland county (N. C.), 73–75

Cumberland gap, 32–33

Cumberland river, 28–29

Cushman, Mary, 176

Cushman, Robert, 171, 174

Dan river, 127

Dasamongwepeuk (Indian village), 160

Dauphin Island (Ala.), 124–25, 132

De Bry, Theodor, 111–12

Declaration of Independence, 197, 198

Degeneration, theory of American, 25

Denton, Daniel, *A Brief Description of New-York* (1670), 64–65, 76–78, 120

Departure: and "center," 180, 183; as commitment to experience, 35; as discovery, 181; as displacement, 154–55; finality of, in exploratory and settlement narratives, 45, 156; and return, 45; in Revolutionary arguments, 196–97; as symbolic act, 7

de Soto, Hernando, 34

Detroit, 49, 124

Discoverer: desire of, to stop time, 43–44; and landscape gardener, 63; language of, 122; as namer, 45; as scientist, 48; struggle of, 27

Discovery: and death, 155–56; and denial of loss, 45; and discontent, 192, 202; as excuse for violence, 42–43; and isolation, 184, 191; and perception, 61, 63, 67; as process of stipulation, 26; and renewal, 60; as result of reading travel books, 39; and "return," 45; vs. settlement, 163–64; and test of reality, 124; and time, 69; and use, 77; as verbal act, 182, 183

Discovery narrative: and the "beyond," 33; categorical nature of, 43; circular form of, 45; as conceptual settlement of American space, 43; defined, 22–25; mixed form of, 44; and national language, 104; struggle toward control in, 27–33; trials of will in, 35

Dismal Swamp, 129

Dispossession: 58, 186. *See also* Loss

Drake, Francis, 106, 111

Dumanoir, Feaucon, 133, 156

El Dorado, Walter Ralegh's search for, 24

Elizabeth I, 24

Ellis, Thomas: as "Gothic" writer, 142; iceberg plate of, 140–41; *A True Report* (1578), 135–43, 152

Emerson, Ralph Waldo: "The

American Scholar," 84–85; *Journal*, 85–86; *Nature*, 82–83

Emigrants: advice to, 95–96, 102–3; alienation of, 120–21; as "makers," 101–2

England: as decadent land, 94–95; poverty of people in, 92; relative closeness of, to America, 89

Evans, Lewis, 48; *A General Map* and the "Analysis" of it (1755), 29–30; *A Map of Pensilvania* (1749), 49

Experience: vs. plan in exploratory narrative, 120–22; simplified, in discovery narrative, 22, 42; as woods in Bacon's *Novum Organum*, 8, 10

Exploitation, theme of: in discovery narrative, 23; in exploratory narrative, 80, 87, 107, 118. *See also* Profit; Use

Exploration: as artistic act, 165, 183–84, 185; defined, 28, 69–75; vs. discovery, 106, 110–11; and isolation, 191; realistic, 133–34; vs. settlement, 162, 166–67, 170; and test of reality, 124

Exploratory narrative: and American historiography, 155, 194; and American literature, 85–87; as answer to Old World doubts, 94–96, 105; commodity as theme in, 82–87; vs. discovery narrative, 121–22; as draft of colonial order, 96–97; fallacies of, 177; hope vs. doom in, 110–11, 114–16, 120–22; lies in, 91, 118; as means of "processing" America, 71; and national language, 104, 193–98; as plan of action, 94, 102; prescription in, 78; pretense of "speaking" for America in, 76–77; as promotional tract, 79, 106–7, 113–14; as prospectus, 87, 91–92; as "script," 78–79, 81; and settlement narrative, 121–22, 127; sophistries in, 93; as syntactic fragment, 94; and time, 69, 74–75, 77, 79–82, 103, 104–5; vision and memory in, 104

Explorer: attitude of, toward change, 75, 81–82; vs. discoverer,

70–75, 78, 107, 122; ethical arguments of, 93–94, 108–9, 117–18; formulative drive of, 85; grammar of, 69–70, 76–79, 80–81, 82–87, 93–94, 141–42, 191; impostures of, 128; pretense to passivity of, 83, 118; vs. surveyor, 130; as tragic figure, 146; view of, toward settlement, 79–80; as visionary, 69, 79, 94, 128

Extremity: of American traveler, 143–44; in Charles Clinton's "Journal," 154; of Columbus, 6, 143; of Humfrey Gilbert, 146–47. *See also* Loss

Fayetteville, N. C., 73–75, 86

Filson, John, *The Discovery, Settlement and Present State of Kentucke* (1784), 32–33

Florida, 54; William Bartram, *Travels* (1791), 59–68

Fort Le Boeuf, Pa., 130

Fort Louis, Ala., 124

Franklin, Benjamin: *The Internal State of America* (date uncertain), 193; *Remarks Concerning the Savages of America* (1784), 202–3

Frémont, John Charles, maps of, 29

French and Indian War: England's gain of land after, 46, 52; as symbol of racial anxiety, 51, 53; as test of English will, 79

Frobisher, Martin, 126–27, 135–43, 144

Frobisher Bay, 137, 139

Frontier, studies of, 14

Fry, Joshua, *A Map of the Inhabited Part of Virginia* (1751), 29–30

Furs, trade in, 90, 98

Garden, Alexander, 57

Georgia: Benjamin Martyn, *An Impartial Enquiry* (1741), 191; Martyn, *Some Account* (1732), 78; Patrick Tailfer, *A True and Historical Narrative* (1741), 191

Gilbert, Sir Humfrey: death of, at sea, 144–52, 157; "Discourse" (1576), 136–37; as explorer, 146

Gorgeana (colony), 184–85

Gorges, Sir Fernando, 184–85

Government, colonial, 34, 124–26, 132–35. See also Community
Granger, Thomas, 172
Great Lakes, 134
Grenville, Sir Richard, 111, 163
Guiana, 23–24

Hakluyt, Richard (elder), Inducements to the Liking of the Voyage (1585), 107
Hakluyt, Richard (younger), 112, 135–36, 160–61, 164, 165; Discourse of Western Planting (1584), 107
Hall, Charles Francis, 139
Hall, Christopher, 140; "The First Voyage of M. Martin Frobisher" (1576), 135–37
Harper's Ferry, W. Va., 32
Harriot, Thomas, 120, 164; anthropological concerns of, 106; A Briefe and True Report (1588), 104–113; interest of, in America, 105–6; lost American writings by, 110–11; plans of, for book with John White, 112; use of catalogs by, 109–10
Hatteras Island, 158, 159
Hayes, Edward, "A Report" (1583), 144–52, 161, 180
Health, as American fact, 33, 35–38, 39–40
Heere, Lucas de, 140
Holme, Thomas, "A Portraiture of the City Philadelphia" (1683), 98–99
Hope: and despair, 165–66; and doom, 111, 120–22; vs. irony, 125, 192; and memory, 158, 170; and realism, 123, 130; vs. ruin, 132; and uncertainty, 110
Hudson, Henry, 138
Hudson river, 193
Hutchinson, Anne, 180
Hyco river, 129

Iconography: in discovery narrative, 21; in exploratory narrative, 74–75; in settlement narrative, 140–41, 162; in travel books, 18
Illinois, 134
Indians: alliance of, with French, 54, 82; Apalachee, 30; capture of whites by, 136, 139, 151; of Carolina, 108, 112, 164; Cartier's relations with, 93; conversion of, 90, 145, 202–3; cultures of, appreciated by whites, 34, 202; defeat of, and white success, 150; engrossment of, by disaffected whites, 186; exclusion of, 201–2; extirpation of, 43–44, 51–52, 200; Fox, 134; kidnapping of, by Frobisher, 139–40; languages of, 2, 48, 106, 109; and liquor, 98, 131; mistreatment of, in land sales, 54–56; as nemesis of traveler, 51–57, 150, 186; open relations of, with whites, 68; of Pennsylvania, 98, 100–101, 131, 202–3; separate place of, in discovery narratives, 42; shrewdness of, 139; Six Nations, 53; as symbol of white anxiety, 82, 121, 131, 149, 180; trade with, 90, 98, 126; wars with white settlers, 42–44, 134, 140, 164; white policy against, 113, 140
Ireland, 89
Irving, Washington, 13
Isle of Shoals, 184
Italy, 88, 90

Jamaica, 6, 18–19, 142–43, 169, 183
James I, 24
Jefferson, Peter, A Map of the Inhabited Part of Virginia (1751), 29–30
Jefferson, Thomas, 34, 43, 45, 47, 50, 58, 155, 156, 186, 188, 200; attack of, on travelers, 25–26; dispute of, with Buffon, 24–25; on Indian languages, 48; on the Natural Bridge, 26–28; Notes on the State of Virginia (1785), 24–33; on the Potomac, 28–33; purchase of Louisiana by, 11; on the West, 25–26
Johnson, Samuel, 115
Jones, Hugh, The Present State of Virginia (1724), 32

Kalm, Pehr (Peter), 47
Kanawha river, 28
Kaskaskia, Ill., 132
Kentucky: John Filson, The Discovery, Settlement and Present State of

Kentucke (1784), 32–33; rumors about, in Thomas Jefferson's *Notes on the State of Virginia,* 26

Kerlérec, Louis Billourart, Chevalier de, 34

La Cosa, Juan de, portolan map (1500), 29

Landscape: division of, into real estate, 76, 96; related to *topos,* 18; in settlement narrative, 163–64; significance of, in travel book, 16. *See also* Space

Lane, Ralph, 105, 106, 108, 163, 164; "Account" of Roanoke (1586), 113

Language: as "alter America," 183–90; of American Indians, 2, 106, 109; *catalogic,* 70, 93–94, 102 (activation of), 95, 101, 107 (and "actors"), 58 (in John Bartram), 90 (in Christopher Carleill), 125–26 (and colonial failures), 99 (and colonial successes), 3 (in Cortés), 83 (in Emerson), 107 (and epistemology), 109–10 (in Thomas Harriot), 28–29 (in Jefferson), 133, 189–90 (as listing of "lacks"), 152–55, 156, 158, 164, 176, 177 (as listing of the lost), 23–27 (purpose of, in discovery narrative), 23–24 (in Walter Ralegh), 24 (reason vs. emotion in), 126–27, 144 (in settlement narrative), 85–87 (in Whitman); changes of, in America, 17, 162; as closed system, 108; and colonization, 70–71, 75, 76–77, 80, 87, 95–97, 107; as cultural tool, 3; as decorum, 4; *descriptive,* 42, 64–65 (as control over events), 3–4 (in Cortés), 22 (in discovery narrative), 76 (in exploratory narrative), 123 (inadequacy of), 62–63 (as means of "discovery"), 31, 42, 70–71, 136 (vs. narrative), 125 (as polemic), 141 (vs. prescriptive); and events, 1, 4, 92, 104, 113, 177, 191–92; extremity of, 6, 143; formulaic, 10, 17–18, 33, 146–47; inadequacy of, 4; and inexpressibility, 3–4, 6, 26–27, 45, 80, 163, 176–77; ironic, 125, 126–31, 136, 142; loss of, 143, 153, 162, 200; as means of control, 5, 27, 45, 46, 90, 93–94; *narrative,* 194 (and American historiography), 5 (and American "tale"), 1–2 (in Columbus), 31, 137 (vs. descriptive), 1–2, 31 (as explanation of events), 82 (in exploratory narrative), 22–23, 64 (lack of, in discovery narrative), 203 (and persuasion in America); orthodox, 14, 195; paratactic vs. hypotactic, 82–83; and perception, 4, 63; as plotting device, 4, 5, 94; and politics, 125, 149–52, 181, 182, 187, 198; predicative, 22, 84, 97, 198; predictive, 5–6, 78, 91, 193; public, 149, 192, 198; reassuring power of, 5, 63; vs. silence, 4, 6, 45, 149, 150, 158, 161, 192; vs. things, 2, 3–4, 6–7, 9–10, 45, 70, 94, 124, 131–32; and "use," 71–72, 76, 102; use of, to name America, 3, 4, 58, 80

La Salle, René Robert Cavelier, Sieur de, 34

Laurens, Henry, 67

Law, John, 133, 134

Law (and legality), 4, 54–55, 101, 121, 134

Lewis and Clark expedition, 25

Leyden, 166–67

Linnaeus (Linné, Carl von), 47

Literary nationalism, 85

Locke, John, 17

Loss: acceptance of, 153–54; denial of, 12–13, 45, 143–52; and gain, 169; as meaning of history for William Bradford, 178; and power, 149; and recovery, 166; as result of transplantation, 10; of Roanoke settlers, 113; and silence, 158; as symbol of the West, 155; of wild plants, 48, 52–53

Louisiana (French colony), 52; Bernard Diron d'Artaguiette, "Journal" (1722–23), 132–35, 152; Jean-Bernard Bossu, *Travels in the Interior of North America* (1768), 33–34; Antoine de la Mothe Cadillac, "Report" to

Pontchartrain (1713), 124–26, 152
Lowlands, 166–67, 173
Loyalists, 201
Lyford, John, 170, 172

Madison, James, 155
Maine, 184–85
Manteo (Indian leader), 159
Maps: as aloof designs, 30; as cognitive organization of the unknown, 26; as drafts of colonial life, 96; vs. landscape in settlement narrative, 129; of Philadelphia, as emblem of success, 99; as spatial ideograms, 29, 141; stasis of, 32; and verbal description, 29–30, 32; of John White, 159
Martyn, Benjamin: *An Impartial Enquiry* (1741), 191; *Some Account* (1732), 78
Maryland, 100; George Alsop, *A Character of the Province of Maryland* (1666), 35–37
Mason, John (Connecticut settler), 185
Mason, John (English sea captain), *A Brief Discourse of the Newfoundland* (1620), 18
Massachusetts Bay, 92, 151; land hunger in, 44, 173
Mather, Cotton, 191
Melville, Herman, *Moby-Dick*, 135
Methodology: historical vs. literary, 15; of the present book, 15–19, 55–56, 113, 120, 123–24, 135, 179–80
Minerals: and European economy, 7; hidden, 79, 91, 125, 127; madness for, 128; in New York, 77; search for, 24, 139; in Veragua, 2
Mississippi river, 54, 132
Mobile, Ala., 134
Mobile Bay, 124–25, 132
Montezuma, palace of, 3
Montreal, 134
More, Sir Thomas, *Utopia*, 146–47
Morison, Samuel Eliot, 137, 174
Morton, Nathaniel, *New England's Memorial* (1669), 194
Morton, Thomas: as excluded figure, 180–87; as "Lord of Mis-

rule," 151; *New English Canaan* (1637), 38, 184, 186; as villain in William Bradford, 167, 172, 180
Mountains: in John Bartram's *Observations*, 50; in Thomas Jefferson's *Notes on the State of Virginia*, 29–33
Mount Wollaston, Mass., 151

Narragansett Bay, 184–85
Natchez, 133–34
Natural Bridge (Va.), 26–28
Nature: activation of, against traveler, 137–39, 146; as allegory of God, 60; as "artist," 31; disorder of, for explorer, 70–71; as "fund" of matter, 79–80, 101–2; and history, 75; vs. human order, 129; as "inviting" realm, 74, 76, 81, 83, 89, 98, 119; as sign of colonial progress, 101; as sign of traveler's condition, 61; "yielding" of, to humanity, 107, 118. *See also* Space
Nauset (Eastham, Mass.), 166–69, 175, 181
New England, 184, 189–90; William Bradford, *Of Plymouth Plantation* (1630–50), 150–52, 165–78; growth of, 193–94; land hunger in, 185; Nathaniel Morton, *New England's Memorial* (1669), 194; Thomas Morton, *New English Canaan* (1637), 38, 184, 186; naming of, 193; and other colonies, 179, 180, 187, 190; John Smith, *The Generall Historie* (1624), 187–90; John Underhill, *Newes from America* (1638), 42–44; Roger Williams, letter to John Mason (1670), 185–86; William Wood, *New Englands Prospect* (1634), 38–42
Newfoundland: Edward Hayes, "A Report" (1583), 144–52; John Mason, *A Briefe Discourse of the Newfoundland* (1620), 18
New France: defeat of, by English, 46; vs. English colonies, 48–49, 92–93, 145; vs. Louisiana, 134
New Hampshire, 44
New Jersey, 53, 76

New Netherland: vs. English colonies, 77; expansion in, 193; Peter Stuyvesant and loss of, 185; Adriaen van der Donck, *A Description of the New Netherlands* (1655), 21–22; van der Donck, *Remonstrance* (1650), 22
New Orleans, 132, 134–35
New York (colony): Daniel Denton, *A Brief Description of New-York* (1670), 64–65, 76–78; expansion in, 193; Charles Wooley, *A Two Years Journal in New-York* (1701), 37–38
Niagara Falls, 45
Nicaragua, 2
North Carolina: Arthur Barlowe, "Discourse" (1584–85), 106–8; William Bartram, *Travels* (1791), 73–75; William Byrd, "A Journey to the Land of Eden" (1733), 127–30; Richard Hakluyt (elder), *Inducements to the Liking of the Voyage* (1585), 107; Richard Hakluyt (younger), *Discourse of Western Planting* (1584), 107; Thomas Harriot, *A Briefe and True Report* (1588), 104–113; Ralph Lane, "Account" of Roanoke (1586), 113; "Scotus Americanus," *Informations Concerning the Province of North Carolina* (1773), 113–22; John White, letter to Hakluyt (1593), 112, 160–61, 164–65; White, report of 1587 voyage, 163–65, 176; White, report of 1590 voyage, 157–60, 165, 189

Oblivion: as affront to white knowledge, 58; as condition of American space, 52–53, 156–57; as condition of American time, 81; denial of, 192; of language, 162–63
Oglethorpe, James, 191
Ohio river, 28, 54
Ontario, Lake, 49
Orinoco river, 183

Paine, Thomas: as autobiographer, 195; *Common Sense* (1776), 194–98; *Crisis* papers (1776–83), 199; *Letter to George Washington* (1796), 199–200; rhetorical stance of, 197, 200–201; view of, regarding American space and time, 194–96
Paradise, America as: 36, 64, 66, 78, 177, 182–83, 186
Parkman, Francis, on Anglo-French rivalry, 48
Paxton Boys, 53
Penn, William: advice of, to emigrants, 95–96; *A Further Account* (1685), 99–103, 165; *Letter to the Traders* (1683), 97–100, 103, 167; modesty of, 95; as projector, 96–99; sale of land by, 97; *Some Account of the Province of Pennsylvania* (1681), 94–97, 116
Pennsylvania: John Bartram, *Observations* (1751), 48–50, 56–57; John Bartram, paper on troublesome plants (1758), 58–59; George Burges, *A Journal of a Surveying Trip* (1795), 130–31; emigration to, 97; land sales in, 97; mountains of, as impediment, 50; Paxton Boys of, 53; William Penn, *A Further Account* (1685), 99–103; Penn, *Letter to the Traders* (1683), 97–100, 103; Penn, *Some Account of the Province of Pennsylvania* (1681), 94–97; Walking Purchase in, 55
Pequot War, 42–44
Perception: appeal to, in William Bartram's *Travels*, 62–63; as "artwork," 31, 84; balanced and idyllic, 34; of cultural differences, 203; as "discovery," 67; elusiveness of, in travel books, 16–17; and epistemology, 107, 141; as eucharistic act in discovery narrative, 23; imperial, 50, 82–84; and language, 124; as means of control, 27, 45; as organic process, 30–31, 60–62; as search for commodities, 107, 109, 128; of "signs," 82–83; and vision, 104, 131
Petersburg, Va., 129
Philadelphia, 32; vs. frontier, 131; laying out of, 98; as sign of success, 98, 101, 103

Pioneer, as sacrificial figure, 13. *See also* Traveler
Plants: collection of, from wilderness, 47–48, 53–54; conversion of, into human products, 71–72, 107–8; as embellishment of journey, 61, 108; as emblems of life, 36, 54, 66, 163–64; escape of, 58; exuberance of, as threat, 57, 58–59; loss of, 48, 52–53; observation of, 62–63; sent to Europe from America, 47; spread of, 58–59, 73; as tools of possession, 77; vs. weeds, 57–59
Plot: of American future, 32–33, 81, 120; of American history and art, 85, 103–4; of American past, 13–14, 155, 179; as design of experience, 135–36, 165; "discovered," 6, 142; double, in settlement narrative, 148, 150–52; expansion of, 91; multiplicity of, in America, 180; perversion of, 81, 166–69; and "plats," 29, 132, 141; and prescription, 78, 177; and providential plan, 147; reinvention of, 191–92; in Revolutionary period, 195; in settlement narrative, 122, 133, 143, 191; static vs. dynamic, 44; as subversion, 151; as vehicle of control, 5, 104, 193; of Western voyage, 37
Plymouth colony, 184, 186, 193; William Bradford, *Of Plymouth Plantation* (1630–50), 150–52, 165–78; design of, 174–75; land hunger in, 44; London partners of, 169–71; loss of settlers from, 58, 180; success and failure in, 155, 166–69; and Virginia Company, 174
Poe, Edgar Allan: "The Domain of Arnheim," 63; "MS. Found in a Bottle," 135, 142, 143
Pontchartrain, Jérôme Phélypeaux, Comte de, 124, 126, 149
Pontiac's Uprising, 53
Portugal, 88
Possession: and dispossession, 58, 186; and language, 182–83; organized facts as sign of, 24; and perception, 84; right to, as moral issue, 148–49

Potomac river, 28–33
Profit: America as source of, 92–94; and irony, 126–28. *See also* Use
Prophecy: as American art, 81–82; and confirmation, 120; and memory in exploratory narrative, 104
Provence, 90
Providence: American God as figure of, 23, 60; and protection against the sea, 42, 142; vs. traveler's own skill, 46

Quakers, 180; in America before Penn, 97; attitude of, toward Indians, 53
Quinn, David B., 112

Ralegh, Sir Walter: American fate of, 24; on Guiana, 23–24; and Thomas Harriot, 105–6, 111; schemes of, for Carolina, 105, 157–65
Reader, role of, in travel books: as Doubting Thomas, 92; as imaginary traveler, 39; as initiate, 41, 62–63; as potential actor, 37, 41, 78–79, 94, 95–96, 102
Regeneration, as American process, 26, 41, 78, 118–19
Regulators, 120
Revolution: allegory of, in Thomas Jefferson's *Notes on the State of Virginia*, 32; allegory of, in George Bancroft's *History*, 103–4; effect of, on Scots emigrants, 120–22; and empire, 46; and national style, 194–201
Rhode Island, 184–85
Richmond, Va., 129
Rivers: as emblem of white settlement, 73–74; as sign of abundance and use, 28–29
Roanoke (colony), 121, 140, 169; Thomas Harriot, *A Briefe and True Report* (1588), 104–13; Ralph Lane, "Account" (1586), 113; Sir Walter Ralegh's failure to visit, 24; John White, letter to Hakluyt (1593), 112, 160–61, 164–65; White, report of 1587 voyage, 163–65; White, report of 1590 voyage, 157–60, 165, 189

Roanoke (river), 128
Robinson, John, 173, 174–76
Rogers, Robert: *A Concise Account of North America* (1765), 46; *Journals* (1765), 18, 49
Ruin(s): and abundance, 163–64; and affirmation, 165–66, 190–91; in William Bartram's *Travels*, 67; of design, 148, 174–75, 191; of language, 143, 162; of nature, 33; psychological, 160, 165, 168, 188, 199–200; and "reconciliation" of Revolution, 201; in Revolutionary period, 197; of settlements, 159–60, 174–75; as theme in settlement narrative, 132, 143, 147, 156, 160, 162, 163–64, 165–66, 168
Rumors: about colonial disasters, 39, 99–100, 105, 117; about the West, 26
Russia, 87–89

Saffin, John, *A Brief and Candid Answer* (1701), 191
St. John's, Newfoundland, 145
St. John's river (Fla.), 72
Salem, Mass., 185
Salt Lake City, 85–86
Sarmiento, Domingo, *Travels in the United States in 1847*, 11–12
Satire: in exploratory narrative, 105; in settlement narrative, 150–51, 165
Science: and empire, 48, 52, 58; as means of rationalizing the unknown, 26; and religion, 60–61; and violence, 57, 66; and wonder, 24–26, 59–60
Scotland, vs. America, 113–22
"Scotus Americanus," *Informations Concerning the Province of North Carolina* (1773), 113–22
Secoton (Indian village), 113, 140, 164
Settle, Dionyse, *A True Report* (1577), 126–27, 131, 135–39, 140
Settlement: and commerce, 90; vs. discovery, 163–64, 165; and exclusion, 149; ideal view of, in exploratory narrative, 79–80, 86; vs. order of nature, 72–73; as organization of American space, 82

Settlement narrative: as autobiography, 165, 167, 175; "centers" in, 168–69, 179–81, 190–91, 194, 201–2; "cluttered" style of, 126; debates in, 105, 180, 190; defined, 123–24; vs. exploratory narrative, 82, 155, 165, 174; inclusion of documents in, 171, 187; ironic shape of, 142; lamentation and vision in, 190–92; as lament or jeremiad, 156, 165, 183, 190; legacy of, 198–203; memory in, 104, 152–56, 158; mixed form of, 44; movement from words to things in, 131–32; as political gesture, 149; as rhetorical act, 144–45, 148, 181–82, 186; "signs" in, 126–27, 136, 156, 158, 159, 162–63; silence in, 143; surveyor's documents as, 130–35; and time, 145, 165; treatment of loss in, 143–44, 152–56, 157–65; triumph of art in, 165–66; and vision, 178; wonder in, 178
Settler: as abandoned figure, 166, 187–90; as active figure, 119; as bringer of bad news, 142; as cataloger of defeats, 34, 152–55; as critic of European illusions, 165; designs of, 96–97; vs. discoverer and explorer, 121–23; "extravagance" of, 44; grammar of, 122, 124, 141–42, 154, 164; humor of, 131–32; and loss, 155; as realist, 123–24; as satirist, 150–52, 165, 172, 186; and "signs," 162–63; vs. surveyor, 130
Sewall, Samuel, *The Selling of Joseph* (1700), 191
Shenandoah river, 28–33, 52
Sherley, James, 169–71
Slaves: denial of language to, 181; as excluded figures, 201–2; as sign of white disaffection, 122, 187; as threat to American settlement, 149; white arguments over, 191
"Small beginnings" theme, 73–75, 86, 90–91, 93, 94–103, 170, 171; inversion of, 136, 143, 168, 176, 196; and "multiplication," 89–94, 167

Smith, James, *Remarkable Occurrences* (1799), 44
Smith, John, 112, 193; as "American voice," 188–89; as displaced discoverer, 190; *The Generall Historie* (1624), 105, 187–90; losses of, 189–90
Spain: and American gold, 7; English trade with, 88, 90; Sir Walter Ralegh's plot against, 24; ships of, attacked by English, 157; troubles of, in America, 145
Space: and the "beyond," 33–35, 68, 82; "breach" in, 32–33, 36, 41, 42; closeness in, as sign of threat, 31; distance in, as symbol, 5, 31, 34, 45, 99–100, 124, 135, 138, 141, 149, 187; effect of, on American writing, 181; location in, as sign of identity, 6, 99, 142–43, 182–83, 184–85, 188–90, 195–96, 199–202; "prospect" of, 38–39, 43–44, 48, 62–63, 74, 81, 118, 196; void of, 30–31, 37, 76, 80, 156–57. *See also* Landscape; Void
Stuyvesant, Peter, 22, 185
Surveyor, as mediating figure, 130–35
Swedes, in Delaware region, 97

Tailfer, Patrick, *A True and Historical Narrative* (1741), 191
Thoreau, Henry David: *The Maine Woods*, 183; *Walden*, 183–84, 186, 192; "Walking," 68
Tombigbee river, 34
Topos (topoi): defined, 17–18, 152; in discovery narrative, 68; in exploratory narrative, 73–75, 77, 103–4, 117, 168, 176; in settlement narrative, 131, 147, 151, 156, 159, 161–62, 164–65, 168–69, 174–75, 176
Towanda creek (Pa.), 56
Tragedy: as comedy, 169; converted into comedy, 93, 144–52, 192; as shape of American journey, 24, 111, 120–22, 160–61, 188
Transformation: "magical," 74–75, 82, 86–87, 90, 97, 103, 116–17, 118, 122, 131, 151, 168, 194, 200; as mythic act, 69; verbal, 80
Translatio motif, 84, 198, 199
Travel: as American ritual, 11–12, 197; in Francis Bacon's *Novum Organum*, 7–10; and "travail," 39–40
Travel book: accumulating force of, 192; as artifact, 15; attacked by Thomas Jefferson, 25–26; complexity of, 2; confrontation with reality in, 18–19, 132; difficulty of writing, 18–19, 36; formulaic quality of, 17–18; imperfection of, 6; influence of, on Revolutionary debates, 198; as "kinetic" literature, 16; as means of "control," 6; shape of, as cultural sign, 55; as structure of language, 6; style of, 10, 17–18; writing of, as play for power, 149
Traveler: as actor in exploratory narrative, 70–71, 93–94; as bringer of bad news, 132–33, 142–43; as chivalric figure, 21, 23, 59, 64–65, 67; competitiveness of, 182; as corrector of Old World lies, 39; as critic of colonial order, 22, 34, 123, 172; as enthusiast, 26; as figure of loss, 143–44; as Fisher King, 54, 188; as hero of order, 32; as iconoclast, 12; as liar, 39, 125; as malcontent in America, 149, 167; and national "tour," 55; as Orpheus, 79–80; as person in touch with world, 9; as social figure and renegade, 12; as victim, 122, 135, 141, 155, 161; as warning figure, 145, 149
Tryon county (N. Y.), 193
Turkey, 88
Turner, Frederick Jackson, 13–14, 193
Turner, Robert, 100

Underhill, John, *Newes from America* (1638), 42–44
U. S. Constitution, as ideal "plat" of nation, 103–4
Use: as explorer's goal, 71–72; idea of, as means of "control," 27; in

Thomas Jefferson's *Notes on the State of Virginia,* 28; and wonder, 72. *See also* Profit

van der Donck, Adriaen, *A Description of the New Netherlands* (1655), 21–22, 68; *Remonstrance* (1650), 22, 34
Veragua, meaning of, 1–2
Vergil, Polydore, 146
Virginia, 52, 113, 129; Thomas Harriot, *A Briefe and True Report* (1588), 104–113; Thomas Jefferson, *Notes on the State of Virginia* (1785), 24–33; John Smith, *The Generall Historie* (1624), 105, 187–90. *See also* Byrd, William
Void: control of, 46; of European space, 88; of experience in America, 104–5, 156, 168, 192; as image of American space, 26, 76, 86–87. *See also* Space; Wasteland

Washington, George, 199
Wasteland: America as, 25, 57, 76; Europe as, 21, 116, 118; as inner state in settlement narrative, 188
Watts, John, 157–58, 160
Weiser, Conrad, 48, 53
Westchester county (N. Y.), 200
Weston, Thomas, 167, 172, 180; writings of, in William Bradford's *Of Plymouth Plantation,* 180
White, John, 168, 174; association of, with Thomas Harriot, 106; Eskimo paintings by, 140, 141; governor of second Roanoke colony, 110–11; letter to Richard Hakluyt (1593), 112, 160–61, 164–65; map of Carolina by, 159; paintings of Carolina natives by, 111–13; report of 1587 voyage, 163–65, 176; report of 1590 voyage, 157–60, 165, 189
Whitman, Walt: compared with Brigham Young by Emerson, 85; "Preface" to *Leaves of Grass,* 85–86; "Starting from Paumanok," 86–87
Wilkes, Charles, 184
Williams, Roger: *The Bloudy Tenent* (1644), 184–186; as excluded figure, 180–87; *A Key into the Language of America* (1643), 184; letter to John Mason (1670), 185–86
Winslow, Edward, 169
Winthrop, John: *Journal* (1630–49), 180; "A Modell of Christian Charity" (1630), 92, 173
Women: exclusion of, in colonial America, 201
Wonder: and alienation, 44; corruption of, 51; vs. enclosure, 77; and enormity, 30; extension of, to human world, 68; and irony, 126–27; as keynote of discovery, 23; as means of "control," 44–45; vs. realism, 123; threats to, in narrative prose, 64; vs. use, 69–73, 83, 98, 106
"The Wonders of Canada" (1768), 33–34, 45–46
Wood, William, *New Enlands Prospect* (1634), 38–43, 56, 68, 82, 102, 138, 186
Woodward, Henry, "Westoe voyage" (1674), 34–35, 68
Wooley, *A Two Years Journal in New-York* (1701), 37–38

Young, Brigham, 85